About the Authors

Cyndie Klopfenstein has a 20-year background in the printing and pre-press industries. She has worked for the past eight years as a corporate trainer for companies that are converting to electronic pre-press. Cyndie also produces a series of videos and other books geared toward the electronic graphics community. She based this book on Que's *Using PowerPoint 4 for Windows*, written by Rich Grace.

Rich Grace is the author of Que's *Using PowerPoint 4 for Windows* and *Word 6 for Windows Quick Reference*, and has penned over 100 magazine articles. He's an experienced Macintosh user and is cultivating a strong interest in real-world multimedia solutions. Rich is currently working on two more book titles and spends his time in San Diego County.

Trademarks

All terms mentioned in this book that are known to be trademarks or service marks have been appropriately capitalized. Que cannot attest to the accuracy of this information. Use of a term in this book should not be regarded as affecting the validity of any trademark or service mark.

Contents at a Glance

Table of Contents

II Text   135

6 Working with Text   137

III Drawing   213

9 Drawing Objects   215

10 Adding Clip Art and Scanned Art   233

11 Selecting, Editing, and Enhancing Objects   245

IV Charts   261

12 Working with Datasheets   263

13 Creating Basic Charts   281

Introduction

Microsoft PowerPoint is among the leaders in a competitive and growing category of computer software: graphics presentations. PowerPoint 4 in particular is appropriately named because the program combines the most powerful features of not one program category, but several. Those features are:

Drawing. PowerPoint 4 offers a wide selection of drawing and art-creation features that rival those of dedicated drawing programs. Although PowerPoint never can replace Adobe Illustrator, for example, many presentation artists may find that PowerPoint is all they need. An extensive clip-art library offers instant art content to the presentation creator.

Charting. PowerPoint 4 offers highly flexible, feature-rich charting and graphing capabilities. You type the numeric data that you want to present (sales for a company department for the four quarters of the year, for example) in a simple datasheet and then choose among dozens of chart styles. PowerPoint 4's charting and graphing capabilities have been substantially enhanced.

Outlining and Word Processing. PowerPoint offers an easy-to-use, intuitive outlining feature that enables you to add any amount of text, choose your favorite fonts and type sizes, and create bulleted lists quickly. A spelling checker is provided, as are search and replace capabilities. You can construct an entire presentation and study its logic in outline view.

An Artist's Palette. PowerPoint uses the graphics power of the Macintosh to offer thousands of professionally created color schemes for your slide shows, as well as hundreds of predefined graphic backgrounds for various presentation motifs. If a predefined scheme doesn't please you, creating your own is remarkably easy.

An Output Program. PowerPoint gets the most out of your output devices. The program handles color printing and slide output with aplomb. You can create overhead transparencies easily. If you want professional color output, use the GraphicsLink program to send your files to Genigraphics Corporation, a service bureau that makes the slide output for you.

Corporate Communications. PowerPoint 4's mission, ultimately, is to empower and expand your delivery of corporate communications. All the tools listed above are designed to provide the most efficient, integrated program available for making corporate communications ring with conviction and authority.

Unlike a drawing or charting package, in which one screen at a time is created, programs like PowerPoint enable you to create extensive multiple-slide presentations. You can create as many slides as your system's memory can accommodate. PowerPoint 4 has perhaps the greatest flexibility of any program in its field for this purpose.

If you have multiple slides in your presentation file, you can use PowerPoint's handy Slide Sorter to rearrange slides simply by dragging and dropping. You can delete and add slides in the Sorter, as well as change the entire color scheme of the presentation. You also can apply different color schemes to individual slides. You can quickly and easily add to your presentation any type of data that your computer can support, including sounds, movie clips, and pictures.

PowerPoint 4 represents a great advance in capabilities from the preceding version, particularly in the way that the program actually works. Every capability and feature in PowerPoint 4 is for the first time integrated into a seamless, interdependent whole. In addition, PowerPoint associates more closely with fellow Microsoft applications than ever before.

You may need to create a presentation from scratch, which may mean doing all the following things:

- Defining a color scheme

- Creating a background for your slide show

- Creating the titles and basic outline for the slides in your show

- Writing the body text for your slides

- Creating three-dimensional pie and column charts for company sales data from imported Excel worksheets

- Adding film clips and sounds

- Defining a specific font for all the titles in your presentation

- Defining another font for your body text and bulleted points

- Adding framing effects to all your objects for a custom effect

- Arranging the objects in your slides for a clean, organized appearance

- Adding a company logo to all the slides in the presentation

- Importing bitmap pictures

- Creating tables

- Spell-checking your presentation

- Saving and printing your presentation slides as color transparencies

And all this has to be done yesterday!

If you had to specify each step in the presentation process by name, you would never get it done. Fortunately, with PowerPoint 4, you don't have to. You can master even the most complex-sounding features rapidly by using the mouse.

When you point to the desired feature or object and select it, you're using a graphical user interface (GUI, pronounced *gooey*): a front end for a program (or even for an entire computer system) that uses the mouse and a color display to simplify the use of your computer. The Macintosh interface, of course, is a popular example of a GUI. The advantage of using Macintosh and other GUIs (such as Windows, for example) is access to another advanced capability: WYSIWYG (what you see is what you get). When a slide show or document appears on your computer screen, WYSIWYG ensures that it bears a close resemblance to what you see on paper—or, in PowerPoint, in the on-screen slide show, color transparencies, or color slides.

Thanks to the GUI, PowerPoint 4 is more powerful and easier to use than ever before. You don't have to be a graphics designer to use PowerPoint. On the contrary, PowerPoint is designed for users who need to apply their expertise—corporate communications—to a presentation and to do it quickly and effectively. To this end, PowerPoint offers more than 100 templates that enable you to create appealing, effective slide shows quickly and easily. PowerPoint's templates contain many of the basic elements of an outstanding slide show, such as attractive color schemes, title fonts, placement of graphic objects, and the logical flow and basic content of the presentation.

PowerPoint 4's new Wizards offer an intelligent and speedy way to create several types of content for presentations—anything from communicating bad news to making progress reports. You can change the words, the outline, and the content of the presentation at will, and thereby craft a slide show that has a top-notch professional appearance. PowerPoint frees you from sweating over the basic details of using the program, allowing you to focus on what's most important: what to say and what images to convey.

PowerPoint 4 combines vast power in a friendly package. You can become a power user almost as soon as you begin, and using the program soon will become second nature. At first, however, you can profit by reading about the program. PowerPoint 4 offers so many features that you're likely to miss some of them unless you take time to seek them out. Helping you discover PowerPoint 4's possibilities for corporate communications is the mission of this book.

What Is in This Book

Like the PowerPoint software itself, *Using PowerPoint 4 for Macintosh* endeavors to make the power of the program easily accessible. The book opens with basic features and functions, and gradually moves to more advanced and complex topics. You should start by learning the basics; when you feel at home with the fundamentals, you can progress to more advanced topics. Be reassured, though; even the most complex features of PowerPoint are surprisingly straightforward and accessible. You can accomplish most tasks in a couple of mouse clicks.

This book is divided into six parts that split the PowerPoint 4 program into discrete areas of study.

Part I, "PowerPoint 4 Basics," introduces the basic features of PowerPoint 4.

Chapter 1, "An Overview of PowerPoint 4 for Macintosh," offers an overview of many of the most significant upgrades and enhancements in the new version of the program, including PowerPoint's new toolbars, Wizards, and drag-and-drop capability.

Chapter 2, "Getting Acquainted with PowerPoint 4," describes how to work with the mouse and keyboard, work with the menus, get help, and understand the new features of PowerPoint 4's user interface that help speed you on the way to successful presentations.

Chapter 3, "Quick Start: Creating a First Presentation," ties many of PowerPoint's most important features together in a basic exercise for creating your first presentation in PowerPoint 4.

Chapter 4, "Setting up Your New Presentation," describes masters and views, the interlocking tools of PowerPoint 4 that help you create the best presentation possible.

Chapter 5, "Using and Creating Templates," describes how to work with templates, which are the fundamental building blocks of presentations.

Part II, "Text," covers PowerPoint's text-handling and text-entry features.

Chapter 6, "Working with Text," describes the basics of entering text, manipulating text objects (by using PowerPoint's enhanced drag-and-drop capability), and using fonts and text styles.

Chapter 7, "Creating Speaker's Notes, Outlines, and Handouts," shows you how to produce the other elements of your presentation: your personal notes for the slide show, your presentation outline, and audience handouts.

Chapter 8, "Working with Tables," shows you how to create, edit, and format tables of text data in Microsoft Word for Macintosh 6 and then bring those tables into PowerPoint.

Part III, "Drawing," covers drawing and creating art objects in PowerPoint.

Chapter 9, "Drawing Objects," shows you how to use PowerPoint's numerous drawing tools.

Chapter 10, "Adding Clip Art and Scanned Art," shows you how to work with PowerPoint's extensive clip-art library, how to place clip art in your slide show, and how to work with images in PowerPoint.

Chapter 11, "Selecting, Editing, and Enhancing Objects," describes the process of using, moving, aligning, and changing object placeholders in PowerPoint slides.

Part IV, "Charts," describes how to create and use charts and organizational charts in PowerPoint.

Chapter 12, "Working with Datasheets," shows you how to edit the building block of every chart that you'll ever create: the numeric datasheet.

Chapter 13, "Creating Basic Charts," explains chart types, the various elements of a chart, and how to change various elements of a chart.

Chapter 14, "Customizing Charts," digs deeper into the process of changing your chart's appearance, offering more detailed discussions of changing chart elements, drawing objects, and adding custom colors to charts.

Chapter 15, "Creating Organizational Charts," introduces the process of creating organizational charts to depict a corporation's or department's structure.

Part V, "Output and Color," focuses on an essential part of PowerPoint: the final output.

Chapter 16, "Printing and Other Kinds of Output," describes how to print the various elements of a presentation, including handouts, notes, and slides, as well as how to use the Genigraphics service bureau for final color-slide output.

Chapter 17, "Working with Color," discusses basic color theory and the way that color really works in PowerPoint, as well as how to apply color to PowerPoint objects.

Part VI, "Advanced PowerPoint 4," discusses advanced topics and techniques for getting the most out of the program.

Chapter 18, "Using Links to Other Applications," discusses how object linking and embedding (OLE) works and how it can help you work more effectively with other data types and applications.

Chapter 19, "Using Advanced Charting Features," further explores sophisticated chart types and chart-customizing techniques.

Chapter 20, "Advanced Presentation Management," discusses adding special effects to presentations and working with multimedia data.

Chapter 21, "Using Advanced Color, Text, and Drawing Features," touches on operations such as scaling objects for different screen resolutions, importing custom color palettes, and recoloring pictures.

Chapter 22, "Customizing PowerPoint," shows you how to create custom toolbars and change PowerPoint's user interface to your liking.

Appendix A, "Installing PowerPoint 4 for Macintosh," shows you how to install PowerPoint.

Appendix B, "Gallery of Presentation Examples," offers a dozen examples of complex, customized PowerPoint slides that demonstrate how you can extend the capabilities of the program.

Who Should Use This Book

Why read a book about PowerPoint 4 if the software is so intuitive? Virtually every feature of PowerPoint can be used and activated with a few mouse clicks—even advanced features such as changing color schemes and rotating charts. PowerPoint doesn't require you to know sophisticated commands or to memorize an arcane set of keystroke combinations; neither is it necessary to know about graphic arts. This book is aimed at anyone who wants to create more effective communications.

Read this book to become acquainted with the myriad possibilities in the PowerPoint software package. You can easily copy a presentation template or any of its default elements and make them your own. To use a presentation template, however, you must know that it's available for your use.

Creating effective, attractive charts is easy in PowerPoint. But how do you know what types of charts to use? Any book about PowerPoint, such as this one, is more a catalog of possibilities than a simple how-to instruction manual. This approach is attempted throughout this book.

Even the most advanced chapters of this book don't plumb the full depths of PowerPoint 4; they merely provide signposts that point in creative directions. If you start using PowerPoint 4 and never read a word about it, it's quite possible to produce serviceable presentations. Over time, you may make many discoveries. But what if you need to harness advanced features and don't have the time to fish around in the software? You certainly will lose much of the program's power, because the program has so much to offer.

This book is aimed at beginning and intermediate users, as well as Macintosh users who appreciate an alternative way to use graphics on their computers. The book is not aimed at graphics specialists or software experts, although members of both groups can profit by reading it. Graphics specialists can learn about an alternative use of computer graphics in the workaday business world; software experts can gain insight about creating high-quality graphics.

Using PowerPoint 4 for Macintosh also is written for corporate-communications specialists and business presenters who want to create their own presentations. This book shows you how to use the program in task-oriented examples. Tips and notes keep you firmly on course and help you get the most out of PowerPoint 4 in the shortest period of time. Liberal use of illustrations depicts many features of the program.

How To Use This Book

PowerPoint is not hard to use; Microsoft has gone to great lengths to make the program more accessible than ever before. You do need to know, however, what the program's features are and what those features can do for you. (The Slide Sorter, for example, is a great idea, but you must know what it is and how to use it. That's where this book comes in.)

You probably won't read this book as you would a novel, from beginning to end. Keep it available as a reference for real-world tasks whenever you use the program. You may use some features frequently and others seldom. *Using PowerPoint 4 for Macintosh* can serve as a reference for features that you only partially remember. Even if you use certain features often, this book still is a source of tips, notes, shortcuts, and troubleshooting ideas. A feature-rich program, no matter how accessible, merits a feature-rich book.

Tips for using Microsoft PowerPoint more effectively are included in the page margins. These tips can help you become more proficient in using the program.

Notes, which appear in highlighted boxes, provide important information about program features and contain cautions about certain aspects of the program.

Short troubleshooting sections try to answer commonly asked questions about the program.

Regardless of the program's ease of use, you still must follow instructions to perform even basic operations. Skipping a step can cause headaches and force you to retrace your steps. When you read a Que book such as *Using PowerPoint 4 for Macintosh*, you learn all the right steps to follow and the exact sequence in which to use them.

Conventions Used in This Book

Some conventions are used in this book to help you learn to use Microsoft PowerPoint 4 quickly.

- You can choose menu commands and dialog-box options by using the mouse or a shortcut key combination (such as ⌘-T). In this book, the instructions are written so that you can use the method with which you are most comfortable. When you see an instruction such as "Open the Edit menu and choose Copy," you can use the mouse to pull down the Edit menu and then click Copy, or you can press ⌘-C to issue the Copy command.

■ Shortcut keys are provided when they are available. The shortcut key ⌘-C, for example, is a shortcut for opening the Edit menu and choosing Copy. Several standard shortcut keys are common to most Macintosh applications—⌘-C for Copy and ⌘-V for Paste, for example—and those key combinations are mentioned where applicable.

■ You click a button or menu command by using the mouse. The word *click* indicates that you should place the mouse pointer on a specific button or command and then click the mouse button one time.

■ Several chapters of this book deal with the process of creating and customizing charts. PowerPoint uses a separate program, Microsoft Graph, to create charts for use in PowerPoint slides. In the chapters that deal with the subject (primarily chapters 12, 13, 14, and 19), the word *chart* is used to describe such objects as bar charts, pie charts, and column charts. Although PowerPoint's graphing and charting application is named Microsoft Graph, all of its menu commands, options, and help menus use the word *chart* in their commands, so that standard is used throughout this book except to refer to the Microsoft Graph program by name.

Part I

PowerPoint 4 Basics

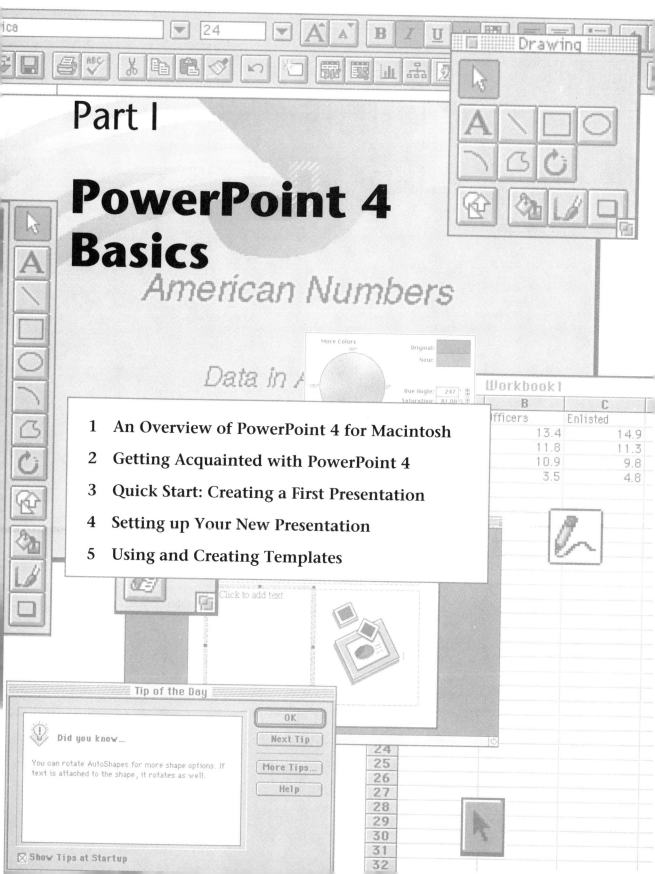

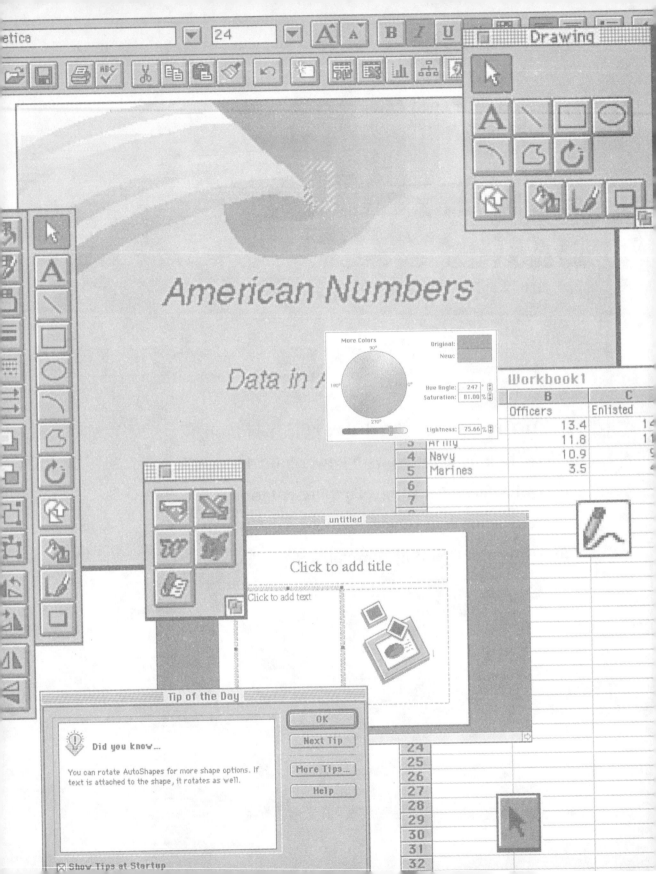

Chapter 1

An Overview of PowerPoint 4 for Macintosh

PowerPoint 4 for Macintosh represents a major upgrade from the preceding version, PowerPoint 3. Although in many ways, the program offers the same functions and methods as its predecessor, Microsoft's presentation package has undergone a facelift and boasts added functionality in many areas. Following are a few of the most important areas of improvement in PowerPoint 4:

- The interface has been enhanced dramatically with new features, including an expanded set of toolbars.

- The user can customize the toolbars, as well as create new toolbars.

- PowerPoint 4's menu bars and standard toolbars give the program nearly identical functionality with its companion programs in the Microsoft Office application suite: Word 6 for Macintosh, Microsoft Mail, and Excel 5 for Macintosh.

- The program's charting capabilities are dramatically improved and expanded, providing greater integration with the PowerPoint main program, an expanded selection of chart types, and easier creation of custom chart types.

- AutoContent and Pick a Look Wizards enable the user to create the basic elements of a presentation quickly and easily.

Version 4 offers many more new features; this short list describes only the major feature enhancements for which most users probably look.

This chapter provides an overview of PowerPoint 4 for Macintosh, including the following:

- Enhanced productivity and ease-of-use features

- Enhanced and integrated charting features

- An organizational-chart feature

- Improved drawing features

- Enhanced color features

- Presentation rehearsal and annotation capability

- Table creation and use of Excel worksheets

PowerPoint is one of the leaders in the growing field of computer presentation applications. Almost everyone who works in a corporate environment is familiar with the idea of a presentation. A presentation, for most people, is a slide show that a speaker uses to help illustrate his or her points. The production of slide shows is the core of the PowerPoint program. Nonetheless, you can make a distinction between a slide show and a presentation. A *slide show* is only one part (although a very important one) of the presentation process. A *presentation*, however, is a slide show combined with hard-copy elements such as speaker's notes, audience handouts, and outlines, which are used to build the structure of the presentation.

A slide show can have many elements, including the following:

- Point-by-point arguments (bulleted lists or body text) that form the backbone of the discussion

- Charts of various kinds (bar charts, pie charts, column charts, and so on), which are used to illustrate statistics and data trends

- Tables, which deliver the actual statistics and categorical explanations

- Graphics and clip art

- Various types of hard copy used to support and round out the presentation

The tools offered in PowerPoint 4 are designed to make the presentation design and production process easier than ever before. All elements of a presentation—the slide show itself, as well as the various forms of hard copy and the outlining tools used to help build the presentation—are united in a seamless whole in the new version of PowerPoint. The various parts of the program are linked in a highly cooperative and collaborative process that, used properly, can help you inform your audience.

The rest of this chapter is devoted to the most important new features of PowerPoint 4. Later chapters of this book cover many small, incremental upgrades in capabilities that have long been part of the program.

Enhanced Productivity and Ease-of-Use Features

Although PowerPoint 4 offers many improvements and enhancements, any user of PowerPoint 3 should feel at home with the new version immediately. Many features have been added to streamline the process of using simple and complex program features, such as shortcut menus, Cue Cards, Wizards, Chart AutoLayouts, and expanded and customizable toolbars.

Shortcut Menus

Many areas of the program are more accessible than ever before through a startlingly simple feature: pressing and holding down the Ctrl key while clicking the mouse button.

Whenever you press and hold down the Ctrl key while clicking an object on the PowerPoint screen (such as a slide background, a drawing, a chart, or a slide title), you display a special shortcut menu similar to the one shown in figure 1.1.

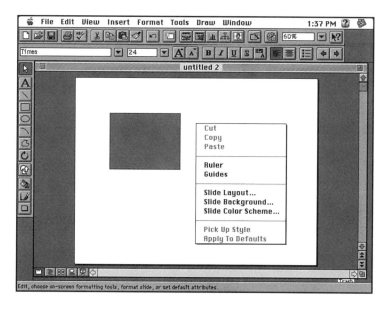

Fig. 1.1
Press Ctrl and click the mouse button to display this shortcut menu.

The greatest advantage of using this method is the extra work it saves you. Perhaps you get tired of continually moving the mouse up to pull down a menu or hunting for the correct menu option. If you point to the desired object on-screen, hold down the Ctrl key, and click the mouse button, that extra work is over.

Additional Toolbars

PowerPoint is one of a new generation of Macintosh applications that allow you to specify the exact appearance of your program screen. PowerPoint 4 offers an expanded set of toolbars, any or all of which can be displayed at any time, as shown in figure 1.2.

Fig. 1.2

When all toolbars are displayed, you may not have much area left to work in.

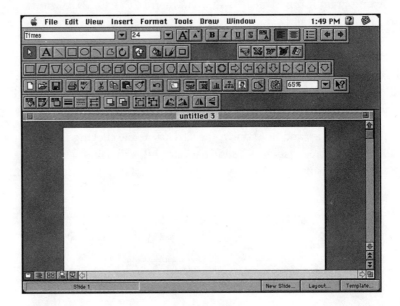

A toolbar arrangement such as the one shown in figure 1.2, however, probably is not to your taste; not many users appreciate having icons occupy half the screen. How does the arrangement shown in figure 1.3 compare?

You can move and rearrange PowerPoint's toolbars at will. Any toolbar can be moved to any margin of the screen, and toolbars can float in the PowerPoint screen, as shown in figure 1.4.

As you can see, you have much more flexibility than before in tailoring your PowerPoint screen. Figure 1.4 also displays another interesting feature of the program: the capability to display and work with more than one presentation at a time.

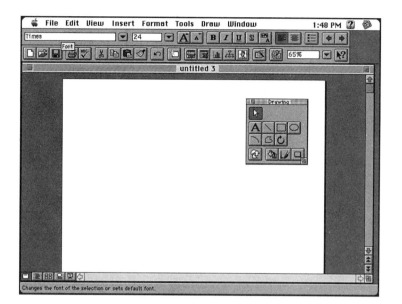

Fig. 1.3
The capability to choose placement and content of toolbars is evidence of PowerPoint's more efficient design.

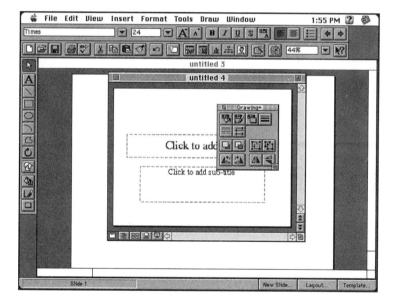

Fig. 1.4
A floating toolbar remains in place even when you switch between open documents.

Among PowerPoint's new toolbars is a Microsoft toolbar that enables you to start any Microsoft application by clicking a button. Programs supported include FoxPro; Publisher; Project; Schedule+; Access; and PowerPoint's Microsoft Office companions, Word and Excel.

PowerPoint's generous assortment of toolbar buttons enables you to assign any PowerPoint function to a button. You also can change any existing toolbar to suit your needs or add any number of new toolbars.

More Help from PowerPoint

PowerPoint 4's ease-of-use enhancements don't stop with mere toolbars and button collections. PowerPoint now provides help every step of the way, from the most basic procedures to the most complex, beginning with PowerPoint's status bar. Whenever you perform an action, choose a menu option, or move the mouse over a toolbar button, a helpful message appears in the status bar at the bottom of the PowerPoint screen, succinctly describing the action that is performed when you click this button.

PowerPoint uses standard menus that bear a close resemblance to those used in Microsoft Word and Excel. In fact, only one menu is different between PowerPoint and Word, which appear to be very different applications (see fig. 1.5).

Fig. 1.5
You'll be treading familiar menu ground in PowerPoint if you're a Word user.

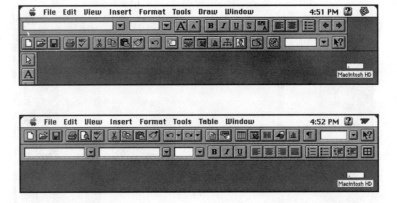

All of PowerPoint's dialog boxes provide a running narrative of the actions that you perform and the options that you choose. You never have a chance to get lost in PowerPoint.

ToolTips is an intelligent, unobtrusive feature that displays a text balloon when you pass the mouse over any toolbar button. Even advanced users appreciate knowing exactly what each button in a crowded custom toolbar means.

Template and Style Wizards

In many workplace situations, you may be forced to produce a presentation on a tight schedule, even if you have no substantial experience in creating presentations. Situations of this kind are where PowerPoint 4's Wizards come in handy.

PowerPoint offers two Wizards to help you get a running start in producing your presentation: the Pick a Look Wizard and the AutoContent Wizard. The Pick a Look Wizard ensures that your presentation has a consistent, attractive appearance, whereas the AutoContent Wizard ensures that the content, style, and structure of your presentation are reasonably complete and organized.

The Pick a Look Wizard provides a nine-step process for choosing a template to define the appearance of your slide show (see fig. 1.6). A template tells PowerPoint how the various elements of your slide show are supposed to look, with specific colors assigned to the various parts of your slides. The Pick a Look Wizard also helps you decide what other presentation elements you want to produce: slide printouts, printer outlines, audience handouts, or speaker's notes to help you keep track of your show while you deliver it.

Fig. 1.6
The Pick a Look Wizard is an extensive template system.

When you begin your presentation, you are given the option to choose the AutoContent Wizard, which provides a four-step procedure for defining the basic message of your presentation (see fig. 1.7). This procedure helps you decide what you're going to say and how you're going to say it, as shown in figure 1.8.

Fig. 1.7
The AutoContent Wizard is an interactive template system.

Fig. 1.8
Use the fields to customize the AutoContent Wizard.

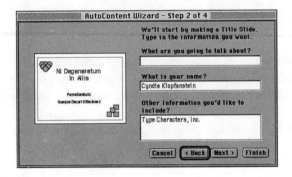

Cue Cards

PowerPoint's Cue Cards, available in the program's Help menu, are easy-to-follow procedures that describe how to perform relatively difficult tasks. Cue Cards cover a long list of common but somewhat complex tasks, including adding a company logo or text to every slide, branching to other presentations, changing colors in a color scheme, and editing PowerPoint clip art. Figure 1.9 shows the basic Cue Cards window.

Fig. 1.9
You can access Cue Cards from the Help menu (the question mark at the right end of the menu bar).

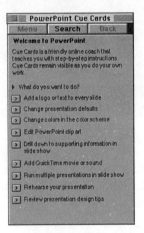

Cue Cards take you through all the steps required to perform a task in PowerPoint. You choose a Cue Card by clicking one of the right-arrow buttons in the Cue Cards window. A step-by-step procedure with a detailed description appears.

AutoLayouts

If you are inserting a slide or beginning a new document, you also can choose AutoLayout options. With this feature, you don't have to design slides yourself; PowerPoint 4 offers 21 slide AutoLayouts that you use to create slide layouts (see fig. 1.10). AutoLayouts bring together five basic slide elements— charts, tables, titles, body text, and objects—in various combinations. To choose a slide AutoLayout, simply double-click it.

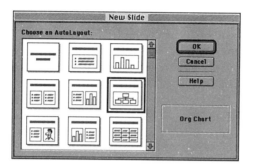

Fig. 1.10
The name listed in the box below the Help button further identifies the selected AutoLayout.

You can, of course, modify any slide layout to suit your needs.

Tighter Application Integration with OLE 2

PowerPoint is not just a remarkably powerful application; it's also part of an even more powerful product called Microsoft Office, which combines Microsoft Word, Microsoft Excel, Microsoft Mail, and PowerPoint in a closely integrated "super app" that makes creating complex documents easy. Complex documents combine many types of data: charts; worksheets; databases; formatted word processing text and layouts; graphics and clip art; and even multimedia elements, such as movie clips and sound files. Many office workers may never create a document that contains all these elements, yet the power is there for them to tap at any time.

PowerPoint, along with all the new Microsoft Office products, supports a powerful new concept called in-place editing. *In-place editing* enables you to use the various programs of the Microsoft Office suite in a single program window; you don't have to open the programs separately and tediously switch among them.

Suppose that you're working in PowerPoint, and you need to use Word 6 to create a table and then paste the table in a slide. All you need to do is click the Insert Microsoft Word Table button in the toolbar. The PowerPoint screen remains, but the PowerPoint toolbars and menus disappear and are replaced by Word toolbars and menus, as shown in figure 1.11.

Fig. 1.11

Click the Insert Microsoft Word Table button to activate Microsoft Word.

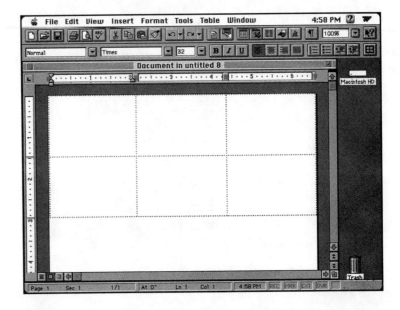

The feature that makes this possible is Microsoft's *OLE* (object linking and embedding) version 2. Version 2 of OLE enables you to copy and paste virtually any type of data between applications that support OLE 2 and to bind the applications that create your data in a mega-application. All the programs in the new version of Microsoft Office—PowerPoint 4, Word 6, Microsoft Mail, and Excel 5—offer this powerful interapplication capability.

PowerPoint's use of objects and its definition of *object* have been greatly expanded. Anything that can be placed in a slide now is considered to be a PowerPoint object, even if the object comes from another program.

Enhanced and Integrated Charting Features

Perhaps one of PowerPoint's greatest improvements is its charting capabilities. PowerPoint offers a new version of Microsoft Graph, the charting program that traditionally has been bundled with PowerPoint. The new version of Graph takes full advantage of OLE 2 to integrate itself much more closely with the main program. For the first time, Graph fully supports PowerPoint's color palettes and color schemes. In fact, most users won't even realize that Graph is a separate application, because it works so closely with PowerPoint 4.

New Chart Types

PowerPoint 4's Graph application offers several new chart types, including a spectacular 3-D surface chart type (see fig. 1.12), which enables you to build topographical maps, adding a new dimension to statistical analysis.

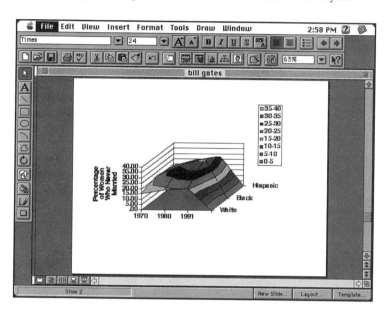

Fig. 1.12
You can create surface charts like this one in Microsoft Graph.

Radar charts are another new chart type, well suited for comparing data (see fig. 1.13).

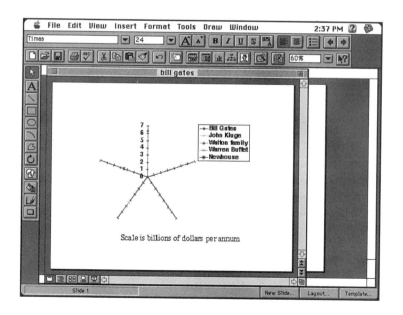

Fig. 1.13
Radar charts offer an unusual way to display data.

A new doughnut chart type is available, offering a variation on the pie charts that are so prevalent in corporate presentations. All the chart types from previous versions of Graph are supported in the new version, including bar, pie, column, area, and line charts (2-D and 3-D). All the chart types include new variations, and PowerPoint 4 offers a remarkably straightforward method for adding special charts as new types. You also can adopt a specific chart as your new default chart type.

Chart Labels, Legends, and Captions

For the first time, Graph allows you to use the mouse to drag chart elements—including axis titles, chart legends, and chart captions—that previously had to stay in specific locations. As a result, manipulating various objects is easier when you edit a chart.

Organizational Charts

PowerPoint also offers an easy-to-use organizational-chart application that enables you to create flow charts, perhaps to show a company's or department's employees and their relationships to one another (see fig. 1.14).

Fig. 1.14
Organizational charts are a new feature of PowerPoint 4.

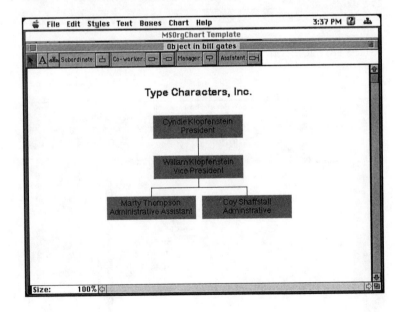

Improved Drawing Features

PowerPoint 4 offers expanded drawing features that put greater artistic power in your hands; you no longer have to use a drawing program to create simple artwork. You now can draw many objects, including squares and rectangles, circles and ellipses, and hard-to-draw AutoShapes (including a starburst and a comic-strip-style text balloon). Other new tools include drop-down color palettes for lines, object fills, and shadows. PowerPoint 4 also offers a special text-rotation feature; you can rotate axis labels 90 degrees in the Microsoft Graph application.

Many drawing features in PowerPoint are replicated in Microsoft Graph. You can fill any shape that you draw in PowerPoint or Graph with colors, shading, and patterns.

Freehand Drawing Tools

A major addition to PowerPoint's drawing capabilities is the Freehand tool. Using this tool, you can draw a shape of any complexity with no restrictions on how the shape must look. To edit a freehand shape, simply drag a point. You can edit a freehand line in the same way.

Editable Curves

PowerPoint's Arc tool enables you to draw a basic curve and then edit that curve by selecting it, opening the Edit menu, and choosing the Object command. Drag any corner handle of the bounding box or side of a curve to lengthen it, shorten it, or change its shape.

Expanded Clip-Art Library

PowerPoint's clip-art library has been expanded to more than 1,000 pieces in various categories, all of which are drawn by graphics professionals at Genigraphics Corporation. PowerPoint offers an improved ClipArt Gallery (see fig. 1.15) that organizes the clip art in *thumbnails* (small reduced views of the clip art), which enable you to preview any piece of artwork before deciding to include it in the presentation. You can use PowerPoint's drawing tools to edit clip art.

Fig. 1.15
Use the ClipArt Gallery to place graphics in your slide presentations.

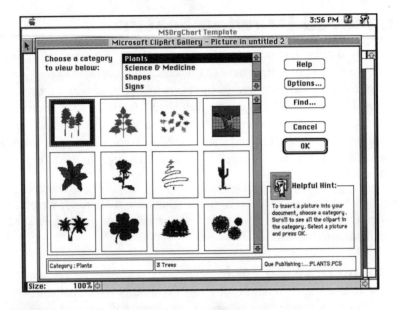

Support for 24-Bit True-Color Pictures

For the first time, PowerPoint includes support for 24-bit true-color graphics in a presentation. Depending on the color depth that your monitor supports, PowerPoint can accept color pictures as easily as it can any other object type.

PowerPoint also offers an intelligent color-scheme feature. You can assign a single background color and title text; PowerPoint automatically offers several sets of colors, making the process of creating custom color sets for your slide shows much easier.

Presentation Rehearsal and Annotation

PowerPoint 4's improved slide-show capabilities facilitate the crucial process of rehearsing and setting the timing of events in your presentation. By watching a digital clock and clicking the mouse button during a presentation, you can trigger all events that occur during the presentation at specific times, so that running your presentation in front of an audience goes off like clockwork.

During your presentation, a member of the audience may ask a question, in which case you can use the Annotate button (in the bottom-right corner of the presentation screen) to help illustrate your point. Clicking this button pauses the presentation and allows you to draw and write with the mouse directly on the presentation screen.

Hidden Slides

You easily can hide single or multiple slides by choosing PowerPoint 4's new Hide Slide command. PowerPoint 4 also takes advantage of object linking and embedding (OLE).

Integrated Table Creation and Use of Excel Worksheets

Along with PowerPoint 4's improved OLE support, buttons (such as the Microsoft Word table and Microsoft Graph buttons) are offered for automatic access to other Microsoft applications to create specific data types for use in your slide show. Particularly if you also own Excel and Word, or the entire Microsoft Office suite, justifying the expense of applications has never been easier. Clicking a toolbar button in PowerPoint enables you to take advantage of Excel's powerful worksheet capabilities, for example, and to insert a worksheet into a slide.

Another toolbar button enables owners of Word 6 for Macintosh to avail themselves of that program's sophisticated table-creation capabilities and to place Word tables in PowerPoint presentations as objects.

Microsoft Graph enables you to import Excel datasheets for use in generating new charts in PowerPoint. You also can import Excel charts for use in PowerPoint slides. When you import an Excel chart, the chart's datasheet information also is imported.

From Here...

From here, you start the task of learning PowerPoint. As noted earlier, the first few chapters of this book cover the basics; later chapters address specific areas of the PowerPoint application in increasing detail. Nonetheless, even the most advanced chapter in this book is easily accessible.

The first few chapters cover the following topics:

■ Chapter 2, "Getting Acquainted with PowerPoint 4," describes the basic mechanics of working with the program (including using the mouse), working in the Macintosh environment, and getting around in the program.

■ Chapter 3, "Quick Start: Creating a First Presentation," takes you through a test drive of PowerPoint 4 by helping you create a presentation.

■ Chapters 4 and 5 delve more deeply into many areas of the program that were introduced in earlier chapters. Chapter 4, "Setting up Your New Presentation," discusses using PowerPoint's various views and masters to create effective presentations. Chapter 5, "Using and Creating Templates," explains the process of using and creating PowerPoint templates.

Chapter 2

Getting Acquainted with PowerPoint 4

Macintosh applications offer you many advantages. A key advantage is that when you know how to use a standard Macintosh application, you know how to activate and use most of the basic features of most other software packages.

This chapter covers the standard Macintosh features offered in PowerPoint 4 and also examines many of the program's most important user-interface features, including the new toolbars and ToolTips.

Using the Mouse

To perform many PowerPoint actions, you can use the mouse or a keyboard command. Because many sophisticated PowerPoint actions can be performed only with a mouse, however, you must have a mouse to use PowerPoint.

Choosing vs. Selecting

When you *choose* an item, you start a program action. To choose an item, you double-click it. To choose PowerPoint 4, for example, you double-click its application icon.

To *select* an item in PowerPoint 4, you click that item only one time. Clicking the PowerPoint 4 application icon one time, for example, selects that icon. Selecting often is called *highlighting* because selected items appear highlighted on-screen. When an item is selected, you can perform many different operations on it, such as formatting text or changing an object's color (discussed in later chapters).

Normally, you can use the mouse to start a PowerPoint feature, especially when the feature is a dialog-box option. Click the option to select it, and then click the OK button (or press Return) to run the feature. Alternatively, you can double-click the option to run the feature. Using the mouse this way speeds the process of using program features. The procedure for using PowerPoint's menus and dialog boxes is covered in "Using PowerPoint's Menus" later in this chapter.

In many situations, you may need to drag the mouse—to move items from one place to another, for example, or to select a group of objects. To drag the mouse, you click and hold down the mouse button and then move, or *drag*, the mouse to a new position on-screen.

Selecting Multiple Objects and Scrolling

Dragging the mouse sometimes creates a box called a *marquee*, which changes size as you move the mouse. Drawing a marquee around several objects in the program selects all those objects at the same time. You also can hold down the Shift key while you click several objects to select all those objects.

Using the mouse, you can move to any area that is visible on-screen by moving the pointer to that position and clicking. Sometimes, however, your PowerPoint slide or program window is not entirely visible on-screen, particularly if you have been moving and resizing windows. To scroll through a slide or program window, use the gray scroll bars on the right side and bottom of each window. Each scroll bar contains two scroll arrows and a scroll box that enable you to advance by single lines (the arrows) or by a page (the scroll box) at a time.

Understanding the Changing Mouse Pointer

The mouse pointer can assume several shapes while you use it. The *arrow pointer* is the most common shape. Use the arrow pointer for tasks such as pointing, choosing items from menus, and selecting objects. When the pointer changes to an *I-beam pointer* (resembling an uppercase *I*), use it to highlight text or to tell PowerPoint that you want to enter new text. As you type, your position is indicated by a vertical bar called the *insertion point*.

When you draw shapes (such as rectangles, ellipses, lines, and freeform polygons) and perform some other functions in the program, the mouse pointer becomes a crosshair. When the program is completing a task and you have to wait, the pointer turns into a watch with a sweep second hand. When you resize windows, the pointer appears as a two-headed arrow. The two-headed arrow is diagonal when you are resizing horizontally and vertically at the same time. In some situations, a four-headed arrow enables you to move items with the keyboard rather than drag them with the mouse.

Manipulating Windows

PowerPoint 4 conforms to all Macintosh standards for minimizing, maximizing, moving, and resizing windows.

The zoom box, which shrinks and enlarges windows, is located in the top-right corner of an open window.

Clicking the close box, in the upper-left corner of an open window, enables you to close a PowerPoint document. If you haven't saved the file, PowerPoint asks whether you want to do so before closing.

You can use PowerPoint commands to manipulate windows in other ways: open and close a window, open multiple files, arrange windows, and so on. These procedures are described later in this chapter.

Starting PowerPoint

Note

For information about PowerPoint installation, see Appendix A, "Installing PowerPoint 4 for Macintosh."

To start the PowerPoint program, follow these steps:

1. Double-click the Microsoft PowerPoint folder to open it, and then double-click the PowerPoint icon (see fig. 2.1).

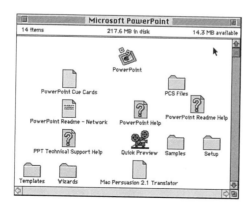

Fig. 2.1
The Microsoft PowerPoint folder is open, showing the PowerPoint icon.

The PowerPoint program starts. If you're starting the program for the first time, PowerPoint's Quick Preview screen appears (see fig. 2.2).

Fig. 2.2
For a brief tour
of PowerPoint's
features, use
Quick Preview.

Click here to start
the Quick Preview

Click here to quit

Click here to get help

2. The Quick Preview is a five-minute tour that helps new users understand some of PowerPoint 4's most important features. To run the Quick Preview, click the Click to Start button. To leave the Quick Preview, click the Quit button.

3. If you clicked the Click to Start button in step 2, the next Quick Preview screen appears. You can step forward and backward through Quick Preview screens by clicking the Next and Back buttons, respectively (see fig. 2.3).

   If you quit the Quick Preview in step 2, the next thing that you see during your first PowerPoint 4 session is a Tip of the Day dialog box, followed by the New Presentation dialog box (see fig. 2.4). In the New Presentation dialog box, you select a Wizard to help you create a new presentation. The Tip of the Day is discussed later in this chapter.

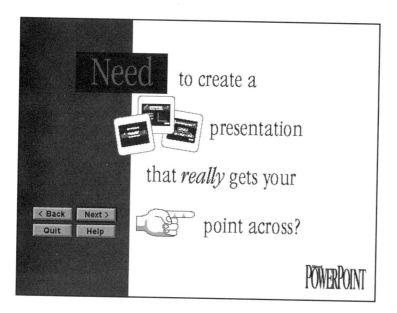

Fig. 2.3
Click the Back and
Next buttons to
move through the
Quick Preview.

PowerPoint 4 Basics

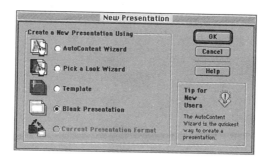

Fig. 2.4
The New Presenta-
tion dialog box
offers several
presentation
options.

The following table describes the options in the New Presentation dialog box.

Option	Description
AutoContent Wizard	Designs the slides you want to use in your new presentation.
Pick a Look Wizard	Designs the appearance of your new presentation.
Template	Selects a template for a presentation.
Blank Presentation	Creates a new, blank presentation.
Current Presentation Format	Opens a new presentation by using the template for a currently displayed presentation. (This option is un- available when you start the program for the firsttime.)

The process of creating a presentation is described in the following sections of this chapter.

Getting Familiar with the PowerPoint Screen

This section introduces the PowerPoint screen and the elements that make it unique. PowerPoint offers many tools and screen elements that require some brief explanation.

The title bar at the top of the PowerPoint program window displays the word Untitled until you save the document and assign a name to it. If an existing file is open, the title bar displays the name of that file, as shown in figure 2.5.

Fig. 2.5
PowerPoint's controls and default toolbars enable you to navigate between slides easily.

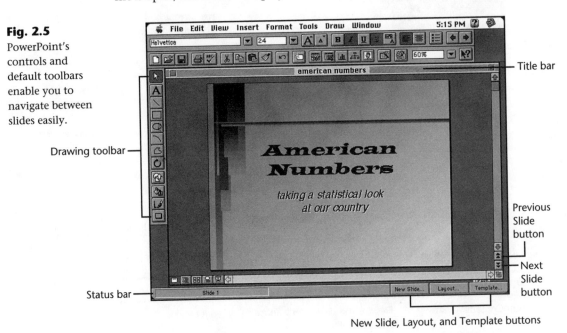

Drawing toolbar

Status bar

Title bar

Previous Slide button

Next Slide button

New Slide, Layout, and Template buttons

The menu bar appears below the title bar, displaying the menus File, Edit, View, Insert, Format, Tools, Draw, and Window.

If the active presentation file isn't maximized in PowerPoint, its own window's title bar appears below the menu bar.

PowerPoint's screen offers several features to help you get started. When you start the program, a set of toolbars appears at the top of the screen, below the menu bar. Another toolbar, called the Drawing toolbar, appears on the left side of the PowerPoint window. (Toolbars are discussed in more detail in "Understanding the Toolbars" later in this chapter.)

At the bottom of the PowerPoint screen is the status bar; the message Slide 1 appears at the left end. The message displayed in the status bar changes whenever you do something with the program or display another slide. If you ever forget which slide you're working on, or which PowerPoint view you're working in, the status bar always tells you where you currently are in PowerPoint.

At the right end of the status bar are three buttons: New Slide, Layout, and Template. These buttons perform the tasks listed in the following table.

Button	Description
New Slide	Inserts a new slide into the presentation.
Layout	Enables you to select a new slide layout.
Template	Enables you to select a new template for your presentation.

The far-right side of the PowerPoint screen is occupied by the Slide Changer and its scroll buttons (double up and down arrows). Clicking the scroll buttons moves you through the slides in your presentation. The Slide Changer also works like a regular scroll bar, except that as you drag the scroll box up or down, new slides appear.

Using the Wizards

The PowerPoint Wizards are tools that help both beginners and seasoned professionals design a presentation from scratch quickly, from the first slide to the last. The AutoContent Wizard provides four short processes that help you create all the slides in your presentation file and assign a basic theme to the presentation (see fig. 2.6).

The Pick a Look Wizard helps you select or design the appearance of your presentation (see fig. 2.7).

PowerPoint 4 Basics

Fig. 2.6
The AutoContent
Wizard provides
the basic content
for many common
presentation
topics.

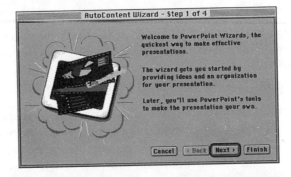

Fig. 2.7
The Pick a Look
Wizard is another
template system
designed to get
you going quickly.

Using Wizards is simple. Choose options at each step, and then click the Next button to move to the next step. Click the Back button if you change your mind and want to use another option in a previous step; click the Finish button if you want PowerPoint to make most of the design decisions for you.

Wizards, as simple as they are, can save you many steps in creating a presentation. Chapter 3, "Quick Start: Creating a First Presentation," provides much more information about using Wizards.

Using the Tip of the Day

The Tip of the Day is a dialog box that opens automatically when you start the program (see fig. 2.8). This dialog box offers simple, useful information about program features and shortcuts for complex tasks.

Tips of the Day usually consist of keyboard or mouse shortcuts, information about basic program operation, or hints about major program functions. PowerPoint has a database of tips that you can flip through by clicking the Next Tip button. If you get tired of seeing the Tip of the Day every time you start the program, click the Show Tips at Startup check box to remove the x.

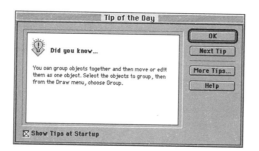

Fig. 2.8
You're not limited
to just one tip a
day; click the Next
Tip button to see
more.

Understanding the Toolbars

Toolbars are among the most important parts of the PowerPoint program.
Version 4 of PowerPoint adds an expanded set of toolbars that you can customize. When you start PowerPoint for the first time, three toolbars are displayed: two at the top of the screen and one on the left side (see fig. 2.9).

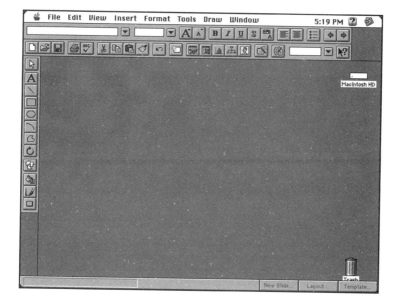

Fig. 2.9
The Standard,
Formatting, and
Drawing toolbars
are set to open by
default.

The three toolbars shown in figure 2.9 are available in all areas of PowerPoint,
including the main program, the charting feature, the Equation Editor, and
the Slide Sorter. The main PowerPoint screen has a default set of seven
toolbars (see fig. 2.10), any or all of which you can display at any time by
opening the View menu and choosing Toolbars.

Fig. 2.10
PowerPoint offers several default toolbars for operations such as drawing, formatting, and creating shapes.

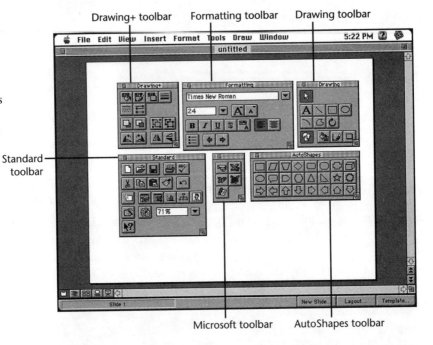

The following table describes the toolbars available in PowerPoint 4.

Toolbar	Description
Standard	Provides buttons for many standard PowerPoint program operations, such as opening, saving, and printing files; handling files; and cutting, copying, and pasting
Formatting	Provides buttons for text-formatting operations, such as bold, italic, justification, and font-selection buttons
Custom	Enables you to add your own buttons (this toolbar is blank until you add buttons)
Drawing	Provides buttons for basic drawing operations, such as drawing basic shapes, arcs, and curves; applying fill colors; and grouping objects
Drawing+	Provides buttons for advanced drawing functions, such as applying fill colors to objects and lines, applying line styles, adding arrowheads, and grouping and ungrouping objects
Microsoft	Provides buttons that activate other Microsoft applications, including Excel and FoxPro (particularly applicable to Microsoft Office owners)
AutoShapes	Provides buttons that draw 24 shapes automatically, including stars, speech balloons, and sunbursts

Using the Toolbars

The toolbars described in the preceding section offer fast access to most of the crucial features of the PowerPoint 4 program. You can use the toolbars only with a mouse or a similar pointing device. To use a toolbar, click the button that represents the command or program function that you want to execute.

As you have learned, not all the toolbars are displayed when you start the program; you decide which toolbars you want to display and where they will appear on-screen.

To display or remove toolbars from the PowerPoint screen, follow these steps:

1. Open the View menu and choose the Toolbars command. The Toolbars dialog box appears (see fig. 2.11).

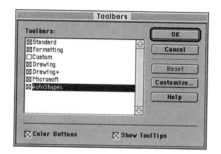

Fig. 2.11
The Toolbars dialog box enables you to specify the toolbars that appear on-screen.

2. The Toolbars list contains seven check-box options. Clicking an empty check box places an x inside it, resulting in the display of the desired toolbar in the program. Clicking any check box that has an x inside it removes the toolbar from the screen.

3. To display color buttons in the toolbars, click the Color Buttons check box. (This option is selected by default.)

4. To display the toolbars, click OK or press Enter.

Another button in the Toolbars dialog box—the Customize button—starts PowerPoint's toolbar-customization feature. Describing this capability is beyond the scope of this chapter, but if you want to learn more, see Chapter 22, "Customizing PowerPoint."

▶ See "Customizing Toolbars," p. 477

When you need information about a particular toolbar button, click the Question Mark button in the Standard toolbar and then click the button for which you need help. PowerPoint displays a help window to show you how to use the button in question. To close the help window, click the close box in the upper-left corner.

PowerPoint 4 Basics

I

Using Floating Toolbars

Floating toolbars are toolbars that you can detach from their normal places at the top or side of the PowerPoint screen so that they appear to float over the presentation. Any toolbar in the PowerPoint program can be detached from the edges of the screen and placed on-screen as a floating toolbar (see fig. 2.12).

Fig. 2.12

Move toolbars or close them to tailor your work area to your needs.

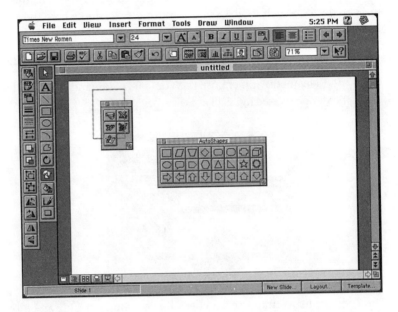

To float a toolbar, simply click any area of the toolbar that isn't occupied by a button (such as the top or bottom end of a toolbar) and drag the toolbar. The toolbar changes shape as you drag it around the screen. When the toolbar is where you want it, release the mouse button.

Buttons in a floating toolbar work exactly the same way as they do in a stationary toolbar, and you can drag floating toolbars to any margin of the PowerPoint screen to relocate them there. You also can drag any edge of a toolbar to reshape it.

When you place toolbars in new locations on-screen or display new toolbars, PowerPoint automatically displays the toolbars in their new configurations when you start the program again. This feature enables you to arrange the screen exactly as you want.

Using ToolTips

ToolTips are simple, unobtrusive forms of Balloon Help that describe the functions of the buttons in the various PowerPoint toolbars. Given the propensity of new programs such as PowerPoint 4 to succumb to "iconitis"—the practice of assigning every possible program function to an icon or button—you may find it hard to keep all the buttons straight. ToolTips are an easy and convenient way to learn all the button functions without getting lost or, worse, doing something in the program that you didn't intend to do.

If the ToolTips feature is activated (as it is by default), a small yellow text box appears as you pass the mouse over any toolbar button on-screen. If you compare the ToolTip with the status bar at the bottom of the PowerPoint screen, you see that the messages are the same.

To turn on the ToolTips feature, open the View menu and choose Toolbars. The Toolbars dialog box appears, listing the toolbars that are available in the program. (As noted earlier, PowerPoint has a default list of seven toolbars, but you're not limited to those, by any means.) Click the Show ToolTips check box at the bottom of the dialog box to place an X in it. Then choose OK (click OK or press Return) to close the dialog box and activate the ToolTips feature.

The ToolTips function whether you're in PowerPoint, in the Graph screen, or in any of the program's views, such as Outline or Slide Sorter. (PowerPoint's various views and screens are discussed later in this chapter.)

Troubleshooting

I can't find the text-formatting buttons in PowerPoint's toolbar.

You probably need to display another toolbar on-screen—namely, the Formatting toolbar. To do so, open the View menu and choose Toolbars; the Toolbars dialog box appears. Click the Formatting check box to place an X in it, and then choose OK. The text-formatting buttons appear on the PowerPoint screen.

I clicked the small box in the upper-right corner of a floating toolbar, and the toolbar disappeared. How do I redisplay the toolbar?

You clicked the toolbar's close box. To redisplay the toolbar, open the View menu and choose Toolbars; the Toolbars dialog box appears. Click the check box for the toolbar that you want to display, and then choose OK. The toolbar appears on the PowerPoint screen.

Using PowerPoint's Menus

PowerPoint's menu bar complements the toolbars, providing access to every function of the program. Earlier, you learned the basic menu names and where the menus are located on the PowerPoint screen; this section covers menus in more detail. (Bear in mind that this is an overview chapter; all the options and functions mentioned here are discussed comprehensively in other chapters.)

Although the toolbars offer fast access to many of PowerPoint's basic features, the menus, with their many options, enable you to access every function of PowerPoint.

Choosing Menu Commands

Each menu in PowerPoint (like menus in all other Macintosh applications) opens when you click its name in the menu bar and hold down the mouse button. This action displays a pull-down menu, so-called because the menu normally is pulled, or dragged, downward from the menu bar at the top of the screen. Some menu options, when chosen, have submenus that pop out slightly to the side of the selected options (see fig. 2.13). These submenus are called *cascading menus*.

Fig. 2.13
An arrow to the right of a menu option indicates the presence of a cascading menu.

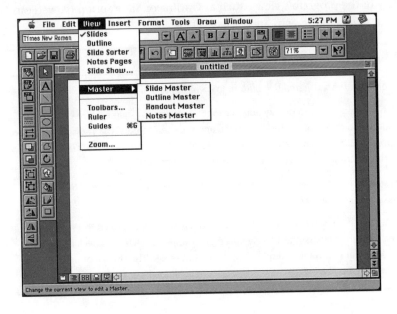

As you see, further options are offered in cascading menus. Cascading menus are indicated in the first-level pull-down menu by small black arrows at the right edge of the menu.

This book discusses menu options in a very specific way. Whenever the text tells you to choose a menu command, that instruction is in the following format:

> Open the Format menu and choose the Font command.

Notice that you *choose* rather than *select* menu options.

Also notice the keyboard equivalents, such as ⌘-N (for creating a new PowerPoint document), listed to the right of some menu options. Instead of choosing one of these options from the menu, you can press the appropriate key combination to choose the option.

Reviewing PowerPoint's Menus

Another advantage of using PowerPoint with other applications (especially with other Microsoft applications) is the fact that its menus closely mirror those of other applications. Other Microsoft programs, such as Word 6 and Excel 5, offer common menus other than just File and Edit—Insert, Window, and Help, for example. Differences exist, of course, but the basics are the same in most programs that run in the Macintosh environment.

Table 2.1 describes PowerPoint's menus.

Table 2.1	PowerPoint Menus
Menu	**Description**
File	The File menu lists PowerPoint's file-handling options, such as New, Open, Close, Save, Print, and Quit. At the bottom of the menu is a list of previously opened files; choose one of these file names to display that file.
Edit	The Edit menu offers access to many of PowerPoint's most important editing features, such as Cut, Paste, Paste Special, Clear, Delete, Find, and Replace.
View	The View menu options—including Slides, Outline, Slide Sorter, and Notes Pages—offer access to the various views and screens within PowerPoint. You also can display the current slide-show presentation from this menu by choosing the Slide Show option.

(continues)

PowerPoint 4 Basics

Table 2.1 Continued	
Menu	**Description**
Insert	The Insert menu offers access to program features for inserting new objects of various types into a presentation. Menu options such as New Slides, Date, Time, and Clip Art are available.
Format	The Format menu lists options for changing and defining every aspect of your presentation, including fonts, presentation templates, color, bulleted text, and text alignment. You also can pick up formats from objects and apply those formats to other objects of the same type by choosing the Pick Up Style option.
Tools	The Tools menu provides access to many of PowerPoint's most powerful add-on features, such as the spelling checker, transition timing for special effects in a presentation, toolbar customization, Smart Quotes, and Smart Cut and Paste.
Draw	The Draw menu gives you access to most of PowerPoint's basic graphics-handling operations, such as grouping and ungrouping objects, layering drawn objects (Send to Back and Send to Front), setting precise sizes and scales for objects, and rotating and flipping objects.
Window	The Fit to Page option in the Window menu resizes the active presentation window to fit the current view. The bottom portion of the Window menu lists the names of the presentations that currently are open.
Help	The Help menu offers access to many kinds of help, including Macintosh Balloon Help (via the Show Balloons option). PowerPoint help options include PowerPoint Contents, PowerPoint Search for Help On, PowerPoint Index, PowerPoint Quick Preview, PowerPoint Tip of the Day, PowerPoint Cue Cards, and PowerPoint Technical Support.

Choosing Dialog-Box Options

When you pull down any menu, you see that certain option names (such as New and Open in the File menu) are followed by an ellipsis (...). Whenever an ellipsis appears after an option in a pull-down menu, choosing that option displays a dialog box that provides more detailed options for the selected menu option.

Note

If an ellipsis does not appear after an option name, PowerPoint immediately executes the appropriate action when you choose that option. If you open the Insert menu and choose the Date command, for example, no dialog box appears; PowerPoint automatically inserts the current date as a text object.

Figures 2.14 and 2.15 show a pair of fairly typical dialog boxes, which contain the various dialog-box elements with which you will work in PowerPoint.

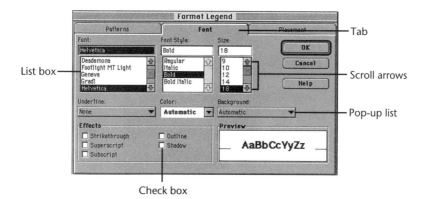

Fig. 2.14
Tabbed dialog boxes have several views. Click a tab to change the view.

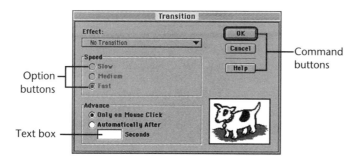

Fig. 2.15
Simple dialog boxes contain only option buttons or check boxes.

As you see, dialog boxes contain a substantial number of elements. The following list describes these elements and how you use them in PowerPoint:

■ *Text box*. A box in which you can type and edit text, dates, and numbers.

To use a text box, click inside it. A blinking vertical bar, called the *insertion point*, appears. The insertion point indicates where the characters that you type appear. You can use the Delete key (or, on some keyboards, the Backspace key) to delete selected text in a text box. To select a word in a text box, click and drag the mouse across the word to highlight it, or double-click the word.

- *Option button.* A button that represents one option in a group of options. (Option buttons sometimes are called *radio buttons*.)

  To choose an option button, click it; a dark dot fills the center of the button, indicating that the option has been chosen.

- *Check box.* A box that represents a feature that you can turn on or off. An x in a check box means that the option is active.

  To select or deselect a check box, click it.

- *List box.* A list or pop-up list that you can scroll to display available alternatives.

  To use a list box, click a list item if it's visible, or click the scroll arrow to display other items and then click the desired item.

- *Command button.* A button that executes or cancels a command. Some command buttons provide access to additional options.

Now that you are familiar with PowerPoint's basic operation, you are ready to learn about some of PowerPoint's most important features.

Understanding PowerPoint Slides

Presentations consist of slides, which are the core of PowerPoint. All the objects that you create for your 35mm slides, overhead transparencies, or on-screen shows are placed and arranged in slides rather than document pages, as in Microsoft Word.

As mentioned earlier in this chapter, you can scroll through slides by using the Slide Changer, which occupies the right edge of the PowerPoint screen when you work with a presentation file. You can view slides full-screen or at magnification factors up to 400 percent. You can cut, paste, and rearrange slides at will, and you can use the mouse to apply new color schemes and templates to them quickly.

Templates are files that help define the continuity of a presentation. These files are discussed in "Understanding PowerPoint Templates" later in this chapter and more extensively later in this book.

Each slide in a presentation has a specific purpose: to deliver a message (or an aspect of a message) efficiently and effectively. Different types of slides have specific designs. When you want to add a new slide to a presentation, PowerPoint gives you several choices, as shown in figure 2.16.

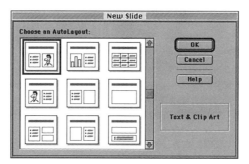

Fig. 2.16
PowerPoint provides several slide-layout options, such as bulleted lists, flow charts, and graphs.

Chapter 3, "Quick Start: Creating a First Presentation," describes how to create new slides in the process of creating a basic presentation. For now, however, examine figure 2.16. The dialog box contains several small thumbnails, each of which represents a slide layout. Some of the thumbnails depict a slide that contains charts; others depict bulleted lists of points, or arguments, to be made in the slide; still others offer combinations. Each of the various slide designs is tailored to convey a particular message.

The AutoContent Wizard, discussed earlier in this chapter, helps you structure the content of a presentation. This Wizard determines the text contents of your slides and therefore can be an important tool to use when you create slides.

Understanding PowerPoint Templates

Templates specify the appearance of your presentation. A template is separate from the actual slide type or content, which can change from slide to slide. In general, a template is the same throughout all slides in a presentation, because it determines the appearance of your slides.

Why use a template? If you're a busy person who suddenly has to pull together a sales pitch for an important meeting in only one hour, you don't want to struggle through the process of creating a layout for your slide show. If you're not a professional artist, or if you're simply pressed for time, use PowerPoint's substantial array of predefined templates, which provide attractive colored backgrounds on which you can create your message.

You can apply a template to an existing presentation, or you can create a new presentation by using the template of an existing presentation. If you have time, you also can create your own templates.

Choosing PowerPoint Template Files

PowerPoint offers a wide variety of templates. Each template was designed for a specific type of output, so templates are grouped in three categories:

- Black-and-white overheads

- Color overheads

- On-screen (video screen) slide-show presentations

These categories simply represent folders of files inside the PowerPoint Folder that contain templates. The following table shows the normal folder names for each category of templates.

Template Category	Folder Name
Black-and-white overheads	B&W Overheads
Color overheads	Color Overheads
Slide-show presentations	On Screen & 35mm Slides

Each set of templates is based on a certain theme, and that theme is repeated in each template in each folder. One of the templates in the On Screen & 35mm Slides folder, for example, is titled BLUDIAGS.PPT; this template displays blue diagonal lines in the slide background. In the B&W Overheads folder, the same template is named BLUDIAGB.PPT, and the Color Overheads folder contains a file named BLUDIAGC.PPT.

To browse through the templates in any of the folders, follow these steps:

1. Open the File menu and choose New. The New Presentation dialog box appears (refer to fig. 2.4).

2. Click the Template option button.

3. Choose OK. The Presentation Template dialog box appears (see fig. 2.17).

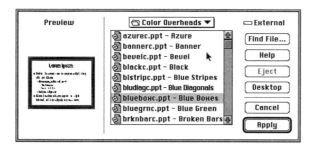

Fig. 2.17
The Presentation Template dialog box enables you to open existing templates provided with PowerPoint.

4. In the list box, double-click the Templates folder (located inside the PowerPoint folder).

5. Double-click a nested folder, such as On Screen & 35mm Slides. When this folder opens, PowerPoint displays a list of template files. (Template file names have the extension PPT, as well as a brief description of the template.)

6. Click any of the listed files. The dialog box displays a thumbnail preview of the selected template (see fig. 2.18).

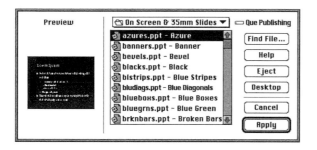

Fig. 2.18
Any of these templates can get you on your way quickly.

7. To return to the presentation without applying a new template, click Cancel or press Esc.

PowerPoint 4 Basics

Note

At times, the thumbnail preview of templates in the Presentation Template dialog box is inadequate. To view the template in an actual slide, follow the steps listed in the following section.

When you create a new presentation, the Pick a Look Wizard can help you choose a template.

You need to know about one more template element: the Slide Master. All templates have Slide Masters, which are used to define common objects that may appear in all your slides, such as a company logo and company name, the time and date when the presentation was created, a border, or a special graphic object.

You also can use Slide Masters to change the basic elements of your template and define new ones. Slide Masters are discussed in greater detail in "Understanding PowerPoint Masters" later in this chapter and in Chapter 4, "Setting up Your New Presentation."

Applying PowerPoint Templates

The process of applying a template to the active presentation is the same as the process of previewing a template, until the last step. Follow these steps:

1. Open the Format menu and choose Presentation Template to display the Presentation Template dialog box.

2. In the Files list, double-click the Templates folder.

3. Double-click a nested folder.

4. Select any of the template files listed.

5. To apply the selected template to the current presentation, click the Apply button. The dialog box closes, and the presentation is reformatted for the new template.

Bear in mind that templates don't affect the content of the presentation or the actual slide layout; they change only the appearance of the slides' background.

Troubleshooting

I followed the steps to apply a template to my presentation, but the layout of the slide in my existing presentation did not change to the layout of the template that I applied.

Applying a template to an existing presentation does not alter the layout or order of the slides in the existing presentation; it changes only the background graphics and color scheme. To change the slide layout, open the Format menu and choose Slide Layout to display the Slide Layout dialog box. Select a new slide layout, and then click Reapply to apply the new layout to the current slide.

I'm unhappy with the new template that I applied to my presentation, and the Undo option in the Edit menu is not available. How can I revert to my original color scheme and slide background?

Open the Format menu and choose Slide Layout. Using the thumbnail graphic or the template file name, locate and choose the template of your original presentation. Then click Apply to apply the template to your presentation.

Locating Template Files

Misplacing files after you save them is easy. To recover a lost file, check the file names listed at the bottom of PowerPoint's File menu. If the desired file isn't there and you can't find it in the normal PowerPoint Template folder, you can use the Find File feature. Open the File menu and choose the Open command to display the Open dialog box; then click the Find File button. PowerPoint's Search dialog box appears. Type the name of the file for which you want to search, choose the drive that you want to search, and then choose OK. PowerPoint lists the folders as it searches them. If your system has more than one drive, you may have to search all of them to find your file.

When your file turns up (if it does) and the program finishes searching, the Find File dialog box appears, displaying the name of the file and the folder in which it's located. If the file doesn't turn up, the Find File dialog box displays the message `No matching files found`, in which case you should try searching another drive. This method should enable you to find a file eventually (assuming that you didn't delete it by accident).

Understanding PowerPoint Masters

You already know about Slide Masters, which define the contents of templates. A few other masters control different parts of a presentation. The Outline Master, the Notes Master, and the Handout Master all play a role in producing effective, powerful messages.

Introducing Slide Masters

Slide Masters control the background of a slide show and define the styles of the text and titles that appear in your presentation. Slide Masters also can contain any objects that you want to use in every slide of a presentation, such as a company logo or graphic object.

To view a Slide Master, follow these steps:

1. Open the presentation whose master you want to view. (Alternatively, simply open a template.)

2. Open the View menu and choose the Master option. A cascading menu appears.

3. From the cascading menu, choose Slide Master. Your current presentation is replaced by its Slide Master.

Figure 2.19 shows an example of a Slide Master. This figure shows the way that slides for the current presentation appear when you add text statements and bulleted lists.

Fig. 2.19
PowerPoint's Slide Masters enable you to add text and graphic elements that appear in all slides in a presentation.

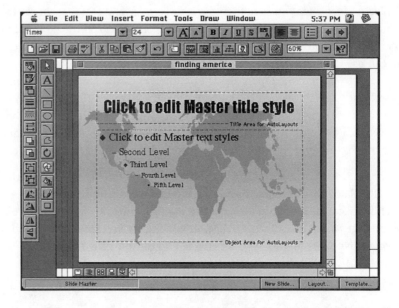

Notice that the Slide Master provides several levels of bullets. You can apply a new font (or any other available text style) to the titles and text, even though the statement Click to edit Master title style doesn't actually appear in any of your slides. That statement is a placeholder that contains the styles for slide titles and the accompanying formatting information.

Introducing Outline Masters

Outline Masters have one key purpose: to help you format and structure the printed outline of your presentation. Figure 2.20 shows a typical Outline Master.

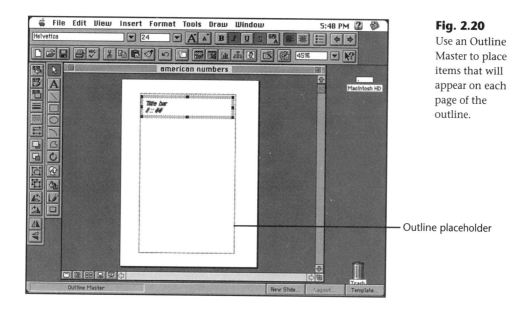

Fig. 2.20
Use an Outline Master to place items that will appear on each page of the outline.

Outline placeholder

A box drawn in dashed lines, called a *placeholder*, contains your outline and any other objects that you add. Like Slide Masters, Outline Masters enable you to add a company logo, date and time information, and other elements that you want to display in every slide.

To view an Outline Master, follow these steps:

1. Open the presentation that you want to edit.

2. Open the View menu and choose the Master option. A cascading menu appears.

3. From the cascading menu, choose Outline Master. Your current presentation is replaced by its Outline Master.

Introducing Notes Masters

PowerPoint's Notes Masters are an extremely handy way for speakers to organize their notes for presentations. Notes Masters combine a miniature view of each slide in a presentation with each slide's text. The Notes Master enables you to create notes pages that organize your presentation. Printed copies of your notes pages help you follow your presentation without being forced to gaze at the screen whenever you need to make a point.

Figure 2.21 shows a typical Notes Master.

Fig. 2.21

The Notes Master displays an image of the slide at the top with room for your notes below.

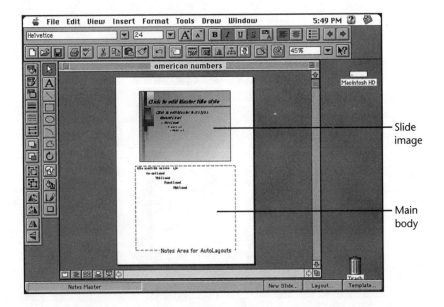

The Notes Master defines the appearance and organization of each notes page. You can add to a Notes Master page numbers that correspond to the slides in your presentation, and you can apply color schemes to the notes. In the master body, you can format your notes just as you do normal text, applying fonts, text styles, text alignment, and so on. You then can print your notes pages.

To view a Notes Master, follow these steps:

1. Open the presentation that you want to edit, or create a new presentation by using a Wizard or opening a new template. (You must have an active presentation open to view any of its masters.)

2. Open the View menu and choose the Master option. A cascading menu appears.

3. From the cascading menu, choose Notes Master. Your current presentation is replaced by the Notes Master.

Introducing Handout Masters

Handout Masters, which are similar to Outline Master, are used to format the handouts that you want to give your audience. A Handout Master displays several slide-image placeholders, which are the overlapping boxes shown in figure 2.22.

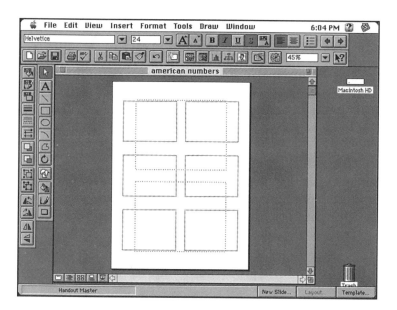

Fig. 2.22
A Handout Master contains place-holders for slides.

As you can with all other masters, you can add background page numbers, dates and times, and graphic objects to your handout pages. You must place these elements outside the placeholders on the master handout page. The text that you type in the Handout Master is included on every page of your handout.

A Handout Master also displays guides and rulers, which can help you design and measure elements in every master and view in PowerPoint. Guides may be familiar to you if you have used a desktop-publishing program; they can help you with object placement and layout for slides, handouts, and other views and masters in PowerPoint.

To view a Handout Master, follow these steps:

1. Open the presentation that you want to edit. (A presentation must be open and active for you to view its Handout Master.)

2. Open the View menu and choose the Master option. A cascading menu appears.

3. From the cascading menu, choose Handout Master. Your current presentation is replaced by its Handout Master.

Understanding PowerPoint Views

The various views in PowerPoint correspond to the masters. PowerPoint has an Outline view, a Slide view, a Notes Pages view, and a special Slide Sorter. Several of these views interact, offering some unique features that put additional power in your hands.

Using the View Buttons

Several view buttons appear just above the status bar in the bottom-left corner of the screen (see fig. 2.23). Each button, when clicked, displays a different view. These view buttons enable you to access not only the various views, but also the various masters.

Fig. 2.23
Click the view buttons to change the view quickly.

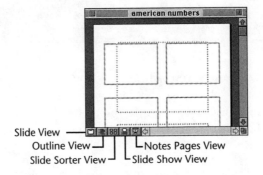

Slide View

Outline View
Slide Sorter View

Notes Pages View
Slide Show View

Clicking the Outline View button, for example, displays the outline of the presentation, showing all the actual text, with the proper indents for each slide. Slide Sorter is a drag-and-drop view that enables you to rearrange slides, somewhat as you do a deck of cards when you're playing solitaire. Notes Pages view enables you to look at and page through all the notes pages that correspond to the slides in your presentation.

In PowerPoint 3, you could use the view buttons to toggle between masters and views. (Masters and views are different, however, as you learn later in this section.) In PowerPoint 4, to access a master, you must hold down the Shift key while you click the view button.

Table 2.2 describes the view buttons.

Table 2.2 PowerPoint View Buttons	
Action	**Result**
Slide View	Individual Slide view
Shift+Slide View	Slide Master
Notes Pages View	Notes Pages view
Shift+Notes	Notes Master
Outline View	Outline view
Shift+Outline	Outline Master
Slide Sorter	Slide Sorter View
Shift+Slide Sorter	Handout Master
Slide Show	Runs the slide show
Shift+Slide Show	Specifies slides to use in show, rehearses timing, and runs slide show

Note

Watch the status bar as you pass the mouse over the view buttons; then hold down the Shift key and pass the mouse over the buttons again. The status bar displays the function of each button. Also, if ToolTips is activated, the ToolTips change as you move the mouse over a button, whether or not you are holding down the Shift key.

Using Slide View

When you create a presentation, you spend most of your time in Slide view. You can page through individual slides by using the Slide Changer at the right side of the screen.

You can use the Slide Changer in several ways. For example, you can page up or down through slides by clicking the scroll arrows at the bottom of the Slide Changer, or you can drag the scroll box up or down the Slide Changer. When you drag, a small slide number pops up next to the Slide Changer (see fig. 2.24). You also can page down through the slides by clicking the vacant area of the Slide Changer.

Fig. 2.24
The Slide Changer
is disguised as the
right scroll bar.

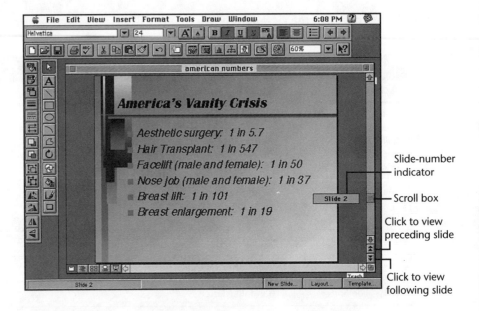

You will do most of your creative work for slides in Slide view. Many of the major creative operations in PowerPoint—including chart creation, drawing, table creation, and text editing—are performed in this view.

Using the Slide Sorter

The Slide Sorter is a quick-and-dirty method of moving slides around and changing their order. As figure 2.25 shows, the Slide Sorter displays rough thumbnails of the slides in your presentation.

To use the Slide Sorter, simply click the Slide Sorter View button just above the status bar at the bottom-left corner of the screen.

When you enter the Slide Sorter, PowerPoint displays the Slide Sorter toolbar. The buttons in this toolbar offer several key elements that you can apply to any slide in your presentation. In addition, two drop-down lists in the toolbar enable you to apply special effects—transitions and builds—to any slide. Although these subjects are discussed in much greater depth in Chapter 20, "Advanced Presentation Management," they merit brief discussion here.

Transitions are special effects that determine how slides appear and disappear during a slide show. You can apply 45 transitional effects to any slide, including fades, wipes, and explodes. You can set transitions to appear randomly, or you can assign a specific transition to a slide. When you apply any transition to a slide in the Slide Sorter, a small icon appears at the bottom of the thumbnail for that slide, indicating that you have applied an effect to it.

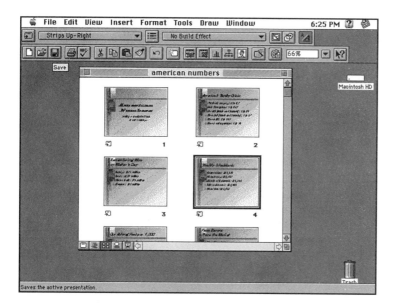

Fig. 2.25
The Slide Sorter is
an efficient way to
track and move
slides.

PowerPoint 4 Basics

As opposed to transitions, which govern how an entire slide appears, *builds* are special effects that you can apply to individual text elements in a slide. PowerPoint offers 30 builds, including effects that make body-text objects fly onto the slide (from the left, right, top, or bottom) or dissolve into the slide. In the Slide Sorter, you apply builds from another drop-down list. You can't apply builds to graphic objects (such as charts or graphics drawn in PowerPoint) or to slide titles; you can apply them only to entries in the slides' body text.

The Slide Sorter is an incredibly effective way to manage slides. You can drag any slide to any position in the slide order; the slide that currently is in that position changes places with the one that you're dragging. You also can delete slides in the Slide Sorter.

> **Note**
>
> Although the Standard toolbar is displayed in the Slide Sorter, some of its buttons work only in other views. Watch the status bar for information about toolbar-button functions.

Using Notes Pages View

As you learned in the discussion of Notes Masters earlier in this chapter, a notes page displays a slide in the upper half of a page; the bottom half of the page displays any notes and narrative that you enter for that slide.

Notes pages are especially helpful when you have more content to communicate for a particular slide than you have space in that slide. (In fact, a good design rule is to limit the amount of information that you convey in any particular slide.) In notes pages, you can place information that elaborates on a slide's contents.

To use Notes Pages view (see fig. 2.26), simply click the Notes Pages View button in the bottom-left corner of the PowerPoint screen, just above the status bar.

Fig. 2.26
Click the Notes Pages View button to switch to this view.

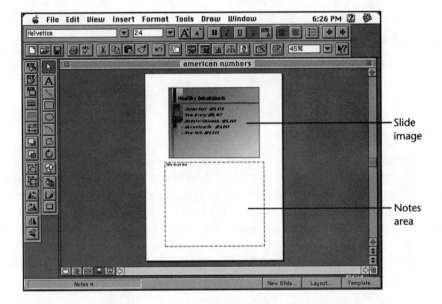

To edit notes in Notes Pages view, click the notes area of the page and then enter, format, and edit notes as you would all other text elements in PowerPoint.

Using Outline View

Outline view provides powerful interaction capabilities with other views in the program, notably Slide view. In Outline view, you can add and delete slides; you also can edit, format, and alter their text content. You can rearrange slides, along with body-text elements, and also indent text (a procedure called promoting and demoting). In fact, until you run the actual slide show, you may not have to use any view other than Outline view, because many key program functions are available in this view (see fig. 2.27).

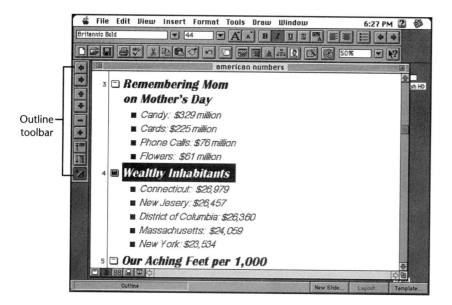

Outline
toolbar

Fig. 2.27
Outline view
makes line editing
easy.

PowerPoint 4 Basics

Outline view is discussed in detail in Chapter 4, "Setting up Your New Presentation." In brief, Outline view is a good place to plan your presentation and to look at the logical progression of your arguments in the presentation.

Using Slide Show View

Slide Show view enables you to preview or rehearse your production. When you click the Slide Show View button, the PowerPoint screen disappears and is replaced by a full-screen display of the current slide. The slide show begins at the currently selected or displayed slide.

When you start the slide show, click the mouse or press the space bar or the Return key to display successive slides. If you have build effects in each slide, PowerPoint displays those effects with each mouse click or keystroke. To end the slide show at any time, press the Esc key.

The features offered in Slide Show view are substantial and go far beyond the space available in this chapter. Slide timing and rehearsals, rearranging, using transitions, and many other features are discussed in detail in Chapter 20, "Advanced Presentation Management."

Getting Help

PowerPoint 4 sports an expanded on-line help system that you can access by using the mouse to pull down the Help menu. The help system provides concise descriptions of PowerPoint topics. The help system explains every PowerPoint feature and also offers suggestions on using those features effectively. In addition, every dialog box in PowerPoint includes a Help button that you can click to display an explanation of the features and options in that dialog box.

Figure 2.28 shows a typical help window.

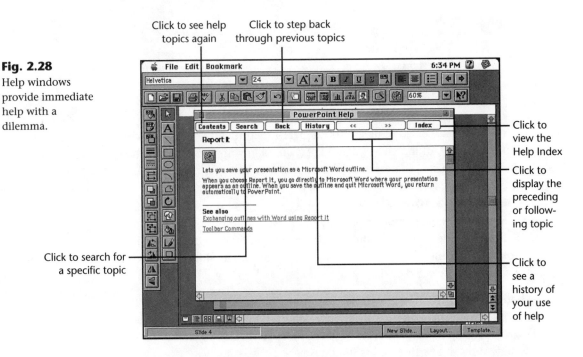

Click to see help topics again

Click to step back through previous topics

Fig. 2.28
Help windows provide immediate help with a dilemma.

Click to search for a specific topic

Click to view the Help Index

Click to display the preceding or following topic

Click to see a history of your use of help

The mouse pointer changes shape in certain areas of the help system. Many terms in a help window, for example, appear in green underlined text (on a color monitor). When you move the mouse over such a term, the pointer changes to a hand with the index finger extended. Clicking one of these terms enables you to jump to helpful text on that topic. This system often is called *hypertext*. (To move back to the preceding topic, click the Back button.)

Also, many terms in PowerPoint help windows have a green dotted underline (again, on a color monitor). Click one of these terms to display a pop-up definition; click outside the definition to close it.

Using Help-Menu Options

The Help menu offers nine options, which are described in the following table.

Option	Description
About Balloon Help	Displays an explanation of Balloon Help
Show/Hide Balloons	Switches Balloon Help on and off
PowerPoint Contents	Displays a table of contents for the help system (the main help screen)
PowerPoint Search for Help On	Activates a search for specific terms and features in PowerPoint
PowerPoint Index	Displays an alphabetical index of help topics
PowerPoint Quick Preview	Demonstrates PowerPoint's features
PowerPoint Tip of the Day	Provides tips on effective program operation
PowerPoint Cue Cards	Displays step-by-step procedures
PowerPoint Technical Support	Displays information about Microsoft technical support

As you can see, PowerPoint's help system is quite extensive and offers several ways to access a particular help topic.

Each of the PowerPoint Help menu options is discussed in greater detail in the following sections.

Balloon Help

When you open the Help menu and choose Show Balloons, help balloons appear when you point to items on-screen. The balloons provide more information about buttons than ToolTips do; therefore, they appear instead of the yellow ToolTips boxes when Balloon Help is activated.

Contents

The Contents option, where many users begin, displays the PowerPoint help screen, which lists three major topic areas and their icons. The following table describes these topic areas.

Topic	Description
Using PowerPoint	Displays information on specific features and procedures
Reference Information	Displays vital information on program, keyboard, and mouse shortcuts, as well as an overview of menu, toolbar, and window commands
Technical Support	Displays detailed information about Microsoft technical-support services

Search for Help On

The Help menu's Search for Help On command automatically takes you to one of the help system's most detailed and useful levels: Search level. Figure 2.29 shows the Search for Help On dialog box.

Fig. 2.29

The PowerPoint Search for Help On command is the fastest way to travel through help data.

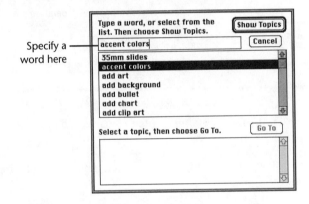

PowerPoint help's Search feature enables you to specify any topic covered in the on-line help system, from menu commands and common PowerPoint terms to procedures for performing various tasks.

The Search list covers almost every topic in the PowerPoint program. Specify a command or word that pertains to the subject on which you need information, and PowerPoint displays the help topic that contains this information.

The easiest way to find a specific topic is to type the name of a feature or a command. The Search list automatically adjusts to display the closest match for the name or command that you type. You also can scroll through the list to find the desired topic.

Click the word in the list and then click the Show Topics button, or double-click the word. In the topics box at the bottom of the Search dialog box, PowerPoint displays the main help topic or topics that contain the information you need.

Click a topic to select it, and then click the Go To button. A new help screen comes up, displaying topic information that may contain the tips and information you want. The hypertext capabilities facilitate fast jumps to almost any topic when you click text that has a green underline (on a color monitor). The Back button enables you to return to any previous level of the help system. The double arrows (<< and >>) enable you to move rapidly through levels of the help system, from the most general to the most specific. You may need to scroll through the text to see all of it.

Index

PowerPoint's Help Index offers another powerful way to reference any topic in the program in an even more direct way than the Search feature does. Figure 2.30 shows the Help Index.

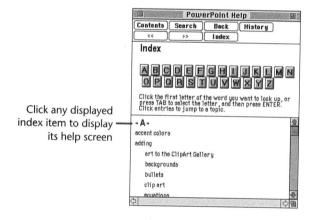

Click any displayed index item to display its help screen

Fig. 2.30
Click a letter (or press Tab to move to the letter) and then press Return to search for help information.

PowerPoint 4's Help Index contains a set of alphabetized buttons. Clicking one of these buttons displays the index section that contains the entries alphabetized under that letter.

To make effective use of the Help Index, follow these steps:

1. Click the button for the first letter of the topic that you want to reference (A to Z).

2. Scroll down the list until you locate your topic, and then click an index entry. The help information for that entry appears.

Quick Preview

PowerPoint's Quick Preview feature, which was described earlier in this chapter, provides a tour of some of PowerPoint's most important features. Quick Preview appears the first time that you run the program, but you can access it from the Help menu at any time.

Tip of the Day

As you learned earlier in this chapter, you can set the Tip of the Day to appear automatically whenever you start the program. You also can access this feature from the Help menu at any time.

Cue Cards

Even for advanced presentation artists, the Cue Cards feature can be extremely handy. Cue Cards are a fairly short list of crucial tasks that normally require tedious menu and point-and-click navigation to master (see fig. 2.31).

Fig. 2.31

Click the arrow buttons to select a Cue Cards topic.

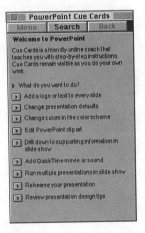

To activate Cue Cards, follow these steps:

1. Create a new presentation or open an existing one.

2. Open the Help menu and choose Cue Cards. The Cue Cards list appears.

3. Click one of the arrow buttons in the Cue Card list.

4. Follow the instructions that appear.

5. If another step is available or implied in the instructions, click the Next button at the bottom of the Cue Card. Click the Menu button on top if you want to reference another Cue Card. Click the Back button if you need to review an instruction.

> **Note**
>
> One useful feature of Cue Cards is the way that they interact with the main PowerPoint program. You can read each step and perform it in the program while keeping the Cue Card displayed on-screen.

PowerPoint Technical Support

This option displays information about support services available through the Microsoft support network, including product training and consultation, electronic services, and phone support.

Quitting Help

To quit the help system, click the close box in the upper-left corner of the help window or press ⌘-W. The help system is a separate program in a window that you can resize as you can any other Macintosh window.

From Here...

This chapter covered only the most basic aspects of PowerPoint. From here, you can go in many directions:

- Chapter 3, "Quick Start: Creating a First Presentation," gives you a chance to test PowerPoint 4 by creating your first presentation.

- Chapter 4, "Setting up Your New Presentation," discusses using views and masters.

- Chapter 5, "Using and Creating Templates," describes the process of working with and creating PowerPoint templates.

- Chapter 7, "Creating Speaker's Notes, Outlines, and Handouts," discusses those features of the program.

Chapter 3

Quick Start: Creating a First Presentation

The last chapter introduced many of the tools that you use to create presentations. In this chapter, you actually make a presentation.

For many people, this chapter may be sufficient for their day-to-day work, because all the basics are covered. The chapter also can be a jumping-off place, however. When you plunge into PowerPoint 4, you may find that the features you explore here trigger many ideas, firing your desire to learn more.

This chapter covers the following subjects in detail:

- Using Wizards to create a presentation design quickly

- Adding common background elements (such as a date or company name) to a template for a presentation

- Creating and working with slides in a presentation

- Adding text and other objects to a presentation

- Creating a chart

- Saving and printing a presentation

Using Wizards

As you learned in Chapter 2, "Getting Acquainted with PowerPoint 4," when you start PowerPoint, you are greeted by the Tip of the Day dialog box. Read the information in this dialog box, and then click the OK button to get it out of the way. The next thing that appears is the New Presentation dialog box (see fig. 3.1).

Fig. 3.1
Choose a template
system or a blank
presentation in
the New Presenta-
tion dialog box.

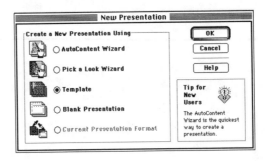

Use the AutoContent Wizard to choose and set up the specific type of presentation (the message and argument to be conveyed), and then use the Pick a
Look Wizard to define the overall appearance of the presentation.

Developing an Outline with the AutoContent Wizard

To start creating the presentation, click the AutoContent Wizard option
button in the New Presentation dialog box. The first dialog box of the
AutoContent Wizard appears (see fig. 3.2). This dialog box shares a few
elements with all the others in the Wizard's dialog-box sequence.

Fig. 3.2
Use the buttons at
the bottom of the
dialog box to
advance through
the steps of the
AutoContent
Wizard.

Use the four buttons displayed at the bottom of the dialog box to move
through the Wizard procedure. After you make your choice, click the Next
button to go to the following dialog box. The Back button (which is not
available in the first dialog box) enables you to backtrack if you change your
mind and want to choose another option. The Cancel button dismisses the
Wizard outright without implementing your choices. The Finish button cuts
the Wizard procedure short but implements the presentation's design, based
on the information that you provided.

The title bar at the top of the dialog box shows the current step of the Wizard
procedure. Figure 3.2, for example, shows that you're in the first of four steps
of the AutoContent Wizard.

The first AutoContent Wizard dialog box simply is an introduction. The following example shows you how to create a structured outline with a specific type of content for your first presentation. Follow these steps:

1. In the first AutoContent Wizard dialog box, click the Next button. The second of the four AutoContent Wizard dialog boxes appears.

2. Enter your own data in the text boxes (see fig. 3.3).

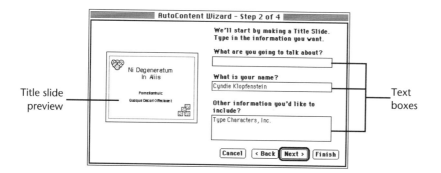

Title slide preview ——

—— Text boxes

Fig. 3.3
The blank text boxes enable you to interact with the AutoContent Wizard.

3. Click the Next button to go to the next step. The third AutoContent Wizard dialog box appears (see fig. 3.4).

Fig. 3.4
In this AutoContent Wizard dialog box, you define the focus of your presentation.

4. Choose a content option by clicking the appropriate button. A preview of the selected option appears in the preview box on the left side of the dialog box.

5. Click the Next button. The final AutoContent Wizard dialog box appears (see fig. 3.5).

6. Click the Finish button to conclude the Wizard procedure. The PowerPoint screen reappears, this time in Outline view.

PowerPoint 4 Basics

Before proceeding further, take a moment to study the example of Outline view shown in figure 3.6.

AutoContent Wizard - Step 4 of 4
Your presentation is well on its way! Press Finish and PowerPoint will create the presentation for you.
Continue to build your presentation by changing the sample text, and add your own slides and ideas.
To choose a different look for your presentation, use the Pick a Look Wizard under the Format menu.
Cancel
< Back
Next >
Finish

Fig. 3.5 This AutoContent Wizard dialog box is the finish line.

Slide titles
Body text
Slide numbers
Slide icon
untitled 2
1 General
Cyndie Klopfenstein
2 Introduction
State the purpose of the discussion
Identify yourself
3 Topics of Discussion
State the main ideas you'll be talking about
4 Topic One
Details about this topic
Supporting information and example
How it relates to your audience
5 Topic two
Details about this topic
Supporting information and example
How it relates to your audience
6 Topic Three
Details about this topic
Supporting information and example
How it relates to your audience
7 Real Life

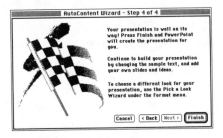

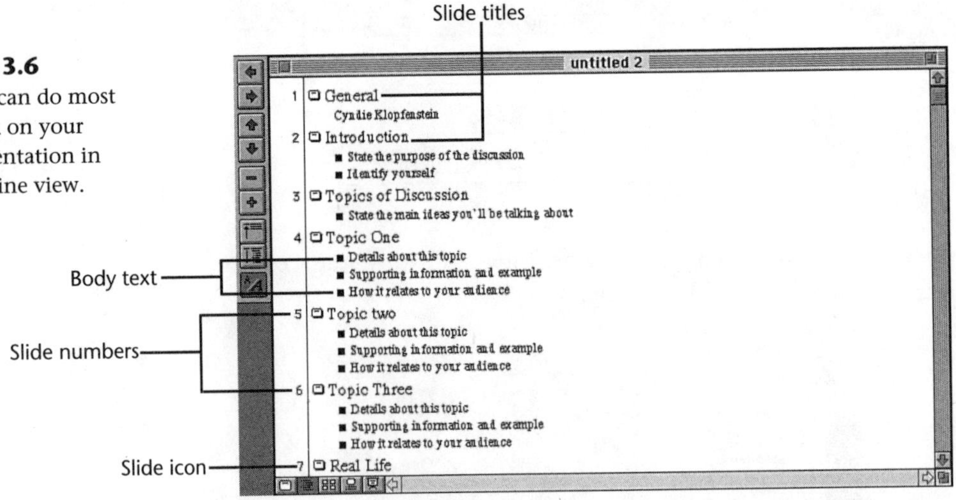

Fig. 3.6 You can do most work on your presentation in Outline view.

Note

After running each Wizard, PowerPoint displays its Cue Cards feature, which coaches you on important and complex procedures in the program. You do not run or use Cue Cards for the current examples. To close the Cue Cards window, click the Cue Card title bar and then press ⌘-W, or click the close box of the Cue Cards window. Bear in mind that you can access Cue Cards from the Help menu at any time.

In Outline view, each slide of the presentation is numbered and marked with a small icon. The slide title is in large type; body text for each slide appears below each slide title.

You're not confined to this outline structure, however; you can make any statement in the outline a slide title in its own right. In many cases, a bulleted statement in the outline may merit a slide of its own. For now, though, the content is relatively unimportant.

Now you're ready to choose the appearance of your presentation.

Choosing the Appearance of Your Presentation

You can start creating a presentation with the Pick a Look Wizard just as easily as you can with the AutoContent Wizard. The two Wizards address different aspects of creating a presentation. The AutoContent Wizard helps you determine the content of your presentation; the Pick a Look Wizard helps you choose a template or graphic design.

> **Note**
>
> When you use the Pick a Look Wizard, you not only define how the slides are going to look, but also set up your notes pages, your handouts, and your Slide Master.

At this point, all you have is an outline. You could design a template from scratch, but unless you have a large time budget for creating the presentation (and is there ever such a thing in the business world?), you need to get the job done quickly and effectively. To do so, use the Pick a Look Wizard.

You can activate the Pick a Look Wizard by clicking its button in the New Presentation dialog box or by clicking its button in the PowerPoint toolbar.

To use the Pick a Look Wizard, follow these steps:

1. Click the Pick a Look Wizard button in the PowerPoint toolbar. The first Pick a Look Wizard dialog box appears (see fig. 3.7).

Fig. 3.7
The Pick a Look Wizard helps you choose a layout.

2. Click the Next button to go to the next step. The second of the Wizard's nine dialog boxes appears (see fig. 3.8).

3. For this example, choose the On-Screen Presentation option.

4. Click the Next button. The third Wizard dialog box appears (see fig. 3.9).

Fig. 3.8
In this dialog box,
you choose a
presentation type.

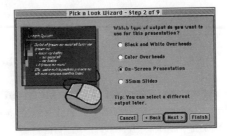

Fig. 3.9
Choose a
background
design in the third
dialog box.

Template list ——

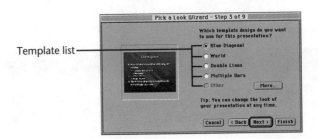

PowerPoint offers 57 template options. Five options appear in this dialog box; the others appear in a different dialog box that you display by clicking the More button.

5. Click the More button to display the Presentation Template dialog box (see fig. 3.10).

Fig. 3.10
This dialog box
offers many more
template options.

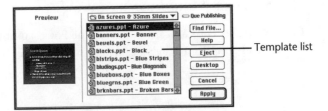

—— Template list

6. For this example, click the Cancel button to return to the Step 3 dialog box. (You can choose any template; all templates work the same way. The remaining steps, however, assume that you do not choose a new template.)

7. Click the Blue Diagonal option button. The preview window on the left side of the dialog box shows the template's appearance.

8. Click the Next button. The fourth Wizard dialog box appears (see fig. 3.11).

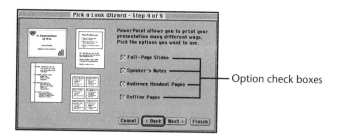

Fig. 3.11
In this dialog box, you choose the types of support material that you will use.

Option check boxes

9. The dialog box asks you to specify the types of printouts that you want to use in the presentation. By default, all the check boxes contain xs, which means that they're all selected.

For this example, leave the options selected, and then click the Next button. The Slide Options dialog box appears, as shown in figure 3.12.

Fig. 3.12
In this dialog box, you choose the objects that will appear on each slide.

10. This dialog box enables you to choose basic background elements for your slide template and master. For this example, choose all the check-box options (click the boxes to place xs in them).

▶ See "Under-standing the Slide Master," p. 110

11. Click the Next button to move to the next step. The Notes Options dialog box appears, as shown in figure 3.13.

12. The Notes Options dialog box displays the same options as the Slide Options dialog box. For this example, choose all the options in this dialog box.

▶ See "Creating Speaker's Notes, Outlines, and Handouts," p. 175

Note

The preview section on the left side of the dialog box shows a typical notes page. By default, the slide appears in the top half of the page, and the actual speaker's notes appear in the bottom half.

Fig. 3.13
This dialog box
adds elements to
the notes pages.

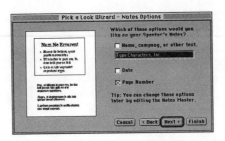

13. Click the Next button to proceed to the next step. The Handout
    Options dialog box appears (see fig. 3.14).

Fig. 3.14
You also can
customize
handouts with the
Pick a Look
Wizard.

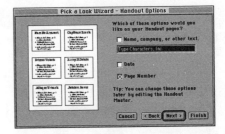

14. The same options as in the preceding dialog boxes are available, this
    time for audience handout sheets. For this example, choose all the
    options.

15. Click Next to move to the next step. The Outline Options dialog box
    appears (see fig. 3.15).

Fig. 3.15
Choose outline
options in this
dialog box.

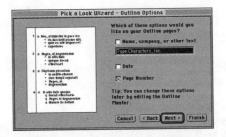

> **Note**
>
> Outline view is one of the most important aspects of PowerPoint, because it represents the organization of the entire presentation in text form. Every slide can be edited and its text contents changed in this view. Points and arguments in each slide can be promoted or demoted in Outline view, and slides can be rearranged as well. Even if you prefer working in Slide view, it's a good idea to refer to Outline view on a regular basis, because it provides a larger view of the presentation. You can use the Outline Master to edit the options at any time.

16. For this example, choose all the options, and then click Next to display the last dialog box.

17. Click the Finish button to exit the Pick a Look Wizard.

Now take a moment to apply your selections to the current document. Open the View menu and choose Slides. A Slide view of the first slide in your presentation appears. If you chose the Blue Diagonal template background in step 7, your screen should resemble figure 3.16.

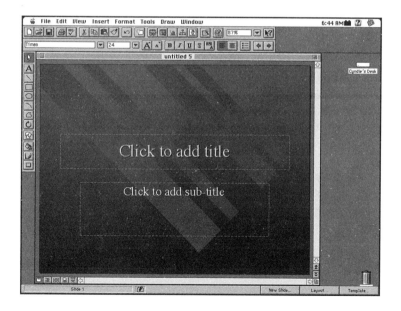

Fig. 3.16
The slide templates now are ready to be customized.

Understanding PowerPoint's Templates

Now that you have created the basis of your first presentation, it may be useful to summarize the components of templates offered in PowerPoint 4 and to explain how they affect your work in the program.

As mentioned earlier, PowerPoint offers 57 predesigned templates. Each template is available in three formats: On-Screen Presentation (one of which you created in the preceding section), Black and White Overhead, and Color Overhead. All templates have certain common elements that are used in every presentation. These elements are:

▶ See "Understanding the Slide Master," p. 110

■ *Slide Master.* The Slide Master sets up the design of every slide in the presentation. Text and objects that you place in the Slide Master appear in all the slides in your presentation.

▶ See "Working with Outlines," p. 187

■ *Outline Master.* The Outline Master organizes each outline page of the presentation.

▶ See "Creating Speaker's Notes," p. 176

■ *Notes Master.* Speaker's-notes pages for a slide provide a reduced image of the slide at the top of the page; your edited notes about the slide and its contents appear at the bottom of the page. You can resize slide images in the Notes Master, so your notes can be as detailed as necessary. The Notes Master contains the elements that appear in every notes page.

▶ See "Creating Handouts," p. 185

■ *Handout Master.* You can produce handouts for distribution to the audience. The Handout Master defines the format and appearance of handout pages, as well as the elements that appear in each handout page, such as a company name, date, or logo. Handouts can be laid out with two, three, or six slides per page.

When you use the Pick a Look Wizard, the four masters are set up automatically. If you don't want to set up all these masters immediately, you can choose a template in the New Presentation dialog box. You also can apply a new template to the current presentation or even create a new presentation with a blank template.

Now that you have the basic framework of the presentation in place, you're ready to add the actual content: charts and text.

Working with Slides

Whether you use a Wizard or a template to set up your presentation, or start with a blank presentation, you may need to add many elements. For example, you may want to add slides. (Your presentation outline expands automatically as you add slides to a presentation.) You may need to edit the text of each slide to suit your subject matter and then format the text to suit your taste. You may want to add a logo or custom chart to all your slides and to place other artwork in a single slide.

The first slide in your new presentation was displayed in Slide view (refer to fig. 3.16). Slide view is not a static display; you can add and edit objects at will in this view, while getting immediate visual feedback. If something doesn't look right, you know it immediately.

The lines of text in the first slide are, quite simply, objects. The slide title, the name, and the job description (the body text) are flexible units that you can edit, reformat, and move around.

At the bottom of the slide are the elements that were placed in the Slide Master when you used the Pick a Look Wizard. These elements include the company name, a page number, and a date. The page number and date are shown in hash marks in Slide view (see fig. 3.17). The hash marks are placeholders for the values in the masters; the elements inside them appear in normal text when you run your slide show.

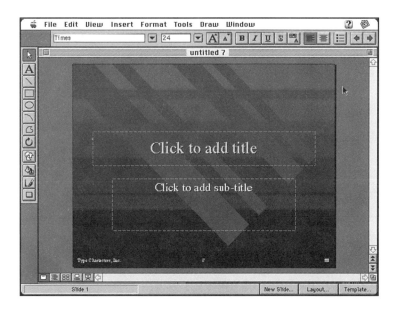

Fig. 3.17
The first slide introduces the presentation topic.

Adding a New Slide with AutoLayouts

AutoLayouts are predefined slide layouts based on the typical objects and data types that you place in slides during the course of creating a presentation. The New Slide dialog box provides a list of AutoLayout thumbnails that include many combinations of charts, bulleted lists, clip art, and slide titles.

As you see in figure 3.18, some AutoLayouts offer simpler slide types than others. Some AutoLayouts combine a title with only a chart or bulleted list of points, and others contain two columns below the title, combining a chart with a bulleted list.

Fig. 3.18
Use the
AutoLayout dialog
box to select a
defined layout.

AutoLayout thumbnails

Description window

Whenever you see a slide layout with chart or clip-art elements, or any other object type offered in an AutoLayout, bear in mind that the layout elements are simply objects. The AutoLayout elements don't contain any data that relates to your subject matter directly; they are items that you edit to construct and illustrate your own logical procession of ideas.

The AutoLayout thumbnails are displayed in rows of three. A description window on the right side of the New Slide dialog box displays the selected layout.

> **Note**
>
> You also can add a new slide by clicking the Insert New Slide button in the PowerPoint toolbar.

To add a new slide to your sample presentation, perform the following steps:

1. Display the first slide in your presentation.

2. Open the Insert menu and choose New Slide, or press ⌘-N. The New Slide dialog box appears (refer to fig. 3.18).

3. The top row of the AutoLayout thumbnail list shows the first three slide layouts. Click the thumbnail at the top right; the description window displays the word Graph.

4. Choose OK. A new slide is inserted into your presentation (see fig. 3.19).

PowerPoint 4 Basics

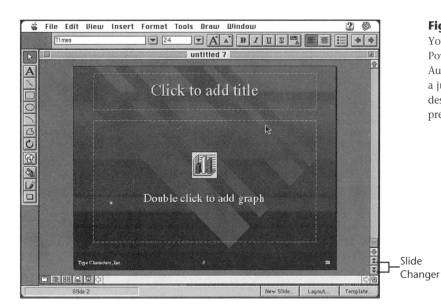

Fig. 3.19
You can use PowerPoint AutoLayouts to get a jump on the design of the presentation.

Slide Changer

The new slide is inserted after the first slide, which was the one that PowerPoint displayed when you started the process of creating a new slide. Whenever you create a new slide, that slide is inserted after the currently displayed slide.

Notice that the bottom of the new slide contains the company name, along with the placeholders for the date and the page number. Two other elements are present: a slide title and a new item called a *chart object*. The chart itself hasn't been created yet; you need to edit it for content to shape your presentation. Even now, you have created only the framework of your presentation.

Moving from One Slide to Another

Now that you have created a new slide, how do you get back to the first one? If you have the extended Macintosh keyboard, you can press the Page Up and Page Down keys. Pressing Page Up displays the preceding slide, and pressing Page Down displays the next slide in the presentation sequence.

You also can use the Slide Changer (refer to fig. 3.19). Click the arrow buttons to move up or down through the slide sequence.

Another way to use the Slide Changer is to drag the scroll box up or down. A slide-number indicator appears as you drag the scroll box.

Working with Text

PowerPoint's text tools offer many powerful features. In both title text and body text, you can change fonts, select font styles and effects (any text font that is available in your system can be used in your slides), adjust the font size, and make many other changes. In the following sections, you expand your knowledge of working with text.

Adding and Editing Text

With the exception of the totally blank slide, all new slides selected in AutoLayout have a placeholder for the title. To add a title to a slide, follow these steps:

1. In Slide view, click the slide title placeholder. The placeholder text Click to add title disappears and is replaced by a text box with a blinking insertion point.

2. Type the title text in this box. Pressing Return adds a blank line for more text.

3. When you finish entering the title, click outside the text box.

Some AutoLayouts have placeholders for bulleted points. To add text to these placeholders, follow these steps:

1. Click the bulleted-list placeholder to get the flashing insertion point.

2. Type the new text.

3. Press Return to add a new bulleted point (see fig. 3.20).

 There may be occasions when you want to add text outside the placeholders. Simply select the Text button in the Drawing toolbar and click anywhere outside the placeholders to get the insertion point.

Text can be easily edited by clicking the text to place the insertion point, and then using the Delete or Forward Delete keys to delete text and typing to add text. You can double-click to quickly select a word and triple-click to select a line of text. Typing replaces selected text.

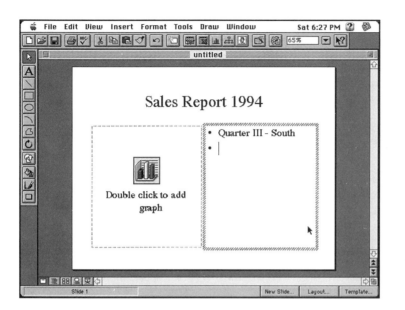

Fig. 3.20
Each time you press Return, a new bullet is added.

Note

Another efficient way to alter and edit text is to use PowerPoint's Outline view. In Outline view, all the text in the presentation is displayed, ready for editing; you don't have to flip back and forth through slides to make changes or to select each text object to edit it. You also can format text in Outline view. Press ⌘-A to select all the text in Outline view.

Formatting Text

To format text, select it with the mouse or keyboard, and then apply the formatting with a command or toolbar tool. The fastest way to format slide text is to use the PowerPoint Formatting toolbar, which simplifies many tedious text-formatting tasks.

▶ See "Formatting Text," p. 151

To apply formatting to selected text, follow these steps:

1. Click the text box in the slide and then select the text or paragraph that you want to format.

2. Click the appropriate toolbar button or press the appropriate shortcut key to apply the desired formatting.

PowerPoint's Formatting toolbar contains Font and Font Size pop-up lists, as well as the buttons described in table 3.1.

	Table 3.1	**PowerPoint Formatting Tools**
Button	**Button Name**	**Description**
A	Increase Font Size	Increases font size to the next predefined point size
A	Decrease Font Size	Decreases font size to the preceding predefined point size
B	Bold	Applies boldfacing to selected text
I	Italic	Applies italics to selected text
U	Underline	Applies underlining to selected text
S	Text Shadow	Applies shadow to selected text
A	Text Color	Displays a pop-up palette of colors that can be applied to selected text
	Left Alignment	Aligns selected text to left margin of placeholder
	Center Alignment	Aligns selected text to center of placeholder
	Bullet On/Off	Adds or deletes bullets from selected text
←	Promote	Promotes selected text (decreases its indent level)
→	Demote	Demotes selected text (increases its indent level)

Notice that if you use a toolbar button, such as Bullet On/Off or Bold, to apply formatting to selected text, you can remove the formatting by clicking the proper button again.

PowerPoint's Format menu offers the same range of choices and options as the Formatting toolbar. Chapter 6, "Working with Text," discusses formatting techniques in greater detail.

Following are some shortcut keys that you can use to format selected text:

Shortcut Key	Description
⌘-B	Boldfaces selected text
⌘-I	Italicizes selected text
⌘-U	Underlines selected text
⌘-equal sign (=)	Subscripts selected text
⌘-Shift-equal sign (=)	Superscripts selected text

Adding Bullets to Text

Bullets can be added to paragraphs in a slide, can be of several different types, and can change according to the level of the bulleted statement.

In PowerPoint, a paragraph is any amount of text that ends with a carriage return. A paragraph can be one word, a few words, a short sentence, or a sequence of sentences of any length; pressing Return at the end creates the paragraph. By definition, bullets are added only to paragraphs.

To add bullets to text, simply select the text and then click the Bullet On/Off button in the Formatting toolbar.

Bullets can be flexible; you can use just about any character as a bullet. To choose a new bullet style for a bulleted list in a slide, follow these steps:

1. Select the bulleted list that you want to change.

2. Open the Format menu and choose Bullet. The Bullet dialog box appears (see fig. 3.21).

Fig. 3.21

Choose a bullet character in the Bullet dialog box.

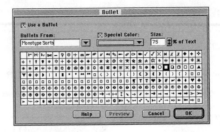

3. Choose any of the following options:

   ■ *Use a Bullet.* When selected, this option applies bullets to the selected paragraphs; when deselected, this option removes bullets.

   ■ *Bullets From.* This pop-up list displays the fonts from which you can choose bullet characters.

   ■ *Special Color.* This pop-up palette displays colors that you can apply to bullets.

   ■ *Size.* This option sets the size of the bullet in relation to the point size of the text font.

4. Click a bullet character in the grid in the dialog box. A small zoom window pops up, giving you a close-up view of the selected character.

5. After you select the bullet and its formatting, choose OK. PowerPoint displays the new bullet characters in your slide.

Working with Objects

Even though the computer press tends to drown the word *object* in reams of verbose terminology, it is a straightforward concept. In PowerPoint 4, an object simply is any type of item—a picture that you draw, a chart that you create in Excel or PowerPoint, a sound that you record and save as a file, or a piece of prerecorded music—that can be cut and pasted between applications and documents or moved around on a slide or between slides.

If you draw a simple graphic in PowerPoint, that graphic is an object. If you create a chart, that chart is an object, too. Pieces of clip art are considered to be objects, and so are snippets of sound.

The following sections discuss some important details of creating and working with the various PowerPoint objects.

Drawn and Text Objects

You can create surprisingly sophisticated drawings in PowerPoint and group those drawings to form, if you will, a meta-object composed of numerous simpler objects. Although they're not usually discussed this way, text items in PowerPoint slides also can be considered to be objects, because they have many of the same simple properties. Text can be cut and pasted, altered, moved around, and deleted; a large number of formatting options also are available for text.

▶ See "Drawing Basic Shapes," p. 216

Objects Created in Other Programs

Any type of data file or item—a Microsoft Word table, an Excel worksheet, a PowerPoint chart, and even a PowerPoint presentation—potentially is an object. Objects such as these can be cut and pasted in the conventional way or through a process called Paste Special, in which an object is embedded in a document.

When an object is embedded in your presentation, it has special properties. The object still can be edited in the application that created it, even though the object may have been created in a program other than PowerPoint. As an example, the charts that you create for use in PowerPoint are created in a separate program called Microsoft Graph. The Graph application appears on top of the main PowerPoint window, enabling you to create the object (a chart). When you complete the chart, Graph closes, and the chart is embedded in your presentation.

This feature, called object linking and embedding (OLE), links PowerPoint, Word, Excel, and other programs in a super-application of sorts. The parts of an OLE document can be used interchangeably, and you can manage all the separate applications in a single window. This feature makes cutting and pasting data between applications easier and more interactive than ever before.

Using the chart example again, you can Paste Special a chart into PowerPoint; when you edit the object (the chart) and click outside it, the object is embedded in your slide. If you later need to edit the chart, all you do is double-click the object; Microsoft Graph starts, enabling you to perform the editing.

Adding Objects to a Slide

For now, you won't be dealing with objects created in Microsoft Word, Excel, or other Macintosh programs. For the purposes of this chapter, objects are any type of data that you can create and use in PowerPoint: drawn artwork, charts, clip art, and so on.

Working with Placeholders

You have already used and manipulated placeholders in this chapter. Place-holders are particularly useful when you use Wizards to create a new presentation. Placeholders of various types set aside space in a slide for specific purposes (see fig. 3.22).

Whenever you create a new slide, and particularly when you use Auto-Layouts, PowerPoint sets up placeholders to help you lay out and properly place objects in the slide. Then you must define each placeholder's content.

Fig. 3.22
Click a place-holder to insert the object listed in the placeholder.

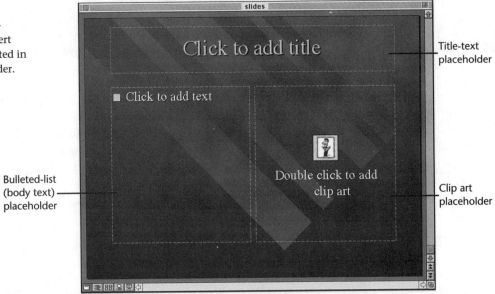

Title-text placeholder

Bulleted-list (body text) placeholder

Clip art placeholder

Inserting an Object

Five buttons in the Standard toolbar allow you to place different types of objects in a slide, as described in the following table.

Button	Button Name	Description
	Insert Microsoft Word Table	Creates and inserts a table from the Microsoft Word for Macintosh application into a PowerPoint slide
	Insert Microsoft Excel Worksheet	Creates and inserts a worksheet from the Microsoft Excel application into a PowerPoint slide

Button	Button Name	Description
📊	Insert Graph	Inserts a graph object created in Microsoft Graph into a PowerPoint slide
📊	Insert Organizational Chart	Creates and inserts an organizational chart into a PowerPoint slide
🖼	Insert Clip Art	Selects and inserts a clip-art image from the ClipArt Gallery into a PowerPoint slide

▶ See "Using the ClipArt Gallery," p. 234

These objects, inserted into a slide, serve not only as objects but also as placeholders. Double-clicking an inserted object enables you to alter that item by using the application that created it.

This section provides only a glance at the possibilities. Various chapters later in this book deal with every aspect of inserting and changing different types of objects.

Creating a Chart

Creating charts is one of the most important operations that you can perform in PowerPoint. Part IV of this book is devoted to the process of creating charts from statistical data; this section simply touches on the basics.

▶ See "Understanding PowerPoint's Charting Feature," p. 263

Charts are commonly used to illustrate statistics of many kinds. Charts can be used to show the progress of a company's stock prices. Charts also can be used to illustrate sales figures or company earnings in conjunction with a company's long-term growth or stock price. In this section, you dig into the basics of creating charts.

Understanding Microsoft Graph

PowerPoint 4 includes a separate charting program called Microsoft Graph 5, which you can use to create charts. In Microsoft Graph, you deal with two specific elements when you make a chart: the chart itself, which is the graphical representation of your data; and the *datasheet*, which contains the actual statistics used to generate the chart.

> **Note**
>
> The charting application in PowerPoint is called Microsoft Graph, but every com-
> mand in the program uses the word *chart*. For that reason, this book uses the word
> *chart* almost exclusively, except when referring to the program Microsoft Graph.
> Also, when you create a new slide from AutoLayouts, one AutoLayout type is called
> Graph. In no other area of PowerPoint (including Help) is the word *graph* used; the
> word *chart* is used to describe features.

Spreadsheet users are familiar with the concept of a datasheet, which essentially is rows and columns of numbers below specific headings that are used
to describe the categories of the data. Figure 3.23 shows a typical datasheet.

Fig. 3.23
Datasheets are the
numbers and text
on which your
chart is based.

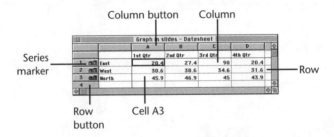

All of Graph's datasheets work essentially the same way: you type numbers in
rows and columns that are structured to fit into one or more series for display
in a chart. Each column and row has a numbered 3-D button that you can
click to select the entire row or column.

▶ See "Under-
standing
Datasheets,"
p. 266

In figure 3.23, notice the small markers for row buttons 1, 2, and 3. These
markers are *series markers*, which indicate that the data displayed in the
datasheet and in the chart is organized in three series of data. This small fact
can have major implications for a datasheet and for a chart, as you learn in
later chapters.

Each rectangular space in a datasheet is called a *cell*. The default datasheet
contains three rows of four cells each. Click any cell in a datasheet to enter a
new value or to edit an existing one.

Starting Graph

This section shows you how to use Microsoft Graph, the charting and graphing *applet* (mini-application) that is bundled with PowerPoint.

Graph is separate from PowerPoint. When you start the Graph application, a
new toolbar appears at the top of the PowerPoint window, and the menu bar
changes.

After you launch PowerPoint, begin a document by choosing a presentation type in the first dialog box, and then choose an AutoLayout. (The blank layout is used in the example in this section.)

Next, double-click the Insert Graph button. The Microsoft Graph application launches, and the Graph toolbar and menu bar appear, along with a default chart and datasheet (see fig. 3.24).

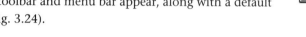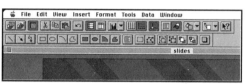

Fig. 3.24
When you launch Graph, Power-Point's menus and toolbars are replaced by those of Graph.

To create a new chart, enter a new set of data values and labels (in other words, edit the datasheet), and select a new chart type, if necessary.

Entering and Deleting Data

The following table lists some shortcut keys that you can use to edit datasheets.

Shortcut Key	Description
Left arrow	Moves to the next cell to the left
Right arrow	Moves to the next cell to the right
Down arrow	Moves to the next row down
Up arrow	Moves to the next row up
Shift-left arrow	Selects each successive cell to the left
Shift-right arrow	Selects each successive cell to the right
Shift-down arrow	Selects each successive cell down through the column
Shift-up arrow	Selects each successive cell up through the column
Delete	Erases the cell's contents

To enter and delete data in a Graph datasheet, follow these simple steps:

1. Click the first cell (row 1, column 1) in the default Graph datasheet.

2. Type a numeric value in that cell, and then move to the next cell in which you want to enter data.

3. Continue entering data until you have entered all the information for the chart that you want to create. Graph changes the drawing each time you press Return.

4. Click outside the borders of the chart drawing to return to PowerPoint.

Selecting and Changing the Chart Type

▶ See "Choosing the Best Chart Type," p. 287

To change the type of chart used in a PowerPoint slide, double-click the chart to start Microsoft Graph. You then can use Graph's toolbar and menu options to edit the chart.

> **Note**
>
> You can create two key types of charts: 2-D and 3-D. Two-dimensional charts are easier to format and work with because they're not as complex, but 3-D charts can be more attractive. The default chart type is a 3-D column chart.

To change a chart type, follow these steps:

1. Click inside the chart to select it.

2. Click the Chart Type down-arrow button in the Graph toolbar. A pop-up list appears, displaying 14 icons that represent the basic chart types (see fig. 3.25).

Fig. 3.25
The Chart Type pop-up list is an easy way to change the style of a chart.

The chart types appear in the drop-down list in this order:

2-D Area	3-D Area
2-D Bar	3-D Bar
2-D Column	3-D Column
2-D Line	3-D Line
2-D Pie	3-D Pie
Scatter	3-D Surface
Doughnut	Radar

3. Choose a chart type from the pop-up list.

The large number of chart types and variations can be quite confusing. To make things even more confusing, certain chart types can be used only for specific types of data. Those issues are covered in other parts of this book.

Pasting the Chart into the Slide

When you finish creating a basic chart, placing that chart in a slide is simple; just click anywhere outside the chart. The Graph toolbar and menu bar disappear, to be replaced by the more familiar PowerPoint screen elements, and the chart is embedded into the slide.

To start Graph and edit the chart, simply double-click the chart.

Saving Your Presentation

Saving a presentation is a very important operation. Any time that you create something new in a PowerPoint presentation, you should save your work.

> **Note**
>
> A good rule of thumb is to save your work every five minutes. Frequent saving minimizes the risk of losing important work.

To save your presentation, follow these steps:

1. With your presentation displayed in any view, open the File menu and choose Save or press ⌘–S. If you're saving the file for the first time, the Save As dialog box appears (see fig. 3.26).

Fig. 3.26

The Save As dialog box is a familiar Macintosh element.

2. Type a title in the Save Presentation As text box.

3. The Save File As Type list should display Presentation (the default setting). You can choose a different format from the pop-up list, if you want.

4. If you want to save your file in a different folder or on a different drive, select the new folder or drive.

5. Choose OK.

Printing a Presentation

PowerPoint offers a substantial number of printing options. If you plan to use several elements in your presentation—for example, an on-screen slide show, audience handouts, and your own set of notes pages—you need to print all those items in advance.

 To print your presentation, open the File menu and choose Print, or press ⌘-P, to display the Print dialog box (see fig. 3.27).

Fig. 3.27

The Print dialog box gives many options for printing your presentation.

The Print dialog box offers the following options:

- *Print What.* This option specifies the type of output: Slides, Notes Pages, Handouts (2 Slides Per Page), Handouts (3 Slides Per Page), Handouts (6 Slides Per Page), or Outline View.

- *Copies.* This option specifies the number of copies of the page or document to be printed (type a number in the text box).

- *Pages.* This option specifies the range of slides to be printed: All or separate slides and ranges of slides.

- *PostScript File.* This option sends output to a PostScript file for downloading at a remote location.

- *Scale to Fit Paper.* This option scales the slide output to the size of the paper that you are using.

- *Print Hidden Slides.* This option enables you to print hidden slides.

- *Pure Black & White.* This option converts shades of black to solid black.

- *Black & White.* This option prints output in white and shades of black only.

Choose the options that you want to use, and then choose OK to start printing.

This section provides only a basic introduction to printing. Chapter 16, "Printing and Other Kinds of Output," discusses every major aspect of printing and many related subjects, such as setting up your presentation for special output, setting up your printer, and troubleshooting printing problems.

Quitting PowerPoint

When you finish working on your presentation, it's a good time to save your work again. Open the File menu and choose Save, or press ⌘-S. Then, to quit the program, open the File menu and choose Quit, or press ⌘-Q.

From Here...

This chapter covered a tremendous amount of ground, providing an overview of almost every major part of PowerPoint 4. For detailed information on certain topics, see the following chapters:

- To learn more about the basic parts of your presentation (including slides, handouts, notes, and outlines), see Chapter 4, "Setting up Your New Presentation."

- Creating and customizing templates is explained in greater detail in Chapter 5, "Using and Creating Templates."

- For an extensive discussion of creating and formatting text, see Chapter 6, "Working with Text."

- To find out more about working with various elements of a presentation, see Chapter 7, "Creating Speaker's Notes, Outlines, and Handouts."

- An entire book could be written on PowerPoint's charting features alone. Chapters 12, 13, 14, and 19 discuss that subject in great detail.

- Chapter 16, "Printing and Other Kinds of Output," discusses all the related issues of printing slides, outlines, notes pages, and other elements of presentations.

Chapter 4

Setting up Your New Presentation

As you saw in the last chapter, a presentation has several major components: notes pages, the outline, the handouts, and finally the slides. The slides are the flashy part, but they should be considered to be only part of the production. If you focus all your attention on working with slides and ignore the other phases of working with PowerPoint 4, you are cheating yourself out of some of the program's most helpful and powerful productivity features.

This chapter explores the following aspects of working with PowerPoint 4:

- The process of starting a new presentation
- PowerPoint's various views
- PowerPoint's masters and how they interact

Understanding the Presentation Process

PowerPoint 4 is considered to be one of the most flexible and most powerful presentation/slide-show packages on the market. But PowerPoint isn't just about slides; it's also about organizing ideas and arguments into the most effective presentation possible. In many situations, you are not displaying great graphics just to dazzle your clients; you are trying to persuade them that your proposed course of action is the best or that they should buy your product.

Although you can produce a presentation by working exclusively in Slides view, doing so defeats the purpose of a large percentage of PowerPoint's features. In fact, if you want to save yourself a lot of work, the wisest way to create the basics of a brand-new presentation is to use the Slide Master, which is one of several masters available in the program. After you use the Slide Master to create the appearance and basic format of your presentation, you can use other masters to expand and change many elements of the presentation. You learn the basics of these techniques in this chapter.

Starting a New Presentation

You do not need to use any templates to create a new presentation. If you are the sort of person who has to do everything yourself, this chapter is where you can begin to do so.

You can start a new presentation in several ways: by using a Wizard, by selecting a template, or by creating your own blank presentation. Because the preceding chapter dealt with Wizards in considerable detail, this chapter focuses on starting from scratch. Although building a new presentation from scratch may sound difficult, it actually is remarkably easy. As you build a presentation in a few simple steps, you begin to see possibilities for exercising your own creativity.

To begin a new presentation, follow these steps:

1. If you have not already done so, launch PowerPoint.

2. Open the File menu and choose New. The New Presentation dialog box appears (see fig. 4.1).

   If you launched PowerPoint in step 1, a similar screen appears after the Tip of the Day. If you read the last chapter, you have seen this dialog box before; you used it to select Wizards. You also can choose three other options: Template, Blank Presentation, and Current Presentation Format.

Fig. 4.1
Begin creating a slide show in the New Presentation dialog box.

3. Choose Blank Presentation, and then choose OK. PowerPoint prompts you to choose the AutoLayout for the first slide, as shown in figure 4.2.

Fig. 4.2
Choose among 21 preformatted layouts in the New Slide dialog box.

4. Click the Title Slide thumbnail (the top-left AutoLayout), and then choose OK. Figure 4.3 shows a typical result: an empty slide with a placeholder for the title text.

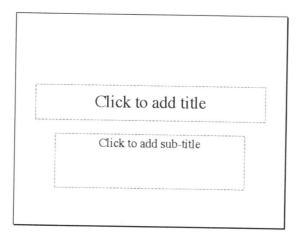

Click to add title

Click to add sub-title

Fig. 4.3
These placeholders are the framework for your text.

5. Open the View menu and choose Master; then choose Slide Master from the cascading menu. The Slide Master appears, displaying the blank title slide (see fig. 4.4). At this time, you can add text and slide formatting to the master.

Fig. 4.4
Items in the Slide
Master appear in
all slides based on
that master.

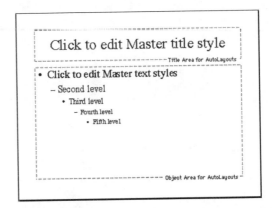

Formatting a Master Slide

After you create a blank master slide, you are ready to apply formatting.
Follow these steps:

1. Open the Format menu and choose Slide Background. The Slide
   Background dialog box appears.

2. In the Shade Styles section, click the Vertical button. More options
   appear in the Variants section of the dialog box.

3. In the Variants section, choose a shading type that works best with your
   planned slide show. You can add a color from the palette that appears
   when you click the Change Color button, and you can use the horizontal scroll bar at the bottom of the dialog box to make your selection
   lighter or darker. (You can change the settings at any time if you opt for
   a different style or decide that the current color and shading options
   make the text illegible.)

4. Click Preview to see the options without dismissing the dialog box (see
   fig. 4.5), or click Apply and then press Return to apply the settings that
   you chose.

Fig. 4.5
The Slides
Background dialog
box enables you to
choose a consis-
tent background
coloring system.

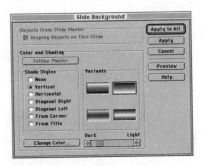

5. You can change the formatting of a single item or a group of items in your Slide Master. To change all items, first select them by opening the Edit menu and choosing Select All or by pressing ⌘-A.

6. Open the Format menu and then choose Font, Line Spacing, Color, Alignment, or some other formatting option. The appropriate dialog box appears.

7. Make your formatting changes, and then click the OK, Apply, or Apply to All button (whichever is appropriate for the dialog box and for the slides in which you want to make the changes).

Tip

To select an individual line of text, triple-click the box that contains the text.

PowerPoint 4 Basics

Note

After you change the formatting (and especially after you change the color), you may need to adjust the background color and shading. You can return to any formatting dialog box to make changes at any time.

When you complete your formatting changes, you have created a new presentation from scratch. All the other slides that you add to the presentation will use the format that you have defined.

Now save your work. Open the File menu and choose Save; then type a file name for your presentation and click the OK button.

You should carry one key point away from this section: the importance of the Slide Master. When you create a new presentation with your own specifications, the Slide Master is where everything should happen. More information on the Slide Master appears in "Understanding the Slide Master" later in this chapter.

Understanding the View Options

Views and masters have considerable similarities. Each primary area of PowerPoint 4—slides, outlines, handouts, and notes pages—has both a master and a view.

Using the View Buttons in the PowerPoint Status Bar

PowerPoint's view buttons are not located in a toolbar; they are located just above the status bar at the bottom of the screen (see fig. 4.6).

Fig. 4.6
Click these
buttons to scroll
through the
different views.

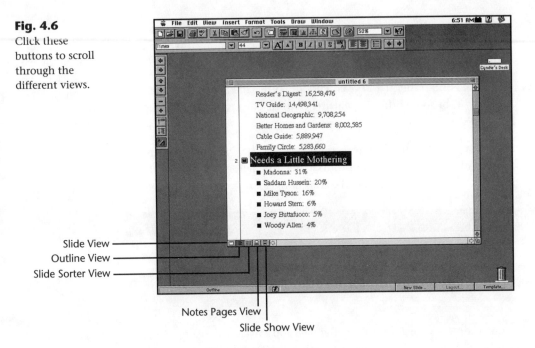

Slide View
Outline View
Slide Sorter View
Notes Pages View
Slide Show View

Table 4.1 describes the view buttons.

Table 4.1   PowerPoint 4's View Buttons

Button Name	Action
Slide View	Changes the view so that you can edit a slide directly.
Outline View	Changes the view to show the title and body text of all slides.
Slide Sorter View	Changes the view to show thumbnails of all slides.
Notes Pages View	Changes the view so that you can edit speaker's notes.
Slide Show View	Changes the view so that you can run or rehearse a slide show.

Clicking any of the five view buttons displays that section of the program.

Using Slide View

Clicking the Slide View button displays the screen in which you edit, change, and add elements in the currently displayed slide. You can use the Slide Changer to page through the slides in your presentation. (Alternatively, if you have an extended Macintosh keyboard, you can press the Page Up and Page Down keys.) Virtually every operation that can be performed on slide objects—creating charts, drawing graphics, placing clip art, entering and formatting text, and so on—can be performed in Slide view. All these issues are discussed in later chapters.

Using Outline View

PowerPoint 4 offers greater flexibility than competing products do because of the various tools that it offers—in particular, the notes pages, the handouts feature, and (especially) the powerful and straightforward outlining capability. Outline view is the key feature that you use to organize your ideas and critique your argument for logical flow and impact. Slide view cannot provide such a viewpoint.

Figure 4.7 shows a sample Outline view.

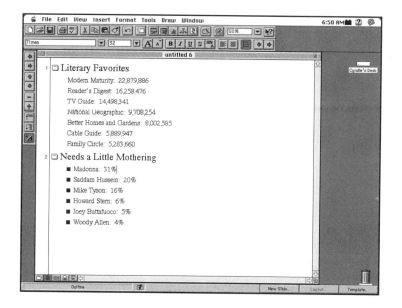

Fig. 4.7
Outline view makes editing text simple.

Outline view enables you to rearrange and edit an entire presentation. Each slide in the presentation is numbered; you can click any slide's number to select it. When a slide is selected, you can drag it to a new location; delete, copy, cut, or paste it; and format the slide's text.

One key element of Outline view is the slide icons shown in figure 4.7. You can drag and drop these icons at any location in the outline—an easy way to rearrange slides. Clicking any slide icon also selects the slide's title and body text so that you can format and edit those elements.

A special toolbar at the left side of the window provides buttons that perform most of the key functions for working with an outline. Table 4.2 describes these buttons in order (top to bottom).

Table 4.2 PowerPoint 4's Outline View Toolbar Buttons

Button	Button Name	Description
	Promote	Moves paragraph up a level in the outline.
	Demote	Moves paragraph down a level in the outline.
	Move Up	Moves selected text up in the slide sequence.
	Move Down	Moves selected text down in the slide sequence.
	Collapse Selection	Hides body text in the Outline view of the selected slide or slides (does not delete it).
	Expand Selection	Restores any body text in selected slides to Outline view.
	Show Titles	Shows only slide titles in the outline.
	Show All	Shows titles and body text for each slide in the outline.
	Show Formatting	Toggles text formatting for titles and body text. If formatting is off, text appears in standard sans-serif characters.

You can insert new slides in Outline view, as the presence of the New Slide button in the bottom-right corner of figure 4.7 indicates. You have no control over slide layout in Outline view, however, so any new slide that you add in this view is a standard title and body-text slide.

To create a new slide in Outline view, place the insertion point at the end of a title line and then press Return. To add a new bullet item in the body text, place the insertion point at the end of a bullet item and then press Return.

Selecting any text for editing enables you to use all the standard text-formatting buttons in the PowerPoint Formatting toolbar. Formatting that you add in Outline view appears in the finished presentation. Some text formatting, however (such as color), is not available in Outline view.

You can promote or demote individual points in a slide in Outline view, as shown in figure 4.8.

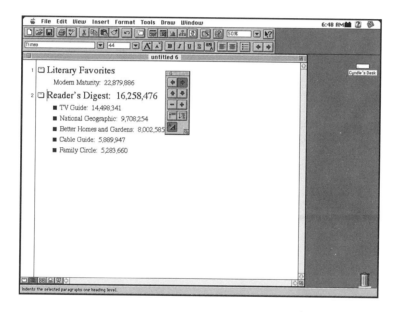

Fig. 4.8
In Outline view, you can promote or demote points to give them more or less emphasis.

Using the Slide Sorter

The Slide Sorter is a very powerful feature of PowerPoint 4. This feature enables you to rearrange slides quickly; just drag and drop, and the slide is in a new location. You also can use the Slide Sorter to apply various special effects to the contents of a slide, including *transition effects*, which determine how a slide appears and disappears on-screen, and *build effects*, which determine how body text (particularly bulleted text) appears in each slide. These powerful special effects give you a wide scope for experimenting with your slides.

◀ See "Working with Slides," p. 79

PowerPoint 4 Basics

To apply transition or build effects in the Slide Sorter, follow these steps:

1. With a presentation displayed, open the View menu and choose Slide Sorter.

2. Click the slide to which you want to apply special effects.

3. Choose the effect that you want from the Transition or Build pop-up menus, which are located in the Slide Sorter toolbar at the top of the screen. (Alternatively, choose Random Effects from either pop-up menu.) The slide thumbnail demonstrates the selected effect.

When you apply effects to slides, small icons appear below the thumbnails of those slides (see fig. 4.9). These icons, which correspond to the Transition and Build buttons in the Slide Sorter toolbar, indicate which effects have been applied to the slide.

Fig. 4.9
Small icons below slides indicate that build or transition effects have been applied.

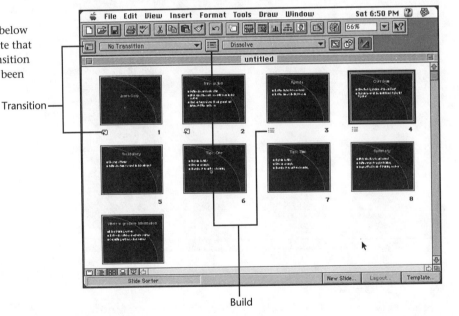

To switch to the Slide Sorter from a different view, use either of the following techniques:

- Click the Slide Sorter button in the lower-left corner of the PowerPoint screen.

- Open the View menu and choose Slide Sorter.

Unlike Outline view, the Slide Sorter enables you to add slides to a presentation. This view also gives you full access to the AutoLayouts. To specify the type of slide that you want to insert, click the New Slide button at the bottom of the PowerPoint screen.

Slide Sorter view also offers a powerful zoom feature that enables you to make the slide thumbnails as large or as small as you want (see fig. 4.10).

Tip

Double-clicking any slide in the Slide Sorter displays that slide in Slide view, where you can edit it.

PowerPoint 4 Basics

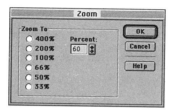

Fig. 4.10

Use the Zoom dialog box to change the size of slides in the Slide Sorter.

Using Notes Pages View

Notes pages are valuable tools for speakers. The capability to write and print extensive notes for each slide in the presentation gives you greater confidence in conducting a slide show.

▶ See "Creating Speaker's Notes," p. 176

As you learned in Chapter 3, "Quick Start: Creating a First Presentation," notes pages generally consist of a slide in the top half of the page and notes about that slide in the bottom half. Figure 4.11 shows a typical notes page.

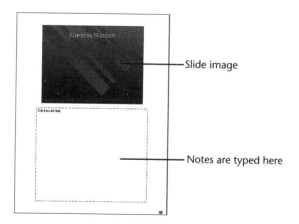

Slide image

Notes are typed here

Fig. 4.11

Notes pages are prompts for use when you show your presentation.

You can place any kind of special information in notes pages: a company name, the date, a logo, and so on. You perform that task in the Notes Master, which is discussed in "Understanding the Notes Master" later in this chapter.

> **Note**
>
> A distinction must be made between the Notes Master and Notes Pages view. You enter your speaker's notes in Notes Pages view. The Notes Master, however, simply defines the general layout of the notes pages, including common elements such as page numbers and logos.

In Notes Pages view, each notes page shows a slide. Below the slide, you can enter and edit notes for that slide. To create a notes page, follow these steps:

1. Click the text placeholder for the desired page. The insertion point appears inside the placeholder.

2. If you want to get a closer look at the text while you enter it, use the zoom feature. Open the View menu and choose Zoom; select a zoom percentage; and choose OK.

3. Type your notes.

▶ See "Creating Text," p.138

The Notes Master determines the basic format of your text; you can alter the text, however, by clicking the Promote and Demote buttons in the Formatting toolbar and by adding bullets to the text. You also can indent the text.

To create indents, open the View menu and choose Ruler to display PowerPoint's ruler; then drag the markers to create the indents you want. (This feature is especially handy for formatting bulleted text.)

Using Slide Show View

To switch to Slide Show view, simply click the Slide Show button above the status bar.

Simply clicking the Slide Show button, however, somewhat limits your ability to control the slide show. If you want greater control of the slide show, open the View menu and choose Slide Show to display the Slide Show dialog box (see fig. 4.12).

Fig. 4.12
Use the Slide Show dialog box to choose additional viewing options.

The Slide Show dialog box offers the following options:

- *All.* Choose this option to show all slides.

- *From* and *To.* Use these options to specify a range of slides to show.

- *Manual Advance.* Choose this option if you want to manually control the display of slides and effects.

- *Use Slide Timings.* Choose this option to use the slide timings built into the presentation.

- *Rehearse New Timings.* Choose this option to create new timings for the slide show.

- *Run Continuously.* When you choose this option, the slide show runs continuously until you press ⌘-Esc.

▶ See "Setting Transition Styles and Transition Timing," p. 445

To run the slide show after you set your options, choose OK.

You can perform rehearsals in Slide Show view to set the precise timing of events that occur in each slide. Use the keystrokes listed in the following table when you want to move through the slide show manually and apply build effects (if any) to the slides.

Keystroke	Action
Return or space bar	Advances to next slide.
Return or space bar	Executes next build effect (if builds are applied).
Page Up	Moves to preceding slide.
Page Down	Advances to next slide.

Understanding the Masters

As you learned in Chapter 2, "Getting Acquainted with PowerPoint 4," the masters are where you create and apply the common elements of your presentation. A presentation template has several masters that are part of the package, as you discovered when you used the AutoContent and Pick a Look Wizards. The masters enable you to access all the components of your template and to change them—for example, to add a company name to handouts (via the Handout Master), to add a company logo to your slides (via the Slide Master), and to adjust the layout of your notes pages (via the Notes Master).

Understanding the Slide Master

The Slide Master provides the basis for the appearance of your presentation. Your template's color scheme, graphic objects, and other common elements of each slide are based here and can be edited and changed here. In this short section, you learn how to perform a few reformatting chores in the Slide Master.

Using the Slide Master

To display the Slide Master, open the View menu and choose Master; then choose Slide Master from the cascading menu. The Slide Master appears (see fig. 4.13).

Fig. 4.13
Use the Slide Master to control the repetitive items of your presentation.

To apply a template to the Slide Master, open the File menu and choose Open; open the Templates folder; and double-click a template name in one of the nested folders.

► See "Using Templates," p. 120

Your Slide Master is composed of several elements that were created when you chose a template style. You can edit, reformat, or move any of these elements. Because this template is used for the rest of the slides in the presentation, each slide will reflect the changes that you make in the Slide Master. The Slide Master is the basis for the entire appearance of your presentation.

You can resize graphic elements by clicking them and then dragging the handles that appear around then. To edit colors and other enhancements, open the Format menu and choose the appropriate option.

Adding and Changing Elements in the Slide Master

This section explores three kinds of changes that you can make in the Slide Master:

- Changing the color and pattern fill of the Slide Master background

- Changing the color and fill of the diagonal graphic

- Changing the title and body-text font

Several options in the Slide Background dialog box enable you to change the slide background: the Shade Styles list; the shading Variants (four thumbnails that show different orientations for the same fill type); the Change Color button, which gives you access to a 90-color palette; and the Dark–Light slider bar, which enables you to change the Slide Master background.

To change the color of the Slide Master background, follow these steps:

1. Open the Format menu and choose Slide Background. The Slide Background dialog box appears, as shown in figure 4.14.

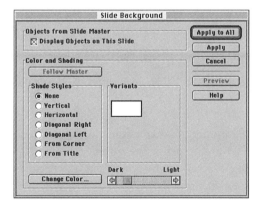

2. Choose an option in the Shade Styles list.

3. Click an option in the Variants section.

Tip
If you don't want to accept the changes that you made, open the Edit menu and choose the Undo command (or press ⌘-Z) to return the Slide Master to its original template form.

Fig. 4.14
The Slide Background dialog box controls the background of individual slides or a series.

PowerPoint 4 Basics

4. Click the Apply to All button. The dialog box closes, and PowerPoint applies the selected options to all the slides in your presentation.

   To apply the background changes to the current slide, click Apply.

To change the color of the template graphics, you first must apply to the Slide Master a template that contains graphics (such as stripes). Then follow these steps:

1. Click the graphic in the Slide Master.

2. Open the Format menu and choose Colors and Lines. The Colors and Lines dialog box appears (see fig. 4.15).

Fig. 4.15
Color and line settings affect all slides based on that master.

3. Choose an option from the Fill pop-up menu. Depending on the option you choose, a new dialog box appears.

4. Make your choices in the new dialog box, and then choose OK to return to the Colors and Lines dialog box.

5. Click the Preview button to view the changes without accepting them.

6. When you are satisfied with your choices, choose OK to apply them to the Slide Master.

Don't forget to save the changes that you made. Open the File menu and choose Save to apply the changes to the current presentation. To save your template changes to a PowerPoint file, open the File menu and choose Save As; then specify a file name and folder.

Now try changing the font used for the Slide Master title and body text. Follow these steps:

1. Select the text.

2. Open the Format menu and choose Font. The Font dialog box appears (see fig. 4.16).

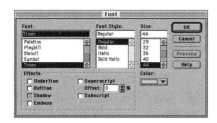

I

PowerPoint 4 Basics

Fig. 4.16
Use this dialog box to specify the font used for any text block.

3. Choose the font and other options that you want to use.

4. Choose OK. The Slide Master displays your changes.

Understanding the Outline Master

The Outline Master differs significantly from Outline view, which shows the outline of your presentation based on the contents of your slides. The Outline Master is used to format your printed outline. The master displays none of the outline's actual content, but it shows the elements that would be common to printed pages of an outline—a company name, page numbers, logos, and the like.

Viewing the Outline Master

To view the Outline Master for the current presentation, open the View menu and choose Master; then choose Outline Master to display the screen shown in figure 4.17.

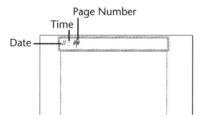

Fig. 4.17
The Outline Master can contain dynamic place-holders for a date, time, and page number.

Using the Outline Master

Using the Outline Master is as straightforward as viewing it. To add a marker to the outline, for example, follow these steps:

▶ See "Working with Outlines," p. 187

1. Open the View menu and choose Masters; then choose Outline Master to display the Outline Master.

2. Open the Insert menu and choose an option such as Date, Page Number, or Time (these elements will appear on each page of the outline).

The appropriate marker appears in the middle of the sample outline page, as shown in figure 4.18.

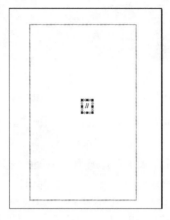

3. Click the border of the marker (don't click inside the border), and drag the marker to an appropriate location. You can use the placeholder margins as a guide, if necessary.

> **Note**
>
> If you repeat step 2 to choose another option while the marker is still selected, PowerPoint adds the new marker to the existing one. If you want the markers to appear in separate locations, click outside the existing marker to deselect it before you choose the new option.

You can reformat the options that you just placed. To format the date, time, or page number, follow these steps:

1. Click the marker to select it; resize handles appear around the marker box.

2. Click and drag the handles to the desired position. (To center the page number, for example, drag the left edge of the box to the left margin and the right edge to the right margin.)

3. Continue to click and drag the handles until the marker box is the size that you want.

4. With the marker object selected, press ⌘-E. The marker text is centered in the marker box.

5. Drag the marker object (by dragging any part of the object that is not a resize handle) to the top or bottom of the page.

> **Note**
>
> When you use the alignment commands or buttons, the marker text is aligned within the marker box, not on the page. If you want to center the page number between the left and right margins, for example, you must drag the left edge of the box to the left margin and the right edge to the right margin, and then make your alignment selection.

If you want to print outlines that contain standard elements (graphics, logos, and so on), make sure that you place inserted objects out of the way of possible printed matter in your outline.

Understanding the Handout Master

The Handout Master is almost as simple as the Outline Master. Although the slide placeholders in the Handout Master seem to be complex, the only time that they ever come into play is when you print the Handout Master. It's as simple to add dates, page numbers, and other elements to the Handout Master as it is to add these elements to other masters.

Viewing the Handout Master

To view the Handout Master for the current presentation, open the View menu and choose Master; then choose Handout Master from the cascading menu. Figure 4.19 shows a typical Handout Master.

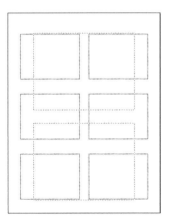

Fig. 4.19
The Handout Master is a collection of slide placeholders.

Using the Handout Master

To insert background objects into the Handout Master, follow these steps:

1. Open the Insert menu and choose Date, Time, or Page Number. A marker appears in the middle of the PowerPoint screen.

2. Drag the marker to an appropriate location on the page. You can use the placeholder margins as a guide, if necessary.

3. Resize the marker, if you want, for convenient formatting and text entry.

Understanding the Notes Master

The Notes Master contains some graphic elements (namely, images of a slide on each notes page) that offer more room for creativity than some of the other masters. You can resize the slide image on each notes page, as well as the placeholder for notes text. As figure 4.20 shows, the Notes Master bears a close resemblance to Notes Pages view, discussed in "Using Notes Pages View" earlier in this chapter.

Fig. 4.20
The Notes Master enables you to move or scale the sample slide.

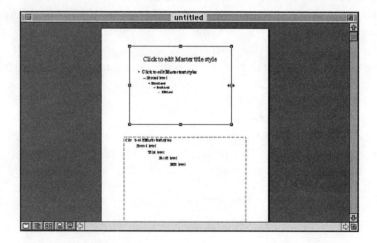

Viewing the Notes Master

To view the Notes Master, open the View menu and choose Master; then choose Notes Master from the cascading menu. The Notes Master appears; it should be similar to figure 4.20.

Using the Notes Master

Using the Notes Master is quite similar to working in Notes Pages view. In fact, because you don't enter notes in the master, using the master actually is simpler.

To make the slide image smaller, follow these steps:

1. Click the slide image to select it. Handles appear around the image.

2. Click and drag a handle to shrink the slide image. The image retains its proportions as you drag.

3. Drag the slide to the desired position on the page.

To reformat the sample text in the Notes Master text placeholder, follow these steps:

1. Click inside the text placeholder.

2. Select the placeholder's contents.

3. Click buttons in the Formatting toolbar to format the text the way you want it. You also can use the zoom feature and the ruler (to format indents). The result may look similar to figure 4.21.

Tip

Use the guides for help in resizing and placing the slide image. To display the guides, open the View menu and choose Guides.

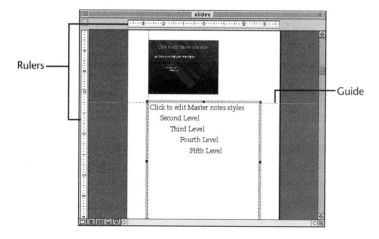

Rulers

Guide

Fig. 4.21

Use the View menu to show guides and rulers and the Format menu to change text attributes.

As you can in the other masters, you can place dates, times, page numbers, and other elements in the Notes Master quickly and easily. To add these objects, follow these steps:

1. Make sure that the notes area isn't selected by clicking outside the text area.

2. Open the Insert menu and choose Date, Time, or Page Number. A marker appears in the middle of the Notes Master page.

3. Drag the marker to an appropriate location. You can use the placeholder margins as a guide, if necessary.

Troubleshooting

I can't display any of the masters.

Make sure that a presentation is open and active.

The formatting of my outline text doesn't show up in Outline view.

Click the Show Formatting button in the Outlining toolbar, which by default appears on the right side of the PowerPoint screen when you're in Outline view.

My notes pages don't have any text placeholders or slides in them.

You can solve this problem easily. Display your Notes Master (not an individual notes page, but the Notes Master for your presentation); then open the Format menu and choose Master Layout to display the Master Layout dialog box, which contains two check boxes: Add Slide Image and Add Notes Text. Click both check boxes to place an X in each of them; then choose OK. Your Notes Master now displays the proper elements for your notes pages.

This technique is common to all the masters. If any of your masters don't have a standard element, odds are that you'll be able to correct the problem in the Master Layout dialog box.

From Here...

This chapter focused on managing information and applying formatting in the various views and masters of PowerPoint. The following chapters build on some of the things that you learned in this chapter:

- Chapter 5, "Using and Creating Templates," discusses templates in detail.

- Chapter 6, "Working with Text," discusses the fine points of working with text in all PowerPoint views.

- Chapter 7, "Creating Speaker's Notes, Outlines, and Handouts," covers those elements of a presentation in detail.

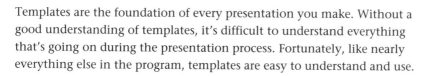

Chapter 5

Using and Creating Templates

Templates are the foundation of every presentation you make. Without a good understanding of templates, it's difficult to understand everything that's going on during the presentation process. Fortunately, like nearly everything else in the program, templates are easy to understand and use.

This chapter shows you how to do the following:

- Apply templates to new and existing presentations

- Inspect the contents of PowerPoint 4's sample presentations and templates

- Define your own default template

- Add company names and logos to your template

In the course of this chapter, Wizards are not used for creating or using presentation templates; rather, this chapter works more behind the scenes to show how things work.

Reviewing Template Elements

Templates consist of four discrete master components, all of which take part in building a complete presentation. Although Chapter 4, "Setting up Your New Presentation," discusses the various masters in detail, their roles in the overall creation of a presentation bear repeating here.

■ *Slide Master:* Defines the appearance of your slide show. Although it's possible for individual slides in your presentation to use a different color scheme from the master, the Slide Master is the visual basis for your slide show. Common slide elements—such as company logos, company names, dates, and page numbers—are placed here.

■ *Outline Master:* Tracks the entire text content of your presentation. In this way, the Outline Master functions very much like a word processor, enabling you to indent text entries, format fonts, and perform many other basic word processing tasks. It's a good idea to use the Outline Master frequently to study the logical flow of your arguments.

■ *Notes Master:* The Notes Master enables you to create a set of speaker's notes for your presentation. Notes are a valuable tool, helping you maintain control of the slide show and of your speech even if you can't see the slide-show screen directly. By default, the top half of each notes page has an image of one slide; text notes are entered in the bottom half. You can rearrange notes pages by reversing the text and slide areas.

■ *Handout Master:* Defines a basic layout of audience handouts. A single handout page can have two, three, or six slides printed on it. The Hand-out Master displays several dashed boxes, which simply indicate where the slides will be printed. You do not edit or interact with the Handout Master; you create handouts by specifying the type of handouts that will be printed.

Tip
Placeholders are generic items in your slides; you can change their contents with a few mouse clicks.

The Slide Master is the core of any slide show. This master contains items called placeholders, which are the building blocks of your slide show. Every slide that you create also has placeholders of various kinds, which you use to define the basic size and location of objects in the slide. In the "Creating Your Own Templates" section later in this chapter, you learn how to use placeholders to define a slide layout.

Using Templates

Templates are used in two ways: to create a new presentation and to change the appearance of an existing presentation.

Selecting a Template To Create a New Presentation

Selecting a template without using a Wizard is identical to selecting a presentation file to edit; in fact, you're doing the same thing. Loading a template simply means loading a presentation file to which you need to add content.

To load a new template, follow these steps:

1. Open the File menu and choose Open or press ⌘-O. The Open dialog box appears, as shown in figure 5.1.

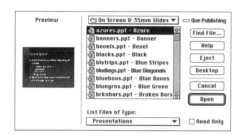

Fig. 5.1
This is a standard Macintosh Open dialog box.

2. Using the standard Macintosh interface, locate the Microsoft PowerPoint folder on your hard disk and, inside that, the folder named Templates. Open Templates and then the folder titled On Screen & 35mm Slides. A long list of PowerPoint templates appears in the Slides folder.

3. Double-click the template that you want to use. A layout appears, ready for you to customize.

You've just opened a new template and in the process created a new presentation without using a Wizard. Opening a template is the same thing as opening a new presentation; the only difference is that you do not name the file yourself. Use the Save As command if you want to avoid overwriting the original template file. If you do not rename the file, the template will reflect any changes that you make in it.

> **Note**
>
> Avoid saving over existing template files. The best and easiest way to do this is to click the Read Only check box in the Open dialog box when you load a new template. If you place an X in this check box, you eliminate the possibility of accidentally overwriting an original template file.

PowerPoint 4 Basics

Modifying an Existing Presentation by Applying a Template

If you have a presentation open and you're not satisfied with the way it looks, you can apply any other template to the existing file. Follow these steps:

1. Open the File menu and choose the presentation that you want to change.

2. Open the Format menu and choose Presentation Template. The Presentation Template dialog box appears, as shown in figure 5.2.

Fig. 5.2
This dialog box should look familiar; it's very similar to the Open dialog box.

3. Using the standard Macintosh interface, locate the PowerPoint folder on your hard disk and, inside that, the folder named Templates. Open Templates and then the folder titled On Screen & 35mm Slides. Inside that folder, you will find many template layouts.

4. Double-click the template that you want to use. The dialog box disappears, and the displayed presentation begins to undergo its facelift. If you have any charts in the presentation, PowerPoint displays this message on-screen:

   ```
   Charts are being updated with the new color scheme
   ```

   After a moment or two, the process is complete, and your presentation gets its new look. Text, default object colors, slide backgrounds, and charts all have a new color scheme.

Importing Outlines from Other Presentation Packages

▶ See "Working with Outlines," p. 187

You can import outlines in several text formats by using the Open dialog box. *RTF* (Rich Text Format, which is a type of text language) is used to import text for outlines.

Many word processing programs support RTF; files must be exported from those programs as RTF files.

To import an RTF file as an outline, follow these steps:

1. Open the PowerPoint File menu and choose Open, or press ⌘-O. The Open dialog box appears.

2. In the List Files of Type list, select All Readable Outlines. The file list in the dialog box changes to display only files of a type that you can import as an outline; these could be RTF or plain-text files.

3. Double-click the name of the file that you want to import.

Clicking the Outline option enables you to locate the desired outline file. Importing the outline automatically converts it to a PowerPoint outline, with slide titles and body text placed appropriately.

Using PowerPoint's Sample Presentations and Templates

PowerPoint provides dozens of sample presentations that you can customize to create your own unique presentation. You also may want to browse through the various templates to gather ideas for formatting and arranging the slides in your presentation. The following sections show you how to get the most from PowerPoint's samples and templates.

Browsing the Folders

As you have already seen in this chapter, PowerPoint has an intuitive folder structure. Everything in the PowerPoint program has a specific place; PowerPoint relies on the files to be where they belong to run properly. Following is a brief overview of the PowerPoint folder structure:

```
Microsoft PowerPoint
    PCS Files
    Samples
    Setup
    Templates
        B&W Overheads
        Color Overheads
        On Screen & 35mm Slides
    Wizards
```

The PowerPoint folder name may be different, depending on what you specified during installation, but all of PowerPoint's subfolders bear the names that are shown here. Don't change them. As mentioned earlier, PowerPoint expects those folders to be named and placed exactly where they are. If they're changed, the program may not work properly.

Caution

Don't change the names of any of PowerPoint's folders. At the very least, the program will not be able to find important features. PowerPoint depends on its files and accompanying applets to be where it expects them to be.

What are the contents of each folder? If you've worked with some of the earlier chapters in this book, you already have some idea of a few of them. The following table provides a sample breakdown of the folder.

Folder	Contents
PowerPoint	This folder contains the PowerPoint executable program; support files; and the default template, which can be the default originally set by the program or a default set by the user.
PCS Files	This folder contains PowerPoint's clip-art files.
Samples	This folder contains several sample PowerPoint presentation files for special applications, such as timeline graphics and flow charts.
Setup	This folder contains PowerPoint's Setup utility, which enables you to install or remove various parts of the program. You still will need the floppy disks or CD-ROM to perform the actual installation.
Templates	This folder contains three subfolders, each of which holds a set of presentation templates that are tailored for a specific purpose.
B&W Overheads	This folder contains template files that are specifically tailored for black-and-white overhead presentations.
Color Overheads	This folder contains template files that are specifically tailored for color overhead presentations.
On Screen & 35mm Slides	This folder contains template files that are specifically tailored for on-screen slide-show presentations and 35mm slide creations.
Wizards	This folder contains several more sample presentations that the Wizards draw upon.

Viewing PowerPoint's Sample Presentations

Two PowerPoint subfolders—the Samples folder and the Wizards folder—each contain a small set of sample presentations that you can draw upon (as can any of the templates that the program offers) for various graphic elements.

Whenever you decide to open another template or finished presentation file, you can preview any files before you apply or open them simply by viewing the thumbnail preview window in the Open dialog box (refer to fig. 5.1).

Clicking a template name in this dialog box displays a thumbnail view of the template. When a template appears that looks good to you, choose OK or double-click the file name to load it.

> **Note**
>
> If you're working on a monochrome or grayscale monitor, the thumbnails and the actual slides will not look nearly as appealing as the actual printed pieces. Don't be afraid to use layouts that seem to be dark; the effect most likely is caused by your monitor.

To load a PowerPoint sample presentation, follow these steps:

1. Open the File menu and choose Open. The Open dialog box appears.

2. Locate the Samples or Wizards folder inside the PowerPoint folder on your hard disk.

    The Samples folder contains five sample presentations: Calendar.ppt - Months, Flowchrt.ppt - Flowcharts, Pintme.ppt - Colors & Patterns, Tables.ppt - 2 to 4 columns, and Timeline.ppt - Gantt Style.

    The Wizards folder contains six more sample files: Badnews.ppt, General.ppt, Progress.ppt, Selling.ppt, Strategy.ppt, and Training.ppt.

3. Select a sample presentation.

4. Click the Read Only check box in the bottom-left corner of the Open dialog box.

5. Choose OK. PowerPoint displays the presentation sample in Outline view, as shown in figure 5.3.

Fig. 5.3
Outline view
sometimes is the
easiest to use,
simply because
it's not laden
with graphics
and colors.

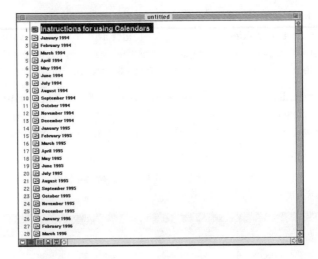

6. Open the View menu and choose Slides, or click the Slide View button in the bottom-left corner of the screen. The sample presentation appears in Slide view, displaying the various graphic elements of the template. Figure 5.4 shows the Calendar.ppt sample presentation.

Fig. 5.4
The sample slide
show appears in
Slide view.

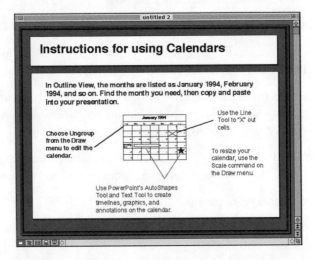

Feel free to explore the other sample presentations. Many of them, particularly those in the Samples folder, display some of the substantial graphic capabilities of PowerPoint.

Reviewing Sample Presentation Slides

Each sample presentation actually conforms to a specific type: a series of body-text slides that, when strung together, constitute a line of argument or a series of points made to deliver a specific message.

To look at the slides in the sample presentation, click the Next Slide button (the double down-arrow button at the bottom of the Slide Changer).

You can view any sample presentation in the same way. To close the sample presentation file, simply click the close box in the upper-left corner of the document window.

Using Elements from Sample Presentations and Templates

PowerPoint offers many templates. Why not use some of the graphic elements of those templates to embellish your own presentations? The process is simple—essentially, a matter of copying and pasting. The key is understanding how to use the template properly. First, you need to open a template that contains elements you may want to use. Follow these steps:

1. Open the File menu and choose Open, or press ⌘-O. The Open dialog box appears.

2. Locate the PowerPoint folder on your hard disk; open the Templates folder and then the On Screen & 35mm Slides folder. The list of templates appears in the list box.

3. Select the template file that you want to copy. This file is the *source* file.

4. Click the Read Only check box in the Open dialog box, to prevent any changes from being saved to the original template file.

5. Choose OK. PowerPoint displays the template file.

Now, to access the graphics elements of the template, you need to display the Slide Master. Follow these steps:

1. Open the View menu and choose Master; then choose Slide Master from the cascading menu. PowerPoint displays the Slide Master.

2. Click anywhere outside the placeholders in the Slide Master; then click the graphic element that you want to copy.

Tip

Press ⌘-A to select the contents of a slide or the Slide Master.

3. Open the Edit menu and choose Copy, or press ⌘-C. PowerPoint copies the graphic object to the Clipboard.

4. Open or display the presentation to which you want to add the new graphic object. This presentation is the *destination* presentation.

5. If you want the object to appear on every page of the presentation, open the View menu and choose Master; then choose Slide Master from the cascading menu.

   If you want to paste the graphic into only one slide, display the desired slide.

6. Open the Edit menu and choose Paste, or press ⌘-V. PowerPoint pastes the graphic into the destination presentation or slide. The graphic automatically conforms to the color palette of the presentation into which it is pasted.

7. Open the File menu and choose Save As, if you want, to save the file.

The body-text object and slide title object can be obscured by the pasted graphic. To correct the problem, make sure that the graphic is selected; then open the Draw menu and choose Send Backward. Each time you choose Send Backward, the object moves back one layer. Objects appear on layers in the order in which they were drawn. Therefore, the first object drawn is on the bottom layer; successive objects are layered on top of the first one.

Perhaps now you can see some of the possibilities for working with graphic objects and other elements from different presentations. You can mix, match, and rearrange items at will. The following section expands on this powerful concept: the capability to create your own templates.

Creating Your Own Templates

In the preceding section, you learned some of the basics of working with template elements and applying those elements to other presentation files. By doing so, you have moved a long way toward creating your own special templates.

Note

If you like the appearance of a presentation file that you create, you can save it as a template for future use. Do not, however, save an existing presentation that contains many slides as a template; the template file will be huge and will contain unwanted slides. The average PowerPoint template file is about 50K to 60K.

To create your own template, follow these steps:

1. Display the presentation that you want to use to create your new template.

2. Open the View menu and choose Master; then choose Slide Master from the cascading menu. The current presentation's Slide Master appears.

3. Open the Edit menu and choose Select All, or press ⌘-A. All objects in the Slide Master are selected.

4. Open the File menu and choose New, or press ⌘-N. The New Presentation dialog box appears (see fig. 5.5).

Fig. 5.5
You are greeted by this dialog box when you choose the New command.

5. Click the Current Presentation Format option button.

6. Choose OK. The New Slide dialog box appears, displaying the slide AutoLayouts.

7. Choose the Title Slide AutoLayout.

8. Choose OK.

To save the new presentation as a slide-show template for later use, follow these steps:

1. Open the File menu and choose Save As. The Save As dialog box appears.

2. In the File Name text box, type the name you want to use.

3. Locate the On Screen & 35mm Slides folder (in the Templates folder, inside the PowerPoint folder).

4. Choose Save, and if the Summary Info dialog box appears, choose OK.

The new file is saved as a template of a reasonable size (about 50K to 60K). You created and saved the template without affecting the contents of the existing presentation on which the new template was based.

Using Placeholders

Placeholders are homes for all the object types in your slides. Titles, body text, graphs, tables, clip art, movie clips, and sounds reside in placeholders. As noted earlier, placeholders are the building blocks of a presentation. Whenever you create a new slide, PowerPoint automatically adds placeholders of specific types, which is why new slide types are called AutoLayouts.

When you create a Graph slide type, for example, PowerPoint adds a chart object to the new slide (see fig. 5.6).

Fig. 5.6
The placeholder at the bottom is ready for you to embed a chart.

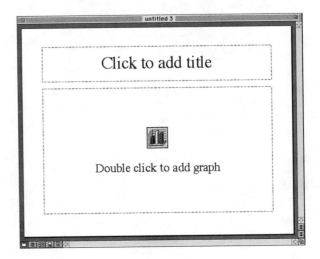

Double-clicking the chart icon in the placeholder starts the Microsoft Graph application, which PowerPoint uses to create charts. The chart object is only a placeholder, however, and doesn't have to hold a chart; it can hold any other object type that is available in your system. All you have to do is select the placeholder and choose a different type of object to place in it.

> **Note**
>
> When you paste a graphic from one presentation to another, the graphic automatically adjusts to the new color palette.

To insert a piece of clip art into the chart placeholder, follow these steps:

1. Click inside the placeholder to select it.

2. Open the Insert menu and choose Clip Art. The ClipArt Gallery appears.

3. In the Choose a Category list, select a category.

4. Click a clip-art thumbnail.

5. Choose OK. PowerPoint inserts the clip art into the placeholder, which assumes the shape of the placed object (see fig. 5.7).

Fig. 5.7
The chart place-holder can contain any object.

Placeholders are generic items in a slide that are capable of holding any object that you can use in PowerPoint. Placeholders can be resized, cut and pasted, copied and reproduced, and deleted; they are flexible, to meet your needs.

PowerPoint 4 Basics

Adding a Company Logo and Company Name to a Template

Earlier in this chapter, you used the Slide Master as the tool for applying and changing templates. The Slide Master also is the key tool in another important task: adding a company name and logo to every slide in your presentation.

▶ See "Using PowerPoint's Drawing Tools," p. 215

Because PowerPoint doesn't offer a selection of company logos in its clip-art collection, you very likely will have to create your own, using PowerPoint or another drawing program. You can create a simple logo from a small text object and a piece of clip art.

To place a company logo in your presentation, follow these steps:

1. Open the View menu and choose Master; then choose Slide Master from the cascading menu. PowerPoint displays the Slide Master for the presentation.

Tip
To place a graphic precisely, display PowerPoint's rulers and use the Zoom feature.

2. Import the file that contains your company logo (open the Insert menu and choose Picture), or use PowerPoint's drawing and clip-art tools to create a logo yourself.

3. Place the graphic object in an acceptable place in your Slide Master (in a corner, for example), as shown in figure 5.8. The logo will appear in the same position in every slide.

Fig. 5.8
The clip art in the lower-right corner could be any graphic or text that you choose.

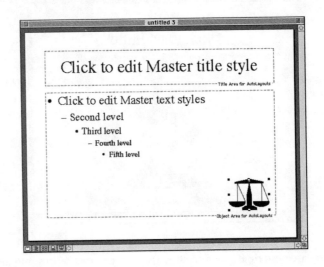

To add text to the Slide Master, follow these steps:

1. Click the Text tool in the Drawing toolbar.

2. Click the location in the Slide Master where you want to place the text. A text placeholder appears, ready for editing.

3. Type the text.

4. Change the font size, if you want, by choosing a different font size from the Font Size pop-up menu, located in the Standard toolbar at the top of the PowerPoint window.

5. Change the color of the text, if you want, by clicking the Text Color button in the Standard toolbar and then choosing a color that stands out well against the Slide Master background.

The graphic and text appear in every slide in the current presentation, providing consistency (see fig. 5.9). The placed objects appear in every slide that is based on this Slide Master.

Fig. 5.9
Slide Masters enable you to add background text and graphic elements to every slide in your presentation.

Saving Your Own Default Presentation

When you add special elements to a template, such as a graphic or text, you may want to save that template as the default to ensure consistency in your presentations.

> **Note**
>
> You may want to create a folder of default templates. Give the templates that you want to save appropriate names, and place them in a folder inside the PowerPoint folder. When you want to use a specific default template, move that file out of the default folder and place it in the PowerPoint folder; then launch PowerPoint.

Using the current template to create a new default presentation is quite easy. Follow these steps:

1. Display the presentation on which you want to base the default template.

2. Open the File menu and choose Save As. The Save As dialog box appears.

3. Select the PowerPoint folder.

4. In the File Name text box, type the file name you want to use.

5. Choose OK. If you have saved a default template before, you may be asked whether you want to replace the existing version. If you do not, move this file or the existing file to another folder.

That's all there is to it. To check your default template, simply create a new presentation.

From Here...

In the past several chapters, you worked with many critical areas in the PowerPoint program. You learned how to create a basic presentation and examined features such as clip art, text, and masters. For more information on these features, see the following chapters:

- Chapter 6, "Working with Text," discusses using PowerPoint's ruler and the fine points of working with text in all PowerPoint views.

- Chapter 7, "Creating Speaker's Notes, Outlines, and Handouts," shows you how to produce and work with those important elements of a presentation.

- Chapter 9, "Drawing Objects," describes how to use PowerPoint's powerful drawing features.

- Chapter 11, "Selecting, Editing, and Enhancing Objects," shows you how to change and edit objects of various types.

Part II

Text

American Numbers

Workbook1

	B	C
	fficers	Enlisted
	13.4	14.9
	11.8	11.3
	10.9	9.8
	3.5	4.8

untitled

Click to add title

Click to add text

Tip of the Day

OK

Next Tip

More Tips...

Help

Did you know...

You can rotate AutoShapes for more shape options. If text is attached to the shape, it rotates as well.

☒ Show Tips at Startup

Chapter 6

Working with Text

In most presentations, bulleted lists and other text charts predominate. Fortunately, PowerPoint makes it easy to create text charts and to apply a consistent format to all text charts in a presentation automatically. Features such as Smart Cut and Paste and Automatic Word Selection simplify common tasks such as copying and moving text. In addition, you can use the following features to eliminate many common inconsistencies in text charts:

- The Slide Master, which enables you to set the basic format—font, type color, bullet shape, tabs, and so on—for the title and body text in all slides in a presentation.

- The Change Case command, which enables you to change selected text to uppercase, lowercase, title case (capitalizes initial letters), or sentence case (capitalizes the initial letter of the first word).

- The Period command, which enables you to add or delete periods at the end of selected paragraphs, such as bulleted-list items.

- The spelling checker, which enables you to check the spelling of all text in your presentation.

In this chapter, you learn how to create and manipulate text in a slide. You also learn many shortcuts for working with text. The chapter also addresses the special features in the preceding list except for the Slide Master, which is discussed in Chapter 4, "Setting up Your New Presentation."

This chapter covers the following major topics:

- Creating text

- Deleting, copying, and moving text

- Formatting text

- Using the spelling checker

- Manipulating and enhancing text placeholders

Understanding Text Placeholders

In PowerPoint, you enter all text in text placeholders, such as those shown in figure 6.1.

Fig. 6.1
Placeholders do not print, whether or not you have edited the contents.

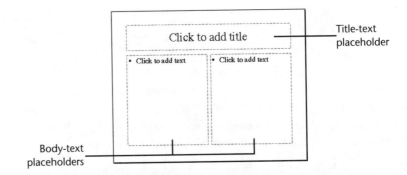

PowerPoint has two types of text placeholders:

- Preset text placeholders, such as those that appear in AutoLayouts. As shown in figure 6.1, these placeholders initially contain the prompt `Click to add title` (for title placeholders) or `Click to add text` (for body-text placeholders). When you add text, the prompt disappears.

- Placeholders that you create by using the Text tool. You could use such placeholders to create labels or other text outside the preset placeholders. Text that you create with the Text tool does not appear in Outline view.

Creating Text

Creating text is as simple as clicking a text placeholder and typing the text. If you are entering title or body text, PowerPoint has created the text placeholders for you. If you are creating a label or other special text, you must create the placeholder before you can type the text. This section describes both procedures.

Creating Title and Body Text

When you create a slide, one of your first steps is selecting the AutoLayout for the type of slide that you are creating. As described in Chapter 3, "Quick Start: Creating a First Presentation," AutoLayouts set up the general layout for each type of slide. The AutoLayout for a bulleted list, for example, includes a placeholder for the chart title and a placeholder for the bulleted list (refer to fig. 6.1). The first time you click the bulleted-list placeholder, a bullet appears; thereafter, a new bullet appears automatically whenever you press Return to start a new item.

◀ See "Working with Text," p. 82

In all AutoLayouts, PowerPoint automatically creates a text placeholder for the title and, if the chart is a text chart, a second text placeholder for the subtitle or body text. Figure 6.2 shows the AutoLayout for a title slide, and figure 6.3 shows the AutoLayout for a chart. These AutoLayout placeholders often are the only text placeholders that you need.

Fig. 6.2
These are title/text placeholders.

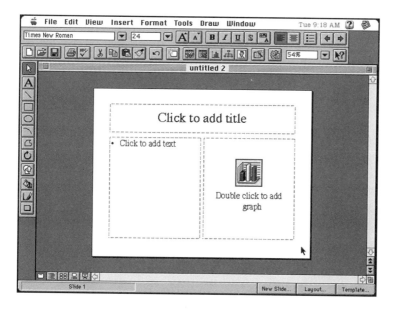

Fig. 6.3
This slide layout contains a text placeholder and a chart placeholder.

To enter text in an AutoLayout placeholder, follow these steps:

1. Click inside the placeholder. The blinking text insertion point appears, and the prompt disappears.

2. Type the text.

Later in this chapter, you learn how to edit and format the text.

> **Note**
>
> The shape of the mouse pointer differs, depending on the type of operation that you are performing. In a text placeholder, the mouse pointer looks like an I-beam. This pointer indicates that you are in an area in which you can enter and edit text.

Creating Labels and Other Special Text

To label an object in a slide or to add special text, such as the date, use the Text tool, which enables you to add text anywhere in a slide.

The procedure for using the Text tool depends on whether you want text that exceeds a certain width to wrap to a new line automatically. For short text, such as labels, this isn't a concern. You add such text by following these steps:

1. Display the slide in Slide view.

2. Click the Text tool (see fig. 6.4).

3. Place the mouse pointer where you want the new text to begin.

4. Click the mouse button to place the insertion point at that location. The gray outline of a text placeholder appears, with the insertion point inside (refer to fig. 6.4).

5. Type the text. The text placeholder expands to accommodate the text.

6. To start another line, press Return. The text box automatically expands to include the next line.

7. Type the text for that line.

Tip
You also can add labels to notes pages, handouts, and outlines. Such labels appear only on those pages, not on the slide. For details, see Chapter 7, "Creating Speaker's Notes, Outlines, and Handouts."

This procedure is suitable for short labels, in which automatic word wrapping isn't necessary. You can use the Text tool, however, to create a text placeholder of a specific size; text automatically wraps to the next line when it exceeds the placeholder width. To create such a placeholder, follow these steps:

1. Display the slide in Slide view.

2. Click the Text tool.

3. Place the mouse pointer where you want the new text to begin.

4. Click and hold down the mouse button to set the left edge of the new text placeholder.

5. Drag the mouse pointer to where you want to fix the right edge of the new placeholder. (Notice that as you drag the mouse, the outline of a text placeholder appears and expands as you move the mouse).

6. Release the mouse button. PowerPoint creates a text placeholder of the selected size that is one line long. The insertion point appears inside the placeholder.

7. Type the text. Any text that exceeds the width of the placeholder automatically wraps to a new line, and the text placeholder automatically expands to include the new line.

You can resize any text placeholder, as described in "Manipulating Text Placeholders" later in this chapter. The text in the placeholder automatically rewraps to fit the new size. If you used the first procedure (which doesn't activate word wrapping) to add text to a slide, you can activate word wrapping simply by resizing that text placeholder.

Tip

To activate word wrapping in any text placeholder, open the Format menu and choose Text Anchor; choose Word-wrap Text in Object; and then choose OK.

Fig. 6.4

Text can be added to a slide without the benefit of a placeholder.

Text tool

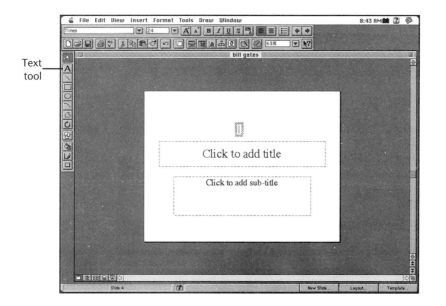

Moving the Insertion Point Within Text and Between Text Placeholders

In a text placeholder, the text that you type appears at the location of the insertion point, which is a vertical bar that blinks on and off. You can move the insertion point by placing the mouse pointer where you want the insertion point to appear and clicking the mouse button. You also can use the keys and key combinations listed in the following table to move the insertion point.

Press...	To Move the Insertion Point...
right arrow	Right one character
left arrow	Left one character
up arrow	Up one line
down arrow	Down one line
⌘-right arrow	Right one word
⌘-left arrow	Left one word
⌘-up arrow	Up one paragraph
⌘-down arrow	Down one paragraph
Home*	To the beginning of the line
End*	To the end of the line

On an extended keyboard.

To move to another text placeholder, just click that placeholder.

Selecting Text

For many operations involving text, you must begin by selecting the text. To make existing text italic, for example, select that text and then choose Italic (see "Changing Text Attributes" later in this chapter). Selected text is highlighted on-screen by a color swash or in reverse video.

Like most Macintosh programs, PowerPoint enables you to use the keyboard or the mouse to select text. This section describes the most common selection techniques.

Mouse Techniques

You can use the mouse to select a single word, a paragraph, or a text block of any length.

To select a word or paragraph, use these techniques:

To Select...	Do This...
A word	Double-click anywhere in the word
A paragraph	Triple-click anywhere in the paragraph

To select a block of text, you can use either of two methods. The first method uses the mouse. Follow these steps:

1. Place the mouse pointer where you want the selection to begin.

2. Press and hold down the mouse button.

3. Drag the mouse pointer to where you want the selection to end.

4. Release the mouse button.

The second method of selecting a block of text uses the mouse and the Shift key. Follow these steps:

1. Place the mouse pointer where you want the selection to begin.

2. Click the mouse button.

3. Place the mouse pointer where you want the selection to end.

4. Simultaneously press the Shift key and click the mouse button again.

Note

If Automatic Word Selection is on, PowerPoint selects an entire word if one letter of the word is selected (see "Automatic Word Selection" later in this section).

Keyboard Technique

To use the keyboard to select text, follow these steps:

1. Place the insertion point where you want the selection to begin.

2. Press and hold down the Shift and ⌘ keys.

3. Press the arrow keys to move the highlight to the end of the text that you want to select. Notice that you can select only entire words.

4. Release the Shift and ⌘ keys.

Automatic Word Selection

Tip
Even when Automatic Word Selection is on, you can select a portion of a word by using the keyboard technique described in the preceding section.

PowerPoint's Automatic Word Selection feature selects a word automatically when any letter of that word is selected, as well as the space or period that follows the word. Automatic Word Selection often speeds editing, because it eliminates the need to carefully position the mouse pointer at the beginning and end of the text that you want to select; instead, you can place the mouse anywhere in the first and last words that you want to select. New Macintosh users will find this feature to be invaluable.

By default, Automatic Word Selection is turned on. To turn it off, follow these steps:

1. Open the Tools menu and choose Options. The Options dialog box appears.

2. Click the Automatic Word Selection check box to remove the x.

3. Choose OK.

Editing Text

No slide presentation is perfect on the first try; chances are that you will edit the text several times before you're satisfied. This section teaches not only basic text-editing techniques, but also PowerPoint shortcuts that can simplify the editing process. If you use a word processing program, many of the editing techniques described in this section will be familiar to you.

Inserting Text

To insert text into an existing text placeholder, place the insertion point where you want to insert the text, and then type the text. Remember that you can use the arrow keys or the mouse to move the insertion point. To use the arrow keys, simply press them (refer to "Moving the Insertion Point Within Text and Between Text Placeholders" earlier in this chapter). To use the mouse, place the mouse pointer where you want to place the insertion point, and then click the mouse button.

Deleting Text

Press the Delete key to delete text. To delete characters one by one, follow these steps:

1. Place the insertion point where you want to begin deleting text.

2. To delete the character to the right of the insertion point, press the Delete Forward key (only on an extended keyboard). To delete the character to the left of the insertion point, press the Delete key.

To delete a block of text, select the block and then press Delete. You also can replace a selected block with new text. To do so, just select the block and then type the new text; PowerPoint automatically deletes the original text and inserts the new text at that location.

Moving or Copying Text

You can move or copy text within a text placeholder and between text placeholders—even between placeholders on different slides. The procedure is the same in each case.

To move text, follow these steps:

1. Select the text that you want to move.

2. Use one of the following methods to cut the text from its current location (see fig. 6.5):

■ Press ⌘-X.

■ Open the Edit menu and choose Cut.

■ Click the Cut button.

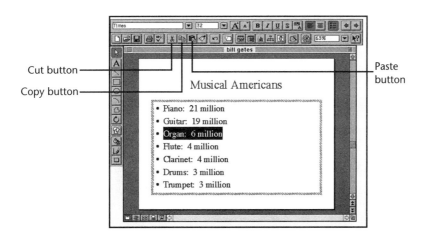

Fig. 6.5
When text is selected, you can use several methods to cut or copy it.

3. Place the insertion point where you want to insert the text.

4. Use one of the following methods to paste the text in its new location (refer to fig. 6.5):

   ■ Press ⌘-V.

   ■ Open the Edit menu and choose Paste.

   ■ Click the Paste button.

To copy text, follow these steps:

1. Select the text that you want to copy.

2. Use one of the following methods to copy the text from its current location:

   ■ Press ⌘-C.

   ■ Open the Edit menu and choose Copy.

   ■ Click the Copy button.

3. Place the insertion point where you want to insert the copied text.

4. Use one of the following methods to paste the copy in its new location:

   ■ Press ⌘-V.

   ■ Open the Edit menu and choose Paste.

   ■ Click the Paste button.

Using PowerPoint's drag-and-drop feature, you also can move or copy selected text to a new location within the text placeholder simply by dragging the text to the new location. You can use the drag-and-drop feature in Slide, Notes Pages, and Outline views. The procedure is the same in each case. Simply follow these steps:

1. Select the text that you want to move or copy.

2. Place the mouse pointer on the selected text. (The pointer should change to an arrow; if it doesn't, move it over the selection until it does.)

3. To move the selected text, click and hold down the mouse button. To copy the text, press and hold down both the ⌘ key and the mouse button.

In both cases, a "shadow" pointer and a box representing the text move with the mouse pointer. If you are copying the text, a plus sign (+) also appears next to the mouse pointer.

4. Move the mouse pointer until the shadow pointer is where you want to insert the text. If the selected text includes a space, you can place the shadow pointer between words but not within words.

5. Release the mouse button to insert the text at that location.

When you move or copy text, PowerPoint's Smart Cut and Paste feature adjusts the spaces before and after words automatically. The Smart Cut and Paste feature appears as an option in the Options dialog box. To display this dialog box, open the Tools menu and choose Options. By default, the Use Smart Cut and Paste option is selected. To disable this feature, click the Use Smart Cut and Paste check box to remove the x and then choose OK.

Moving List Items Up and Down

To simplify editing further, PowerPoint enables you to move list items up or down in the list quickly. Follow these steps:

1. Click anywhere in the bulleted list.

2. Move the mouse pointer left of the list item until the pointer looks like a four-sided arrow.

3. Click and hold down the mouse button. The list item is highlighted.

4. Drag the mouse pointer where you want to insert the item. As you drag the pointer, it changes to a double-sided arrow. A horizontal line indicates the pointer's location in the list.

5. Release the mouse button.

Changing the Case of Text

If many people are involved in a presentation, inconsistencies in the text are common. Inconsistent use of letter case is one of the most frequent problems; it also used to be one of the most time-consuming to fix because you had to retype the text in the correct case. Not any more. PowerPoint includes an automated Change Case feature that enables you to change selected text to any of the following cases:

■ *Lowercase.* these are lowercase letters.

■ *Uppercase.* THESE ARE UPPERCASE LETTERS.

- *Title case.* Title Case Uses Initial Capital Letters, As Shown Here.

- *Sentence case.* Sentence case capitalizes only the initial letter of the first word, as in a sentence.

You also can toggle the cases in selected text so that lowercase letters change to uppercase and uppercase letters change to lowercase. To change the case of text, follow these steps:

1. Select the text that you want to change.

2. Open the Format menu and choose Change Case. The Change Case dialog box appears.

3. Select the case that you want to use.

4. Choose OK.

Adding or Removing Periods at the End of List Items

Another common inconsistency is the use of periods at the end of list items. Inevitably, some lists do not conform to your convention. As you may have guessed, PowerPoint also simplifies the task of fixing this problem. You can add or remove periods from the end of list items quickly. Follow these steps:

1. Select the items that you want to change.

2. Open the Format menu and choose Periods. The Periods dialog box appears.

3. Choose Add Periods or Remove Periods.

4. Choose OK.

Finding and Replacing Text

PowerPoint's Find feature and Find and Replace feature enable you to search for text and replace it with different text quickly. Use the Find feature to search for text that appears only in a specific slide.

To search for text, follow these steps:

1. Open the slide presentation that you want to search.

2. Open the Edit menu and choose Find, or press ⌘-F. The Find dialog box appears, as shown in figure 6.6.

Fig. 6.6
The Find dialog
box searches each
slide for a match.

3. In the Find What text box, type the text that you want to find.

4. To find only text that matches the case that you entered, choose the Match Case option. If you enter **CAMP** in the Find What text box and choose Match Case, for example, PowerPoint finds only *CAMP*. If you don't choose Match Case, PowerPoint finds *CAMP, Camp, camp*, and all other occurrences of the word *camp*.

5. To find only whole words that match the text that you entered, choose the Find Whole Words Only option. PowerPoint finds only matching words that are preceded and followed by a space or punctuation.

6. Click the Find Next button. PowerPoint moves to the first occurrence of text that matches the Find criteria.

7. To find the next match, repeat step 6.

8. When you finish searching, click Close, or click the close box in the upper-left corner of the dialog box.

Tip
To display the
last four words
for which you
searched, click the
Find What button
in the Find or
Replace dialog box.

To search for text and replace it with different text, follow these steps:

1. Open the slide presentation that you want to search.

2. Open the Edit menu and choose Replace, or press ⌘-H. The Replace dialog box appears.

3. In the Find What text box, type the text that you want to find.

4. To find only text that matches the case that you entered, choose the Match Case option. To find only whole words that match the text that you entered, choose the Find Whole Words Only option.

5. In the Replace With text box, type the text that you want to replace the original text.

6. To replace all occurrences of the original text with the new text, click the Replace All button. PowerPoint does not prompt you to confirm that you want to replace the text.

   To choose the cases in which the new text replaces the original text, click the Find Next button. PowerPoint moves to the first occurrence of text that matches the Find criteria. If you want to replace that text, click the Replace button. To find the next occurrence, repeat this step.

7. When you finish, click Close, or click the close box in the upper-left corner of the Replace dialog box.

Troubleshooting

Is there a fast way to delete all text in a placeholder?

With the insertion point in the placeholder, press ⌘-A to select all text in the place-holder; then press the Delete key.

To conserve space, I want to use " and ' as inch and foot symbols. But whenever I press the " and ' keys, I get real quotation marks. How can I get inch and foot symbols?

Disable the Smart Quotes feature, which automatically enters true double and single quotation marks when you press the " and ' keys. To disable the feature, open the Tools menu and choose Options; the Options dialog box appears. Click the Replace Straight Quotes with Smart Quotes check box to remove the X, and then choose OK.

This action doesn't change true quotation marks that already appear in the presenta-tion—only quotation marks that you subsequently enter. If you need true quotation marks later, simply check the Replace Straight Quotes with Smart Quotes check box.

How can I select part of a word, rather than the whole word?

The easiest way is to use the keyboard: Place the insertion point where you want the selection to begin; then press and hold down the Shift key while you press the arrow keys to extend your selection. When you finish selecting text, release the Shift key. (If you are selecting more than one word at a time, you may not be able to select part of the final word in the sequence because of your Option settings in the Tools menu. Deselect the Automatic Word Selection option in the Options dialog box.)

Tip

The Macintosh keyboard also has "hidden" quota-tion marks and apostrophes; to access them, press Option and Shift-Option in con-junction with the bracket keys ([and]). To see the locations of these and other hidden characters, open the Apple menu and choose Key Caps.

Replacing Fonts

Suppose that you develop a presentation for several of your company's offices and then find that some of the offices cannot print the fonts that you used. With PowerPoint, you can quickly replace these fonts with other fonts that the office can print. Follow these steps:

1. Open the presentation that you want to change.

2. Open the Tools menu and choose Replace Fonts. The Replace Fonts dialog box appears.

3. Click the Replace button to list the fonts used in the presentation, and then select the font that you want to replace.

4. Click the With button to list available fonts, and then select the replacement font.

5. Choose Replace. PowerPoint replaces the font throughout the presentation.

Formatting Text

The Slide Master sets the default format for the title and body text in a slide: the text font, size, and color; the bullet shape, size, and color; and the tabs, line spacing, and justification. If you want a format to affect all slides in your presentation, set that format in the Slide Master. PowerPoint automatically reformats all slides according to the new Slide Master format.

◀ See "Under-standing the Slide Master," p. 110

To change the characteristics of individual words or paragraphs in a slide, however, you must make the changes in the slide itself. A common example is when you emphasize key words by making them boldface or by changing their color. Formats that you enter in individual slides are preserved even if you change the format for the corresponding text in the Slide Master.

Changing Text Attributes

PowerPoint gives you great flexibility in choosing the appearance of your text, allowing you to change the following text attributes:

■ *Font.* In PowerPoint, a font is a type family, such as Times Roman or Helvetica (see fig. 6.7). You can choose one of the TrueType fonts installed with PowerPoint or any other font installed on your system.

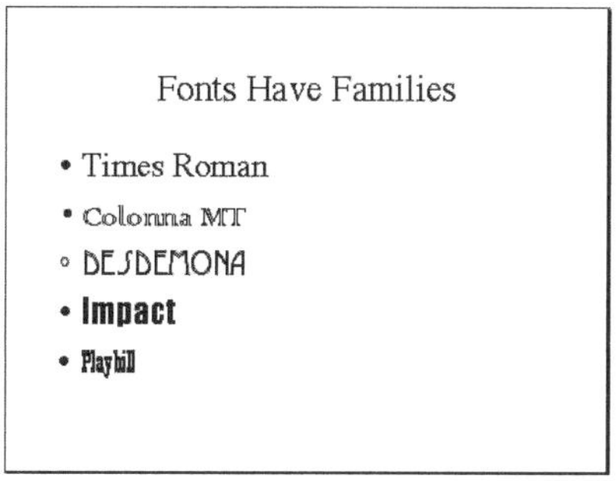

Fonts Have Families

• Times Roman
• Colonna MT
◦ DESDEMONA
• **Impact**
• Playbill

Fig. 6.7
The name of a font generally refers to its family. A font includes the bold, italic, and bold italic versions.

> **Note**
>
> TrueType fonts are not recommended if you are planning to print to a PostScript device. Type 1 (PostScript) fonts work best and most reliably when you print to a typical PostScript laser printer or imagesetter.

- *Font style.* You can make text plain, bold, italic, or both bold and italic. As figure 6.8 shows, plain text is the upright, medium-weight text that you normally see; bold text is darker than plain text; and italic text slants to the right.

Fig. 6.8
Style is applied to a font, so a family includes bold, but bold also is a style.

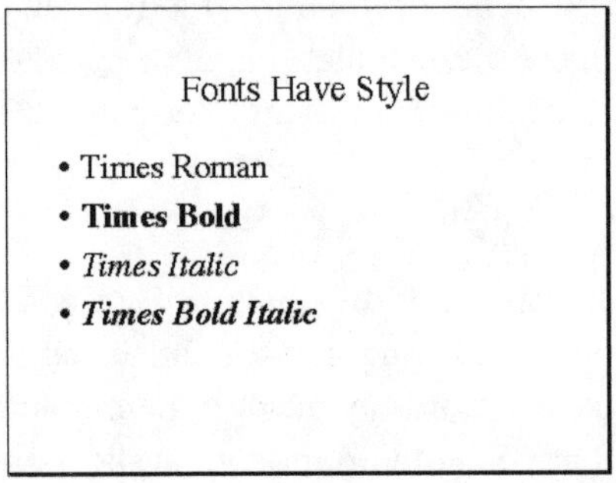

Fonts Have Style

- Times Roman
- **Times Bold**
- *Times Italic*
- ***Times Bold Italic***

- *Font size.* Font size is expressed in *points*; 1 point equals 1/72 inch. The size of the font that you are reading now, for example, is 9 points.

- *Color.* Color is one of the most powerful graphic elements in a slide. You can use predefined colors or custom colors that you create.

- *Special effects.* You can underline, superscript, subscript, shadow, or emboss text (see fig. 6.9). Shadowed text appears to have a drop shadow behind it; embossed text appears to be raised.

Fig. 6.9
Special effects are available for fonts.

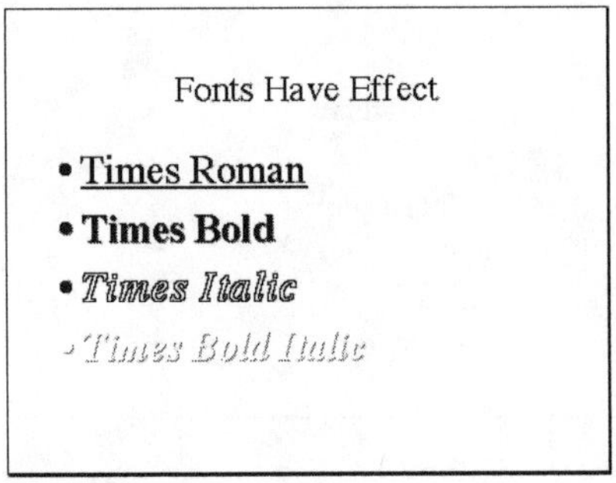

Fonts Have Effect

- <u>Times Roman</u>
- **Times Bold**
- *Times Italic*
- *Times Bold Italic*

With so many possibilities, you may be confused about the appropriate use of text attributes. The cardinal rule of presentation design is "Keep it simple." If you remember this rule as you design your slides, you will create a more effective presentation; the audience will focus on the content of the presentation instead of on a busy design. For help in designing your presentation, try using the Pick a Look Wizard or one of PowerPoint's many professionally designed templates.

◀ See "Using Wizards," p. 69

◀ See "Using Templates," p. 120

PowerPoint enables you to use menus, the Formatting toolbar, or keyboard shortcuts to change text characteristics. The toolbar and keyboard shortcuts are the fastest methods, but you cannot use them to apply some special effects, such as embossing and superscript. To apply these special effects, you must use menu commands.

Tip

If the Formatting toolbar doesn't appear on-screen, open the View menu and choose Toolbars; choose Formatting; and then choose OK.

Table 6.1 describes the buttons in the Formatting toolbar (see fig. 6.10). To use a button to format text, select the text and then click the button.

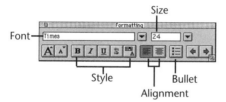

Fig. 6.10

The floating Formatting toolbar, which normally appears at the top of the document area, can be moved on-screen.

Table 6.1 Buttons and Menus That Change Text Appearance		
Button or Menu	**Button or Menu Name**	**Description**
Book Antiqua	Font	Click the down arrow to display a list of fonts, and then select a font. The four most recently used fonts appear at the top of the list.
44	Font Size	Click the down arrow to display a list of font sizes, and then select a size. Alternatively, type the size in the text box.
A⬆	Increase Font Size	Click this button to increase the font size incrementally.
A⬇	Decrease Font Size	Click this button to decrease the font size incrementally.

(continues)

Table 6.1 Continued		
Button or Menu	**Button or Menu Name**	**Description**
B	Bold	Click this button to toggle boldface style on and off.
I	Italic	Click this button to toggle italic style on and off.
U	Underline	Click this button to toggle underlining on and off.
S	Text Shadow	Click this button to toggle the drop-shadow effect on and off.
A	Text Color	Click this button to display a color palette; then select a color.

Table 6.2 lists the keyboard shortcuts. To use these shortcuts to format text, select the text and then press the appropriate key(s).

Table 6.2 Keyboard Shortcuts for Changing Text Appearance	
Style	**Keys**
Bold	⌘-B
Italic	⌘-I
Underline	⌘-U

To use menu commands to change text attributes, follow these steps:

1. Select the text that you want to change.

2. Open the Format menu and choose Font. The Font dialog box appears.

3. Make your changes in the dialog box. If you choose Superscript or Subscript, type in the Offset box the percentage by which you want the superscript or subscript text to be offset; for subscript text, enter a negative number. To apply a different color, click the Color button to display a palette, and then select the color.

4. Choose OK.

Copying Text Styles

After you format text—as red 30-point italic Times, for example—you can copy the text style to any other text. Copying text styles not only saves you steps, but also saves you from having to remember detailed styles.

To use the Standard toolbar to copy a style, follow these steps:

1. Select any word that has the format that you want to copy.

2. In the Standard toolbar, click the Format Painter button (see fig. 6.11). To apply the format to more than one selection, double-click the button.

3. Select the text that you want to format with the copied style.

4. Click the mouse button.

5. If you are applying the format to more than one selection (that is, if you double-clicked the Format Painter button in step 2), repeat steps 3 and 4. When you finish, click the Format Painter button.

Format Painter button

Tip
Unless you are experienced in type design, use the same font for title and body text throughout a presentation. Set the font in the Slide Master (refer to Chapter 4, "Setting up Your New Presentation").

Fig. 6.11
The Standard toolbar can also be dragged around the work area.

To use menus to copy a style, follow these steps:

1. Select any word that has the format that you want to copy.

2. Open the Format menu and choose Pick Up Text Style.

3. Select the text that you want to format with the copied style.

4. Open the Format menu and choose Apply Style.

Changing Bullet Characteristics

You can change the shape, color, and size of the bullets that you use in bulleted lists. Bullet size is given as a percentage of the text size. A bullet size of 80, for example, means that the font size used for the bullet is 80 percent of the text-font size.

To change bullet characteristics, follow these steps:

1. Select all items whose bullets you want to change.

2. Open the Format menu and choose Bullet. The Bullet dialog box appears (see fig. 6.12).

Fig. 6.12
In this dialog box, you can select a character to be used as a bullet.

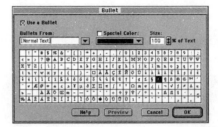

3. To change the bullet character, click the desired character in the character palette (refer to fig. 6.12).

   To choose a character in a different font, click the Bullets From button to list the fonts, and select a font. When the characters in that font appear in the character palette, select the character that you want to use.

4. To change the bullet color, click the Special Color check box and then select a color from the pop-up menu.

5. To change the bullet size, type a new size in the Size box, or click the arrow buttons to increase or decrease the percentage displayed in that box.

6. Choose OK.

Setting Tabs and Indents

Tip
Use decimal tabs to set up numbered lists. A decimal tab makes the numbers align left of the decimal point and the text align right of the decimal point.

Tabs and indents enable you to control the way that text aligns in a chart. If your presentation includes columns of text, you can use tabs to set up the column format—the location of the columns and the alignment of text within the columns.

To set up a bulleted or numbered list, in which you want text to align at a point inside the left margin, use a paragraph indent. The AutoLayouts for bulleted lists, for example, use indents to set the placement of bullets and the text aligned to the right of the bullets.

Understanding the Ruler

You set tabs and indents with the PowerPoint ruler, which you can display in slide or Notes Pages view. To display the ruler for a paragraph, place the insertion point in the paragraph; then open the View menu and choose Ruler. The ruler appears below the main menu bar and any toolbars that are displayed (see fig. 6.13).

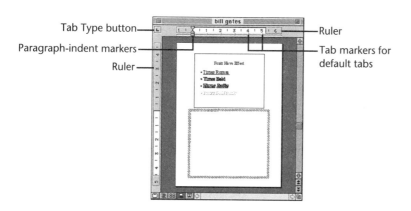

Fig. 6.13
The tab ruler is available in Notes Pages and Slides views.

The ruler has the following features:

- *Tab Type button.* Click the Tab Type button to cycle through the four tab types:

Button	Button Name	Description
L	Left	Aligns the left end of text at the tab
⌐	Right	Aligns the right end of text at the tab
⊥	Center	Centers text on the tab
⊥	Decimal	Centers text on a decimal point

- *Tab markers.* The default tabs, which are left tabs spaced at one-inch intervals, are marked by ticks at the bottom of the ruler (refer to fig. 6.13). Tabs that you set are indicated in the ruler by the icon for that tab type (left, right, center, or decimal).

■ *Paragraph-indent markers*. The top marker shows the indent for the first line of text in the selected paragraph (refer to fig. 6.13). The bottom marker shows the indent for the rest of the paragraph. When both markers are aligned, all lines of text in a paragraph are indented equally. For most text placeholders, the default setting for both markers is zero inches—that is, there is no indent, so all text in paragraphs aligns at the left margin of the placeholder. In the AutoLayouts for bulleted lists, default indents are set for the bulleted-list items.

Changing the Default Tabs

You can change the default tabs for a placeholder to any evenly spaced interval; this capability enables you to set up evenly spaced columns across a chart. Remember that the default tabs are left tabs. If you want to use a different type of tab—for example, a decimal tab to align numbers on a decimal point—you must set a specific tab of that type, as described in the following section.

To change the default tab interval, follow these steps:

1. Place the insertion point anywhere in the placeholder that you want to change.

2. If the ruler isn't displayed, open the View menu and choose Ruler.

3. Click and drag the first tab marker to the place in the ruler where you want to set the first tab.

4. Release the mouse button. The other tab markers adjust to be evenly spaced at the interval determined by the first tab marker.

> **Note**
>
> If you don't click the tab marker precisely, you insert a tab rather than reset the default interval. If you accidentally insert a tab, you can delete it by dragging it off the ruler.

Setting Specific Tabs

You can override the default tabs by setting your own. The tab type can be left, right, center, or decimal. When you set a tab, PowerPoint ignores all default tabs that precede that tab. If you set a tab at three inches, for example, pressing Tab moves the insertion point directly to the three-inch tab, rather than to the first default tab (at one inch).

To set individual tabs, follow these steps:

1. Place the insertion point in the paragraph that you want to change, or select two or more paragraphs.

2. If the ruler isn't displayed, open the View menu and choose Ruler.

3. Depending on the changes that you want to make, use one or more of the following procedures:

   - *To add a tab:* Click the Tab Type button until it displays the icon for the appropriate tab type; then click the ruler where you want to set the tab. To insert more than one tab of that type, click every location where you want to set a tab.

   - *To move a tab:* Click and drag the tab marker to a new location in the ruler.

   - *To delete a tab:* Drag the tab marker off the ruler.

4. To hide the ruler, open the View menu and choose Ruler (the ruler toggles on and off). Hiding the ruler doesn't affect the tab settings.

Tip

To select all text in a placeholder, place the insertion point anywhere in the placeholder and then press ⌘-A.

Setting Indents

PowerPoint enables you to choose one indent for the first line of a paragraph and another indent for subsequent lines of the paragraph. You can set up the indents so that the first line begins either to the right or the left of the subsequent lines. In the first example in this section, the first line begins to the right; this indent is a standard *paragraph indent*. In the second and third examples, the first line begins to the left; this type of indent is called a *hanging indent*.

Example 1:

The first line in this paragraph is indented. Subsequent lines in the paragraph automatically begin at the normal left margin.

Example 2:

This is a hanging indent. Notice that the first line begins to the left of subsequent lines.

Example 3:

■ This also is a hanging indent. The bullet, which is the beginning of the first line, begins to the left of subsequent lines. In bulleted lists, the first line of text automatically moves right so that it aligns with other text in the paragraph.

To change paragraph indents, follow these steps:

1. Place the insertion point in the paragraph that you want to change, or select two or more paragraphs.

2. If the ruler isn't displayed, open the View menu and choose Ruler.

3. Depending on the changes that you want to make, use one or more of the following procedures:

■ *To change the indent for the first line of text in the selected paragraphs:* Drag the top indent marker to where you want the text to align on the left.

■ *To change the indent for the remaining text in the selected paragraphs:* Drag the bottom indent marker to where you want the text to align on the left.

■ *To use the same indent for all lines of text in the selected paragraphs:* Align the top and bottom indent markers, and then drag the bottom (square) half of the bottom marker to move both indent markers to where you want the text to align on the left.

Note

PowerPoint enables you to use up to five indent levels in a text placeholder. Each level is defined by one set of indent markers. To display the indent markers for the levels that are already used in a placeholder, place the insertion point in any paragraph in the placeholder, and then display the ruler. To display the indent markers for a level that hasn't been used yet, place the insertion point in a blank line, and then click the Demote button to demote the line to that level. The rightmost indent markers on the ruler define the settings for that indent level.

Moving to Tab Stops and Indents

In most placeholders, you can press Tab to move to a tab stop. In placeholders that contain bulleted lists, however, you must press Option-Tab; in those placeholders, pressing Tab indents the text. In any placeholder, press Delete to move back one tab stop.

To move the insertion point to the next indent, click the Demote button. (In bulleted lists, you also can press Tab.) In AutoLayouts for bulleted lists, the Demote button inserts a bullet and indents the text. To move the insertion point back an indent, click the Promote button. (In bulleted lists, you also can press Shift-Tab.)

Tab settings do not affect indents. When you indent list items by clicking the Demote button, the insertion point moves only to indent stops, ignoring tab stops. Similarly, if you set up indents to indent the first line of a paragraph automatically, the first line begins at the indent, regardless of whether you set a tab before that indent.

Indent settings, however, do affect tabs. When you press Tab, the insertion point moves to the next tab stop or indent.

Setting Margins

Margins in a text placeholder are similar to page margins: all text lies between the margins, which are measured from the edge of the placeholder. In PowerPoint, you can change the left and right margins jointly, but not separately. Similarly, you can change the top and bottom margins jointly, but not separately.

To change the margins in a text placeholder, follow these steps:

1. Click the text placeholder that you want to change.

2. Open the Format menu and choose Text Anchor. The Text Anchor dialog box appears.

3. To change the left and right margins, type a new measurement (in inches) in the top text box in the Box Margins section. Alternatively, you can click the buttons to the right of the text box to increase or decrease the measurement in 0.05-inch increments.

4. To change the top and bottom margins, type a new measurement (in inches) in the bottom text box in the Box Margins section. Alternatively, you can click the buttons to the right of the text box to increase or decrease the measurement in 0.05-inch increments.

5. Choose OK to close the dialog box.

Aligning Text

You can align text on the right, on the left, on both the right and the left (fully justified), or in the center. Generally, lists are best aligned left. Full justification, however, can be used to give a more formal appearance. Titles and subtitles can be left-aligned, right-aligned, or centered.

  You can choose left or center alignment by clicking the Left Alignment or Center Alignment button in the Formatting toolbar.

To change the alignment of text, select the paragraphs that you want to change; open the Format menu and choose Alignment; and then choose Left, Center, Right, or Justify from the cascading menu.

> **Note**
>
> A paragraph cannot have more than one type of alignment.

Setting Line and Paragraph Spacing

Line spacing is the distance from the baseline of one line of text to the baseline of the next line of text. *Paragraph spacing* is additional space that you can add before and after paragraphs.

To change line or paragraph spacing, follow these steps:

1. Select the paragraphs that you want to change.

2. Open the Format menu and choose Line Spacing. The Line Spacing dialog box appears.

3. To change line spacing, type a new measurement in the Line Spacing text box. Alternatively, click the buttons next to the text box to increase or decrease line spacing by 0.05-line increments.

4. To change paragraph spacing, type a new measurement in either or both of the Before Paragraph and After Paragraph text boxes. Alternatively, click the buttons next to those text boxes to increase or decrease spacing by 0.05-line increments.

5. Choose OK. The dialog box closes, and the text is reformatted.

Tip

The default unit of measure is lines. If you prefer to use points as the unit of measurement, click the down arrow to open the pop-up Lines menu and then choose Points.

Using True Quotation Marks

When you use PowerPoint's Smart Quotes feature, pressing the " or ' key inserts true quotation marks (", ') rather than straight quotation marks (", '). PowerPoint is even smart enough to recognize when the quotation mark should be an opening or closing quotation mark.

On occasions, however, you may want to use straight quotation marks—as inch and foot symbols, for example. In such a case, disable the Smart Quotes feature by following these steps:

1. Open the Tools menu and choose Options. The Options dialog box appears.

2. Click the Replace Straight Quotes with Smart Quotes check box to remove the x.

3. Choose OK.

Disabling this feature does not affect any true quotation marks that you already have typed.

> **Note**
>
> As discussed earlier in this chapter, you can type Smart Quotes when the feature is disabled by locating the mark you need in Key Caps (Apple menu). Copy and paste the mark or type it from your keyboard by pressing the Shift and Shift-Option keys along with the bracket keys ([and]).

Creating a Bulleted List

If a text placeholder contains a simple list (that is, a list without bullets), you can change the list to a bulleted list. Follow these steps:

1. Select all items in the list.

2. Open the Format menu and choose Bullet. The Bullet dialog box appears.

3. Choose the Use a Bullet option.

4. If you want, change the bullet character (the default for first-level list items is a round bullet), color, or size. (For details, refer to "Changing Bullet Characteristics" earlier in this chapter.)

5. Choose OK. The dialog box closes, and bullets precede the selected items.

II

Text

If necessary, change the indent settings to adjust the space between the bullets and the text. (For information on setting indents, refer to "Setting Tabs and Indents" earlier in this chapter.)

If you intend to use the default bullet character, color, and size, you can change to a bulleted list even more quickly. Simply select the list items and then click the Bullet On/Off button in the Formatting toolbar (see fig. 6.14). To remove the bullets, select the items and then click the Bullet On/Off button again.

Fig. 6.14
The Bullet button is in the lower-left corner of this floating toolbar.

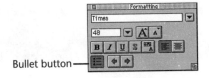

Bullet button ——

  After you have a bulleted list, you can click the Promote and Demote buttons to add items below the main items. To list secondary items below a main item, follow these steps:

1. Place the insertion point at the end of the item to which you are adding the new list.

2. Press Return to insert a new line. A bullet automatically appears.

3. Press Tab. PowerPoint automatically indents the bullet below the preceding line. If the text is in a placeholder that you created, the bullet character does not change. (You can change it later, as described in the section "Changing Bullet Characteristics" earlier in this chapter.)

   Also, the indent may not be correct; in placeholders that you create, for example, there typically is no space between the bullet and the text. To fix this problem, you must create a hanging indent (refer to "Setting Indents" earlier in this chapter).

4. Type the text for the item.

5. When you finish, press Return. The insertion point moves to a new line that is indented the same way as the preceding item.

6. Continue adding items until the list is finished.

You can have up to five levels of lists in a placeholder, but you should limit yourself to two levels in the same slide; an audience can't digest much more than that in the short time that a slide is shown. If you must add more levels, the procedure is the same as that for adding a secondary list.

To promote an item one level, click the item and then press Shift-Tab.

Troubleshooting

When I press Tab, PowerPoint inserts a bullet and indents the text. How do I just tab?

You are getting an indent because you are in a bulleted list. In bulleted lists, pressing Tab has the same effect as clicking the Demote button. To tab in bulleted lists, press ⌘-Tab.

How do I make text wrap to a new line automatically?

In most placeholders, word wrapping occurs automatically. In some placeholders created with the Text tool, however, word wrapping is not automatic. To activate word wrapping, open the Format menu and choose Text Anchor; choose Word-wrap Text in Object; and then choose OK. (For more information on word wrapping, refer to "Creating Labels and Other Special Text" earlier in this chapter.)

How can I increase or decrease the space between the text and the edge of the place-holder (or between text and a border I created around the text)?

Change the placeholder margins. For instructions, refer to "Setting Margins" earlier in this chapter.

What's the best way to emphasize text in a slide?

In color slides, make the text a warm color, such as red or yellow (but don't mix red with green, because some people are red–green color blind). In black-and-white slides, make the text bold or italic; bold provides a greater degree of emphasis than italic does. Some designers also use underlining for emphasis. Don't use other special effects, such as shadows or embossing, unless they fit well with the slide design.

Using the Spelling Checker

Always check the spelling in a presentation before the audience sees it; few things are more embarrassing than an 18-inch-high typo. To check the spelling, use PowerPoint's spelling checker, which checks both spelling and letter case.

Note

By default, PowerPoint suggests corrections when it detects a potential error. If your spelling checker is slow, you can speed it by disabling this feature. Open the Tools menu and choose Options; deselect Always Suggest; and then choose OK.

To use the spelling checker, follow these steps:

1. Open the presentation that you want to check.

2. Open the Tools menu and choose Spelling.

PowerPoint begins checking the spelling. If the program detects a potential error, the Spelling dialog box appears. As figure 6.15 shows, the potential error appears in the Not in Dictionary box.

Fig. 6.15

Use the buttons in this dialog box to correct or skip misspelled words.

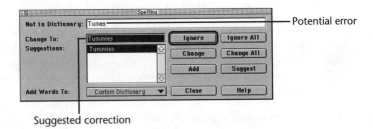

A suggested spelling or case appears in the Change To text box (unless you have disabled the Always Suggest feature). Below this suggestion, PowerPoint may display a list of additional suggestions. You can take any of the following actions:

- To continue without correcting the word, choose the Ignore button.

- To ignore this occurrence and all further occurrences of this word, click the Ignore All button.

- To correct only this occurrence of the word, select one of the suggested alternatives or type the correction in the Change To text box, and then choose the Change button.

- To correct this occurrence and all further occurrences of the word, select one of the suggested alternatives or type the correction in the Change To text box, and then click the Change All button. PowerPoint makes the changes without prompting you to confirm each change.

- To add the word in the Change To text box to the dictionary listed in the Add Words To text box, click the Add button. If the word differs from the word that is highlighted in the slide, PowerPoint also replaces the highlighted word with the correct word. To select a different dictionary, click the down arrow next to the Add Words To text box and then choose a dictionary from the pop-up menu.

■ If the Always Suggest feature is disabled and you want PowerPoint to suggest a correct spelling, click the Suggest button.

After you make your selection, the spelling checker continues checking the presentation. When it finishes checking the entire presentation, the spelling checker displays a message to that effect. Choose OK to close the dialog box.

After using the spelling checker, carefully proof the presentation for errors that a spelling checker can't detect. No spelling checker can tell you, for example, that *Sales Sour in 1994* should be *Sales Soar in 1994.*

Manipulating Text Placeholders

A text placeholder is an object in PowerPoint; as such, you can treat it like any other object. You can resize, move, or copy a text placeholder; you also can enhance it with a border or different background that separates text areas in the slide. This section describes the basics of manipulating text placeholders as objects.

▶ See "Enhancing Placeholders and Objects," p. 252

Resizing a Text Placeholder

After you enter text in a placeholder, you may find that it appears unbalanced or has awkward line breaks; for example, a bulleted-list item may wrap so that only one word is on the last line. You sometimes can improve the appearance by resizing the text placeholder or by forcing the words to wrap at a different location (or not at all).

In the examples shown in figures 6.16 and 6.17, widening the placeholder lets more items fit on one line. In figures 6.18 and 6.19, narrowing the placeholder forces the long item to wrap to another line.

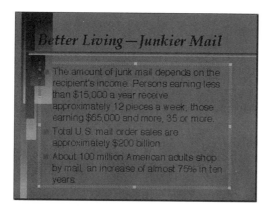

Fig. 6.16
The word *approximately* is forced to the next line because the placeholder box is too narrow.

Fig. 6.17
Widening the placeholder makes *approximately* move up to the preceding line.

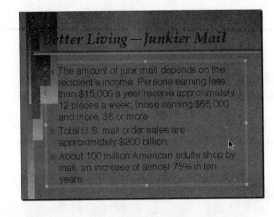

Fig. 6.18
The length of the last line throws off the balance of the slide.

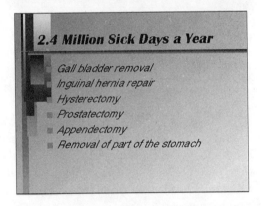

Fig. 6.19
Shortening the placeholder and then centering it on the page makes the text look more level.

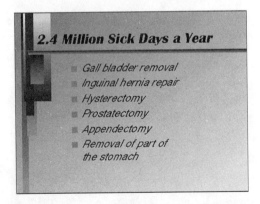

You also can resize the length of a placeholder. You may leave additional space, for example, to indicate to a colleague the approximate space allotted for entering the remaining text.

Remember that the placeholders that you create automatically adjust their length to fit the text. You must disable this feature before you can change the length of such a placeholder. To do so, follow these steps:

1. Click anywhere inside the text placeholder.

2. Open the Format menu and choose Text Anchor. The Text Anchor dialog box appears.

3. Choose the Adjust Object Size to Fit Text option.

4. Choose OK.

Note

The text placeholders in AutoLayouts already have this option disabled.

To resize a text placeholder, follow these steps:

1. To display the gray outline of the text placeholder, click anywhere in the text within that placeholder.

2. Click the gray placeholder to select it. Sizing handles appear, as shown in figure 6.20.

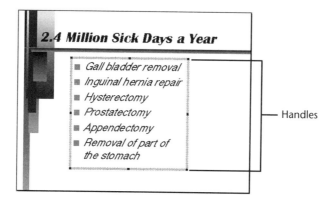

Fig. 6.20
Use the handles to resize the place-holder.

3. Place the mouse pointer on the sizing handle at the side or corner that you want to move in or out. The pointer changes to a double-headed arrow.

4. Drag the sizing handle in or out to shrink or expand the text place-holder.

Moving or Copying a Text Placeholder

Moving and copying a text placeholder is similar to moving and copying text; you select the placeholder and use the mouse to move or copy the original to the new location. When you move or copy a text placeholder, all text inside also is moved or copied.

To move or copy a text placeholder, follow these steps:

1. Display the gray outline of the text placeholder by clicking anywhere in the text within that placeholder.

2. Click the gray placeholder to select it. (You will know that it's selected when you see the resizing handles.)

3. Place the mouse pointer on the gray outline, being careful to avoid the sizing handles. The mouse pointer must look like a single-headed arrow.

4. To move the placeholder, click and drag the placeholder to the new location; then release the mouse button. Alternatively, you can press the arrow keys to move the placeholder.

   To copy the placeholder, press and hold down the ⌘ key. Notice that a plus sign appears next to the mouse pointer. Continuing to hold down the ⌘ key, click and hold down the mouse button, drag the copy to the new location, and then release the mouse button and the ⌘ key.

Deleting a Text Placeholder

You can delete any text placeholder by selecting it and then pressing the Delete key. Text in the placeholder also is deleted.

 If you delete a placeholder accidentally, you often can restore it—and its text—by using the Undo command, which reverses the last edit you made. To use this command, open the Edit menu and choose Undo, or press ⌘-Z.

Creating a Border for Text

To emphasize or visually separate a text area from the rest of a slide, you can create a border around the text. The border appears just inside the boundaries of the text placeholder.

To create a border, follow these steps:

1. Click anywhere in the text around which you want to create the border. The gray placeholder outline appears.

2. Click the gray placeholder outline to select it.

3. Open the Format menu and choose Colors and Lines. The Colors and Lines dialog box appears, as shown in figure 6.21.

Line and border styles

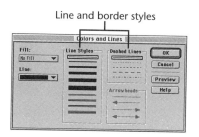

Fig. 6.21
You can use line styles to create borders along the inside edge of placeholders.

4. In the Line Styles section, select a line style.

5. To make the line dashed as well, select one of the styles in the Dashed Lines section.

6. To change the border color (the default is black), click the down arrow next to the Line box to display the color selections, and then select a color.

7. Choose OK. The dialog box closes and the border appears just inside the text placeholder.

The default shape for a border is a rectangle, but you can change the shape by following these steps:

▶ See "Enhancing Placeholders and Objects," p. 252

1. Create the border as described earlier in this section.

2. If the text placeholder isn't selected, select it.

3. Open the Draw menu and choose Change AutoShape. PowerPoint displays the AutoShapes, shown in figure 6.22.

4. Select the AutoShape that you want to use. The border changes to the new shape. (The outline of the text placeholder remains rectangular; the change doesn't affect the border.) Text rewraps automatically to fit the new shape. If the text can't fit within the shape, it extends below it.

II

Text

Fig. 6.22
AutoShapes
change the shape
of a bordered
placeholder.

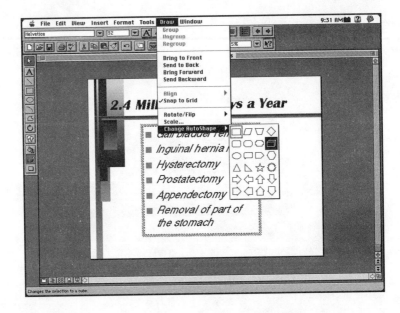

Changing the Background Color of the Text Placeholder

▶ See "Changing
a Slide's Color
Scheme,"
p. 375

To further emphasize a text area, you can change the background color of the text placeholder. To choose a different background color that is appropriate for the text color, follow these steps:

1. Click anywhere in the text for which you want to change the background color. The gray outline of the text placeholder appears.

2. Click the gray placeholder outline to select it.

3. Open the Format menu and choose Colors and Lines. The Colors and Lines dialog box appears.

4. Click the down arrow next to the Fill box to display the color selections, and then select a color.

5. Choose OK. The dialog box closes, and the background color appears inside the text placeholder.

Troubleshooting

I resized a text placeholder, and now the title and body-text placeholders no longer align. How do I realign them?

Align text placeholders the same way that you align graphic objects. Select one placeholder by clicking its gray border, place the mouse pointer on text in the other placeholder, and press and hold down the ⌘ and Shift keys while clicking the mouse button. This action selects the second placeholder and keeps the first placeholder selected. Release the keys; then open the Draw menu and choose Align. In the cascading menu that appears, choose the alignment (for example, Left).

The text in a placeholder extends beyond the placeholder. How do I fix it?

You have several options: you can reduce the font size, resize the placeholder, or edit the text so that it fits. If you can edit the text without compromising clarity, that method is best (in slide presentations, text should be as concise as possible). If you reduce the font size, make sure that the audience at the back of the room can read the smaller text. To resize the placeholder so that it fits the text automatically, click the placeholder; then open the Format menu and choose Text Anchor. In the dialog box that appears, choose the Adjust Object Size to Fit Text option, and then choose OK.

From Here...

In this chapter, you learned the basics of working with text and many time-saving features for editing text. For information on related topics, read the following chapters:

- Chapter 8, "Working with Tables," describes how to create Microsoft Word tables.

- Chapter 11, "Selecting, Editing, and Enhancing Objects," shows how to place text inside objects.

- Chapter 13, "Creating Basic Charts," explains how to add legends and labels to charts.

- Chapter 21, "Using Advanced Color, Text, and Drawing Features," describes the special Equation Editor.

Chapter 7

Creating Speaker's Notes, Outlines, and Handouts

An effective slide presentation flows logically from one slide to the next, with each slide illustrating a few key points. To help you prepare and give an effective presentation, PowerPoint offers some powerful tools: outlining, speaker's notes, and handouts.

In this chapter, you learn how to:

- Create and print speaker's notes and handouts
- Develop an outline for a slide presentation
- Create a slide presentation from an outline

Outlining helps you organize and focus your thoughts. Because PowerPoint allows you to create slides directly from your outline, following the outline is a snap. After you complete a draft presentation, you can return to the outline—which automatically reflects any changes that you made in the presentation—and modify, rearrange, or delete slides as necessary.

Speaker's notes, called *notes pages* in PowerPoint, are pages that display a slide and any notes you have for that slide. You may add notes, for example, to remind you of the key points that the slide illustrates. Such notes help you focus during your presentation and reduce the chance that you might accidentally skip an important topic.

You can make your presentation even more effective by providing your audience with *handouts*, which are printouts of the slides. Handouts relieve audience members of the need to take extensive notes, so they can focus on your presentation instead. Handouts also provide a common reference for participants in question-and-answer sessions.

In this chapter, you learn how to create and print speaker's notes, handouts, and outlines, as well as how to use an outline to develop a presentation. You also learn how to use the master pages (Notes Master, Handout Master, and Outline Master), which enable you to globally change the layout of speaker's notes, handouts, and outlines. The tools that you learn about in this chapter improve the effectiveness of any slide presentation.

Creating Speaker's Notes

You can create speaker's notes for any slide in a presentation. As figure 7.1 shows, a notes page displays the slide at the top of the page. Below the slide is a notes box in which you can type notes on that slide.

Fig. 7.1
Use notes pages when you need to include additional explanation of the slide content.

Notes typically are most useful for bar charts, pie charts, and other graphical slides that have no text to explicitly state the main points illustrated in the slides. In such cases, you can use the notes pages to list the points that you want to make. Although text charts (such as bullet charts) usually state the key points in the text, you may find it helpful to add notes regarding sub-themes or the transition to the next slide.

Creating a Notes Page for a Slide

To create a notes page for a slide, follow these steps:

1. Display the slide for which you want to create a notes page.

2. Open the View menu and then choose Notes Pages, or click the Notes Pages View button (see fig. 7.2). PowerPoint displays the notes page for the slide, as shown in figure 7.3.

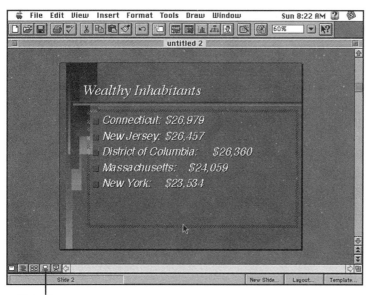

Notes Pages
View button

Fig. 7.2
In Slide view, you can click the Notes Pages View button in the bottom-left corner of the screen.

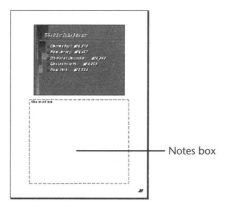

Notes box

Fig. 7.3
The top of the notes page contains an image of the slide.

3. Click the notes box. The insertion point appears in the notes box.

4. Type your notes.

5. Open the File menu and choose Save, or press ⌘-S, to save your notes page. The page is saved with your presentation.

> **Note**
>
> If you are saving a new presentation, the Save As dialog box appears. In the File Name text box, type a file name; then choose OK.

Modifying Notes Pages

PowerPoint provides a default font, color scheme, and layout for notes pages. You can change these elements for an individual notes page or globally change all notes pages in your presentation. You also can modify individual page or all pages to include graphics and labels.

To modify an individual notes page, follow these steps:

Tip
If you don't like your changes, you can revert to the default settings. Open the Format menu and choose Notes Layout; choose Reapply Master; and then choose OK.

1. Display the slide for which you want to modify the notes page.

2. Open the View menu and choose Notes Pages, or click the Notes Page View button.

3. Depending on what you want to modify, follow one or more of the procedures described in the following text.

To change the text font, format, or color: Modify text in a notes page as you would text in a slide.

◀ See "Formatting Text," p. 151

◀ See "Creating Labels and Other Special Text," p. 140

To add labels or a graphic: Add these elements as you would add them to a slide.

To move the slide or notes box to a different position: To select the slide, click it; to select the notes box, click the text area to display the gray placeholder of the notes box, and then click the gray border. A selection box encloses the slide or notes box, as shown in figure 7.4. Click inside the selection box, and drag the slide or notes box to the new location. (Be careful not to click and drag a sizing handle.)

Fig. 7.4
The slide and the notes placeholders can be moved.

To resize the slide or notes box: To select the slide, click it; to select the notes placeholder, click the text area to display the gray border of the notes placeholder, and then click the gray border. The selection box appears. Click a sizing handle (see fig. 7.5), and drag the handle until the slide or box is the correct size. Notice that the mouse pointer becomes a double-headed arrow when it is on a sizing handle.

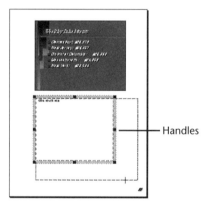

Handles

Fig. 7.5
The dotted line represents the size that the object will be when you release the mouse button.

To crop the slide: Click the slide. The selection box encloses the slide. Then open the Tools menu and choose Crop Picture. The crop pointer appears (see fig. 7.6). Click and drag any handle to crop the picture.

Fig. 7.6
Drag a corner
handle to crop a
side. Press the
Option key to
crop all sides from
the center.

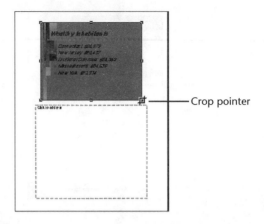

————Crop pointer

◀ See "Manipu-
lating Text
Placeholders,"
p. 167

To add a border or shadow to the notes box or slide image: Add these elements as
you would add them to a slide.

To change the background color of the notes box: Change the color as you would
change it for any text placeholder.

To change the background design of the notes page: Open the Format menu and
choose Notes Background. The Notes Background dialog box appears, as
shown in figure 7.7. You can use this dialog box to change or shade the background color of the notes pages.

Fig. 7.7
In this dialog box,
you can choose a
background color
and variant for the
notes pages.

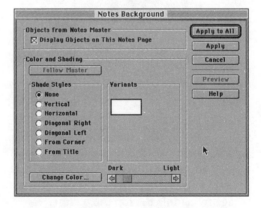

■ To change the background color, click the Change Color button. The
Background Color dialog box appears. Choose a color from the color
palette, and then choose OK. (To display more colors in the Background
Color dialog box, click the More Colors button.)

■ To use a shaded background, choose the direction of shading (Vertical or Diagonal Right, for example) in the Shade Styles section. If that style has one or more variations, those variations appear in the Variants box; choose the variation that you want. To adjust the lightness or darkness of the shading, drag the scroll box below the Variants box. To darken (add more black to) the shading, drag the scroll box left; to lighten (add more white to) the shading, drag the scroll box right.

You also can use the Notes Background dialog box to hide graphic objects, including any text that you added with the Text tool. To do so, deselect the Display Objects on This Notes Page check box.

After you make your changes in the Notes Background dialog box, you can apply the changes to the current notes page or to all notes pages in the presentation. To apply the changes only to the displayed notes page, click the Apply button. To apply the changes to all notes pages, choose the Apply to All button. To cancel the changes, click the Cancel button.

You can revert to the default color and shading settings (those set by the Notes Master page) at any time by choosing Follow Master in the Notes Background dialog box.

To change the notes color scheme: Open the Format menu and choose Notes Color Scheme. The Notes Color Scheme dialog box appears, as shown in figure 7.8.

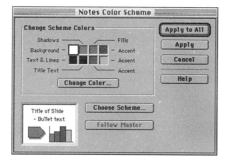

Fig. 7.8
This dialog box enables you to change the overall use of color.

The Change Scheme Colors palette in this dialog box shows the current colors for the title text, the background, and other elements of the notes page. In this palette, the Accent colors refer to additional fill colors, such as those used for additional bars in bar charts. To change a color, double-click the color, or single-click the color and then click the Change Color button. In the dialog box that appears, choose a color from the color palette. (To see more colors, click More Colors.) You return to the Notes Color Scheme dialog box, where the new color scheme is previewed in a thumbnail in the lower-left corner.

If you aren't comfortable creating your own color scheme, PowerPoint can suggest one. In the Notes Color Scheme dialog box, click the Choose Scheme button. The Choose Scheme dialog box appears. In the Background Color box, select a color for the notes background. Based on your choice, compatible colors for the body text and the chart lines appear in the Text and Line Color box. Choose one of these colors. Based on your selections, PowerPoint displays four suggested color schemes in the Other Scheme Colors box. To choose one of these schemes, select it and then choose OK. You return to the Notes Color Scheme dialog box, which now reflects the new color scheme.

After you make your changes in the Notes Color Scheme dialog box, you can apply the changes to the current notes page or to all notes pages in the presentation. To apply the changes only to the current notes page, click the Apply button. To apply the changes to all notes pages, choose the Apply to All button. To cancel the changes, click the Cancel button. You can revert to the default color scheme (set in the Notes Master) at any time by choosing Follow Master in the Notes Color Scheme dialog box.

To change the font, color scheme, or layout for all notes pages in a presentation, use the Notes Master. This method enables you to make the changes one time, because changes in the Notes Master page automatically apply to all notes pages in that presentation. You also can use the Notes Master to add graphics or text (such as the date or page number) that you want to apply to all notes pages in your presentation.

To use the Notes Master, follow these steps:

1. Open the presentation for which you want to modify the Notes Master.

2. Open the View menu and choose Master; then choose Notes Master from the cascading menu. The Notes Master appears, as shown in figure 7.9.

3. Follow one or more of the procedures for modifying individual notes pages, listed earlier in this section. If you want to move or resize the notes box, you can select the notes box in the Notes Master page simply by clicking the dashed border of the box.

Fig. 7.9
Changes made in
the master are
reflected in all the
notes pages.

4. Open the File menu and choose Save, or press ⌘-S, to save the new
format. The new master page is saved with your presentation, and all
notes pages in the presentation are modified according to the new settings in the Notes Master.

Inserting the Date, Time, and Page Number

To have the date, time, or page number automatically appear on all notes
pages, you must use the Notes Master. Follow these steps:

1. To insert the date, time, or page number in the notes box, position the
insertion point where you want that element to appear. To insert the
date, time, or page number outside the notes box, click the Text tool
(shown in fig. 7.10); position the insertion point where you want the
date, time, or page number to appear; and then click the mouse button
to create a text placeholder.

Text tool

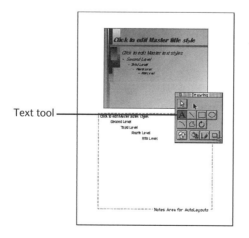

Fig. 7.10
Move the floating
Drawing toolbar to
the area where you
are working.

2. Open the Insert menu and choose Date, Time, or Page Number.

If you choose Date, the symbol // appears at the insertion-point location; if you choose Time, the symbol :: appears; and if you choose Page Number, the symbol ## appears. In the notes pages themselves, these symbols are replaced by the actual date, time, or page number.

> **Note**
>
> You can change the type size and font of the date, time, and page-number symbols in the Notes Master page just as you do other text.

Printing Notes Pages

To print your notes pages, follow these steps:

1. Open the File menu and choose Print, or press ⌘-P. The Print dialog box appears.

2. From the Print What pop-up menu, select Notes Pages (see fig. 7.11).

3. Make any other selections that you want.

4. Choose OK.

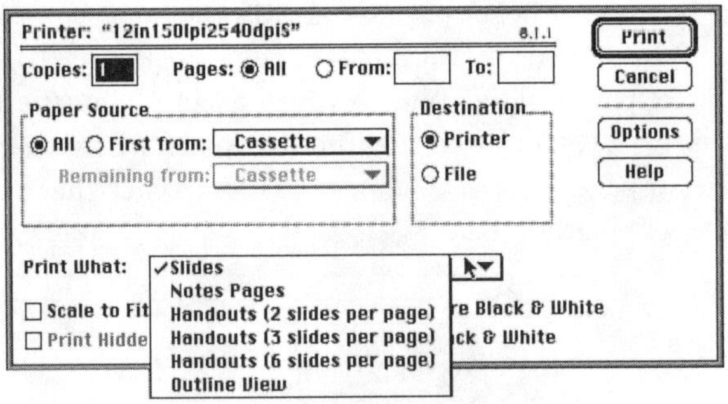

Fig. 7.11
The pop-up menu affords you the opportunity to specify which part of the presentation to print.

Printer: "12in150lpi2540dpiS"	8.l.l

Print

Cancel

Copies: 1   Pages: ● All ○ From: _____ To: _____

Paper Source
● All ○ First from: [Cassette ▼]
　Remaining from: [Cassette ▼]

Destination
● Printer
○ File

Options

Help

Print What:
　✓ Slides
　　Notes Pages
☐ Scale to Fit　Handouts (2 slides per page)　re Black & White
☐ Print Hidde　Handouts (3 slides per page)　ck & White
　　Handouts (6 slides per page)
　　Outline View

Troubleshooting

I accidentally deleted the slide image (or notes box). Can I restore it?

You can restore the slide image or notes box at any time. Open the Format menu and choose Notes Layout; the Notes Layout dialog box appears. Choose Add Slide Image or Add Notes Text (or both), and then choose OK. If the notes box that you deleted contained text, the text won't be restored. Slide images, however, are restored.

Alternatively, if the deletion was your last action, you can use the Undo command, which reverses your last action. To use this command, open the Edit menu and choose Undo, or press ⌘-Z.

I changed the background and color scheme of a notes page. Can I change it back to the default format used in other notes pages?

Yes. To restore the default background color and shading, open the Format menu and choose Notes Background; the Notes Background dialog box appears. Choose Follow Master, and then click the Apply button. (To restore the default background for all notes pages in a presentation, choose the Apply to All button.)

To restore the default color scheme, open the Format menu and choose Notes Color Scheme; the Notes Color Scheme dialog box appears. Choose Follow Master, and then click the Apply button. (To restore the default color scheme for all notes pages in a presentation, choose the Apply to All button.)

I chose Preview in the Notes Background dialog box, but nothing happened.

The Notes Background dialog box probably is hiding the preview image. To move the dialog box, click the dialog-box title bar and drag the dialog box to the lower-right corner of your screen. (You can drag the dialog box so that most of it is off the screen.)

Creating Handouts

By providing handouts of your slides, you enable audience members to focus on your presentation rather than on taking notes. Handouts can display two, three, or six slides per page. You select the layout when you print the handouts, as discussed later in this section. To allow room for notes on handouts, choose the three-slide layout.

Adding Text and Graphics to Handout Pages

You can add text and graphics to handout pages by using the Handout Master. Use the Handout Master, for example, to add the company logo and the date of the presentation to handouts. Any text or graphics that you add to the Handout Master appears on every handout page. Unlike notes pages, handout pages cannot be edited individually.

To add text or graphics to the Handout Master, follow these steps:

1. Open the presentation for which you want to modify the Handout Master.

2. Open the View menu and choose Master; then choose Handout Master from the cascading menu. The Handout Master page appears, as shown in figure 7.12. Placeholders on the page show the layout for two, three, and six slides per page. (The three-slides-per-page layout is on the left side.)

Fig. 7.12
The placeholders in the Handout Master are for slides.

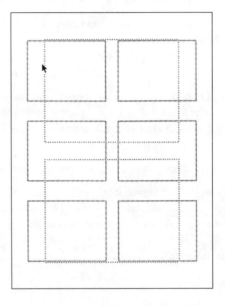

▶ See "Drawing Basic Shapes," p. 216

3. Add graphics, such as PowerPoint's AutoShapes, or import artwork from PowerPoint's ClipArt Gallery. You also can create your own images, using the basic drawing tools in the Drawing toolbar.

4. To add text, click the Text tool; position the insertion point where you want the text to appear; click the mouse button to create a text place-holder; and type the text. You can format the text as you would text in any slide.

Tip
To enlarge your view of the text area, increase the zoom percentage.

Be sure to place any graphics and text outside the placeholders for the layout that you intend to use; otherwise, the slide images print over the graphics and text.

Printing Handouts

To select the number of slides per handout and print the handouts, follow these steps:

1. Open the File menu and choose Print, or press ⌘-P. The Print dialog box appears.

2. From the Print What pop-up menu, select one of the following options:

   - Handouts (2 slides per page)

   - Handouts (3 slides per page)

   - Handouts (6 slides per page)

3. Make any other selections that you want.

4. Choose OK.

Working with Outlines

The first step in planning a presentation is preparing an outline. PowerPoint provides all the tools you need to create and manipulate an outline; you even can create slides directly from the outline.

Creating an Outline

To create an outline, you use Outline view. To display this view, open the View menu and choose Outline, or click the Outline View button (see fig. 7.13). If you are starting a new presentation, Outline view displays the number 1 and a slide icon in the left margin, as shown in figure 7.14.

Outline View button

Fig. 7.13
In Slide view, click the Outline View button to switch to Outline view.

To create an outline for a new presentation, follow these steps:

1. Type the title of the first slide in your presentation, and then press Return. A slide icon appears for slide 2.

2. To enter a bullet point below the title, keep the insertion point in the line for slide 2, and then click the Demote button. PowerPoint automatically indents the line and inserts a bullet. Pressing the Tab key also demotes a bullet point.

3. Type the text for that bulleted point.

Fig. 7.14
With a new
presentation,
there's not much
yet to find in
Outline view.

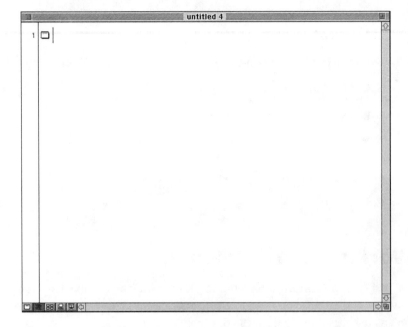

4. To add another bullet point, press Return. PowerPoint automatically indents the next line and inserts the bullet.

5. Repeat steps 3 and 4 until you have entered all the bulleted points.

> **Note**
>
> An outline can have up to five levels below each slide title. Each level is indented from the preceding level. To demote an item one level, place the insertion point in the item and then click the Demote button or press the Tab key. To promote an item one level, place the insertion point in the item and then click the Promote button or press Shift-Tab.

Tip
To insert a new
line at the same
level as the preced-
ing line but with-
out a bullet, press
Shift-Return.

6. At the end of the last bulleted point for the slide, press Option-Return to create the next slide.

7. Type the title of the next slide.

8. Repeat steps 2 through 7 to complete your outline.

You also can use Outline view to review the outline of an existing presentation. Open the presentation and click the Outline View button in the status bar. The slide presentation appears as an outline, with the title and main text displayed for each slide. (The outline does not show graphic objects or text that you entered with the Text tool.)

After you have an outline, you can use it to create, delete, modify, and rearrange slides, as described in the following sections.

Using the Outline Tools

Outline view includes a special toolbar, shown in figure 7.15, that makes creating, modifying, and reviewing an outline easy.

Fig. 7.15
You can make the Outlining toolbar a floating toolbar by dragging it toward the center of the screen.

Note

If the toolbar isn't displayed, open the View menu and choose Toolbars; the Toolbars dialog box appears. Choose the Outlining option, and then choose OK.

Table 7.1 describes the buttons in this toolbar.

Table 7.1	Outlining Toolbar Buttons	
Button	**Button Name**	**Description**
⬅	Promote	Promotes, by one level, the paragraph that contains the insertion point. The paragraph moves left one indent, and the bullet character changes to match other bullets at that level.
➡	Demote	Demotes, by one level, the paragraph that contains the insertion point. The paragraph moves right one indent, and the bullet character changes to match other bullets at that level.
⬆	Move Up	Moves the paragraph that contains the insertion point above the preceding item.
⬇	Move Down	Moves the paragraph that contains the insertion point below the next item.

(continues)

Table 7.1 Continued

Button	Button Name	Description
	Collapse Selection	Collapses all levels of text for a slide, so that only the slide title appears. A line below the slide title indicates that the text is collapsed. To use this button, place the insertion point anywhere in the text for that slide (at any level of text), and then click the button.
	Expand Selection	Expands text that has been collapsed. To use this button, place the insertion point in the slide-title text, and then click the button.
	Show Titles	Collapses all levels of text for all slides, so that only slide titles appear. The insertion point can be anywhere in the outline when you click this button.
	Show Formatting	Enables you to display actual character formatting (font and type size, for example) or plain text. Plain text, which is a smaller type size, enables you to see more of the outline on-screen. The insertion point can be anywhere in the outline when you click this button.
	Show All	Expands the outline so all levels of text for all slides appear. The insertion point can be anywhere in the outline when you click this button.

Using Outline View To Create Slides

When you create an outline, PowerPoint automatically creates slides with the titles and text that you entered in the outline. To view one of the slides in Slide view, place the insertion point in the slide title in Outline view; then open the View menu and choose Slides or click the Slide View button in the status bar. To display the following or preceding slide in the outline, click the Next Slide or Previous Slide button. (These buttons are near the bottom of the right-hand scroll bar. The Next Slide button displays a double arrowhead pointing down, and the Previous Slide button displays a double arrowhead pointing up.)

In Slide view, you can edit the slide. Outline view automatically adjusts to reflect any changes that you make in Slide view, so you need not worry about having different versions of the presentations. After you edit slide in Slide view, you may want to redisplay the presentation in Outline view to obtain an overall view of the changes.

You also can create a presentation from an imported outline. To import an outline, follow these steps:

1. Open the File menu and choose Open, or press ⌘-O. The Open File dialog box appears.

2. In the List Files of Type pop-up menu, select All Readable Outlines. PowerPoint lists files that you can open as outlines.

3. Select the outline file that you want to import.

4. Choose OK.

Manipulating Text in Outline View

You can edit text (except labels) in Outline view just as you can in Slide view. To make text italic, for example, select the text and then click the Italic button in the toolbar. Any changes you make to text in Outline view appear on the slide.

◀ See "Editing Text," p. 144

You cannot add graphics or labels in Outline view. To add these elements to a slide, you first must switch to Slide view.

Rearranging and Deleting Slides in Outline View

Outline view enables you to rearrange and delete slides in your presentation easily. To select a slide to move or delete, click the slide icon for that slide. PowerPoint highlights the icon and all outline text associated with that slide.

To move the slide, drag the slide icon up or down to the new position in the presentation. PowerPoint automatically reorders the other slides. To delete the slide, select it and then press the Delete key. When you move or delete a slide, PowerPoint moves or deletes the entire slide, including all text and graphics that it contains.

Adding Text and Graphics to All Outline Pages

Use the Outline Master to add text and graphic objects that you want to appear on all outline pages. Follow these steps:

1. Open the presentation for which you want to modify the Outline Master.

2. Open the View menu and choose Master; then choose Outline Master from the cascading menu. The Outline Master page appears, as shown in figure 7.16. A placeholder on the page shows the text area for the outline.

II

Text

Fig. 7.16
In the Outline Master, you do not see the text that is entered in the slides.

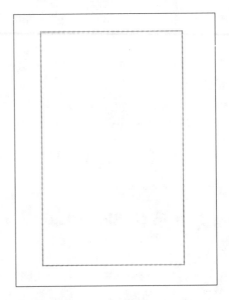

▶ See "Drawing Basic Shapes," p. 216

3. Add graphics, draw, or import artwork to suit your design.

4. To add text, click the Text tool; position the insertion point where you want the text to appear; click the mouse button to create a text placeholder; and type the text. You can format the text as you would text in any slide.

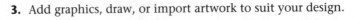

Note

Be sure to place any graphics and text outside the placeholder for the outline text; otherwise, the outline text may print over the graphics and text.

Printing an Outline

An outline prints as it appears in Outline view. If you selected plain text and collapsed the entries, for example, the printed outline also is plain text with collapsed entries. The outline also prints at the same scale as the zoom scale in Outline view. Before you print an outline, therefore, make sure that Outline view has the settings that you want for the printed handout.

To print an outline, follow these steps:

1. Open the File menu and choose Print, or press ⌘-P. The Print dialog box appears.

2. In the Print What pop-up menu, select Outline View.

3. Make any other selections that you want.

4. Choose OK.

Troubleshooting

I changed the indent or tab settings in my text chart, but Outline view doesn't reflect those changes. Can I change the tab or indent settings in Outline view?

No. Outline view has default tab and indent settings that cannot be changed. When you return to Slide view, however, your charts retain the tab and indent settings that you selected.

I used the Text tool to add text to my chart, but the text doesn't appear in Outline view. How can I display it in Outline view?

You cannot. Outline view doesn't show text that you created with the Text tool or any graphic objects.

From Here...

For other information related to speaker's notes, handouts, and outlines, turn to the following chapters:

- Chapter 6, "Working with Text," covers most aspects of creating and editing text, including selecting, editing, and formatting text; searching for and replacing text; and using the spelling checker.

- Chapter 9, "Drawing Objects," Chapter 10, "Adding Clip Art and Scanned Art," and Chapter 11, "Selecting, Editing, and Enhancing Objects," describe how to add graphics to a slide. The procedures in these chapters also apply to adding graphics to master pages.

Chapter 8

Working with Tables

Using tables is a way to communicate some types of information effectively. You can use a table to list a group of specific points with explanatory notes beside them. Although you can show this same information by using a text box and tabs for spacing, the table makes your job much easier by enabling you to place your text easily and format it as needed. By using a table, you can align text in perfectly aligned rows and columns, thereby displaying information in a form that your audience can grasp quickly. From within PowerPoint, you can use the power of Microsoft Word's capability to create and manipulate tables.

In this chapter, you learn how to do the following things:

- Open the Word table function and select the table size
- Enter, format, and edit information in the table
- Adjust column and row widths in the table
- Add borders to the table
- Paste the table into a slide

To use the Microsoft Word table option, you must have Word 6 for Macintosh installed on your computer. If you do not have that program, this feature is not active.

PowerPoint and Microsoft Word are capable of working together. When you want to place a table in a slide, clicking the Table button activates Word and places a table frame in your slide. You actually use Word 6 (and Word's menus and functions) to create the table and then insert it into PowerPoint.

Starting Table Creation

When you insert a table into PowerPoint from Word, the menus and most of the toolbar buttons on-screen change from PowerPoint menus and tools to Word menus and buttons. Some buttons remain in the main toolbar but cannot be used until you create your table and insert it into a slide.

You use two basic methods to insert a Word table into your PowerPoint slide: choosing menu commands and clicking toolbar buttons. The result is the same for either method; you have a table displayed in your slide.

Starting Table Creation from the Menu

By using menu commands, you can create a larger table easily. Follow these steps:

1. Display the slide into which you want to insert a table.

2. Open the Insert menu and choose Microsoft Word Table. The Insert Word Table dialog box appears, as shown in figure 8.1.

Fig. 8.1
In this dialog box, you specify the number of rows and columns of the Word table.

3. In the Number of Columns text box, type the number of columns that you need for your table. Alternatively, click the arrow buttons to the right of the text box to increase or decrease the number of columns.

> **Note**
>
> The maximum number of columns that you can insert when you create your table is 15. You can add columns later.

4. In the Number of Rows text box, type the number of rows that you need for your table. Alternatively, click the arrow buttons to increase or decrease the number of rows.

> **Note**
>
> The maximum number of rows that you can insert from this dialog box is five. You can add rows later.

5. Choose OK. PowerPoint automatically accesses Word's table function and displays a blank table inside a table box.

Figure 8.2 shows a table that is three columns by four rows.

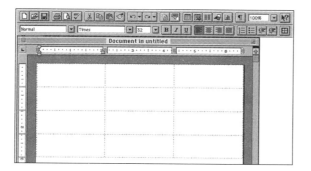

Fig. 8.2
The Word table is ready for you to add text.

Starting Table Creation with the Toolbar

The main toolbar contains a button named Insert Microsoft Word Table. To use this button to insert a table, follow these steps:

1. Click the Insert Microsoft Word Table button, and hold down the mouse button. The grid box appears, as shown in figure 8.3.

Fig. 8.3
This button in the PowerPoint toolbar is a shortcut that bypasses the Insert menu.

2. Drag the mouse pointer across the grid box to indicate the number of columns and rows that you want in your table.

As you drag across the grid boxes from the upper-left corner, the boxes remain selected, and the word Cancel at the bottom of the grid box is replaced by the number of rows and columns that you have selected. 1 × 1 Table, for example, indicates that you have selected one row and one column.

3. When you have selected the number of rows and columns that you want to use, release the mouse button. PowerPoint accesses Word's table functions and displays an empty table grid in your slide (refer to fig. 8.2).

Note

The grid box seems to indicate that the largest table you can construct is four rows and five columns. You can increase the number of rows, however, by dragging the mouse pointer to the box that indicates the number of rows and columns. PowerPoint adds another row. To add more rows, continue to drag down. Likewise, you can create additional columns by dragging the mouse pointer past the right edge of the grid. The largest table that you can create with this method is five rows by nine columns. You can add more rows and columns later.

Troubleshooting

When I click the Insert Microsoft Word Table button, nothing happens, or I get an error message.

Make sure that you have version 6 of Microsoft Word for Macintosh correctly installed on your computer.

I can't see the table grid lines on-screen.

Choose the Table menu and the Gridlines command. A check mark appears next to the command and the grid lines appear on-screen.

Editing Tables

When you change the structure of a table—by adding rows and columns, for example, or by adding text, formatting, charts, worksheets, or pictures—you are editing the table. In this section, you learn to enter text, edit text, and move from cell to cell. You also learn to use the Word toolbars to edit a table.

Inserting Rows and Columns

If you decide that the table you have created is too small to display the information you need, you can add rows and columns. When you are setting up the table format, you need to remember to include a row and/or column for row and column labels, if needed.

To add rows and columns, follow these steps:

1. Add a row to your table by using one of the following methods:

   ■ Click the Insert Rows button in the toolbar.

   ■ Open the Table menu and choose Insert Rows.

■ Place the mouse pointer inside the table frame, hold down the Ctrl key, and then click and hold down the mouse button; a shortcut menu appears. Choose the Insert Rows option.

2. Add a column by moving the mouse pointer to the top of a column. The mouse pointer changes to a down arrow called the Add Additional Column icon, as shown in figure 8.4.

Add Additional
Column icon

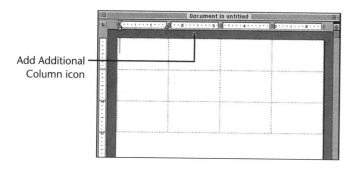

Fig. 8.4
The black arrow above the second column is the Add Additional Column icon.

3. Hold down the Ctrl key, and then click and hold down the mouse button to display a shortcut menu. Choose the Insert Columns option. PowerPoint inserts another column. Alternatively, open the Table menu and choose Insert Columns.

Using the Microsoft Word Toolbars

When you add or edit a Microsoft Word table in PowerPoint, many of the toolbar buttons are replaced by Word toolbar buttons (see fig. 8.5), and many menu options are replaced by Microsoft Word menu options.

As you move the mouse pointer across the toolbar buttons, you notice that some buttons are not available to you. The following message appears in the status bar at the bottom of your screen:

```
This command is not available because this document is being edited
in another application.
```

These options become available after you complete your table.

Fig. 8.5
The Word toolbars
appear when you
insert a table.

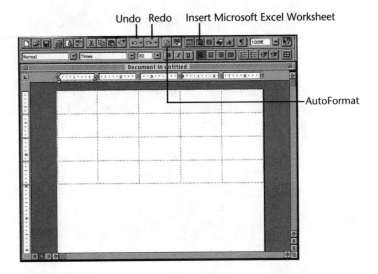

The first toolbar contains a mix of PowerPoint and Microsoft Word buttons. Among the new buttons are the following:

■ *Undo.* This button enables you to undo your last action. Clicking the down-arrow button beside the Undo button displays a list of all the actions that you have completed, starting with the most recent, since you opened the table.

■ *Redo.* This button enables you to redo your last undone action. Clicking the down-arrow button beside the Redo button displays a list of all the actions that you have undone since you opened the table. The list begins with the most recently undone action.

■ *AutoFormat.* This button enables you to format your text automatically or to apply an existing style to your table.

■ *Insert Rows.* This button enables you to insert a row above the current insertion-point location. If you have a three-row table and want to add a new row 2, for example, place the insertion point in the current row 2, and then click the Insert Rows button. A new row is inserted; the old rows 2 and 3 move down one position and become rows 3 and 4, respectively.

■ *Insert Microsoft Excel Worksheet.* This button inserts a selected Excel worksheet at the current insertion-point location. (The button is available only if you have Excel installed on your computer.)

The second Word toolbar includes buttons that are similar to those in the PowerPoint Standard toolbar. You can use these buttons to format text by setting styles, fonts, font size, text alignment, and borders. These options are discussed in greater detail later in this chapter, in the "Formatting Tables" section.

Typing Table Entries

By default, when you create a table, the insertion point is located in the first cell—the upper-left corner of the table. Entering text in a cell is a simple matter of typing. If you have moved the insertion point, click the first cell and begin typing. Generally, the top row is used for headings.

Figure 8.6 shows text entered in the default font and font size.

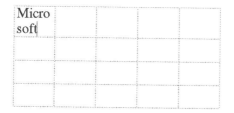

Fig. 8.6
Click a cell and begin typing to add text to the table.

Notice that the text does not go past the right cell border; text automatically wraps to the next line, regardless of where the word normally breaks. Also notice that the cell height is adjusted downward to fit all the text. You learn to adjust fonts later in this chapter, in "Changing the Font Style."

Moving from Cell to Cell

You can move from cell to cell in a couple of ways: you can click the next cell in which you want to enter text, or you can press the Tab key. The Tab key moves the insertion point from the current cell to the next cell in the same row. If the insertion point is in the last cell of a row, pressing Tab creates a new row. Additionally, you can press Shift-Tab to move to the preceding cell or to the last cell in the preceding row.

◄ See "Working with Text," p. 82

A third method of moving to another cell is pressing the arrow keys on your keyboard, as described in the following table.

II

Text

Key	Action
←	Moves the insertion point to the cell to the left of the current cell. If the insertion point is located in a cell that contains text, the insertion point moves one letter at a time to the left. When the insertion point reaches the beginning of the text in a cell, it moves to the next cell to the left.
→	Moves the insertion point to the next cell to the right of the current cell.
↑	Moves the insertion point to the cell above the current cell. When the insertion point reaches thefirst row, your computer simply beeps if you press this key again.
↓	Moves the insertion point to the cell below the current cell.

Formatting Tables

When you start to enter information into your table, you quickly see whether the default format settings are adequate for your needs. More often than not, you need to make some adjustments.

◄ See "Working with Text," p. 82

The default font used for the text, for example, may be too large. By applying formatting to text, you can make it look better; make it easier to read; and, more importantly, give the message that you are trying to convey greater impact.

Selecting Table Entries

To adjust the formatting of existing text in a table, you first must select the text. PowerPoint enables you to select an entire row or column, or the entire table. This capability can be especially helpful when you need to make global changes.

To select the text in a single cell, click and drag through all the text that you want to format. (This procedure is the same one you use to select text within a placeholder in PowerPoint.)

Tip
You also can select a row of text by clicking and dragging across the row.

To select an entire row of text, follow these steps:

1. Place the insertion point in the row that you want to select. The cell in which you place the insertion point doesn't matter, so long as the cell is located in the row that you want to select.

2. Open the Table menu and choose Select Row. All the text in the selected row is highlighted.

3. Click anywhere in the table frame to deselect the text.

To select an entire column of text, follow these steps:

1. Place the insertion point in a cell of the column that you want to select.

2. Open the Table menu and choose Select Column. The text in the selected column is highlighted, as shown in figure 8.7.

Fig. 8.7
Use the Select Column command to select all the text in a column.

Changing the Font

You can use any of the fonts that are installed in your system in a table. By using different fonts for the various parts of your table, you can emphasize specific information.

Some fonts are easier to read than others. You may need to experiment a little to see which font is best for your presentation.

To change a font style, follow these steps:

1. Select the text for which you want to change the font.

2. Click the down-arrow button next to the Font text box in the second toolbar at the top of your screen. A pop-up menu appears, listing the fonts that are available.

3. Select the font that you want to use. The font name is now listed in the Font text box, and the selected text changes to the chosen font.

The text remains selected until you click the table frame. While text remains selected, you can change the font again or make other changes in the text.

You also can apply bold, italic, underline, and other formatting attributes to text. Simply select the text and then click the appropriate button in the toolbar or choose the Format menu's Font command.

Tip
You also can select a column of text by placing the mouse pointer at the top of the column. When the mouse pointer changes to a down arrow, click to select the entire column.

Changing the Font Size

In addition to changing the font, you can change the sizes of many fonts. Some fonts, such as Los Angeles, come only in two sizes (10 and 12); but most fonts, such as Times, Bookman, and Helvetica, come in a variety of sizes (from 8 point to 72 or 96).

Fonts are measured by *points*. There are 72 points in an inch, so a 36-point font is approximately one-half inch tall. The measurement is attained by measuring letters from their *descenders* (the bottoms of the characters *y, g, j, p,* and *q*) to the tops of their *ascenders* (the tops of characters such as *h, d,* and *b*).

To change the size of your text, follow these steps:

1. Select the text that you want to change.

2. Click the down-arrow button next to the Font Size text box to display a list of the sizes available for the font that is applied to the selected text.

3. Select an appropriate font size. As soon as you release the mouse button, that size is applied to the selected text. You can change the size again as long as the text remains selected.

You can choose a type style, font, and other formatting even before you begin typing. Click the cell; choose the appropriate formatting, using menu commands or toolbar buttons; and then type the text. The text is formatted as you specified.

Changing Column Width

PowerPoint enables you to adjust the width of selected columns or all columns in your table. This capability is useful when the information entered in different columns is of various lengths. Each column can be a different width, if necessary, to hold your entries.

To adjust the width of a single column in your table, follow these steps:

1. Place the mouse pointer on the right guideline of the column that you want to change. The mouse pointer changes to a double vertical line with arrows pointing left and right.

2. Drag the guideline to the new location (see fig. 8.8).

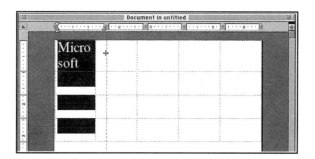

Fig. 8.8
Drag the guideline
to change the
width of a column.

Note

This method adjusts only the selected column border; all other columns are compressed in the available space. The outside table frame is not adjusted.

To adjust the width of several adjacent columns, follow these steps:

1. Place the mouse pointer at the top of the first column. When the mouse pointer changes to the down-arrow column selector, click and drag across the columns that you want to adjust to select them.

2. Double-click a vertical guideline of any selected columns. PowerPoint automatically adjusts the columns so that they fit the longest line of data.

To adjust all the columns of your table to fit your information automatically, follow these steps:

1. Open the Table menu and choose Select Table.

2. Open the Table menu and choose Cell Height and Width. The Cell Height and Width dialog box appears. Click the Column tab, as shown in figure 8.9.

Tip
Move the mouse
pointer to a col-
umn marker in the
horizontal ruler;
then hold down
the Ctrl key and
mouse button.
PowerPoint dis-
plays, in the ruler,
the actual mea-
surement of each
column.

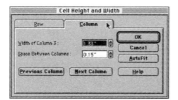

Fig. 8.9
This is a tabbed
dialog box; you
move through the
views by clicking
the tabs.

3. Make any changes that you want. You can change the width of a column or the height of a row, or both. When you click the Column tab, you can make the following changes:

- *Width of Columns.* You can specify an exact width, in inches, for the selected column or table. If only a single column is selected, the column number is displayed. The maximum width you can enter is 22.

- *Space Between Columns.* Use this option to specify the amount of white space, in inches, that you want between your columns. (This space also is called the gutter.) Again, the maximum width that you can enter is 22.

- *Previous Column.* This option enables you to select the preceding column in your table without closing the dialog box, selecting the column, and then reopening the dialog box.

- *Next Column.* This option enables you to select the next column in your table, again without closing the dialog box and starting over.

- *AutoFit.* This option changes the column size to fit the longest text in the column, taking into account the size of the table frame. This option does not automatically increase the size of the table frame.

4. Click the AutoFit button. Figure 8.10 shows an adjusted table.

Fig. 8.10
AutoFit compensates for the longest line in a column.

Adjusting Row Height

In addition to changing a column's width, you can change a row's height. Adjusting the height of a row is similar to changing the width of a column. All the individual cells of a row are the same height, but each row can have its own height.

To adjust the height of a row, follow these steps:

1. Place the mouse pointer on the vertical ruler.

2. Select the row marker for the row that you want to adjust. The mouse pointer changes to a vertical double arrow.

3. Click and drag the row marker up or down the ruler. The row guideline moves with the marker.

4. When the row is the size that you want, release the mouse button.

You also can use the Cell Height and Width dialog box to change the height of a row or rows. To use this dialog box, follow these steps:

1. Select the row or rows that you want to adjust.

2. Open the Table menu and choose Cell Height and Width. The Cell Height and Width dialog box appears. Click the Row tab, as shown in figure 8.11.

Fig. 8.11
This area of the dialog box is for adjusting the height of cells.

3. You can choose any of the following options for adjusting rows:

    ■ *Height of Rows.* Select one of the three options that are available. (The number next to `Height of Rows` indicates the number of the rows that are selected.)

    ■ *Auto.* This option adjusts the row width automatically to fit the text that is entered. If no text is entered, this option does not appear.

    ■ *At Least.* Choose this option from the Height of Row drop-down list. This option adjusts the row width to the number entered in the At text box. If the contents of the row are wider than this setting, the row is adjusted to fit.

- *Exactly*. Choose this option from the Height of Row drop-down list. This option fixes the row height to the number entered in the At text box. If the contents of the row are taller than the row height, the contents are adjusted to fit.

- *Indent from Left*. Enter the distance from the left edge of the column that you want to indent your text. This setting helps separate your columns.

- *Alignment*. Choose the appropriate alignment for your rows in relation to the slide's page margins.

- *Allow Row to Break Across Pages*. When you choose this option, the text in a row can be broken across a page, if necessary.

4. When you finish making choices in the dialog box, choose OK. Your table is adjusted automatically.

Changing Cell-Data Alignment

Change the alignment of text within a cell or selected cells is easy. Changing the alignment of text also enhances the readability of your presentation.

The following table describes the alignment buttons that are available in the Formatting toolbar.

Button	Button Name	Description
	Left Alignment	Aligns the selected text with the left margin of the cell.
	Center Alignment	Centers the selected text within the cell.
	Right Alignment	Aligns the selected text with the right margin of the cell.
	Justify	Aligns the selected text with the left and right edges of the cell. When text is justified, words may be stretched, with extra space inserted between letters, so that the text fills the cell. The font size does not change—only the spacing between letters and words.

To change the alignment of text in your table, follow these steps:

1. Select the text that you want to align.

2. Click the appropriate button (Left, Center, Right Align or Justify) in the Formatting toolbar. The selected text is aligned in relation to the edges of the cell.

Adding Borders to a Table

By adding borders and shading to your table, you can help draw attention to the entire table or to selected portions of the table. Use the table functions to accomplish this task. The grid lines of the table that are displayed do not print and are not visible when you return to PowerPoint. If you want to shade cells or place lines around or within your table, you must add borders using the Borders toolbar.

To add borders and shading to your table, follow these steps:

1. Click the Borders button in the Formatting toolbar. A new toolbar appears below the Formatting toolbar.

2. Select the entire table.

3. Click the down-arrow button next to the Line Style text box to display a pop-up menu of line styles, and select a line weight.

> **Note**
>
> Like font sizes, line weights are measured in points. One point is approximately 1/72 inch.

4. Click the Outside Border button. The border appears around the table.

5. Click the Inside Border button if you want to border each cell independently. Your table may look like figure 8.12.

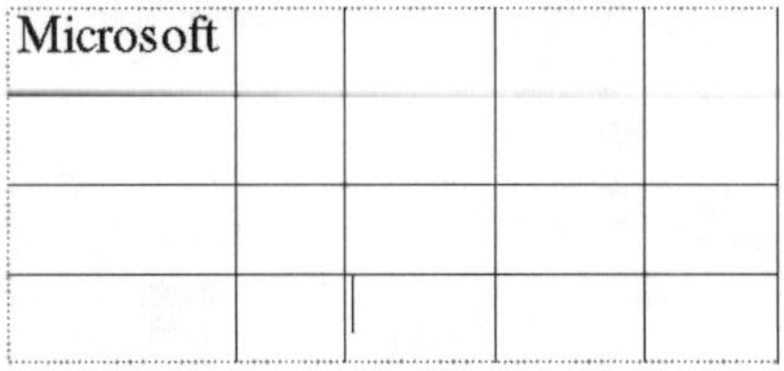

Fig. 8.12
The Inside Border button divides cells with lines that print.

Microsoft			

Troubleshooting

When I tried to resize a column by dragging the down-arrow column selector, only one cell in one row changed size; the rest of the cells in the column stayed the same size.

When you use the column selector in the ruler to select a row, only the selected row is affected when the column border is moved. You can avoid this problem by dragging the column guideline instead of the column selector or by deselecting the row first.

Each column is a different size. How do I get them all evenly spaced?

With the columns in question selected, open the Table menu and choose Cell Height and Width. Choose Column. In the Width text box, enter one width for all columns.

Pasting the Table into the Slide

After your table is complete, you can paste the table into the slide. Although you used Microsoft Word to create the table, it actually is an embedded object in PowerPoint; this table is not a file that you will find the next time you open Microsoft Word.

An embedded object can be copied to a disk and then run on a computer that does not have the program in which the object was created (in this case, Microsoft Word).

To paste the table into your slide, simply click outside the table frame. After a few seconds, the Microsoft Word menus and toolbars are replaced by the PowerPoint menus and toolbars. Figure 8.13 shows a completed table pasted into a slide.

If you need to edit the table at any time, simply display the slide and double-click the table.

	1987	1988	1989	1990	1991	1992
Climbers	817	916	1,009	998	935	1,024
Successes	251	551	517	573	553	398
Deaths	2	2	6	3	0	11

Fig. 8.13
You can edit a table by double-clicking inside the table boundaries.

Creating a Chart from a Table

If your table contains labels and numbers, you can create a chart from this information. Select the cells that contain the data you want to use, and then click the Insert Graph button in the toolbar. Microsoft Word opens Microsoft Graph, which uses the selected information to create a chart. Like the Microsoft Word table, the Microsoft Graph chart is an embedded object.

When you embed the chart in the Word table, the chart is displayed below the table. You may need to resize the table frame to make sure that everything fits in your slide.

From Here...

Now that you have learned to create, edit, and insert a Microsoft Word table into a PowerPoint presentation, you are ready to learn about additional features, such as charting, drawing, and creating links to other applications. Refer to the following chapters for more information about these subjects:

- Chapter 9, "Drawing Objects," shows you how to draw and place objects in a slide.

- Chapter 13, "Creating Basic Charts," shows you how to create charts by using datasheets and how to customize your charts.

- Chapter 18, "Using Links to Other Applications," shows you how to take full advantage of PowerPoint's linking and embedding features.

II

Text

Part III

Drawing

American Numbers

Click to add title

Click to add text

Tip of the Day

Did you know...

You can rotate AutoShapes for more shape options. If text is attached to the shape, it rotates as well.

OK

Next Tip

More Tips...

Help

☒ Show Tips at Startup

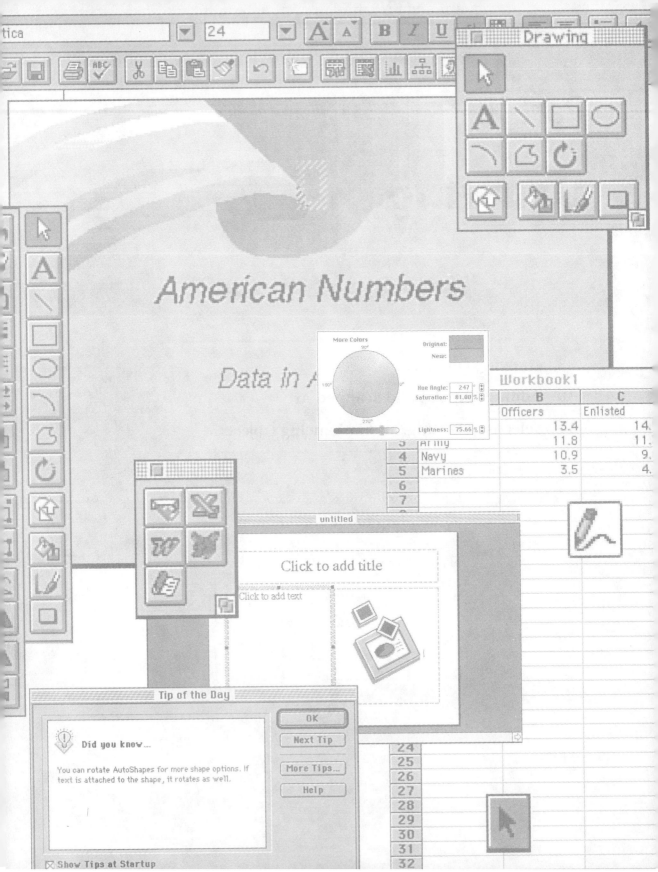

Chapter 9

Drawing Objects

When you have set the basic structure of your presentation, and you know what you want to say and how you want to present your subject, it is time to take your visual effects another step forward. PowerPoint provides a complete set of drawing tools. You also can perform freehand drawing and use a set of AutoShapes.

In this chapter, you learn to do the following things:

- Draw lines, arcs, polygons, and use AutoShapes

- Use vertical, horizontal, and 45-degree-angle lines

- Draw lines, arcs, and polygons from a center point

- Use guides, grids, and edges to align objects

With PowerPoint, you can use shapes and colors to emphasize a specific point or piece of information. You can scale figures, rotate them, or apply shadows to them. In this chapter, you learn to use the PowerPoint drawing tools to create a presentation that can inform and persuade your audience.

Using PowerPoint's Drawing Tools

PowerPoint's professional drawing tools enable you to draw and revise shapes, lines, text, and pictures to create a professional presentation. Each object that you draw for a slide is infinitely adjustable.

The PowerPoint window contains a complete set of drawing tools in the Drawing toolbar. By default, this toolbar is located at the left side of your window and contains 12 buttons. You can add tools to the toolbar at any time, move the toolbar, or make it a free-floating object.

Table 9.1 describes the 12 Drawing toolbar tools.

Table 9.1 Drawing Toolbar Tools		
Tool	**Tool Name**	**Description**
▲	Selection	Selects any object. This tool is selected by default.
A	Text	Enables you to create text.
╲	Line	Enables you to draw a single straight line.
▭	Rectangle	Enables you to draw rectangles and squares.
◯	Ellipse	Enables you to draw ellipses and circles.
⌐	Arc	Enables you to draw curved lines from two selected points.
⬠	Freeform	Enables you to draw a many-sided figure, continuing to draw lines until you connect the beginning point with the end point.
↻	Free Rotate	Enables you to rotate an object by one of the four corner points. Any object can be rotated in a 360-degree circle.
⬚	AutoShapes	Displays a palette from which you can choose a shape. You can manipulate these shapes as you can all other shapes and lines.
▨	Fill On/Off	Applies the default fill pattern to the selected object, or removes the fill.
✎	Line On/Off	Applies the default line type to the selected line object, or removes the line.
▫	Shadow On/Off	Applies the default shadow type to the selected object, or removes the shadow.

Drawing Basic Shapes

Many of the most complicated drawings start with the simplest elements: the line, the arc, and the polygon. By using these lines and shape as the basis of your drawings, you can create the emphasis that you want for your slides.

To create even more complex drawings, you can combine different pieces of drawings in a single drawing.

◀ See "Working with Objects," p. 86

Drawing Lines

The line is the most basic object, because lines compose all other objects. To draw a line, follow these steps:

1. Open the slide in which you want to draw.

2. Click the Line tool in the Drawing toolbar.

3. Move the mouse pointer into the slide to choose a beginning point for the line. Notice that the mouse pointer changes to a crosshair when you place it in the slide.

4. Click to anchor the beginning point of the line, and then drag the mouse to locate the end point of the line.

5. Release the mouse button to anchor the line's end point, as shown in figure 9.1. Drawn lines have two handles: one at the beginning anchor point and one at the ending anchor point. Both handles can be edited.

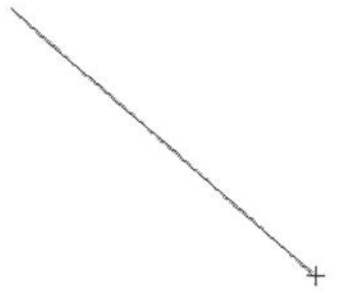

Fig. 9.1
Draw the line by dragging the cross from the beginning to the end of the line.

You can manipulate any PowerPoint object and move it anywhere in a slide. You can resize, move, or tilt a line quickly. To adjust a line, follow these steps:

1. Click the Selection tool.

2. Place the mouse pointer at the center of the line, and then click and hold down the mouse button. The solid line changes to a dotted line.

3. Drag the line to its new location. To constrain the line, hold the Shift key while creating it.

To change the length of the line, click one of the handles and hold the mouse button down; then drag the handle. You can extend the line by dragging the handle away from the center of the line; alternatively, you can reduce the length of the line by dragging the handle toward the center of the line. To change the angle of the line, drag the handle to a new position. The opposite handle, or end point, remains stationary during these movements.

III

Drawing

Drawing Arcs

Not every line is a straight line, of course, and not every item that you want to show in your slide can be illustrated in straight lines. PowerPoint gives you the capability to draw *arcs*, which are curved lines between two points. You can edit an arc the same way you do a straight line.

To draw an arc or curved line, follow these steps:

1. Click the Arc tool in the Drawing toolbar.

2. Place the mouse pointer where you want to begin the arc, and then click and hold down the mouse button. The mouse pointer changes to a crosshair.

3. Drag the cross to anchor the end point of your arc, and then release the mouse button.

Your arc may look something like the one shown in figure 9.2.

Fig. 9.2
Arcs are drawn exactly like lines. Click to begin, drag, and click to end.

Tip
You can turn an arc into a full or partial circle. Select the arc, open the Edit menu and choose Edit Arc, and then drag one of the arc end points.

To edit the arc, click the Selection tool and Select the arc. Handles appear in a rectangle around the arc. Point to a handle, and the Selection tool changes to a double-headed arrow. Drag any of the handles to resize or reposition the arc.

Don't hesitate to experiment with your drawing. Try dragging each of the handles to see what happens. As you try each movement, you gain confidence in your drawing abilities.

Figure 9.3 shows two arcs with the same beginning point.

Fig. 9.3
Draw multiple arcs to create an interesting effect.

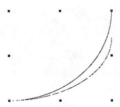

Drawing Polygons

Polygons, or freeform shapes, can be used to draw many objects. A polygon can be closed or open. A polygon is closed if its beginning and end points meet; a polygon is open if its beginning and end points do not meet.

To draw a polygon, follow these steps:

1. Click the Freeform tool in the Drawing toolbar.

2. Move the mouse pointer to the slide, and click to anchor the beginning point. Do not hold the mouse button down.

> **Note**
>
> If you hold down the mouse button, the mouse pointer changes to a pencil. You then can drag the mouse to draw as though it were a pencil. You may want to try this method, but it takes a very steady hand to draw successfully in this manner. Double-click the mouse button to end a freehand line.

Tip

If you are drawing a complex shape, try increasing the magnification of your slide to 200 percent or more so that you can see the smaller lines easily. Decrease the magnification to see the entire drawing.

3. Move the mouse pointer to the next corner of the polygon, and click the mouse button again to anchor that point. Hold the Shift key while drawing to constrain the line.

4. To finish the polygon, do one of the following things:

- Close the polygon by clicking the beginning point. The mouse pointer changes from a crosshair to an arrow. PowerPoint applies the default fill pattern or color and displays the eight resizing handles around the polygon.

- Double-click the mouse button.

- Click the mouse at the end of the line or shape and then press the Return key.

Any of these actions completes a polygon, open or closed, displaying the eight resizing handles around the polygon. The mouse pointer changes back to the Selection tool.

Figure 9.4 shows an open polygon and a closed polygon. The open polygon is considered to be open because the beginning and end points do not meet.

III

Drawing

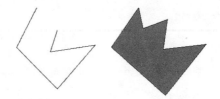

Fig. 9.4
Closed polygons
are automatically
filled with the
default color and
outlined with the
default line.

Drawing Rectangles and Ellipses

In addition to lines, arcs, and polygons, you can draw regular circles, ellipses (ovals), squares, and rectangles. By using the appropriate tools, you can draw precise figures without the jagged edges and bumps associated with the freeform objects.

To use the Ellipse and Rectangle tools, follow these steps:

1. Click the Ellipse or Rectangle tool.

2. Move the mouse pointer to the slide (the pointer becomes a crosshair), click to anchor the beginning point, and drag the mouse to draw the object. The outline of the ellipse or rectangle follows the mouse so you can adjust as you draw. Hold the Shift key as you draw to constrain the shape to a circle or a square.

Tip
Think of an ellipse
as being a curved
rectangle. Click
and hold down
the mouse button
where you want to
place one of the
ellipse's "corners."

3. Release the mouse button when the object is the size and proportion that you want; this action anchors the end point.

The shape that you drew may look like one of those shown in figure 9.5. Remember that you can always drag the shape to another location or adjust its size and proportion.

Fig. 9.5
Ellipses can be
longer than they
are tall, or vice
versa. You also can
draw circles.

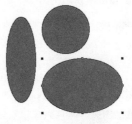

Enhancing an Object with Fills, Colors, and Shadows

In addition to drawing an object, you can enhance an object by applying colors, fill patterns, and shadows. By using color, you can make your presentation more attractive and emphasize a particular point or object. You can apply various fill patterns in lieu of using color. And you can use shadows to give your slides a more three-dimensional effect. PowerPoint enables you to adjust shadows to produce the appearance of depth.

Adding Fill Patterns and Colors

To add fill patterns and colors to a slide, follow these steps:

1. Select an object. An object is selected when the eight handles appear, defining the object's *bounding box*.

2. Hold down the Ctrl key, and then click and hold down the mouse button to display the object's attributes menu, which appears where the mouse pointer is located.

3. Choose the Colors and Lines option. The Colors and Lines dialog box appears, as shown in figure 9.6.

Tip
Be sure that the mouse pointer is located inside the object that you want to work with, not just inside the bounding box of handles.

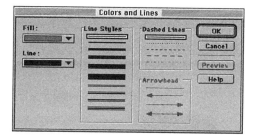

Fig. 9.6
The Colors and Lines dialog box works the same way for all shapes.

III

Drawing

> **Note**
>
> Each drawn object consists of two parts. The border is made up of a continuous line. A rectangle's border, for example, is one line shaped like a rectangle. The second part of an object is its interior, made up of color or patterned fill. You can change the attributes of the two parts of an object in the Colors and Lines dialog box.

4. Choose options in the following sections of the dialog box:

■ *Dashed Lines.* Select one of the four styles of dashed lines. The selected style is applied to the border of the selected object, not to the border of the bounding box. A solid line is selected by default.

■ *Arrowhead.* Select one of the three styles of arrowheads when you want to add an arrowhead to a selected line. An arrowhead can be added to the left end, the right end, or both ends of a line. By default, a solid line without arrowheads is selected.

> **Note**
>
> The Arrowhead option is available only for an object that has two end points, such as a line, an arc, or an open polygon. You cannot add arrowheads to a rectangle, an ellipse, or a closed polygon.

■ *Line Styles.* You can choose among six solid lines of various widths and four other styles of multiple lines.

■ *Fill.* The Fill pop-up menu is exactly like the Fill Color menu you can choose from the Drawing+ toolbar.

■ *Line.* The Line pop-up menu is exactly like the Line Color menu you can choose from the Drawing+ toolbar.

5. Open the Fill pop-up menu and choose Pattern; the Pattern Fill dialog box appears (see fig. 9.7). Select a fill pattern, and then choose OK. The selected pattern appears in the Fill box of the Colors and Lines dialog box.

Fig. 9.7
Choose a fill
pattern in this
dialog box.

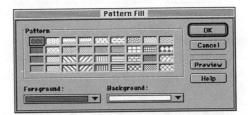

6. Open the Fill pop-up menu and choose one of the following options:

■ *One of eight color-block selections.* These options are the default color settings that are always available.

■ *No Fill.* Choose this option if you do not want to use a fill pattern or color. This option also makes the interior of the object transparent, so that you can see any objects that are behind it.

■ *Background.* Choose this option to apply the default background color or pattern to the selected object.

■ *Shaded.* Choosing this option displays the Shaded Fill dialog box, in which you can choose specialized shading effects.

■ *Pattern.* Choosing this option displays the Pattern Fill dialog box, in which you can choose among 36 pattern options, as well as background and foreground color options.

■ *Other Color.* Choosing this option displays the Other Color dialog box, which contains a palette of 88 colors. Click the More Colors button to display the More Colors dialog box in which you can mix your own colors. Your options are limited only by your monitor.

7. Open the Line pop-up menu and choose a line option. You can select a color for your line from the default block of eight colors, or add colors by using the Other Color dialog box. You also can choose the No Line option, which displays your object without a line around it.

▶ See "Applying Colors to Individual Objects," p. 378

Caution

If you create an object that has the same fill pattern or color as the slide and then choose the No Line option, the object disappears into the background. Only by clicking around the object can you hope to select it.

---

8. Choose OK to close the Colors and Lines dialog box.

Adding Shadows

Placing a shadow behind an object adds a three-dimensional effect to the object. To add a shadow, follow these steps:

1. Select the object to which you want to apply a shadow.

2. Open the Format menu and choose Shadow. The Shadow dialog box appears (see fig. 9.8).

Tip
Make sure that your shadows appear to come from the same light source, so that all are facing the same direction.

III

Drawing

Fig. 9.8
Add shadows to
objects by using
the Shadows
dialog box.

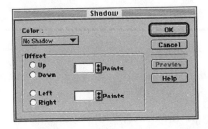

3. Open the Color pop-up menu and choose a color that is darker than your object and its background. This menu contains the eight default color blocks and the options No Shadow, Embossed, and Other Color.

4. In the Offset section, you control the perceived location of the light source and the distance of your object from the background. If the light source is supposed to be coming from above and left of the object, for example, your shadow should be offset down and to the right. In this case, click the Down and Right buttons.

5. To make your object appear farther from the background, increase the numbers in the Points text boxes. If you want your object to appear closer to the background, decrease the numbers.

6. Click the Up button and enter the number of points that you want the shadow to appear from your object.

7. Click the Right button and enter the number of points that you want the shadow to appear from your object.

8. Choose OK to apply the shadow.

Figure 9.9 shows a shadow applied to an object in a slide.

Fig. 9.9
Shadows can be
offset by small
amounts or large
amounts,
depending on the
emphasis that
you want.

Using AutoShapes

PowerPoint comes with a set of predefined shapes called *AutoShapes*. These shapes can be adjusted in size, and many include an additional adjustment handle.

AutoShapes are located in the AutoShapes toolbar. Click an AutoShape to place that object in your slide.

You already have used two AutoShapes that appear in the Drawing toolbar: the Ellipse and the Rectangle. You use the other AutoShapes the same way.

The AutoShapes toolbar contains 24 AutoShapes, including a starburst, a star, several arrows, a cross, a box, and a balloon.

You can combine AutoShapes with one another and with freeform shapes to create complex objects. To use AutoShapes, follow these steps:

1. Click the AutoShapes tool in the Drawing toolbar. The AutoShapes toolbar appears. By default, the AutoShapes toolbar is a floating toolbar.

2. Click an AutoShape, and then move the mouse pointer to the slide.

3. Click and drag the tool to define the shape. As you drag, the shape enlarges and changes proportions. When you're happy with the shape, release the mouse button.

4. If you want to edit the shape, drag the adjustment handle (a small un-shaded diamond) until you are satisfied with the result.

Although not all AutoShapes have an adjustment handle, all AutoShapes have the normal complement of eight resizing handles.

Tip
Convert the AutoShapes toolbar from a floating toolbar to a horizontal or vertical toolbar by dragging it toward an edge of your screen. Change it back by double-clicking the toolbar border.

Rotating Objects

Any object created in PowerPoint—even title bars and text boxes—can be rotated with the Free Rotate button. The capability to rotate an object gives you a great deal of creative freedom; you no longer are limited to displaying objects and text in a single horizontal plane.

You can draw objects, add text, and then move and rotate these objects. To use the Free Rotate tool, follow these steps:

1. Draw an object in the slide and then select it.

III

Drawing

2. Click the Free Rotate tool in the Drawing toolbar. The mouse pointer changes to circular rotating arrows.

3. Position the pointer over a handle of the selected object and the pointer changes to a four-headed arrow. Click one of the handles of the object, and drag the object to rotate it.

Figure 9.10 shows an object that has been rotated.

Fig. 9.10
This is a rotated AutoShape; drag the four-headed pointer to rotate the object.

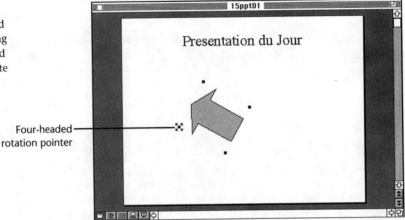

Four-headed rotation pointer

You are not limited to rotating one object at a time. Select several objects; open the Draw menu and choose Group; then click the Free Rotate tool and rotate the group as a unit. You can use this method to place text inside an AutoShape and then rotate the text.

Drawing Objects Precisely

When you are creating a presentation, neatness counts almost as much as content. The last thing you want to do is distract your audience with sloppy drawings. The following sections show you how to use PowerPoint's drawing tools in a very precise manner.

Drawing Vertical, Horizontal, and 45-Degree-Angle Lines

At times, you will not want to draw lines freehand. You may want lines that are exactly horizontal, vertical, or at a 45-degree angle, but you may not need a rectangle or right triangle for your drawing. You can draw such lines easily in PowerPoint.

To draw horizontal, vertical, and 45-degree-angle lines, follow these steps:

1. Click the Line tool in the Drawing toolbar.

2. Move the mouse pointer to the slide.

3. Hold down the Shift key, click and hold down the mouse button, and drag to draw your line.

Drawing Uniform Shapes

Uniform (regular shapes) include squares and circles. You cannot turn a freeform shape into a uniform shape. Without PowerPoint's special capabilities to draw uniform shapes, you would have to click the Ellipse button and try to approximate the shape as closely as possible. Unless you have an extremely accurate eye and steady hand, this procedure can be quite difficult.

To draw uniform shapes, follow these steps:

1. Click a drawing tool in the Drawing toolbar.

2. Move the mouse pointer to the slide.

3. Hold down the Shift key, click and hold down the mouse button, and then drag to draw the object.

4. Click to define the end point.

Note

You can turn a nonuniform shape, such as an ellipse or rectangle, into a regular shape by double-clicking any of the object's resizing handles. This method changes a shape into a uniform shape along the shorter of the up/down and left/right axes.

Drawing Objects from a Center Point

You can draw objects from the center outward. This technique can be used for all objects except those drawn with the Freeform tool.

To draw an object from a center point, follow these steps:

1. Click the drawing tool that you want to use.

2. Place the mouse pointer in the slide where you want the center point of the object to be.

III

Drawing

Tip
You can draw a regular object (square or circle) from the center point out by pressing the Option and Shift keys in combination: Option-Shift-drag object.

3. Hold down the Option key and the mouse button, and drag to draw the object.

4. When the object is the desired size, release the Option key and the mouse button.

Note

If you are drawing with the Option key, make sure you hold the key down until after you release the mouse button. If you accidentally release the Option key before you are done drawing, just press it again and complete the drawing.

Troubleshooting

How do I delete a drawn object?

Click the object to select it, and then press the Delete key.

I made a mistake in a freeform drawing. How do I correct it?

Simply press the Delete key. This action deletes the last end point that you drew. You can back up as far as necessary by pressing the Delete key. You can delete up to, but not including, the beginning point.

I want to move or resize several objects at the same time, without making them a group. Can I do this?

Yes, you can. Click the Selection tool. Draw a selection box that surrounds all the objects that you want to treat as a group temporarily. Each object's handles appear. Drag any of these handles to resize all the objects at the same time. To move all the objects, click and drag them to the new location.

When I try to select several objects at the same time, I seem to miss one or another. Why?

Be sure that when you draw your selection box around the objects, you enclose all the objects that you want to select. If you miss even a small corner of an object, that object will not be included with the group.

I drew an object and made it invisible by choosing No Fill and No Line. How do I find this object again?

Open the Edit menu and choose Select All. Handles appear around each object in your slide, including the invisible object. Hold down the Option key, click one of the resize handles, and change the line or fill type.

Aligning Objects

PowerPoint offers two helpful tools for aligning objects: guides and grid lines. You access these tools through menu commands.

Using Guides

To give your slides the most professional appearance possible, you may want to align some or all of your objects. Guides help you by providing vertical and horizontal axis lines. You can move the guides from their origination point at the exact center of your slide; PowerPoint tells you how far from the center point you have moved the guide.

To align objects, follow these steps:

1. Open the View menu and choose Guides. Two dotted lines—one vertical and one horizontal—appear in your slide, intersecting at the exact center of your slide, as shown in figure 9.11.

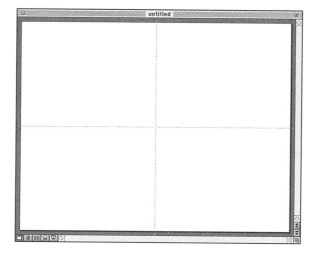

Fig. 9.11
The guides appear at the exact center of the slide by default, but you can move them.

2. Click and drag the horizontal guide downward. As you drag the line, the mouse pointer changes to a number. As you drag the line, notice that the number increases. An arrow appears to the right of or below the mouse-pointer number, indicating whether you are above, below, left, or right of the center point.

3. Drag the line down until you reach the point at which you want to align your objects; then release the mouse button.

III

Drawing

4. Move the objects until they are similarly positioned along the horizontal guide. If you move the objects across the line slowly, they snap to the guide as though they were magnetized.

> **Note**
>
> If you need to align different groups of objects at different points, place the guides for the first group, and align those objects; then move the guides for the next group, and align those objects. The first group of objects does not move with the guides. When an object has been aligned in a specific position, moving the guides has no effect unless you move the object again.

5. Open the View menu and choose Guides. The guides disappear.

Using Grid Lines

PowerPoint comes with an alignment method called the grid. You can turn the grid on or off at any time. The grid consists of a series of invisible lines, both horizontal and vertical, across your slide screen that are 1/12 of an inch apart. When the grid is turned on, your objects automatically snap to the closest grid line as though they were magnetized.

> **Note**
>
> The grid is turned on by default. A check mark appears beside the Snap to Grid command in the Draw menu. To turn the grid option off, choose the Snap to Grid command; the check mark disappears.

Depending on the measurement system that you chose for PowerPoint, you have either 12 grid lines per inch or 5 grid lines per centimeter. To see how the grid works, follow these steps:

1. Draw two rectangles with which to experiment.

2. Drag one rectangle to a new position on the slide.

3. Now drag the second rectangle in close proximity. The grid forces the second rectangle to snap to the same spot.

To see how objects move without the grid lines, follow these steps:

1. Open the Draw menu and choose Snap to Grid to turn off the grid lines. The check mark disappears.

2. Select one of the rectangles again and drag it to a new position. Notice that the movement now is smooth and not jerky. PowerPoint no longer snaps the object from one grid line to the next.

3. Now drag the other rectangle in close proximity of the first. Try to align the two objects. It is difficult to align them exactly without the grid.

From Here...

Now that you are familiar with drawing and placing objects in slides, you are ready to add color to your drawings and add clip art to your slides. To learn to use color and clip art, refer to the following chapters:

- Chapter 10, "Adding Clip Art and Scanned Art," shows you how to use the PowerPoint ClipArt Gallery and how to place clip-art pictures.

- Chapter 14, "Customizing Charts," shows you the basics of using color in slide charts.

- Chapter 17, "Working with Color," builds your color skills to increase the impact of your presentations.

III

Drawing

Chapter 10

Adding Clip Art and Scanned Art

PowerPoint comes with a variety of professionally drawn pictures, called *clip art*, that you can use in your slides. Clip art saves you time when you need to put together a polished presentation in a hurry. The PowerPoint Macintosh version stores these drawings in files with a PCS extension and a short description.

In this chapter, you learn to do the following things:

- Insert clip art from the ClipArt Gallery

- Search for and organize clip art in the ClipArt Gallery

- Insert clip art from another application

- Add scanned art to a slide

PowerPoint goes further by allowing you to use pictures from other sources. By using a scanner with special software, for example, you can scan your company's logo in a bitmap file and include it in a presentation. You also can include pictures from other applications, such as word processing, spreadsheet, and desktop-publishing programs. PowerPoint can read several file formats that are used for storing pictures. In this chapter, you learn more about some of these formats. The chapter also discusses scanners and the use of scanned art in presentations.

Clip art is organized and accessed through the ClipArt Gallery, a utility that optionally is installed with PowerPoint. In this chapter, you learn how to use this utility to insert pictures into a slide. You also learn how to add and organize pictures in the ClipArt Gallery.

III

Drawing

Using the ClipArt Gallery

More than 500 clip-art pictures are included with PowerPoint, so there is a good chance that one or two pictures will work well in your presentation. If you don't find what you're looking for in the clip art included with PowerPoint, you can use pictures from other applications.

PowerPoint's ClipArt Gallery allows you to manage a large collection of clip art organized in several predefined categories, including business, landscapes, communications, and animals. You can use the ClipArt Gallery to organize every picture in your collection, not just on your hard disk, but also on floppy disks. Like a library, the ClipArt Gallery maintains an index that lists the location of each picture in the gallery. This feature enables you to keep track of a large collection of useful artwork without using valuable hard-disk space.

 To access the ClipArt Gallery, open the Insert menu and choose Clip Art. If you are accessing the ClipArt Gallery for the first time, PowerPoint must create a clip-art database for the ClipArt Gallery to use in locating clip art. Click Yes in the dialog box that appears. Keep in mind that this process could take a few minutes. After PowerPoint creates the clip-art database, the ClipArt

Fig. 10.1
The size of the ClipArt Gallery is limited only by your disk space.

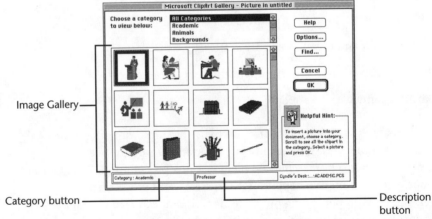

Image Gallery

Category button

Description button

Gallery dialog box appears, as shown in figure 10.1.

To display pictures in categories, make a selection in the Choose a Category to View Below list at the top of the dialog box. The default selection is All Categories. The grid section just below the list is the Image Gallery, which displays pictures assigned to the current category.

At the bottom of the ClipArt Gallery dialog box are two large buttons. When you select a new category, the name of that category is displayed on the left button, which is the Category button. If you move to another picture in the gallery, the description of that picture is displayed on the right button, which is the Description button. You use the Category and Description buttons to change the category name or picture description, as described in "Deleting and Renaming Categories" later in this chapter.

Another useful feature is the Helpful Hint section, located in the lower-right corner of the dialog box. Helpful Hint sections appear in many major PowerPoint dialog boxes. A Helpful Hint section tells you how to perform the principal task associated with the current dialog box—in this case, selecting and placing a piece of clip art in a slide.

Placing Clip Art from the ClipArt Gallery in a Slide

You use the ClipArt Gallery dialog box to place clip art in a slide. To place clip art in a slide, open a presentation and then follow these steps:

1. Open the Insert menu and choose Clip Art. The ClipArt Gallery dialog box appears.

2. Select a category in the Choose a Category to View Below list. The default selection is All Categories.

3. Scroll through the pictures in the Image Gallery, and make a selection by clicking the desired picture.

4. Choose OK.

Note

To place clip art from somewhere other than the ClipArt Gallery in a slide, open the Insert menu and choose Insert Picture. A dialog box appears, displaying a file list. Use the Macintosh interface to locate the file, and then double-click the file name.

Searching for Clip Art

You can search the ClipArt Gallery for a specific picture or group of pictures. When you click the Find button in the ClipArt Gallery dialog box, the Find Picture dialog box appears. The Find Picture dialog box enables you to narrow or expand your search criteria by category, text used in the picture description, file name, and file type.

III

Drawing

To search for clip art, follow these steps:

1. Open the Insert menu and choose Clip Art. The ClipArt Gallery dialog box appears.

2. Click the Find button. The Find Pictures dialog box appears, as shown in figure 10.2.

Fig. 10.2
Type the search criteria in the text boxes.

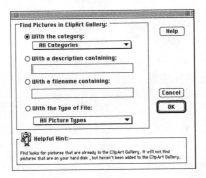

3. Open the With the Category pop-up menu and choose a category.

4. In the With a Description Containing text box, type a word or partial word.

   You use this option to perform a search based on the text in a picture description. Typing the word **jet**, for example, causes PowerPoint to search for all pictures in the gallery that have this word in their descriptions.

5. (Optional) In the With a Filename Containing text box, type a full or partial file name to further narrow the search.

   This option enables you to change the name or delete a category without affecting the pictures associated with the category.

6. Open the With the Type of File pop-up menu and choose a file type.

   You use this option to locate pictures that are saved in a different file format than those in the ClipArt Gallery. The default selection is All Picture Types.

7. Choose OK. The ClipArt Gallery displays the pictures that match your search criteria.

Managing the ClipArt Gallery

Clicking the Options button in the ClipArt Gallery dialog box causes the Options dialog box to appear (see fig. 10.3).

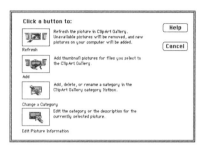

Fig. 10.3
Use this dialog box to manage the ClipArt Gallery.

You use this dialog box to manage the ClipArt Gallery by adding and deleting clip art and clip-art categories. The Options dialog box divides these operations among four buttons: Refresh, Add, Change a Category, and Edit Picture Information. Table 10.1 briefly describes these options.

Table 10.1 Options for Managing the ClipArt Gallery	
Option	**Description**
Refresh	Updates the ClipArt Gallery, removing previously recorded entries that can no longer be found and adding entries for new pictures.
Add	Enables you to add a specific picture or group of pictures to the ClipArt Gallery.
Change a Category	Enables you to change the name or delete a category without affecting the pictures associated with the category.
Edit Picture Information	Enables you to change the description of a picture or reassign the picture to different category.

Adding Clip Art from Other Applications

You can take advantage of object linking and embedding (*OLE*) to add pictures, text, graphs, or tables to your presentations. Embedding inserts the object into your presentation; linking inserts a reference to the object into your presentation.

III

Drawing

When an object such as a chart is linked to your presentation, all copies of the object are updated whenever changes are made in the original. Use linking when you need to update several copies of the same data immediately.

Use embedding when you want to make changes in an object quickly. Because the object actually is inserted into the presentation file, there are no links to consider; you simply double-click the object and make your change in the application that appears. Keep in mind that presentations with embedded objects take more room on your hard drive than do those that contain linked objects.

Many Macintosh applications, such as word processing and spreadsheet programs, come with a variety of pictures saved in various file formats. In programs that enable you to create and edit images, such as desktop-publishing programs, you have the option to save images in multiple formats.

PowerPoint's ClipArt Gallery allows you to add pictures in several file formats to your clip-art collection. Many of these file formats are native to a specific software package.

Click the Add button in the Options dialog box to search for and add one or more clip-art files to the ClipArt Gallery. When you click Add, the Add ClipArt dialog box appears. Use this dialog box to specify a drive, folder, and file type to locate. Files that match the specified file type are displayed on the left side of the Add ClipArt dialog box. You can click a file and then click the Picture Preview button to display the contents of the file.

To add clip art from another application to the PowerPoint ClipArt Gallery, follow these steps:

1. Open the Insert menu and choose Clip Art. The ClipArt Gallery dialog box appears.

2. Click the Options button. The Options dialog box appears.

3. Click the Add button to display the Add ClipArt dialog box (see fig. 10.4).

Fig. 10.4
Use the Add ClipArt dialog box to add non-PowerPoint clip art to the ClipArt Gallery.

4. Select a picture name in the list box.

If you select only one picture, you then can click the Picture Preview button to display the picture.

> **Note**
>
> If you have clip art located in other folders or on another hard disk, click the Drives box and select a new drive, and then double-click a folder name. The files in that folder appear in the list box of the Add ClipArt dialog box.

5. Choose OK.

If you selected more than one picture, PowerPoint asks whether you want to assign each picture to a category. Click Yes if you want to be prompted for a category for each picture. Otherwise, PowerPoint adds all the pictures to the All Categories group.

6. If you are prompted, enter a category and description for the picture in the dialog box that appears next. Then choose Add to add the picture to the ClipArt Gallery.

To skip a picture and move on to the next one, click the Don't Add button.

Deleting and Renaming Categories

Click the Change a Category button in the Options dialog box to rename or delete an existing category. The Change a Category dialog box appears. You can use this dialog box to rename or delete a category.

> **Note**
>
> When you delete a category, PowerPoint does not delete the pictures that previously were assigned to that category; it places those pictures in the All Categories list.

To delete a category, follow these steps:

1. Open the Insert menu and choose Clip Art. The ClipArt Gallery dialog box appears.

2. Click the Options button. The Options dialog box appears.

III

Drawing

3. Click the Change a Category button to display the Change a Category dialog box (see fig. 10.5).

Fig. 10.5
When you customize a category, you also may want to change the name.

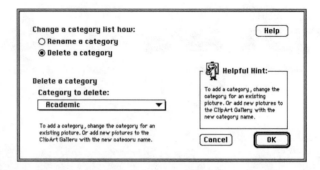

4. In the Change a Category section of the dialog box, select Delete a Category.

5. Choose the category that you want to delete.

6. Choose OK. PowerPoint prompts you to confirm the deletion.

7. Click Yes to delete the category or No to cancel the operation.

When you rename a category, all pictures that were grouped under the old category are reassigned to the new category. Follow these steps to rename a category:

1. Open the Insert menu and choose Clip Art. The ClipArt Gallery dialog box appears.

2. Click the Options button to display the Options dialog box.

3. Click the Add button to display the Add a Category dialog box.

4. In the Change a Category section of the dialog box, select Rename a Category.

5. Open the Old Category Name pop-up menu and choose the old category name.

6. In the New Category Name text box, type a new name.

7. Choose OK.

Moving Pictures to a New Category

The Edit Picture Information option in the Options dialog box displays the Edit Picture Information dialog box. You use this dialog box to edit a picture's description or to move the current picture to a new category. Another way to access the Edit Picture Information dialog box is to click the Category or Description button at the bottom of the ClipArt Gallery dialog box.

To move a picture to a new category, follow these steps:

1. Open the Insert menu and choose Clip Art. The ClipArt Gallery dialog box appears.

2. Choose the picture that you want to move from the ClipArt Gallery.

3. Click the Category button at the bottom of the ClipArt Gallery dialog box. The Edit Picture Information dialog box appears, as shown in figure 10.6.

4. Open the Category pop-up menu and choose a new category.

5. Choose OK. PowerPoint moves the selected picture to the specified category.

Fig. 10.6
Use this dialog box to change the description of a picture.

Note

You can use the Edit Picture Information dialog box to create a new category. Simply type a new category in the New text box and choose OK. PowerPoint adds the selected clip art to the new category.

III

Drawing

Refreshing the ClipArt Gallery

When you click the Refresh button in the Options dialog box, PowerPoint searches your hard drive for new clip art, optionally adding it to the ClipArt Gallery. Entries for unavailable pictures are removed from the gallery.

Earlier in this chapter, you learned that the ClipArt Gallery records the locations of the pictures in your collection. You may need to move pictures located in a certain folder to a new location on your hard drive, or even to a floppy disk, to conserve space. When you do so, it is a good idea to update the ClipArt Gallery.

To refresh the ClipArt Gallery, follow these steps:

1. Open the Insert menu and choose Clip Art. The ClipArt Gallery dialog box appears.

2. Click the Options button. The Options dialog box appears.

3. Click the Refresh button. The ClipArt Gallery prompts you to specify which drives to search.

> **Note**
>
> Change a picture's description by clicking the Description button in the ClipArt Gallery dialog box and typing the description in the Edit Picture Information dialog box. Choose OK to complete the process. Use this feature to perform precise searches based on picture descriptions.

4. Choose OK to begin the operation.

5. If new art is found, PowerPoint asks whether you want to assign a category and description to the art. Make your choice, and then choose OK to continue.

6. If you are prompted, enter a category and (optionally) a description. Then click Add to add the picture to the ClipArt Gallery.

   To skip the picture and move to the next one, click the Don't Add button.

Entries for clip art in the ClipArt Gallery that cannot be found are deleted.

Adding Scanned Art

Scanners enable you to copy important material such as company logos, drawings, photographs, and text into your computer directly from paper. There are two basic types of scanners: hand-held and flatbed scanners. Flatbed scanners offer a wide range of options and features, but many of them cost as much as a personal computer. Hand-held scanners, on the other hand, tend to be priced much lower, making them popular accessories for Macintoshes.

Both types of scanners work the same way; they copy an image and save it to a file on your computer. Some flatbed scanners allow you to scan color as well as black-and-white images. Hand-held scanners produce images that appear in shades of gray.

The software that usually comes with the scanner manages the scanning operation and also enables you to edit and print the image. Most software packages enable you to save scanned images in several file formats.

Before you can place a scanned image in a slide, you must add that image to the ClipArt Gallery, optionally assigning the picture to a category and giving it a description. For instructions, refer to "Adding Clip Art from Other Applications" earlier in this chapter.

To add the scanned picture to a slide, refer to "Placing Clip Art from the ClipArt Gallery in a Slide" earlier in this chapter.

Troubleshooting

I attempted to add a new image to the ClipArt Gallery, but there are too many files to scroll through to find the name of the image that I want.

Use the Type of File pop-up menu to specify the file format of the file you need. If the image was created by a drawing package such as Adobe Illustrator, change the file type to Illustrator (EPS).

I used PowerPoint's setup program to add more clip-art images to my system, but when I try to access them from PowerPoint, they don't show up in the ClipArt Gallery.

To use the new images, you must tell PowerPoint where they are located on your disk drive. In the ClipArt Gallery dialog box, click the Options button to display the Options dialog box; then click the Refresh button to scan the drive for the images. The images are added to the ClipArt Gallery, and you then can add them to your slide presentations.

(continues)

III

Drawing

(continued)

My company has grown quickly and I have numerous divisional logos that I'd like to use in PowerPoint. I used the Add feature of the ClipArt Gallery to create a new category for the logos, but my company has gone public and changed its name. The category name that I used for the images is no longer correct. How do I change it?

In the ClipArt Gallery dialog box, click Options to display the Options dialog box; then click Change a Category to rename the category to match your new company name.

I mistakenly deleted a category of images in the ClipArt Gallery, and I need an image from the deleted category.

The images in the category that you deleted are not gone, just relocated. The images from deleted categories are assigned to the All Categories category. Scroll through All Categories to find the image that you need. To re-create the category that you deleted, follow the instructions in "Moving Pictures to a New Category" earlier in this chapter.

From Here...

In this chapter, you learned how to place clip art and other types of pictures in presentations. You also may want to explore the following chapters:

- Chapter 9, "Drawing Objects," shows you how to draw and place objects in your slide.

- Chapter 11, "Selecting, Editing, and Enhancing Objects," shows you how to edit and manipulate objects, such as clip art, in PowerPoint.

- Chapter 18, "Using Links to Other Applications," shows you how to take full advantage of PowerPoint's linking and embedding features.

Selecting, Editing, and Enhancing Objects

PowerPoint handles many types of data in a surprisingly generic way. Every data type that you can possibly include in a PowerPoint presentation—charts, drawings, imported pictures, clip art, body text, organizational charts, movies, and sound—is considered to be an object in PowerPoint. With rare exceptions, PowerPoint handles all these data types in similar ways; you manipulate and change the data types in slides in the same way.

This chapter covers the basic mechanics of handling objects in the PowerPoint screen. Specifically, this chapter covers the following topics:

- Selecting, deleting, and moving objects

- Copying and pasting objects

- Rotating and flipping objects

- Applying background colors, patterns, and shading to objects

- Layering and grouping objects

Understanding Placeholders

You became acquainted with the term *placeholder* in chapters 4 and 5. A placeholder reserves space in a slide for a specific type of object. Most object types in a PowerPoint slide are contained in placeholders, which are the main tools that you use to manipulate PowerPoint objects.

PowerPoint uses seven types of placeholders, which are described in the following table.

III

Drawing

Placeholder Type	Description
Graph	Contains charts created in Microsoft Graph
Organizational Chart	Contains charts created in Microsoft's OrgChart application
Table	Contains tables created in Microsoft Word
Body Text	Contains body text for slides edited directly in PowerPoint
Title	Contains slide title text
Object	Contains various types of embedded and linked objects, such as sounds, movie clips, imported pictures, and Excel worksheets

Figure 11.1 shows an AutoLayout slide that contains three types of place-holders.

Fig. 11.1
Placeholders are
the default objects
in AutoLayout.

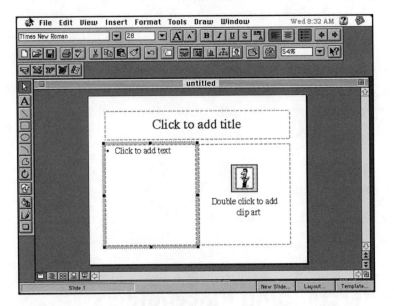

Manipulating Objects

Placeholders are not objects themselves, but they are capable of containing objects of various kinds.

When a placeholder or object is selected, PowerPoint displays around it eight small boxes called *handles* and a selection box (also called a *bounding box*).

Many features described in this chapter require the use of the two drawing toolbars in the standard toolbar set of PowerPoint 4. To place the Drawing and Drawing+ toolbars on the PowerPoint screen (if they are not already on-screen), follow these steps:

1. Open the View menu and choose Toolbars. The Toolbars dialog box appears.

2. Click the Drawing and Drawing+ check boxes in the Toolbars list.

3. Choose OK. The Drawing and Drawing+ toolbars appear on the PowerPoint screen. You can drag them to a more convenient place, if necessary.

Selecting Multiple Objects

Selecting a single object is as simple as clicking it. You can select multiple objects in several ways. Display the slide that contains the objects that you want to select, and then use one of the following methods:

- Click the Selection tool, and then drag the mouse diagonally across the displayed slide from one corner to the other, drawing a box around the objects that you want to select. This procedure is called *marqueeing* or *drawing a marquee*. (Dragging horizontally and then vertically may have the same effect but takes a little more time.)

  All the objects in the slide that the marquee completely encompasses are selected.

- Hold down the Shift key and click an object. Then, continuing to hold down the Shift key, click successive objects until you have selected all the objects that you want to use.

  Tip
  To select all objects in a slide when you're working in Slide view, press ⌘-A.

- To select all objects in a slide, open the Edit menu and choose Select All, or press ⌘-A.

Copying and Pasting Objects

To copy and paste any object, follow these steps:

1. Select the desired object by clicking it.

2. Open the Edit menu and choose Copy.

3. Display the slide in which you want to paste the copied object.

4. Open the Edit menu and choose Paste. This action pastes a copy of the object into the current slide.

Tip
You also can press
⌘-C to copy a
selected object.

Tip
You also can press
⌘-V to paste a
copied object.

The Edit menu also contains the Paste Special command. When you choose this command, the Paste Special dialog box appears (see fig. 11.2).

In the Paste As list, select the object type to be pasted into the slide. If the selected object is a graphic, chart, or imported picture, you can paste it either as an object or as a simple picture. If the object is of a specific type that is generated in another program, that specific object type appears in the Paste As list.

If you paste the object as a plain object, it retains all the typical properties of an object of its type, which could be a PowerPoint object (such as a title text object), a chunk of body text, or just about anything else.

Fig. 11.2
The Paste Special
dialog box lists the
paste options.

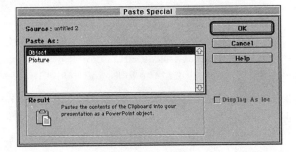

If the object is a bitmap Paintbrush picture, you can paste it into the slide as an object. To edit the object, double-click the picture; Paintbrush launches, and you can make changes in the picture.

If you paste the object as a picture, the pasted item is placed in the slide as a simple bitmap. You cannot double-click such an object to edit it.

The Paste As list includes any object type that your system supports—for example, a chart created in Microsoft Graph, an OrgChart, a Word table, an Excel datasheet, or other data imported from another program. If the object is a simple PowerPoint object, such as a title or body text from a slide, you see only the Object and Picture options in the Paste As list. Although you can paste a text object or title into a slide, doing so is not a good idea, because the text or title becomes much harder to manipulate.

You can display the pasted object as an icon by choosing the Display as Icon option.

Rotating and Flipping Drawn and Text Objects

PowerPoint 4 enables you to rotate text objects, such as titles and body text, as well as objects drawn in the PowerPoint screen. Objects such as imported pictures, sound-file objects, movie clips, and charts cannot be directly rotated because they were created in other programs.

◀ See "Rotating Objects," p. 225

Figure 11.3 shows three types of objects that can be rotated in a PowerPoint slide.

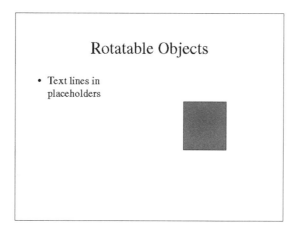

Fig. 11.3
All text and graphic objects created in PowerPoint can be rotated.

Whether you are rotating text bullets, titles, or graphic objects, the procedure for rotating is the same. Follow these steps:

1. Click the object that you want to rotate.

2. Click the Free Rotate button in PowerPoint's Drawing toolbar. The mouse pointer changes its shape to a pair of arrows circling each other. In addition, the selected object now has four handles—one at each corner—instead of eight, and the status bar at the bottom of the PowerPoint screen reads Position the mouse pointer over any corner handle.

3. Place the mouse pointer on one of the four handles. The mouse pointer changes to a four-arrow pointer, and the status bar reads Drag to rotate the selection; press Shift key to constrain angle.

4. Click and drag to rotate the selected object. As you drag, the message in the status bar changes to Rotated by X degree(s). (X is the number of degrees by which the object has been rotated.)

III

Drawing

Tip
To rotate the object in 45-degree increments, hold down the Shift key while you drag the object.

5. When you finish rotating the object, click the Free Rotate button again or click an empty part of the slide.

> **Note**
>
> You can rotate more than one object at a time. Simply hold down the Shift key, select the objects that you want to rotate, and click the Free Rotate button. Then click a handle of any selected object and drag the object. All selected objects are rotated at the same angle.

Moving and Aligning Objects

Objects are moved according to their type and depending on whether they have colors, patterns, or shading fills.

To move text and nontext objects, follow these steps:

1. Click the edge of the text object. Its selection box appears.

2. To move a text object or any other object that has a fill applied to it, click and drag the object.

   To move a nontext object (such as a chart object, clip-art placeholder, or other placeholder that has no fill), click and drag the edge of the object.

> **Note**
>
> When you select a rotated object, it returns to its original position. While the object is selected, you can move, format, or edit it. When you deselect or move the object, it reverts to the rotated position.

◀ See "Aligning Objects," p. 229 Placeholders and objects can be aligned in a slide in many ways: by their bottom edges, tops, left sides, or right sides. If you have two objects that you can't seem to get lined up properly or just want to align them quickly, follow these steps:

1. Select the objects that you want to align.

2. Open the Draw menu and choose Align to display a cascading menu (see fig. 11.4).

3. Choose one of the following alignment options:

- *Lefts* aligns objects by their left sides.

- *Centers* aligns objects by their centers.

- *Rights* aligns objects by their right sides.

- *Tops* aligns objects by their top edges.

- *Middles* aligns objects by their middles.

- *Bottoms* aligns objects by their bottom edges.

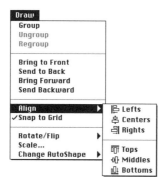

Fig. 11.4
Align options are a
fast way to make
multiple objects
line up.

Resizing Objects

You can resize most types of objects in two ways: proportionally or randomly.
Resizing is most effective with placeholders that can hold objects such as
imported pictures, clip art, charts, and multimedia data (such as movie clips).
Clicking and dragging a corner handle of any of those placeholders automatically resizes the object proportionally if the object already is inside the placeholder. The object (and the placeholder that contains it) retains its shape
regardless of its size. Holding down the Shift key while resizing an object has
no effect on the resizing process.

Some object types—such as imported pictures, movie clips, and charts created
in Microsoft Graph—can be resized only proportionally. Other object types,
such as clip-art placeholders, can be resized in any way that you can move
the mouse.

Resizing Placeholders Proportionally

You can resize empty placeholders of any kind proportionally by holding
down the Shift key while you drag the mouse. This method retains the default shape of the placeholder (usually a square or rectangle) but shrinks or
enlarges it, depending on the direction in which the mouse is moved.

III

Drawing

Resizing Placeholders Randomly

To resize an empty placeholder randomly, click and drag a handle. You then can reshape and resize the placeholder at will.

Resizing an empty placeholder at random does not affect the quality or proportions of an inserted object, such as a bitmap picture or clip-art object. This procedure merely affects the size of the object when it is inserted into the placeholder.

Deleting Objects

Deleting objects can be a two-step process. First, you must delete the contents of the placeholder (the actual object); then, if you want, you can delete the placeholder.

To delete an object, follow these steps:

1. Click the border of the object that you want to delete.

2. Open the Edit menu and choose Clear, or press the Delete key. The object contents are deleted, and the placeholder that contained the object appears, selected for deletion.

3. To remove the placeholder, open the Edit menu and choose Clear or Cut, or press the Delete key.

> **Note**
>
> If the object that you are deleting is an object drawn with PowerPoint's drawing tools, which don't use placeholders, press the Delete key to remove the drawn object.

Enhancing Placeholders and Objects

You can use PowerPoint 4's drawing tools to enhance object placeholders in much the same way that you enhance the objects themselves. You can add line styles to placeholder borders, add color fills and shading to their backgrounds, and align them for an organized appearance.

You also can apply shadows to placeholders. The colors that are available for placeholder color fills are the same ones that you use for drawings, chart objects, and slide backgrounds.

Framing and Shadowing Object Placeholders

You can apply line weights and styles to the borders of placeholders for clip art, text, titles, and other objects. In addition, you can apply shadows to placeholders to emphasize the objects that they contain.

To apply a line style to an object placeholder, follow these steps:

1. Click the border of the placeholder to select it.

2. Click the Line Style tool in PowerPoint's Drawing+ toolbar. A pop-up menu of line styles and weights appears.

3. Select a line style and line weight. PowerPoint applies your choices to the selected placeholder.

> **Note**
>
> You can combine dashed lines and line styles to a selected placeholder by clicking first the Line Style button and then the Dashed Lines button in the Drawing+ toolbar.

To add a shadow to a placeholder, follow these steps:

1. Click the border of the placeholder to select it.

2. Open the Format menu and choose Shadow. The Shadow dialog box appears (see fig. 11.5).

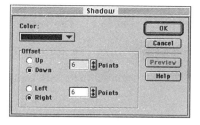

Fig. 11.5
The Shadow dialog box enables you to customize the color and offset of object shadows.

3. Choose any of the following options:

■ *Color.* This pop-up palette offers the basic presentation colors, the No Shadow option, an Embossed shadow style, and the Other Color option (for adding colors from the expanded Other Color table).

III

Drawing

- *Offset.* This option specifies the offset (the amount of space between the shadow and the back of the placeholder or object).

- *Up or Down.* This option sets the shadow to project up or down from the object by a specified number of points.

- *Left or Right.* This option sets the shadow to project left or right from the object by a specified number of points.

4. Choose OK.

Figure 11.6 shows a typical shadowed placeholder.

Fig. 11.6
The shadow effect
in a placeholder
applies to the
placeholder's text
elements.

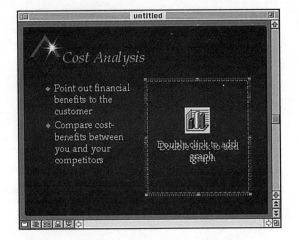

Filling, Shading, and Patterning Objects

You can apply a fill to any placeholder or object—a chart object, an empty placeholder for a piece of clip art, a title, or a body-text object. The fill can be any style, such as a solid color, a shading, or a pattern fill.

You add shading, shadows, patterns, and color fills to placeholders by using the same techniques that you use to add these enhancements to drawn objects. Line styles and color and shading fills can be combined to give a placeholder an attractive appearance, particularly if the placeholder is used for a text object (such as body text or the title).

To add solid, shaded, or pattern fills to placeholder objects, follow these steps:

1. Click the border of the text-object placeholder to select it.

2. Click the Fill Color button in the Drawing+ toolbar. A pop-up color palette and option list appears (see fig. 11.7).

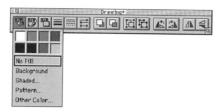

Fig. 11.7
The Drawing+
toolbar enables
you to choose
numerous fill
options for the
selected object.

3. Choose a color from the palette. PowerPoint applies that fill color to the placeholder's background.

4. Click the Fill Color button in the Drawing+ toolbar again. A pop-up menu appears.

5. Choose Shaded. The Shaded Fill dialog box appears (see fig. 11.8).

Fig. 11.8
In this dialog box,
you select a
shading type and
color for the
shading.

6. Choose an option in the Shade Styles section (Vertical is selected by default), and then click OK to close the dialog box.

7. Click the Dashed Lines button in the Drawing+ toolbar. A pop-up menu appears.

8. Choose a line style for the border of the placeholder. PowerPoint applies that line style.

> **Note**
>
> PowerPoint applies shading not to the actual text, but to its placeholder.

III

Drawing

Layering Objects

Object placeholders can be layered and often must be layered a certain way if the objects are to be visible. Every object that you place in a slide occupies its own layer. Whether you have 3 objects in a slide or 100, you can move each object backward or forward to any level.

Figure 11.9 shows a simple example of object-placeholder layering.

Fig. 11.9
Watch objects that overlap so that corners aren't hidden.

To reverse the order of object layering, follow these steps:

1. Click the bottom object to select it.

2. Click the Bring Forward button in the Drawing+ toolbar. PowerPoint brings the selected object forward one layer, as shown in figure 11.10.

3. Click the Bring Forward button again, if necessary, until the object reaches the desired layer.

To move an object back through the layers, follow these steps:

1. Click the top object to select it.

2. Click the Send Backward button in the Drawing+ toolbar. PowerPoint places the object behind the layer directly below it, as shown in figure 11.11.

3. Click the Send Backward button again, if necessary, until the object reaches the desired layer.

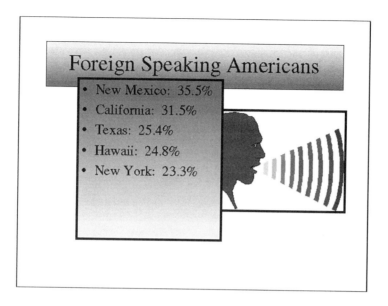

Fig. 11.10
The text object
now covers part of
the clip-art layer.

These layering steps apply to all objects in a PowerPoint slide: placeholders,
the objects that you put in those placeholders, and drawn objects. You can
layer object placeholders. You also can draw objects in PowerPoint and layer
those objects.

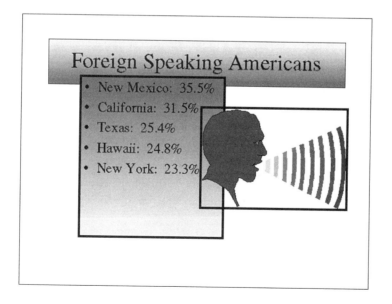

Fig. 11.11
The object can be
returned to its
original layer or
moved farther
back.

III

Drawing

Grouping Objects

You can group placeholders and drawn objects for easier moving and manipulation. Grouping object placeholders works exactly the same way as grouping drawn objects. Follow these steps:

1. Hold down the Shift key and click the objects in the slide that you want to group. (You must select two or more objects.)

2. Open the Draw menu and choose Group. PowerPoint groups the selected objects and displays handles around the area that the selected objects occupy.

Scaling Objects

PowerPoint's Scale feature is an easy and efficient way to resize pictures, charts, movie clips, and other objects in PowerPoint slides. This feature enables you to do several things:

- Resize, by a specific percentage, any selected object (or multiple selected objects)

- Resize an object to an optimum size, based on the screen resolution of your slide show

- Restore a resized picture or object to its original proportions

The Scale feature resizes objects and retains their original proportions; you see no distortion of the object during resizing.

To rescale an object, follow these steps:

1. Select the object(s) that you want to rescale.

2. Open the Draw menu and choose Scale. The Scale dialog box appears.

3. In the Scale To text box, type the percentage by which you want to resize the object or group. To enlarge the object or group, type a number larger than 100; to reduce the object or group, type a number smaller than 100.

4. If you want to make sure that the picture returns to the size that it was when it was imported, choose the Relative to Original Picture Size option. When this option is selected, a scale of 100 means that the picture is resized to its original proportions.

5. If you are creating a slide show, and you want to size the selected object or objects to the best size for the screen when you give the actual presentation, choose the Best Scale for Slide Show option. This option is especially handy for multimedia movie clips.

▶ See "Inserting Video Clips," p. 449

6. To check your scaling changes before closing the dialog box, click the Preview button.

7. When you're satisfied with your scaling choices, choose OK.

Troubleshooting

When I click a title placeholder and try to drag it, it won't move.

You can move placeholders by dragging them by their insides or by their borders. If a placeholder won't move when you drag its interior, the placeholder was placed in your Slide Master and consequently appears in all the slides in your presentation. You must drag such a placeholder by its border to move it.

I'd like to move objects smoothly and make fine adjustments in their positions.

You can do several things. First, open the Draw menu and look at the Snap to Grid menu option. If a check mark appears next to this option, choose the option to turn it off. Second, open the View menu and choose the Ruler and Guides options. The ruler and the guidelines are the tools that you need to place your objects as accurately as possible. After that, adjustments are mostly a matter of your taste.

I resized a picture and accidentally distorted it. How can I fix it?

To fix a distorted picture, select it, and then open the Draw menu and choose Scale to display the Scale dialog box. Choose the Relative to Original Picture Size option, and then choose OK. The picture returns to its original shape. (This process is called restoring the aspect ratio.)

From Here...

You have just completed a major section of this book. The preceding chapters covered many of the tools and basic techniques for working with drawn objects; this chapter wrapped up the process by covering the basic operations for handling and changing object placeholders.

III

Drawing

The next section of this book deals with vastly improved and enhanced features of PowerPoint 4: charting and graphing. Read the following chapters:

- Chapter 12, "Working with Datasheets," describes how to create and edit datasheets in Microsoft Graph.

- Chapter 13, "Creating Basic Charts," discusses how to create, edit, and modify basic chart types and their elements.

- Chapter 14, "Customizing Charts," shows you how to change and customize charts in detail. The chapter also touches on some of the more sophisticated chart types.

- Chapter 17, "Working with Color," discusses PowerPoint's various color palettes and shows you how to use some advanced color and fill techniques for various objects in slides.

- Chapter 19, "Using Advanced Charting Features," discusses chart types and the powerful editing features of Microsoft Graph.

Part IV

Charts

American Numbers

Click to add title

Click to add text

Tip of the Day

Did you know...

You can rotate AutoShapes for more shape options. If text is attached to the shape, it rotates as well.

OK

Next Tip

More Tips...

Help

☒ Show Tips at Startup

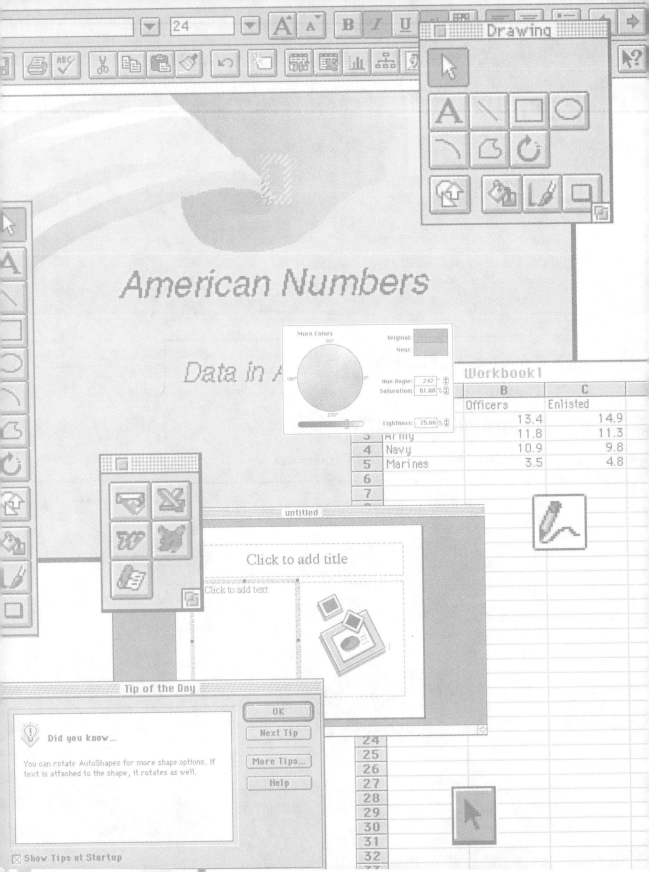

Chapter 12

Working with Datasheets

Charting is one of the key capabilities of PowerPoint 4. Charts are created from rows and columns of numeric data. In PowerPoint, those rows and columns are called a *datasheet*. The process of creating and editing datasheets is the key to effective charting in PowerPoint.

This chapter starts by discussing how datasheets are created and used. Creating datasheets is quite similar to creating tables. Datasheets, however, are used solely to create charts and are not intended for direct display in a slide. Thus, you must begin by starting PowerPoint's Graph program to create a new datasheet and chart or to edit an existing datasheet.

In this chapter, you learn how to do the following things:

- Start PowerPoint's charting feature

- Place data series in rows or columns

- Edit datasheets

- Work with rows and columns

- Format chart data

Understanding PowerPoint's Charting Feature

PowerPoint has undergone a major change in its charting features in version 4. To understand the profound improvement in PowerPoint's charting

▶ See "Under-
standing
Object Linking
and Embed-
ding (OLE),"
p. 396

capabilities, you need to compare the current version of the program with the preceding version.

In PowerPoint 3, charting was performed in a program called Microsoft Graph, a separate program intended to be used in other Microsoft applications, such as PowerPoint and Microsoft Word. In version 3, a technique called object linking and embedding (*OLE*) was used to place charts in PowerPoint slides. Whenever you double-click a chart in PowerPoint 3 to change it, Microsoft Graph pops up in a separate window.

Although PowerPoint 4 is similar to version 3, it is different in subtle but important ways. When you install PowerPoint 4, you also install Microsoft Graph, which uses object linking and embedding to place charts in PowerPoint slides. The major difference is that when you double-click a chart to change or edit it in PowerPoint 4, Graph does not appear in a separate window; instead, it takes over the PowerPoint 4 screen.

The Graph program takes over the screen because PowerPoint and Microsoft Graph use a newer version of object linking and embedding, called OLE 2. If you have Microsoft Word for Macintosh and used it to create tables in Chapter 8, "Working with Tables," you know that Word also takes over the PowerPoint screen.

The new version of Graph bundled with PowerPoint works exactly the same way. You don't see the name Microsoft Graph when you start Graph to create charts for your slides. Graph doesn't look like a separate application at all, but it is, just like Microsoft Word. Accordingly, this chapter (and all other chapters that talk about charting) refers to Microsoft Graph as being a separate program.

Starting the Charting Application

To create a new datasheet and chart, follow these steps:

1. Open the presentation in which you want to embed a new chart object.

2. Display the slide in which you want to insert a chart.

3. Click the Insert Graph button in the PowerPoint toolbar. The Microsoft Graph application program starts. The Microsoft Graph Standard toolbar appears at the top of the PowerPoint screen, and a new datasheet is displayed with a chart object behind it (see fig. 12.1). The PowerPoint menu bar also changes to display a new set of menus.

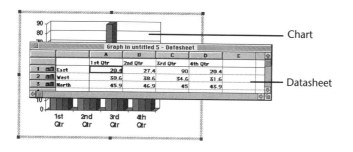

Chart

Datasheet

Fig. 12.1
This figure shows
the default
datasheet and
graph.

> **Note**
>
> You can create a new slide with a chart object embedded in it by clicking the New
> Slide button at the bottom of the PowerPoint screen and then choosing a slide
> template with an embedded chart object. When the slide is created, a column chart
> icon appears in the middle of the chart object, with the caption `Double click to add`
> `chart`.

Graph's Standard toolbar offers buttons that perform many functions.
Buttons that change the appearance of datasheets are available in Graph's
Formatting toolbar, which by default is not displayed. Because you will need
this toolbar later, open the View menu and choose the Toolbars command;
the Toolbars dialog box appears. Click the Formatting check box to place an x
in the check box, and then choose OK. PowerPoint displays the second
toolbar.

Notice that the new datasheet has a set of default values that make up the
sample data displayed. The chart shown just behind it is a default 3-D
column chart. The following sections lead you through the process of editing
the chart and choosing different chart types to reflect changes in your
datasheet.

To modify an existing chart in a slide, follow these steps:

1. Display the slide that contains the chart you want to edit.

2. Double-click the chart object. The Graph toolbar appears. The chart is
   still displayed, and the datasheet from which the chart was created also
   appears, ready to be edited.

In many cases, the datasheet may not appear automatically. If this is the case,
simply click the Datasheet button in the toolbar. The datasheet appears.

Understanding Datasheets

◀ See "Editing Tables," p.198

The process of creating and editing datasheets is quite simple and closely resembles editing tables. The key difference is that datasheets are used only to create charts for display in your presentation. Unlike tables, datasheets are not displayed in slides after you edit them, so you must double-click an existing chart before the associated datasheet appears.

Each rectangle in a datasheet that contains an entry is called a *cell*. Some cells, such as the ones displayed on the top row and the left column of the datasheet shown in figure 12.2, are designed to hold text that is used to label each row and column in the chart. Most other cells hold data values.

In many PowerPoint charts, several categories of data are compared. Each category of data is called a *data series*. In the sample datasheet shown in figure 12.2, the series are labeled East, West, and North. Each series has four values, which are labeled 1st Qtr, 2nd Qtr, 3rd Qtr, and 4th Qtr. The time-period labels are displayed in the top row of the datasheet. Those labels are called a measurement scale or timeline.

Rows and columns are numbered as they are in typical spreadsheet programs. The rows in figure 12.2 are labeled 1 through 3, and the columns are labeled A through D.

Fig. 12.2
Datasheets simplify entering and editing the data for a chart.

Series labels ⟶

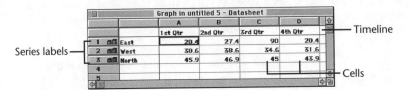

⟶ Timeline

⟶ Cells

Placing Data Series in Rows or Columns

An important aspect of editing charts is understanding where to place data values for the best effect. A data series can be defined as being a single set of values that have a specific relationship to one another. In most charts, data values are placed in rows in the datasheet to create each series. Each successive value represents another entry for the series on the timeline represented in the chart. By default, PowerPoint places data series in rows, as shown in figure 12.3.

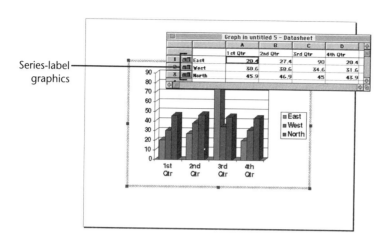

Series-label
graphics

Fig. 12.3
The default style
puts the data series
text in rows.

A small graphic appears next to each row label, indicating the chart type in which each series appears. In figure 12.3, the series-label graphics indicate that 3-D columns are used and show the colors used for each series. Putting the series in rows emphasizes the timeline values (1st Qtr, 2nd Qtr, 3rd Qtr, and 4th Qtr in the figure), each of which compares the figures for East, West, and North for each quarter. Placing the data series in rows creates the best and most workable chart, in most cases. Chapter 13, "Creating Basic Charts," discusses the few exceptions to this rule.

In some cases, however, you may want to emphasize the East, West, and North data sets by using the yearly quarters, rather than the regions, as the data series. The data for each quarter is broken down by columns in the datasheet (with one value from each series for each quarter), so the data series need to be redefined in columns.

Tip
Look at the label graphics to see whether the data series are organized in rows or columns.

To redefine data series in rows as data series in columns, follow these steps:

1. Display the slide that contains the chart you want to change.

2. Double-click the chart to select it and launch Microsoft Graph.

3. Click the Datasheet button in the Graph toolbar to display the datasheet.

4. Click the By Column button in the Graph toolbar.

Notice that the series-label graphics migrate to column labels A through D in the datasheet. This change indicates that the series labels have been transferred to columns. In this example, the series are now the quarters, rather than the regions.

The chart also reflects these changes. The four sets of three columns shown in figure 12.3 become three sets of four columns in figure 12.4. Also notice that the East, West, and North labels appear on the axis at the bottom of the chart, replacing the original quarter labels. The data for each region, rather than the data for each quarter, is broken down in columns in the datasheet.

Fig. 12.4
You can transpose the rows and columns by clicking the By Column button.

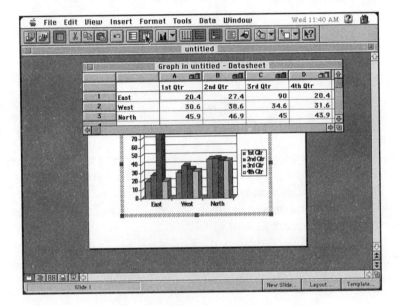

Editing Datasheets

In PowerPoint 4, editing a datasheet is a relatively painless process. PowerPoint's default datasheet offers a set of data series that you can delete or simply type over when you want to enter new values.

When you edit a datasheet, follow these generic rules:

- Use the arrow keys to move from one cell to another.

- To move to the next cell in a row, press the Tab key.

- To remove a cell's contents, select the cell and then press the Delete key.

> **Note**
>
> Pressing the space bar also erases an entry, but it leaves a space-bar character in the datasheet cell.

- When the desired cell is selected, simply type the new value or entry; the old one is overwritten.

To enter new information in the default datasheet, follow these steps:

1. Click the cell labeled 1st Qtr.
2. Type the desired text for the timeline, and then press Tab or the right-arrow key to move to the cell labeled 2nd Qtr. Type the next label.
3. Click the cell labeled East, and type a new series label. Press the down-arrow or Return key to edit or add series labels.
4. To change the data in the table, click cell A1. Then type the new data and press Tab, Return, or the arrow keys to move through the cells, adding more data to the chart.

When you finish entering data, you may have a datasheet that looks similar to the example shown in figure 12.5.

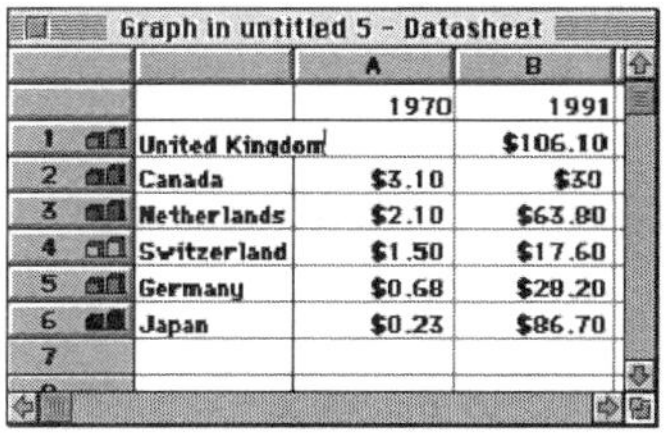
Graph in untitled 5 - Datasheet

		A	B
		1970	1991
1	United Kingdom		$106.10
2	Canada	$3.10	$30
3	Netherlands	$2.10	$63.80
4	Switzerland	$1.50	$17.60
5	Germany	$0.68	$28.20
6	Japan	$0.23	$86.70
7			

Fig. 12.5
The label *United Kingdom* is too long for the cell.

Notice that in the datasheet shown in figure 12.5, the column that contains the series labels is too narrow for the label *United Kingdom*. You learn how to solve this problem in "Changing the Column Width" later in this chapter.

Editing Cells

Editing a cell is quite simple, but keep these rules in mind:

- To edit a cell without overwriting its contents, double-click the cell and then place the insertion point where you want to begin editing.
- To edit and overwrite the contents of a cell, click the cell to select it and then begin typing.

Tip
You can erase a cell entry in many ways. Using the Delete key, however, is a good habit, as well as the quickest way to get the job done.

You may not want to overwrite the contents of a cell to change them. In the example shown in figure 12.5, for example, you could simply change *United Kingdom* to *UK*.

To edit a cell without overwriting its contents, follow these steps:

1. Double-click the cell that contains the text that you want to edit. The insertion point appears in the text. The cell contents, which are highlighted, may seem to pop out and overlap the next cell to the right. (Don't worry; the contents of that cell are not affected.)

2. Click to place the insertion point where you want to begin editing.

3. Edit the text.

> **Note**
>
> When editing a cell, you can use the Delete Forward key (located next to the End key) to remove characters to the right of the insertion point. (Some Mac keyboards do not offer a Delete Forward key.)

Copying Cells

Copying cell contents to another cell is a simple process, but you need to be aware of a subtle trick. In many Macintosh programs, you probably are accustomed to double-clicking a word to select it before you delete, copy, or move it. When you edit datasheets in PowerPoint 4, however, you cannot use that procedure. When you double-click a cell, the contents are highlighted, but the Cut and Paste commands (⌘-C and ⌘-V, respectively) do not work. To copy cell contents to the Clipboard, single-click the desired cell and then use the Copy command.

To copy cell contents to another cell, follow these steps:

1. Click the cell that contains the data you want to copy. A bold border appears around the cell.

2. Open the Edit menu and choose Copy, or press ⌘-C.

3. Click the datasheet cell in which you want to place the copied text.

4. Open the Edit menu and choose Paste, or press ⌘-V.

To use an alternative method of copying a cell's contents, follow these steps:

1. Hold down the Option key and then click the cell that contains the data you want to copy. The Edit shortcut menu appears.

2. Choose the Copy command. PowerPoint copies the cell's contents to the Clipboard, from which you can paste that data into a new cell.

Dragging and Dropping Cells

You can drag and drop a cell's contents to another location in the datasheet. Select the cell, and then click and drag the cell by its border to the new location in the datasheet.

To drag and drop a copy of a cell to a new location while leaving the original cell in place, hold down the Option key while you drag.

Troubleshooting

Even though I double-click a cell value to select it, I can't use any menu commands on it.

For many operations in PowerPoint 4, you cannot double-click a cell to select it; most menu commands that deal with editing and formatting are unavailable. Single-click the cell instead, and the menu commands will be available.

I can't drag and drop a cell.

The drag-and-drop feature may be turned off. To activate this feature, open the Tools menu and choose Options. The Options dialog box appears. Click the Datasheet Options tab, if necessary, to see the datasheet options. If the Cell Drag and Drop option is not selected, click its check box to select it, and then choose OK. You now should be able to use the drag-and-drop feature in your datasheets.

Working with Rows and Columns

Datasheets allow you to edit individual cells and their values. In PowerPoint 4, the process of editing and working with rows and columns of data has been simplified. You can alter each cell in a datasheet; in addition, you can copy and move an entire row or column, several selected rows and columns, or groups of selected cells. You also can select columns, rows, and cells for exclusion from a chart.

Selecting Rows and Columns

Selecting rows and columns for editing and moving is a straightforward process. Datasheets in PowerPoint 4 have a series of 3-D buttons along the top and left sides; each series of buttons represents one column or one row of data. Clicking one of these buttons automatically selects the entire row or column. Buttons that represent rows are marked with numbers; buttons that represent columns are marked with letters.

Use the following techniques to select rows and columns:

- To select an entire row, click the numbered button (1, 2, 3, and so on) to the left of the row that you want to select.

- To select an entire column, click the lettered button (A, B, C, and so on) at the top of the row.

- To select more than one row or column without selecting the entire chart, hold down the Shift key as you click each button.

 When you have selected the row(s) or column(s), open the Edit menu and choose Copy, or press ⌘-C, to copy the contents to the Clipboard.

You also can select a group of cells by clicking and dragging the mouse over all the cells that you want to include in the group. All the selected cells are highlighted; you then can copy and paste them in other places in the datasheet.

Clearing Rows and Columns

As you learned earlier, problems can arise when you edit a datasheet, particularly when you delete rows and columns of data. Simply selecting the cells to be deleted and pressing the Delete key does not work. The easiest way to delete rows or columns is to follow these steps:

1. Select the rows or columns that you want to delete by dragging across the row or column headings.

2. Open the Edit menu and choose Delete, or press ⌘-K.

If you don't select the entire row or column, a dialog box appears, containing options for shifting the cells left or up and for deleting the entire row or column. Pressing ⌘-K is not enough to remove the column; you need to clean up the datasheet and remove the superfluous column space from the chart. Follow these steps:

1. Click the column button at the top of the datasheet for the data that you want to delete.

2. Press the Delete key, or press ⌘-K. The label graphic disappears from the column, and the empty column space disappears from the accompanying chart.

You use the same procedure to remove datasheet rows.

Another quick way to get rid of rows or columns is to Option-click. Follow these steps:

1. Place the mouse pointer (which should be in the shape of a cross) on a row or column button.

2. Hold down the Option key and click the mouse button. The entire column is selected, and the Edit shortcut menu appears.

3. Choose the Cut or Delete command from the Edit shortcut menu. The row or column is deleted.

One limitation of this method is that you cannot Option-click to select more than one cell, column, or row at a time; you can select only a single cell, column, or row.

Inserting New Rows and Columns

If you discover that you need another row or column in your datasheet, adding one is simple. You can use several methods, including the following:

■ To insert a new row above any other row, click the row button (1, 2, 3, and so on) for the row above the place where you want to insert a new one. Then open the Insert menu and choose Cells.

■ To insert a new column to the left of any other column, click the column button for the column before which you want to insert a new one. Then open the Insert menu and choose Cells.

Suppose that you want to add a new row to the top of the datasheet. You need to reset the chart for series in rows and then add the new row. Follow these steps:

1. Click the By Row button in the Graph toolbar. PowerPoint returns the series to the rows in the datasheet.

2. Click the row button to select the entire datasheet row.

3. Open the Insert menu and choose Cells. A new row is inserted above the selected row, which moves down to row 2. You now can add another data series to the chart.

Notice that the chart itself does not yet change or add any space for more columns.

As you enter values in the added row, the chart adjusts to include a fourth column. The new columns in the series are assigned a new color automatically, and the name of the row is added to the legend.

You don't have to select an entire row or column to insert a new one. Follow these steps:

1. Click any cell in the row (except its row number) above which you want to insert a row.

2. Open the Insert menu and choose Cells. The Insert dialog box appears (see fig. 12.6).

Fig. 12.6
The Insert Cells dialog box is available only if the datasheet is open.

3. Choose one of the following options:

   ■ *Shift Cells Right* enables you to shift the selected cell (or cells) to the right by one cell (or column).

   ■ *Shift Cells Down* enables you to shift the selected cell or cells down by one row.

   ■ *Entire Row* inserts an entire row into the datasheet.

   ■ *Entire Column* inserts an entire column into the datasheet.

4. Choose OK.

Dragging and Dropping Rows and Columns

Graph's datasheet editor also enables you to drag and drop cells, groups of cells, rows, and columns. This feature was not included in earlier versions of Microsoft Graph.

To drag and drop one or more rows or columns, follow these steps:

1. Select the cell, row, or column that you want to move to a new location in the datasheet.

2. Click and drag the cell, row, or column to the new location, making sure that you do not overwrite datasheet elements you want to keep. (If you do so accidentally, open the Edit menu and choose Undo Drag and Drop.)

Formatting Chart Data

Datasheets bear a resemblance to conventional worksheets, because chart data can be formatted in a variety of ways. You can apply different fonts to the datasheet to change its appearance. You can change the style of numbers used in the datasheet. You can set the alignment of cell data and adjust column width. With one exception—formatting numbers—these operations do not affect the chart that you are creating with the datasheet; they simply improve the datasheet's readability.

Changing the Numeric Format

Changing the numeric format of the chart is simply a matter of specifying that you want your data values to be in a specific format. Numbering systems are available in a wide variety of formats and can be closely associated with the type of chart that you are trying to create.

Table 12.1 lists the numbering categories available for use in PowerPoint 4.

Table 12.1 Numbering Categories	
Category	**Description**
Accounting	Used in ledger sheets and accounting charts
Currency	Adds currency signs to dollar values
Custom	No default numbers are provided; you create your own numbering system
Date	Provides formatting for various dating standards (MM/DD/YY and others)
Fraction	Used for stock quotes and open-high-low-close stock charts
General	The PowerPoint default; automatically adjusts numbers to the most precise value
Number	Various standard number formats, up to eight figures with commas
Percentage	Attaches percent signs to datasheet values
Scientific	Offers scientific notation for datasheet values
Time	Formatting for various timing standards (HH:MM:SS and others)
Text	Standard Arabic text numbers

Each category has a selection of specialized numbering types. Sometimes, if a number format is too long for the cell that holds the data value, the number is displayed in scientific notation. At other times, if the number is too big to be displayed at all, it is displayed as a series of pound signs (#), in which case the column must be widened to display the data value properly.

Each numbering format affects the actual value in different ways. Table 12.2 shows a partial listing of number, date, and time formats.

Table 12.2 Number Formatting Examples	
Type	**Result**
General	5
0	5
0.00	5.00
#.##0	5
#,##0.00	5.00
$#,##0_);[Red]($#.##0)	$5
$#,##0.00_);($#,##0.00)	$5.00
$#,##0.00_;[Red]$(#,##0.00)	$5.00
0%	500%
0.00%	500.00%
0.00E+00	500E+00
m/d/yy	1/5/94
d-mmm-yy	5-Jan-94
mmm-yy	Jan-94
h:mm AM/PM	12:00 AM
h:mm:ss AM/PM	12:00:00 AM
h:mm	12:00
h:mm:ss	12:00:00
m/d/yy h:mm	1/5/94 12:00

When you change the numeric format in a datasheet, the values displayed on the y-axis (the value-measurement axis) in the accompanying chart change to reflect the new number format.

To change the number format for one cell in a datasheet, follow these steps:

1. Hold down the Ctrl key and then click the cell to select it and display the shortcut menu. This process is called *Ctrl-clicking*.

> **Note**
>
> You also can click the cell to select it and then open the Format menu and choose Number. Don't make the conventional mistake of double-clicking the cell to select it; if you do, the Number command will be unavailable.

2. Open the Format menu and choose Number. The Number Format dialog box appears (see fig. 12.7).

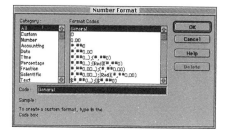

Fig. 12.7
Numbers have a default format. To customize them, use the Number Format dialog box.

3. Select a numbering category, and then choose a numbering format.

> **Note**
>
> Although many number formats look rather complex, you can see their result in the Sample section just below the Category list. The formatting code that you select is displayed in the Code box. You can customize any numbering code in the Code box by deleting or adding formatting characters.

4. Choose OK.

To change the numbering format for all cells in a datasheet, drag the mouse over the desired cells to select them; then Ctrl-click any of the selected cells and choose the Number command from the shortcut menu or open the Format menu and choose Number.

To change the numbering format for a single row or column, click the row or column button to select that row or column; then open the Format menu and choose Number, or Ctrl-click the selected cells and choose Number from the shortcut menu.

As you may have noticed, there are several ways to perform just about any basic operation in a datasheet. Most people are accustomed to using the mouse to pull down menus and choose options. Using the Ctrl-click method is a minor conceptual leap, but this method can save time by cutting the steps required to choose values and formatting options in half.

Changing the Font

Changing the font in a datasheet is simply a cosmetic process to improve the datasheet's appearance. Changing the font in a datasheet does not affect the chart; text elements in a chart must have their fonts changed separately. Selecting datasheet elements and changing their font works much the same way as changing number formats.

PowerPoint 4 supports both TrueType and Adobe fonts for datasheets and charts. You can change the font only for an entire datasheet; you cannot change the font or text formatting (boldface, italics, underlining, and so on) for one cell, row, or column.

To change the fonts displayed in a datasheet, follow these steps:

1. Ctrl-click any cell that contains a datasheet value. The shortcut menu pops up.

2. Choose the Font command to display the Font dialog box.

3. Perform any of the following actions:

    ■ Choose a new font by clicking a name in the Font list.

    ■ Choose a new font style: Bold, Italic, Regular, Bold Italic, or whatever is shown in the list. (Some fonts that you have installed in your system may not have all those options available.)

    ■ Choose a new font size.

    ■ Choose an underline style: Single, Double, or None.

    ■ Change the font color to any color available in the palette.

    ■ Choose any of three effects: Strikethrough, Superscript, or Subscript.

4. When the options are set properly, choose OK.

You also can use the buttons in the Formatting toolbar to add bold, italic, and underline formatting and to change the font and the font size. A pop-up menu in the Formatting toolbar offers quick access to any font that is installed in your system.

Changing the Column Width

In an earlier example, the entry *United Kingdom* in the sample datasheet was too large for the margins of the cell in which it was entered. You can change the column width to display the entire contents of such a cell; you cannot adjust the margins of individual cells.

To adjust the width of a selected column, follow these steps:

1. Click the column button for the column that you want to adjust.

2. Open the Format menu and choose Column Width. The Column Width dialog box appears.

3. Do one of the following things:

   ■ Adjust the width manually by entering a new value.

   ■ Click the Best Fit button for automatic adjustment of the column to the width needed to accommodate the entry.

   ■ Choose the Use Standard Width option to adjust the column to the default width values in the datasheet.

4. Choose OK. The width of the column is adjusted to the size that you specified. Figure 12.8 shows the result of this change.

Tip
To fit the column width to the data automatically, double-click the right border of the label cell above the column, or click and drag the border.

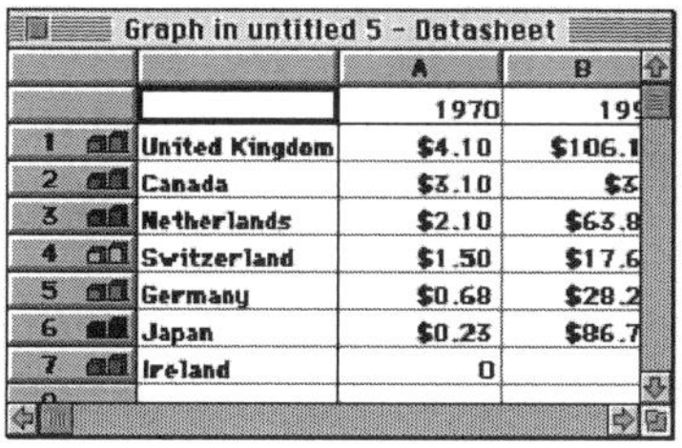

Fig. 12.8
The Best Fit option widens the column to accommodate the longest entry.

Troubleshooting

I can't drag and drop any rows or columns of data.

You're probably trying to click a selected row to drag it. That won't work. Click the row or column button to select the entire row or column; click and drag the margin to move the selected row or column to the desired location on the datasheet; then release the mouse button. Drag and drop works slightly differently in Graph datasheets than it does in other applications. The method also works for individual cells or blocks of cells in a datasheet, except for the method of selection.

I selected a column and used the Font command in the Format menu to change the font of the column, but the entire datasheet font changed. How do I change the font of a single column?

Unfortunately, you can't select different fonts for different columns or cells. The Font command applies to the entire datasheet.

From Here...

Now that you are familiar with working with datasheets and arranging data, you are ready to begin building PowerPoint charts. To learn how to work with charts, refer to the following chapters:

■ Chapter 13, "Creating Basic Charts," builds on what you learned about datasheets in this chapter and takes you through the process of creating bar, column, pie, and other chart types from datasheet values.

■ Chapter 14, "Customizing Charts," shows you how to add special elements and effects to charts.

■ Chapter 19, "Using Advanced Charting Features," offers more information about PowerPoint's powerful chart customization features.

■ Chapter 22, "Customizing PowerPoint," shows you how to add toolbar buttons for many functions that were covered in this chapter.

Chapter 13

Creating Basic Charts

As you learned in Chapter 12, "Working with Datasheets," PowerPoint's charting capabilities have been greatly enhanced and more effectively integrated into the program in version 4. For native PowerPoint 4 use, a dramatically enhanced charting engine offers better color-scheme integration, a wider selection of chart types, greater flexibility in chart formatting, and many other features. Microsoft Graph objects created in PowerPoint 3 still are supported, but any use of PowerPoint 4 quickly reveals the advantages that its charting engine offers over the obsolescent Microsoft Graph program used in PowerPoint 3.

The sophisticated charting options of PowerPoint 4 can help you convey powerful images to your viewers—or, just as easily, confuse them. The key is to make the right choices, to place in the chart only the information that is necessary to illuminate your ideas. In addition to presenting a road map of basic and essential charting features, this chapter offers brief design tips to help you create the most effective charts for your presentations.

In this chapter, you learn to do the following things:

- Create several basic types of charts

- Select chart types for the best effect

- Add and edit various chart elements, such as labels, titles, and other objects

- Change the colors and patterns of various chart elements

- Add a chart to a slide

> **Note**
>
> Throughout this chapter, please bear in mind that Graph is a separate program from PowerPoint. Whenever you use the program to create and modify charts, the Microsoft Graph program takes over the PowerPoint screen and displays its own toolbars. If this issue is a little confusing, please read the first section of Chapter 12, "Working with Datasheets," which offers a more complete description of the basic operation of Microsoft Graph.

Using Chart AutoFormats

Chart AutoFormats create every major predefined chart type that is available in PowerPoint 4. Use the AutoFormat dialog box for high-speed chart selection.

Figure 13.1 shows the AutoFormat dialog box.

Fig. 13.1
Use the chart AutoFormat dialog box to quickly access predefined chart styles.

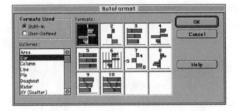

The AutoFormat dialog box is the key to accessing the greatest possible number of chart types. In figure 13.1, for example, 10 types of 2-D bar charts are displayed. Each chart type is displayed in a thumbnail picture, each of which is numbered (1 to 10). Double-clicking any of the thumbnails changes the selected chart to the new format.

To the left of the thumbnails is the Galleries list box, which contains every chart category available in PowerPoint. When you select a different category in this list box, a different set of thumbnails appears.

Table 13.1 lists the AutoFormat chart types.

IV

Charts

Table 13.1	Chart AutoFormat Types	
2-D/3-D	**Galleries Type**	**No. of AutoFormats**
2-D	Area	5
	Bar	10
	Column	10
	Line	10
	Pie	7
	Doughnut	7
	Radar	6
	XY (Scatter)	6
	Combination	6
3-D	Area	8
	Bar	5
	Column	8
	Line	4
	Pie	7
	Surface	4

To choose a chart AutoFormat, perform the following steps:

1. Double-click the chart in the PowerPoint slide to launch Graph. (The process works for an existing chart or for a new one that you just created.)

2. Open the Format menu and choose AutoFormat. The AutoFormat dialog box appears.

3. Select a chart type in the Galleries list. A new set of thumbnails appears in the Formats section.

4. Click the thumbnail that shows the desired chart type.

5. Choose OK.

You can use other methods to choose chart types—for example, you can click the Chart Type button in the Graph toolbar to display a list of 15 basic chart types—but AutoFormats give you the fastest access to the greatest number of options for any chart type.

▶ See "Using
Alternative
Chart Types,"
p. 416

Bear in mind that you are not limited to the charting choices displayed in the AutoFormat thumbnails. The Formats Used buttons (shown as Built-In and User-Defined in fig. 13.1) in the top-left corner of the dialog box offer more opportunities, particularly the User-Defined button. You can create as many custom chart types as you have room for on your hard disk.

Understanding the Elements of a Chart

Chart elements simply are the parts that compose a chart in a slide, such as the legend, title, data series labels, and so on. You can manipulate and format these elements to produce a desired effect. Some chart styles in the AutoFormat dialog box differ from others solely on the basis of certain elements—whether certain text labels are displayed, for example, or whether grid lines are used in the background of a chart. The next several sections discuss those elements and explain how to work with them.

Knowing the basic elements of a chart is the key to effective design and customization. This knowledge will help you when you explore chart creation and modification later in this chapter (and later in this book). Most chart types share the elements and principles described in the following sections.

The various chart elements fall into two categories: those that are common in 2-D charts, and those that are unique to 3-D charts.

Two-Dimensional Chart Elements

Figure 13.2 shows a sample 2-D column chart.

The following list describes the elements shown in figure 13.2.

- *X-axis:* the horizontal axis, which is normally shown on the bottom of the chart. Each series has a single column for each increment along the x-axis.

- *X-axis title:* identifies the x-axis and what each axis label represents. In figure 13.2, the x-axis title is *1993*.

- *X-axis labels:* labels for the increments along the x-axis. The audience uses the labels to determine what data is represented in each bar. In figure 13.2, the x-axis labels are 1st Qtr, 2nd Qtr, and so on.

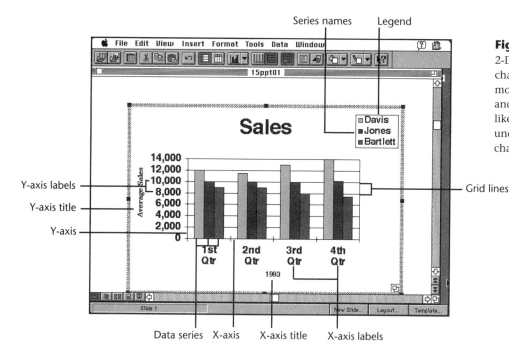

Fig. 13.2
2-D column charts are the most common and, therefore, likely the best-understood charts.

- *Y-axis:* the vertical axis against which the height of each column is measured. The increments and range of the y-axis are directly based on the values in your data. In figure 13.2, the increments of the y-axis are evenly spaced from the bottom to the top of the range in increments of 2,000 from 0 to 14,000.

- *Y-axis title:* identifies the y-axis and what each axis label represents. In figure 13.2, the data values, and hence the columns in the chart, are shown as Average Sales.

- *Y-axis labels:* labels for the increments along the y-axis. The labels on the y-axis in figure 13.2 simply show the values of each increment, from 0 to 14,000. In this example, the viewer compares the height of each column to the axis and labels to learn the approximate average sales.

- *Data series:* a group or set of data defined by a specific criteria, such as all the data values associated with a company. PowerPoint displays all the columns of one series in the same color and relative location in the chart.

- *Legend:* provides information about the data in a chart, including the name for each series and the color for the columns (or bars, or pie slices, or whatever chart type you select). The legend in figure 13.2

Tip
For most purposes, you should use no more than four series in a chart to keep the chart from becoming crowded or cluttered. If you have more than four series, consider using two or more charts.

indicates which series represents each sales person and displays the color for the columns of each series.

- *Series names:* provide information about what the data series represent. The series names are shown in the legend of the chart.

- *Frame:* displays behind the chart and works as a boundary to encompass the columns in the chart. Grid lines can be added to a frame to further identify values.

- *Grid lines:* display on the frame; they extend from each axis across the frame.

- *Tick marks:* show the location of an increment on each chart axis.

Three-Dimensional Chart Elements

The x- and y-axis elements described in the preceding section apply to all charts that you can create in Microsoft PowerPoint. The x- and y-axes define 2-D charts: charts that have no visual depth. Three-dimensional charts, however, have a third axis, called the *z-axis*. The z-axis helps create the depth that defines a 3-D chart.

In many cases, a 3-D chart may not be absolutely necessary, but it can be used to provide attractiveness and impact. In other cases, a 3-D chart offers compelling advantages.

Figure 13.3 shows a sample 3-D column chart.

Fig. 13.3
3-D charts put a little spin on the typical 2-D type.

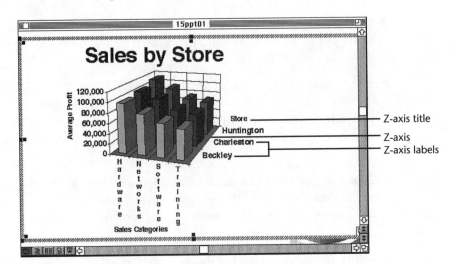

The following list describes the elements that are unique to 3-D charts.

- *Z-axis:* In a 3-D chart, the z-axis is actually the vertical axis—unlike 2-D charts, in which the y-axis is the vertical one. Imagine a 2-D chart pushed over, with the previously vertical y-axis now lying on the "floor." The z-axis is then drawn perpendicular to the plane created by the x- and y-axes. The z-axis lends depth to the chart, and is generally labeled with a series of tick-mark labels, used in turn to measure values.

- *Z-axis title:* identifies the z-axis and what each axis label represents. Figure 13.3 shows that the z-axis title is average profit.

- *Z-axis labels:* labels for the value increments along the z-axis.

> **Note**
>
> In 3-D charts, you normally use the x- and z-axes to provide clues about the data presented in your chart. Most 3-D charts don't provide all three axis titles or enable you to attach labels or increments to them. Adding a title to just one of the axes, however, can provide all the information about the contents of a chart that you need.

- *Object depth:* Object depth is the thickness of the column or other object from the front of the chart to the back. Two-dimensional charts are flat and have no depth.

- *Floor depth:* Floor depth gauges how deep the bottom of the chart is and shows how much room there is between each series.

Choosing the Best Chart Type

Specific chart types represent data in particular ways. You choose the chart type depending on the type of data you are using. This section offers some simple guidelines that may help you make decisions about basic chart types.

Audiences appreciate bar and column charts for their visual simplicity and their common frame of reference: the size or length of horizontal bars that represent the data values. When audience members walk out of the conference room, they tend to remember images of bars and how they differ in size, rather than recall specific values and percentages. The secret to creating effective bar charts is simplicity. Bar charts enable you to compare different items over a period of time. You can use both *bar and column charts*—2-D and 3-D alike—to display more than one series of data. Bar and column charts of both types can have special subtypes, such as stacked bars and stacked columns. Also, 3-D column charts can place each series in its own rank, making direct comparisons of values in each series and still showing the relationship of those values to the other series in the chart.

Pie charts, on the other hand, are most effective when you want to display one set of data values for direct comparison to the whole. A pie chart is effective when, for example, you are conveying information such as a set of companies' market share in a particular business for one year. You can pull a single slice of a pie chart away from the rest to emphasize a value. Using too many values in a pie chart, however, can make a slide crowded and unreadable.

Line charts offer a tremendous number of options. You can display multiple data series in a line chart, and you can display a line chart in 2-D and 3-D format. One specialized line-chart type is the stock chart, otherwise known as an *open-high-low-close* (OHLC) chart. OHLC charts show the progress of a company's stock prices over a certain period. These charts are unique in that they can display a large number of data sets—as anyone who has seen a Dow Jones stock-price history can attest.

Using Column Charts

The options available for column charts reflect major enhancements of the charting features in PowerPoint 4. You can choose among ten 2-D column chart types and eight 3-D chart types. After you enter the chart data in the datasheet, you can begin to create the chart.

> **Note**
>
> Remember that Microsoft Graph is an OLE 2 application that appears in the PowerPoint screen.

To create a 2-D column chart, follow these steps:

1. With a slide presentation open, click the Insert Graph button in the PowerPoint toolbar. Microsoft Graph launches, displaying a datasheet.

2. Enter the chart data in the datasheet.

3. Open the Format menu and choose AutoFormat. The AutoFormat dialog box appears.

4. In the Galleries list box, select Column. A set of 10 thumbnails appears in the Formats section.

5. For a basic 2-D column chart type, click one of these thumbnails to select it. For most simple data sets, either type 1 or 2 will do.

6. Choose OK.

Tip
You can double-click a thumbnail to select it and apply that chart type to the chart.

To create a stacked column chart, follow these steps:

1. With a slide presentation open, click the Insert Graph button in the PowerPoint toolbar. Microsoft Graph launches, displaying a datasheet in which you can enter the statistical data.

2. Enter the data for your chart.

3. Open the Format menu and choose AutoFormat. The AutoFormat dialog box appears.

4. In the Galleries list, select Column. A set of 10 thumbnails appears in the Formats section.

5. Select a stacked column chart type in the set of thumbnails.

6. Choose OK. A stacked column chart appears; it should be similar to the one shown in figure 13.4.

Tip
Place dominant statistics or series values at the bottom of a stacked column chart to draw attention to them. To do this, place the series that contains those numbers in the top row of the datasheet.

In the figure, a legend has been added to provide information about the series values. For more information on adding legends to a chart, see "Adding and Moving a Legend" later in this chapter.

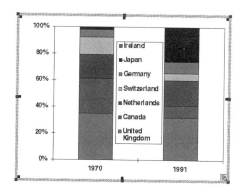

Fig. 13.4
Displaying data in stacked columns compares parts to the whole as well as to each other.

Using Pie Charts

◄ See "Editing Datasheets," p. 268

Pie charts are an exceptional option for comparing parts to the whole. With a pie chart, you can show only one data series.

To create a pie chart, follow these steps:

1. With a PowerPoint presentation open, click the Insert Graph button in the toolbar. Microsoft Graph launches, providing a datasheet that is ready for your pie-chart data.

2. Enter the data in the datasheet.

3. Open the Format menu and choose AutoFormat. The AutoFormat dialog box appears.

4. In the Galleries list, select Pie. A set of seven new thumbnails appears in the Formats section.

5. Select a chart type.

6. Choose OK.

In many cases, the default pie size is too small. You can edit an embedded chart, just as you can all other PowerPoint objects, by changing information in the datasheet or by changing the size of the chart.

To delete items from an embedded chart, follow these steps:

1. Double-click the chart to launch Microsoft Graph.

2. Click the item to select it, and then press the Delete key.

3. Click outside the chart area to place the chart in a slide and return to PowerPoint.

To change the size of an embedded chart, follow these steps:

1. Click anywhere in the chart. Eight handles appear, showing the boundaries of the embedded chart.

2. Click one of the corner handles, and drag the handle out (to make the chart larger) or in (to make the chart smaller).

3. When the chart is the size that you want, release the mouse button.

You can repeat this resizing technique until you're comfortable with the results. Notice that the labels resize with the pie automatically.

To move an embedded chart, follow these steps:

1. Click inside the bounding box of the chart, and hold down the mouse button. Handles appear at the corners and centered between the corners.

2. Drag the bounding box until the chart is where you want it in the slide.

3. Release the mouse button.

Tip
To select a pie chart for moving or resizing, click just outside its contents.

IV

Charts

This section covers only the beginning aspects of working with charts. You can use many other techniques to change and customize charts in PowerPoint 4; those techniques are discussed in later chapters.

Using Bar Charts

Bar charts are commonly used in presentations. In PowerPoint 4, ten 2-D bar charts and five 3-D bar chart types are available. All the default bar-chart types provided in Microsoft Graph are horizontal bars; you do not have to worry about mixing up bars and columns, because column chart types always are vertical.

To select and use a 2-D bar chart, follow these steps:

1. With a PowerPoint presentation open, click the Insert Graph button in the toolbar. Microsoft Graph launches, displaying a datasheet in which you can enter the statistical values for your chart.

2. Enter the data in the datasheet.

3. Open the Format menu and choose AutoFormat. The AutoFormat dialog box appears.

4. In the Galleries list box, select Bar. A set of 10 bar-chart thumbnails appears in the Formats section.

5. Select a bar-chart thumbnail.

6. Choose OK or double-click the thumbnail. The chart appears in the Microsoft Graph window.

7. Click the Datasheet button in the Graph toolbar to display the datasheet (see fig. 13.5). Notice that the label graphics on the row selection buttons have changed to tiny horizontal bars—one set for each data series. This change provides a clue to the way that bar charts work.

Fig. 13.5
Bar charts are an
easy-to-follow
alternative to
column charts.

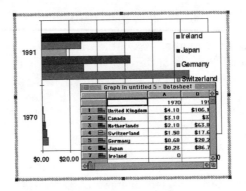

The process of choosing and using a bar chart is much the same as for other types. Nevertheless, bar charts display one significant difference from other chart types: the x- and y-axes are switched. The x-axis labels are displayed at the side of the chart rather than at the bottom, and y-axis labels are displayed along the bottom.

Two-dimensional and 3-D bar charts have a few oddities that set them apart from other chart types, as described in the following list:

■ *X-axis.* In bar charts, PowerPoint displays x-axis values on the vertical axis, shown along the side of the chart. In horizontal bar charts (as in other chart types), the x-axis still can be used to denote categories and series labels.

■ *X-axis title.* The title identifies the x-axis (vertical, in this case) and what each axis label represents.

■ *X-axis labels.* The labels identify the increments along the x-axis. The viewer uses the labels to determine what data is represented in each bar.

In 3-D bar graphs, the y-axis defines the depth of the chart. Y-axis labels are not available for this chart type.

Figure 13.6 shows a 3-D bar chart in which the horizontal-axis labels actually are the z-axis labels.

In a 3-D bar chart, the z-axis is the horizontal axis; in a 2-D bar chart, the y-axis is horizontal. Imagine a 2-D bar chart rotated 90 degrees, with the horizontal y-axis rotating 90 degrees to the "back" while still lying on the "floor." The vertical x-axis rotates in place. The z-axis then is drawn in the position previously occupied by the y-axis, perpendicular to the vertical plane created by the x- and y-axes. This axis generally is labeled with another series of tick-mark labels.

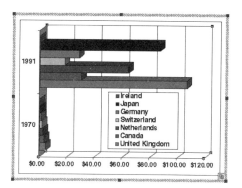

Fig. 13.6
Once again, the
3-D option adds
zip to an otherwise
simplistic chart.

Three-dimensional bar charts are a special case. Notice that the z-axis also provides the scale for measuring the bars in your 3-D bar chart (as it does for every other 3-D chart in this book); it's just "lying down" in this chart type. In 3-D bar charts, the overworked z-axis takes a rest.

Using Other Types of Charts

PowerPoint 4 offers a wide selection of chart types, including 2-D and 3-D line charts, XY scatter charts, combination charts, doughnut charts, 3-D surface charts, and radar charts. A complete breakdown of all chart types and their uses is beyond the scope of this chapter and this book. Brief accounts, however, appear in later chapters.

▶ See "Under-
standing Alter-
native Chart
Types," p. 416

Line charts are an interesting, subtle option that helps your audience draw visual conclusions from your numeric data (see fig. 13.7). Use a line chart to show trends or changes in data over time. A line chart emphasizes the rate of change rather than the amount of change. To show uneven rates of change, try using an XY chart.

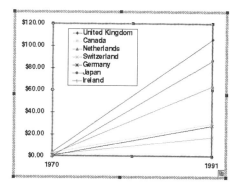

Fig. 13.7
This data doesn't
fare well in a line
chart, but data
that contains
many variables is a
perfect candidate.

XY charts are useful when you have a two or more data series that represent uneven clusters of data, such as with scientific data. XY charts plot their data against two axes—the x- and y-axes—to show the relationship between the data series. You must enter data in pairs to create an XY chart; the first data set determines the point along the x-axis and the second set determines the point along the y-axis.

▶ See "Understanding Alternative Chart Types," p. 416

In Graph, stock charts are not available as a separate AutoFormats option; they are grouped with line charts. Nonetheless, these charts are so unique that they are discussed in detail later in this book. The same is true of combination charts, which may be the most challenging charts that you ever create.

Stock charts require different data sets from other chart types. A high-low-close stock chart, for example, requires three series of data: low stock-price values, high values, and closing values. An open-high-low-close (OHLC) chart requires all those series plus an open series, which represents the price at which the stock opened trading for the given period. The four series can be tremendously long; the Dow Jones stock-price poster that you can see in any stockbroker's office is a classic case of an OHLC chart.

▶ See "Understanding Alternative Chart Types," p. 416

Combination charts, on the other hand, can combine stock-price information with profit, sales, or market-share statistics to provide a compelling picture of the overall fortunes of a company. Generally, combination charts combine columns with lines or columns of OHLC numbers and require two distinct data sets.

Changing Elements of a Chart

Now that you have learned the basics of creating charts, you're ready to examine the chart-customization features of Microsoft Graph. Even the simplest charts contain a few elements; by the time you finish this chapter, you'll be familiar with all of them.

You begin to notice changes in one of the options in Graph's Format menu as you select different chart elements to edit. For example, when you double-click a chart in a slide to start Microsoft Graph, the top item in the Format menu is Selected Chart Area, as shown in figure 13.8.

Fig. 13.8

When an entire chart is selected, the Format menu enables you to edit the object as a whole.

When you click the chart's legend, the menu item changes to Selected Legend, as shown in figure 13.9.

Fig. 13.9
With the legend selected, the Format menu changes.

If you press Esc and then select a chart axis, the menu item changes to Selected Axis, as shown in figure 13.10.

Fig. 13.10
Select an Axis and the command changes on the Format menu.

A pattern is emerging. Whenever you decide to change a chart element and select it, the Format menu changes its top option to accommodate the selected object.

An earlier chapter of this book discussed the structure of PowerPoint's menus. PowerPoint's menu bars are replaced when different parts of the program (such as Graph) are activated; and depending on the items selected in a chart, certain menu items change, too. All the element-changing and formatting features are centralized in the Format menu's dynamic Selected menu option; therefore, you can use this menu's options to customize and add elements to a chart.

Note

Alternatively, you can select chart elements for editing by holding down the Ctrl key while you click chart elements to select them. When you Ctrl-click a chart element (axis, legend, and so on), a shortcut menu appears, offering all the formatting options that you can access and use in other ways. The shortcut-menu options work exactly the same as the options in the Format menu. Over time, you may prefer the mouse method to the menu method.

Selecting Objects in a Chart

You select objects in a chart the same way that you select objects in a PowerPoint slide. You can select almost all the objects in a chart: axes, chart bars, pie slices, columns, lines, and anything else that represents a data series or data value; chart and axis titles; grid lines; and legends. For many types of chart objects, you use similar formatting methods. In every case, you must select a chart object before you can change it.

> **Note**
>
> You can use three mouse methods on chart objects: single-clicking to select them, double-clicking to display formatting options, and Ctrl-clicking to display a shortcut menu.

Figure 13.11 shows a selected 2-D pie chart. The bounding box and handles indicate that the chart is selected. Drag a handle to resize the chart; drag the bounding box to move the chart and its labels.

Fig. 13.11
The handles that surround the chart are used for resizing.

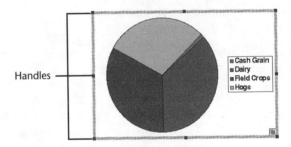

Handles

The following section describes the elements that you can add and change within a chart.

Adding a Title to a Chart

You can add titles to any chart to help explain its contents. Titles are a real help to an audience; therefore, you should always (or almost always) use them.

To add a chart title, follow these steps:

1. Open the PowerPoint presentation that contains the chart to which you want to add a title.

2. Double-click the chart object to select it and to launch Microsoft Graph. The chart object is selected automatically.

3. Open the Insert menu and choose Titles. The Titles dialog box appears, as shown in figure 13.12.

IV

Fig. 13.12
The Titles dialog box enables you to add titles to the chart and the axes.

Charts

Note

The last two options in the Titles dialog box are not available unless you're working with a combination chart. Sometimes, particularly when you're working with a pie chart, only the Chart Title option is available (but because a pie chart has no axes, this stands to reason).

4. Click the Chart Title check box to select that option.

5. Choose OK. The word *Title* appears, selected, in your chart.

6. Type a new title, and then click outside the Title object to deselect the title.

Choosing Axis Line Weights and Tick Marks

You can change axis line weights to emphasize an axis or to enhance its visibility. You also can use tick marks to help the viewer measure values and to separate groups of data values into appropriate categories.

Chart types that normally display axes (bar, column, scatter, XY, combination, and other types) can have different line weights and tick marks. To apply those elements, follow these steps:

1. Click the chart axis to select it. (Make sure that you click the axis; otherwise, you may select another chart element instead.)

2. Open the Format menu and choose Selected Axis. The Format Axis dialog box appears (see fig. 13.13).

3. Click the Patterns tab.

4. To change the line weight of the selected axis, open the Weight pop-up menu and choose an option. (The lightest line weight is at the top of the menu, and the heaviest weight is at the bottom.)

Fig. 13.13
Click the Patterns
tab to see this area
of the Format
dialog box.

5. To assign and place labels for tick marks on the selected axis, choose one of the following options in the Tick-Mark Labels area of the dialog box:

   ■ *None:* displays no tick marks

   ■ *Low:* displays tick-mark labels

   ■ *High:* displays tick-mark labels above the chart

   ■ *Next to Axis:* places labels next to axis (for x-axis, effect is same as for Low)

Tip
Minor tick marks
are an important
measurement tool
for precise values
and are as easy to
select as major tick
marks.

6. In the Tick Mark Type section of the dialog box, choose Major to assign major tick marks or Minor to assign minor tick marks.

7. Choose one of the following tick-mark options:

   ■ *None:* displays no tick marks

   ■ *Inside:* displays tick marks on the inside of the axis

   ■ *Outside:* displays tick marks on the outside of the axis

   ■ *Cross:* displays tick marks that cross the axis

8. Choose OK.

Tick marks are frequently used in good charts. Tick marks are useful for measuring values on the x-axis and for separating categories in the y-axis for easier viewing, as figure 13.14 shows.

Major tick marks are placed at each major increment on the axis scale. If your scale is measured by tens (10, 20, 30, 40, and so on), a major-increment tick mark is placed at each one. Minor tick marks, which are used for more precise value measurements, appear as smaller marks in the axis.

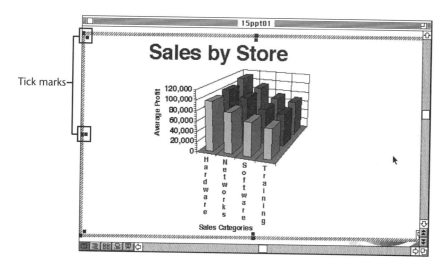

Tick marks—

Fig. 13.14
Tick marks help
the viewer follow
the values.

Choosing Colors and Pattern Fills for Chart Elements

Applying different colors and pattern fills is one of the most important chart-customizing procedures that you can perform. Although PowerPoint's built-in templates automatically assign specific colors to certain chart elements, you are not limited to those predefined choices; you can use any color that is available in the current palette for any chart object. Like many other chart features, color largely is a matter of taste.

Generally, chart objects should have colors that help them stand out from the slide background and the chart background. A *pattern fill* simply is a graphic pattern that is used to fill an object to its borders. Colors work exactly the same way. You can fill objects such as bars, columns, and data markers with distinctive colors that set them apart from other data sets.

PowerPoint 4 offers substantially enhanced color and pattern options, providing support for a 64-color palette in all templates (PowerPoint 3 supported only 16 colors) and easier access to many pattern fills, which you can combine with colors to create custom effects.

To make color and pattern selection easier, follow these general rules:

- You can change the colors (and, usually, the patterns) used to fill any object in a chart.

- Objects generally are split into two parts for color changes: borders and areas. *Borders* are the outside edges of objects; you can apply line weights, colors, and line styles to them. *Areas* are the interiors of objects; you can fill them with colors and patterns.

- Single-clicking any chart object selects it for color and pattern changes.

- When a chart object is selected, the easiest way to make color and pattern changes is to open the Format menu and choose the Selected command. When you do so, the Patterns tab automatically appears, enabling you to make changes.

When you change the color or pattern of one chart object, you can use the same method to change just about anything else in the chart. To change the color of a chart background, for example, follow these steps:

1. Click an area of the chart that is not occupied by any chart object.

2. Open the Format menu and choose Selected Chart Area. The Format Chart Area dialog box appears, with the Patterns tab displayed.

3. In the Border section, choose one of the following options:

   - *Automatic:* applies the default border color

   - *None:* removes the border from display

   - *Custom:* defines custom border settings

   - *Style:* assigns a new line style

   - *Color:* assigns a new line color

   - *Weight:* assigns a new line weight

   - *Shadow:* adds a shadow effect to the border of the object

4. In the Area section, choose one of the following options:

   - *Automatic:* displays the default color automatically

   - *None:* ensures a transparent chart background or object background

   - *Color:* displays the current color palette

   - *Pattern:* displays the color palette and 18 pattern fills

5. To apply your choices, choose OK.

This section touches on the basics of handling color in PowerPoint. You can customize palettes; define, mix, and apply new colors; and manipulate entire color schemes to change the appearance of an entire presentation. Later chapters of this book touch on many subjects associated with color.

Choosing Fonts

You can use Microsoft Graph's Fonts feature to select the type, style, size, color, and background for the fonts used in your chart. Fonts are used in many elements of a chart, including legends, axis labels, chart titles, tick-mark labels, and comments. You can, in fact, apply font changes to any chart element that contains text; you can change those elements individually without affecting other elements of the chart.

To change the fonts in a chart, follow these steps:

1. Select the line, legend, axis, or other chart item that contains the text that you want to change.

2. Open the Format menu and choose Font; alternatively, double-click the text you want to format. The Font tab appears in a dialog box, as shown in figure 13.15. (In the figure, an axis is selected, but it could be almost any other chart element.)

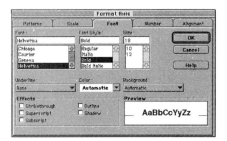

Fig. 13.15
The Font tab enables you to change an object's text attributes.

3. In the Font list, select a new font.

> **Note**
>
> The Preview section changes to reflect each change that you make.

4. In the Font Style list, select a new style: Bold, Italic, Regular, Bold Italic, or whatever else appears in the list. (Not all options may be available for some fonts installed in your system.)

5. Choose a new font size.

6. Choose an underline style.

7. Change the font color to any color available in the palette.

8. Choose an option in the Effects section.

9. To apply your changes, choose OK.

For some chart objects, another option is available in the Font tab: Background. You can set the background color of an axis title, chart title, or the background of the chart itself to be opaque or transparent, or to use a specific color or pattern (or any combination).

Adding and Editing Axis Labels

You add an axis label the same way that you add a chart title. An axis label explains what the axis increments measure and therefore can be extremely helpful in many charts.

Tip

You can attach a label to an axis without selecting the axis first.

To add or edit labels on an axis, follow these steps:

1. With a PowerPoint presentation open, double-click the chart object to launch Microsoft Graph.

2. Open the Insert menu and choose Titles. The Titles dialog box appears.

3. Choose the Value (Y) Axis or Category (X) Axis option. You can choose the X Axis if you are formatting a 3-D chart.

4. Choose OK. The axis label(s) appears, remaining selected in the chart.

Tip

Click and drag a handle to resize or change the shape of a selected axis label.

After you insert an axis label, you can change the font and make other formatting adjustments. You also can rotate an axis label if it interferes with the readability of tick-mark labels (an axis label longer than a few letters may very well do so, particularly on a vertical axis label). Figure 13.16 shows an axis label that needs to be adjusted.

Fig. 13.16

The title *Percentage* doesn't have enough room, but it would fit if it were rotated.

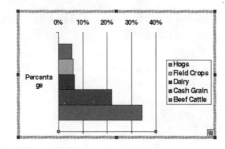

To adjust an axis label, follow these steps:

1. With the axis label selected, open the Format menu and choose Font or double-click the axis label. The Format Axis Title dialog box appears, with the Font tab displayed.

2. Choose a new font type, size, style, color, and background fill. (In this respect, axis labels are treated just like any other objects.)

3. After you choose font options, click the Alignment tab to display the options shown in figure 13.17.

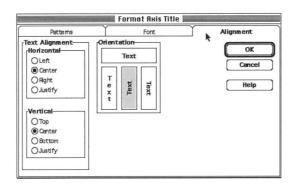

Fig. 13.17
Rotating an axis label often keeps it from running over other objects.

4. To change the alignment of text on the axis, choose among the following options in the Text Alignment section of the dialog box:

   Horizontal options

   ■ *Left:* left-aligns title text in the text box

   ■ *Center:* centers title text in the text box

   ■ *Right:* right-aligns title text in the text box

   ■ *Justify:* justifies title text in the text box

   Vertical options

   ■ *Top:* aligns text at the top of the text box

   ■ *Center:* aligns text midway between the top and the bottom of the text box

   ■ *Bottom:* aligns text at the bottom edge of the text box

   ■ *Justify:* justifies the text in the text box vertically

Tip
You can rotate axis labels—and often should—to avoid overwriting tick-mark labels on an axis.

5. To rotate the axis label by 90 degrees, click one of the four icons in the Orientation area of the dialog box.

   Rotation can be normal or spun 90 degrees to the left or right, or the text can be aligned with each letter below the previous one. In some ways, a rotated axis label can be very attractive on a chart.

6. Choose OK to apply your changes.

Adding and Moving a Legend

The *legend*—the small box in your chart that identifies the data series—appears in the upper-right corner by default, but you can move it to any other location in the chart. You also can resize the legend and change its font.

Many chart types don't add legends automatically; some charts, such as labeled pie charts, really don't require them. Nonetheless, adding a legend is simple. Follow these steps:

1. With a PowerPoint presentation open, double-click the chart that you want to edit. Microsoft Graph launches.

2. Open the Insert menu and choose Legend. PowerPoint automatically inserts a legend into the chart, showing the series names and the colors assigned to them.

You can move the legend to any location in the chart simply by dragging it. Alternatively, you can let Graph find the best location for it. Follow these steps:

1. Select the legend and open the Format menu and choose Selected Legend; alternatively, double-click the legend box. The Format Legend dialog box appears.

2. Click the Placement tab to display the options shown in figure 13.18.

Fig. 13.18
Use this dialog box for a shortcut method of moving and aligning the legend.

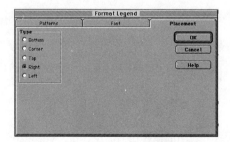

3. Choose one of the Type options: Bottom, Corner, Top, Right, or Left. If you choose Top, for example, PowerPoint formats the legend as a single-row legend and places it above the center of the chart.

4. Choose OK to apply your changes.

> **Note**
>
> If you happen to click inside the legend after it's selected, you see that one of your legend entries is selected. You then can format that entry individually, just as you would any other text element in a chart.

Troubleshooting

My columns or bars are in the wrong order.

It's quite possible that your data series is set up as Series By Column rather than Series By Row. Click the By Row button in Graph's Standard toolbar.

My axis labels still interfere with value labels on the axis.

Despite specifying a rotated axis label or a different font size for the label, you still may experience problems in positioning an axis label properly. To fix the problem, click the area that contains the actual chart (the region between the x- and y-axes of the chart) to select it. Then drag a handle to resize the chart. The label moves along with the chart border. Finally, click the axis label, and then drag the border to move it. (You may have to experiment to get it right.)

I can't add axis titles to my pie chart.

The only title that you can add to a pie chart is a chart title. Pie charts have no axes; therefore, you can't attach titles to them. Most pie-chart types listed in the AutoFormat dialog box automatically attach percentage labels or slice labels, or both, to a chart.

Inserting the Chart into Your Slide

Inserting your completed chart into a slide is simple: just click anywhere outside the selected chart object. The PowerPoint screen reappears, and the chart is embedded in the slide.

From Here...

This chapter covered most of the basic steps in creating charts. In later chapters, you learn about the chart-customization features of PowerPoint 4. For more information, read these chapters:

- Chapter 14, "Customizing Charts," shows you how to add special elements and effects to charts.

- Chapter 19, "Using Advanced Charting Features," offers more information about chart customization and specialized charts.

- Chapter 22, "Customizing PowerPoint," shows you how to add toolbar buttons for many functions that you performed in this chapter.

Chapter 14

Customizing Charts

With the dramatic improvements of PowerPoint 4's charting facilities, Microsoft's presentation software has come of age. When you move beyond the basic chart-creation features to chart customization, color handling, and the creation and saving of custom chart types, more of the true strengths of the PowerPoint 4 upgrade become apparent. This chapter builds on the basic element creation and manipulation features discussed in the preceding chapter.

▶ See "Understanding Alternative Chart Types," p. 416

This chapter covers the following topics:

- Adding arrow pointers and colored polygons to a chart

- Rotating a chart

- Drawing various objects in a chart

- Adding colors, shading, and shadowing to drawn objects

- Understanding and applying color palettes in a chart

Customizing Chart Elements

Besides the numerous chart elements discussed in the preceding chapter, many other elements can add further effects and a custom appearance to any PowerPoint chart. This section shows you how to display additional elements in your chart and how to customize those elements.

Displaying Gridlines

The column chart shown in figure 14.1 could benefit from a few additional touches. One of those touches is gridlines. Gridlines rest inside the vertical plane created by the x- and y-axes in 2-D charts and can provide more accurate measurement of data values. Gridlines can be used in conjunction with tick marks (and perform much the same function) or instead of tick marks.

Fig. 14.1
These columns vary so much in height that discerning the values is difficult.

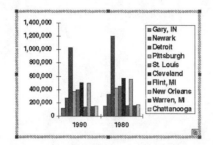

Gridlines bear another similarity to tick marks: you can specify them in major and minor increments. Figure 14.2 shows the chart with major y-axis gridlines added. Notice that the gridlines intersect with the major tick marks on the y-axis.

Fig. 14.2
Gridlines help the reader follow the values.

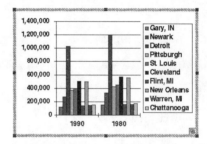

Gridlines are available as an option for most chart types, including bar, column, line, area, and scatter charts in 2-D and 3-D formats.

To add gridlines to a chart, follow these steps:

1. Double-click the chart. The Graph toolbar appears, and the chart is selected.

2. Open the Insert menu and choose Gridlines. The Gridlines dialog box appears, as shown in figure 14.3.

Fig. 14.3
Use the Gridlines dialog box to add major and minor gridlines to any or all axes.

IV

Charts

> **Note**
>
> The four options offered for 2-D chart types are for major and minor gridlines on the x- and y-axes. As you soon will see, going nuts with gridlines usually isn't a good idea; you can render a chart almost unreadable by using too many of them.

3. Choose the options you want.

4. Choose OK. Your chart now may be similar to figure 14.2.

At this point, the gridlines have enhanced the readability of the column chart. The values of each column are much easier to estimate.

To demonstrate how too many gridlines can damage the readability of a chart, try enabling the major and minor x-axis gridlines along with the y-axis minor gridlines, as shown in figure 14.4.

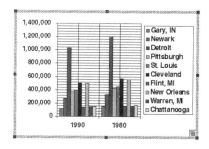

Fig. 14.4
Too many gridlines make the chart cluttered.

The chart still is functional, but viewers are distracted by the additional work of reading a closely packed succession of gridlines to see the columns' values. Also, if you are working with an interlaced monitor or displaying a slide show on a large television screen, the packed horizontal gridlines can be painful to view for both you and your audience.

You can use major and minor gridlines effectively in a chart, however. To do so, you may need to adjust the scale of the gridlines in your chart.

Adjusting Gridline Scales

Changing the gridline scale for a chart is simple. To adjust the y-axis gridline scale for easier reading of minor gridlines, follow these steps:

1. Click any of the y-axis gridlines displayed in the chart (major or minor).

2. Open the Format menu and choose Selected Gridlines. The Format Gridlines dialog box appears, displaying two tabs: Patterns and Scale.

3. Click the Scale tab.

4. Choose among the following scale options for the y-axis gridlines:

   ■ *Minimum:* sets the minimum y-axis data value to appear on the axis

   ■ *Maximum:* sets the maximum y-axis data value to appear on the axis

   ■ *Major Unit:* sets the increment for each major gridline

   ■ *Minor Unit:* sets the increment for each minor gridline

   ■ *Category [X] Axis Crosses At:* sets y-axis placement where axis crosses the chart; the option changes to Floor [XY] Plane if you are using a 3-D chart and specifies the value at which the floor crosses the z-axis.

   ■ *Logarithmic Scale:* useful for charts that have widely ranging values

   ■ *Values in Reverse Order:* switches the Value [Y] axis increments from top to bottom or bottom to top; reverses position of x-axis

   ■ *Category [X] Axis Crosses Maximum Value:* places the x-axis at the highest y-axis value in the chart if the chart is resized; the option changes to Floor [XY] Plane if you are using a 3-D chart.

> **Note**
>
> Although the sheer number of options may be daunting, this dialog box enables you to do a great deal of experimentation with very little trouble. You can use the Format Gridlines dialog box to execute some very sophisticated effects—custom effects that are surprisingly simple to create.

5. Choose OK.

Figure 14.5 shows a chart after options were selected in the Format Gridlines dialog box.

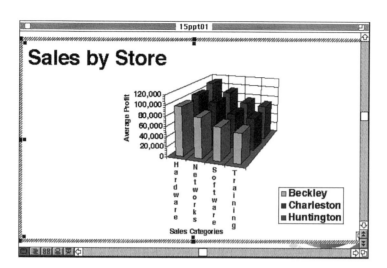

Fig. 14.5
Changing the frequency of tick marks along the y-axis makes a chart more legible.

IV

Charts

As you can see, you can use both major and minor gridlines in designing a powerful chart. When you use proper minor-gridline increments, column values are even easier to estimate; the chart isn't cluttered with distracting horizontal lines.

Displaying Data Labels

At times, it may be helpful to an audience to see explicit data values in your chart. The two preceding sections on gridlines discussed one method of providing accurate visual estimates. If you do not want to provide estimations but do want to display concrete number values in your chart, you can attach data labels to your columns or other types of data markers in your chart.

Note

Data-value labels are applied to one series at a time.

To display actual values as data labels in your chart, follow these steps:

1. Click the data-series marker (a column, bar, or other type of object that represents a data value in the chart) to select it. All markers that belong to the same series are selected.

2. Open the Format menu and choose Selected Data Series. The Format Data Series dialog box appears.

3. Click the Data Labels tab to display the options shown in figure 14.6.

Fig. 14.6
Modify the data-series labels in this dialog box.

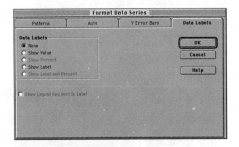

4. Choose one of the following options:

   ■ *Show Value:* displays data values in the chart

   ■ *Show Percent:* available only for pie charts; displays percentages represented by pie slices

   ■ *Show Label:* displays category label

   ■ *Show Label and Percent:* displays value and category label percentage

5. Choose OK.

6. Repeat the process for each data series in your chart.

Tip
You also can double-click any data label to display the Format Data Label dialog box.

If the font for the labels is too big, you can reduce it to a more appropriate size. Click any label for each data series; then open the Format menu and choose Font. The Format Data Label dialog box appears, displaying the Font tab. Choose a new size from the Size list, and then choose OK.

In figure 14.7, gridlines aren't applied because they are unnecessary. Placing the data-value labels above specific columns makes it crystal-clear what the columns represent.

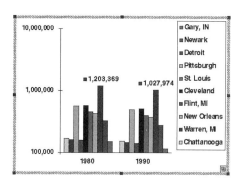

Fig. 14.7
When you use
labels, gridlines are
not necessary.

Adding Arrows

You can use arrows, with various styles of arrowheads, to draw attention to an outstanding or interesting feature of a chart. After you place an arrow in a chart, you must enter the text to be used with the arrow (if desired) in Slide view in PowerPoint.

To add an arrow, follow these steps:

1. With the PowerPoint presentation open, double-click the chart to launch Microsoft Graph.

2. Open the View menu and choose Toolbars. The Toolbars dialog box appears.

3. Choose the Drawing option in the Toolbars list, and then choose OK. This option displays the Drawing toolbar for use while you edit the chart.

4. Click an Arrow tool in the Drawing toolbar. The mouse pointer becomes a crosshair pointer.

5. Click and drag the mouse from the desired starting place of the arrow to the desired end point. When you release the mouse, an arrow appears (see fig. 14.8). The arrowhead is located at the point where you finished drawing the line for the arrow and released the mouse button.

6. Click anywhere outside the chart to embed the chart in the slide.

Fig 14.8
Arrows help point
out important
aspects of a chart.

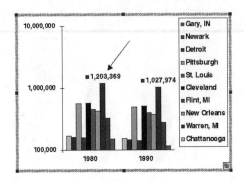

To add a caption to the arrow, follow these steps:

1. Click the Text tool in the PowerPoint Drawing toolbar.

2. Click the slide where you want to place the text caption. A new text object appears.

3. Type the text.

4. Click outside the text object to add the text box to the chart. The result may resemble figure 14.9.

Fig. 14.9
Arrow labels
are added in
PowerPoint,
not Graph.

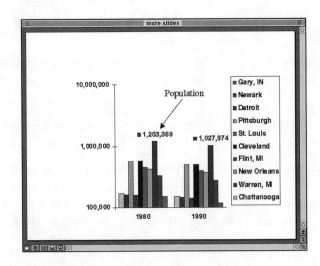

Note

Sometimes, you must leave Graph if you want to add a text caption to an arrow. This is true for any text object that isn't directly related to a series value, for an axis, or for any chart object that has a direct provision for a text label.

Several arrowhead types are available. To change the arrowhead style of an existing arrow, follow these steps:

1. With the PowerPoint presentation open, double-click the embedded chart in the slide. Microsoft Graph launches.

2. Click the arrow to select it.

3. Open the Format menu and choose Selected Object or double-click the arrow. The Format Object dialog box appears.

4. If it isn't already displayed, click the Patterns tab.

You also can change the line style of the arrow; to change the line style, follow these steps:

1. In the Format Object dialog box, Patterns tab, choose from among the following options:

    ■ *Automatic:* displays the default line and arrowhead

    ■ *None:* removes line from display

    ■ *Custom:* defines custom line style, color, and weight settings

    ■ *Style:* assigns a line style

    ■ *Color:* assigns a line color

    ■ *Weight:* assigns a line weight

2. If you want to change the arrowhead style, choose from among the following options:

    ■ *Style:* assigns an arrowhead style

    ■ *Width:* assigns an arrowhead width

    ■ *Length:* assigns an arrowhead length

3. Choose OK.

Tip
You also can double-click the arrow to display the Format Object dialog box, with the Patterns tab displayed.

Tip
The Sample box displays a sample of the arrow style.

IV

Charts

The Properties tab in the Format Object dialog box offers an interesting feature. When the Object Positioning option is selected, the selected object can be resized with the chart automatically, or it can retain its size if the chart is reduced or enlarged. If resizing is turned off (choose the Don't Size with Chart option), the selected arrow or other object stays its original size if the chart is resized. If the Size with Chart option is on, the arrow or other object is resized to retain its aspect ratio to the rest of the chart.

Changing Axes

Chart axes can play a role in customizing a chart's appearance. Earlier in this chapter, you learned how to scale gridlines to different increments. Scaling an axis works very much the same way—which stands to reason, because a gridline scale is identical to that of an axis. In 2-D charts, the x- and y-axis scales have differing properties, just as the x and y gridlines do.

Scaling Axes

Changing the scale for the x-axis involves changing the frequency at which labels appear on the axis. Frequently, you create charts that have more than three categories on the x-axis; sometimes, you can create charts that have more x-axis categories than you display. If, for example, you can create a column chart that depicts the quarterly sales of a firm for the past five years, you can have up to 20 categories on the x-axis. Displaying all the x-axis category labels isn't always necessary, however; the effect can be distracting to the viewer, and the labels may clutter the chart.

To adjust the scale for the x-axis, follow these steps:

1. Click the x-axis to select it.

2. Open the Format menu and choose Selected Axis. The Format Axis dialog box appears.

3. Click the Scale tab to display the options shown in figure 14.10.

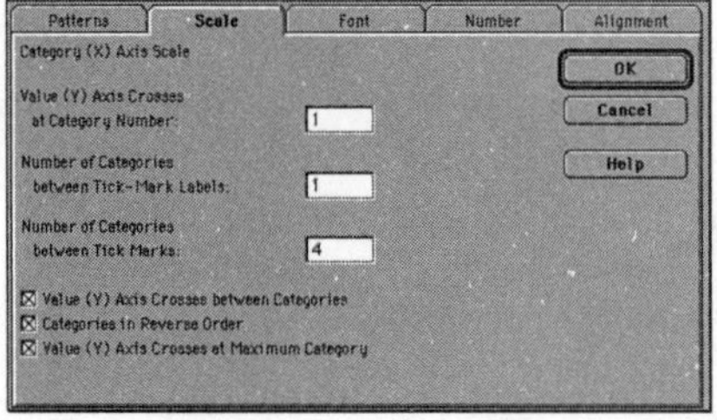

Fig. 14.10
This dialog box controls the settings for the x-axis.

IV

Charts

4. Choose from among the following Scale options for the x-axis:

   ■ *Value [Y] Axis Crosses Category Number:* If this option is set to 1, the y-axis remains in its customary position at the left side of the chart. The y-axis can be placed anywhere else, though, with major effects on the custom appearance of the chart.

   ■ *Number of Categories Between Tick-Mark Labels:* If set to 1, this option means that each x-axis category bears a label in the chart. If this option is set to 2, every other category is labeled; if this option is set to 4, every fourth category is labeled; and so on.

   ■ *Number of Categories Between Tick-Marks:* When this option is set to 1, every category on the x-axis has a tick mark. Setting this option to a higher number (such as 2) means that every other category (first, third, fifth) has a tick-mark assignment in the chart for the x-axis.

   ■ *Value [Y] Axis Crosses Between Categories:* This option enables you to place the y-axis somewhere along the x-axis (the *category axis*), the location of which is determined by the value that you enter in the Value [Y] Axis Crosses at Category Number box.

   ■ *Categories in Reverse Order:* This option sets the categories in reverse order on the x-axis.

   ■ *Value [Y] Axis Crosses at Maximum Category:* This option places the y-axis to cross at the highest value on the x-axis, placing the y-axis on the other side of the chart.

5. When you finish making selections, choose OK.

As you can see, you have a great deal of room for experimentation just in this single area; you can completely alter the appearance of a simple column chart.

Changing the scale for the y-axis (the *value axis*) is somewhat more straight-forward. To change the scale for the y-axis in a 2-D chart, follow these steps:

1. Click the y-axis to select it.

2. Open the Format menu and choose Selected Axis or double-click the y-axis. The Format Axis dialog box appears.

3. Click the Scale tab.

   4. Choose among the following Scale options for the y-axis:

   ■ *Minimum:* sets minimum y-axis value

   ■ *Maximum:* sets maximum y-axis value

   ■ *Major Unit:* sets the increment for each major tick mark

   ■ *Minor Unit:* sets the increment for each minor tick mark

   ■ *Category [X] Axis Crosses At:* places y-axis where x-axis crosses the chart (the default is 0, so the x-axis is placed at the bottom of the chart)

   ■ *Logarithmic Scale:* useful for charts that have widely ranging values

   ■ *Values in Reverse:* switches the axis order increments from top to bottom or bottom to top; reverses position of x-axis

   ■ *Category [X] Axis Crosses at Maximum Value:* places the x-axis at the highest y-axis value in the chart

   5. Choose OK.

As mentioned earlier, you can do many things to charts just by adjusting the axis placement and label values. Although there isn't space in this chapter to do justice to all the possibilities, the examples shown in figures 14.11 and 14.12 illustrate some of the things that you can do to change the appearance of even the simplest column chart.

Fig. 14.11
Using only major gridlines helps keep this chart simple.

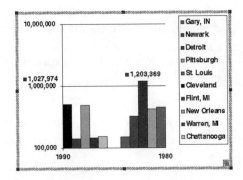

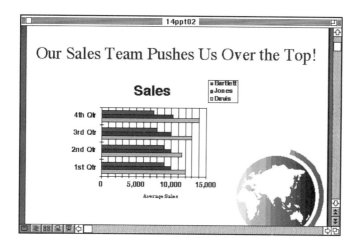

Fig. 14.12
Bar charts are
simple to read—
especially with a
bit of custom-
ization.

Hiding Axes

Hiding axes is a more straightforward process than changing the display style
of axes, which is by itself a way of designing custom charts. In figure 14.13,
the y-axis and its labels have been removed from the chart, creating a pleasing minimalist effect.

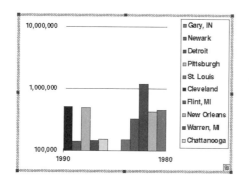

Fig. 14.13
In some charts,
the fewer lines,
the better.

To hide the y-axis, follow these steps:

1. Click the y-axis to select it.

2. Open the Format menu and choose Selected Axis. The Format Axis
   dialog box appears.

3. Click the Patterns tab, if it is not already displayed.

4. To remove the y-axis from the chart display, choose the None option in
   the Axis options list.

5. In the Tick-Mark Labels section, choose None to remove the tick-mark increment labels from the chart.

6. Choose OK.

Troubleshooting

I can't add text captions to my arrows in Graph.

Unfortunately, text captions are not available in the Graph program. After you add your arrow, you must embed the chart in your slide and add the text caption in PowerPoint.

Some series values are too big for my chart.

You may need to use a logarithmic scale, which is a particularly handy feature if your chart displays two widely ranging sets of data—for example, sales figures for the 10–15 age group and for the 60–65 age group. If you set up your age groups on the x-axis, the age groups will be so far apart on the x-axis that they will distort the chart.

You can solve this problem by using an x-axis logarithmic scale. If one set of sales figures is an order of magnitude greater than another (one company has $10 million in sales, whereas another has $150 million, for example), you can apply a logarithmic scale to the y-axis. You can even apply it to both axes, if necessary.

To apply a logarithmic scale to a selected axis, follow these steps:

1. Click the axis that you want to scale.

2. Open the Format menu and choose Selected Axis. The Format Axis dialog box appears.

3. Click the Scale tab.

4. Choose the Logarithmic Scale option.

5. Choose OK.

The selected axis is automatically adjusted to encompass the values. The data markers also are adjusted to be more proportional on the chart, while still providing visual measurement. You can click a gridline (if any gridlines are displayed on the desired axis) to do the same thing.

Colorizing Charts

PowerPoint 4 has broken through some of the most grievous limitations of earlier versions of the program. One of the most important features is color-scheme congruence. In earlier versions of PowerPoint, the Graph program did not support the color palettes in the actual PowerPoint program. This lack of support turned out to be a major design flaw; whenever you needed to edit a chart, Graph would reset the color palette to a set of default colors that had nothing to do with PowerPoint itself. Every time you used Graph, you had to painstakingly reset all the object colors in the chart to the desired values.

In PowerPoint 4, the situation has changed. Despite the fact that Graph still is a separate program, color schemes are completely consistent between Graph and PowerPoint. Graph seamlessly transports the color scheme from the template in PowerPoint to its own charting facilities and conforms to those facilities whenever you create new chart elements. You still can assign your own colors to chart elements of every description, but PowerPoint 4 offers a much more intelligent color-handling system, especially for charts.

This section addresses PowerPoint's enhanced color support, its improved color palettes, its method of assigning specific colors to individual chart elements, and other features.

Understanding the Basic Color Palette

PowerPoint offers an expanded color palette of 56 colors plus 18 patterns. You can apply these colors and patterns to chart objects in borders and fills. The palette enables you to create custom effects and differentiate series values from one another.

▶ See "Studying PowerPoint's Basic Color Palette," p. 370

To display the color palette in Graph, follow these steps:

1. With the chart displayed in Graph, open the Tools menu and choose Options. The Graph Options dialog box appears.

2. Click the Color tab to display the options shown in figure 14.14.

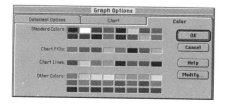

Fig. 14.14
Color and color schemes appear in the Color tab of the Graph Options dialog box.

The 56 colors in the palette are split into four categories:

- *Standard Colors*. This 16-color palette is composed of the 16 basic Macintosh System colors.

- *Chart Fills*. This eight-color palette is used for color fills in data-series markers.

- *Chart Lines*. This eight-color palette is used to color lines and borders in a chart.

- *Other Colors*. This 24-color palette is a group of "leftover" colors that are matched to the current palette and template.

▶ See "Applying Color to Individual Objects," p. 378

Any of the colors in any palette can be used for any other purpose, but the colors assigned to a specific palette generally are the ones that are best suited for their assigned task. Color palettes—and the individual colors in those palettes—also change depending on the template that you use to create your presentation.

▶ See "Tips for Using Colors and Patterns Effectively," p. 459

The Color tab enables you to modify any color or palette. You even can copy a color or palette from one slide to another, allowing for consistency of custom colors in your slides.

Selecting and Coloring Chart Elements

Most chart elements consist of two parts: borders and areas. Objects of these types include the following:

- Data markers, such as columns, bars, and pie slices

- Drawn objects, such as polygons and freeform shapes

- Floors and backgrounds of charts

Choosing color and pattern fills for object areas and changing the line color of borders are generic processes for all object types. You can change the style, color, and weight of borders for a selected object, as well as the pattern and color of an object's area.

To change the color fill for a data series, follow these steps:

1. With the PowerPoint presentation open, double-click the chart to launch Graph.

2. Click any item in the data series that you want to change. Single-clicking one series item selects the entire series.

3. Open the Format menu and choose Selected Data Series. The Format Data Series dialog box appears, displaying the Patterns tab (see fig. 14.15).

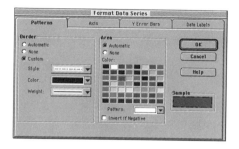

Fig. 14.15
In the Patterns tab, you can apply a border to a data series.

4. If you want, choose one of the following border options:

- *Automatic:* automatically displays border

- *None:* removes border

- *Custom:* defines custom border settings

- *Style:* assigns a border style

- *Color:* assigns a border color

- *Weight:* assigns a border weight

5. To change the color of the selected area, choose among these options:

- *Automatic:* displays the area in the default color

- *None:* removes the area from display (in effect makes the object transparent)

- *Color:* displays a thumbnail of the 56-color palette; click any color to assign it to the selected object

Tip
Choose the Automatic option if you want to clear custom formatting and return to the default settings.

6. If you want to assign a pattern to the selected area, select a pattern from the Pattern pop-up menu. The top-left pattern is a transparent one and shows only the color that already is chosen.

Note

Patterns can change the appearance of the color in a chart.

Tip

If you want to
return to the
original color,
open the Edit
menu and choose
Undo Format
Series, or press
⌘-Z.

7. If you want to invert the pattern assigned in step 6, choose the Invert
   if Negative option. This option inverts the pattern ascribed to a series
   value if that value happens to be a negative number (such as a company
   that lost money during the quarter); otherwise, the option does not
   affect the colors or patterns in the chart.

8. Choose OK. The series should be redrawn in the new color.

Note

When you change the colors of data markers in a series, you can make a distinction
between changing the color of all the markers in a series and changing the color of a
single data marker. This somewhat tricky step involves using the mouse.

Click the series data marker that you want to change; the entire series is selected.
Pause for a second or two, and then click the same data marker; only that marker is
selected this time. Next, open the Format menu and choose Selected Data Point; in
the Format Data Point dialog box that appears, change the border or area of the data
marker, and then choose OK. The functions are the same as for a series.

Rotating Three-Dimensional Charts

Rotating charts is fun; it's also one of the fastest, most flexible ways to customize a 3-D chart. You can use the mouse or the keyboard to rotate a chart.

Although you can rotate only 3-D charts, you can convert 2-D charts to 3-D
for rotation. To change a 2-D chart to a 3-D chart, follow these steps:

1. With the PowerPoint presentation open, double-click the 2-D chart in
   the slide to launch Graph.

2. Open the Format menu and choose AutoFormat. The AutoFormat dialog box appears.

3. In the Galleries list, select 3-D. A set of thumbnails, each representing a
   3-D type, appears in the Formats section.

Tip

You also can
double-click a
thumbnail to
select it and re-
turn to Graph.

4. Choose a chart type.

5. Choose OK.

6. Click outside the chart to embed the chart in the slide. Your 3-D chart
   may resemble the chart shown in figure 14.16.

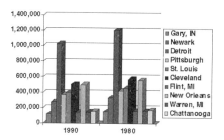

Fig. 14.16
Create a 3-D chart
or change a 2-D
chart to a 3-D
chart.

Assigning Explicit Rotation Values to Charts

The Graph program offers flexible, powerful, and surprisingly simple methods of rotating charts. You can make many adjustments, including viewing elevation, perspective adjustment, and left and right rotation values. The title of this section is no accident.

It's also quite easy (almost too easy) to rotate a chart solely by using the mouse.

To gain a thorough understanding of how 3-D chart rotation works, you start by assigning explicit values to change the view of your 3-D chart.

The basic 3-D column chart is rather attractive to begin with. To enhance it, start by using the keyboard to specify rotation values. Follow these steps:

1. With the PowerPoint presentation open, double-click the chart to launch Graph.

2. Open the Format menu and choose 3-D View. The Format 3-D View dialog box appears, as shown in figure 14.17.

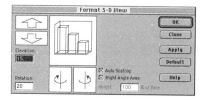

Fig. 14.17
Rotating a 3-D
chart gives it a
new perspective.

3. Choose among the following options for formatting 3-D chart views:

   ■ *Elevation.* This option adjusts the view elevation (like a bird's-eye view). Two arrow buttons are provided to adjust the elevation value by increments of 5; you also can type a number in the Elevation text box.

■ *Rotation.* This option rotates the chart along the horizontal axis. Two arrow buttons adjust the rotation values by increments of 5; you also can type the number that you want.

■ *Auto Scaling.* This option (selected by default) is used in changing a 2-D chart to 3-D; it helps retain the size of the chart when the conversion is made.

■ *Right Angle.* This option (selected by default) controls axis orientation, showing axes at right angles to one another. If this option is disabled, 3-D perspective features are enabled.

■ *Height.* This option adjusts the base and perspective of your 3-D chart. If the Auto Scaling and Right Angle Axes options are selected (xs appear in the check boxes), you cannot make perspective adjustments, and this option is not available. Perspective is used primarily to adjust the height of your chart view.

4. Choose OK. Your chart may resemble figure 14.18.

Fig. 14.18
Rotating the chart puts a different slant on the view.

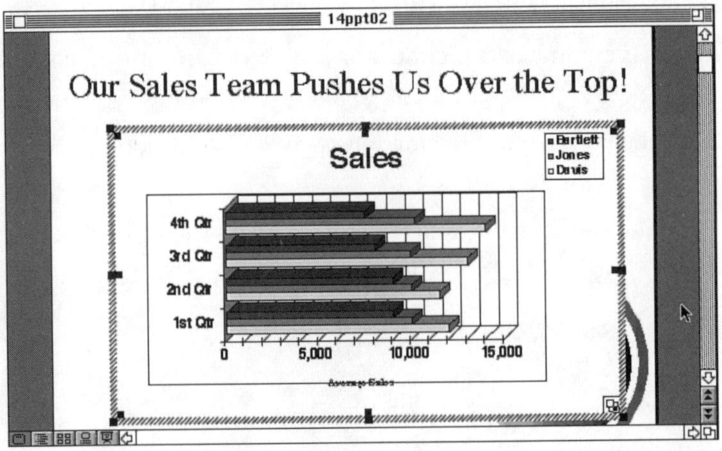

Tip
To restore the rotation defaults for a 3-D chart, click the Default button in the Format 3-D View dialog box and then choose OK.

As you see, even the minor adjustments that you just performed significantly change a chart's appearance. You have plenty of room for experimentation.

Rotating Charts with the Mouse

You also can rotate a 3-D chart with the mouse, with somewhat more unpredictable but amusing and interesting results. You simply drag the mouse, view the results, and undo the action that you just performed if the adjustment isn't to your liking; then you can repeat the process until you get it right.

To rotate a 3-D chart with the mouse, follow these steps:

1. With the PowerPoint presentation open, double-click the chart to launch Graph.

2. Click the intersection of any two axes of the chart (but not any of the data markers).

3. Click any corner handle of the selected chart, and hold down the mouse button. The mouse pointer changes to a small crosshair pointer.

4. Drag the mouse in any direction. The 3-D chart changes to a transparent wire-frame box, which rotates according to the movement of the mouse.

5. Release the mouse button. The chart may resemble figure 14.19.

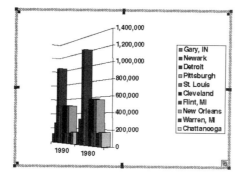

Fig. 14.19
Rotate until you find a view that suits your purposes.

After you wreak havoc on what previously was a perfectly respectable 3-D chart, you can check the actual rotation values by opening the Format menu and choosing 3-D View. The Format 3-D View dialog box appears, with the Elevation and Rotation values reflecting the new position of the chart.

If the result isn't to your liking, open the Edit menu and choose Undo, or press ⌘-Z.

Adjusting for Three-Dimensional Perspective

Three-dimensional perspective is another feature available for those who just cannot leave a perfectly nice 3-D chart alone. Perspective, in combination with rotation and elevation, is another fun adjustment to play around with. Three-dimensional perspective changes the viewing angle from the perspective of the viewer.

To change the 3-D perspective of a chart, follow these steps:

1. With the PowerPoint presentation open, double-click the chart to launch Graph.

2. Open the Format menu and choose 3-D View. The Format 3-D View dialog box appears.

3. To activate the Perspective option, click the Right Angle Axes check box to remove the x. The Perspective feature appears in the dialog box, as shown in figure 14.20.

> **Note**
>
> The Perspective option is not available unless the Right Angle Axes option is deselected.

Fig. 14.20
Adjust Perspective in the Format 3-D View dialog box.

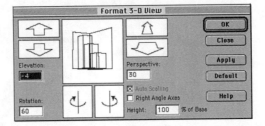

4. Enter a value in the Perspective box.

5. Choose OK.

Perspective has specific (and radical) effects on a 3-D chart. More perspective makes data markers at the back of a chart smaller than the markers at the front of the chart, which creates an impression of distance to the data markers at the back.

Perspective is handy when you have a large number of data values to display, because it creates a better sense of visual proportion. This option also is a remarkably powerful way to customize any 3-D chart type that can benefit from it (3-D pie charts are the exception). The perspective value that you specify is the ratio of the front of the chart to the back of the chart; the value can range from 0 to 100.

IV

Charts

This section and the preceding sections should give you some idea of the possibilities inherent in 3-D chart creation. You used one simple chart type—3-D Columns—to create many special effects.

Drawing Shapes and Graphics in Charts

PowerPoint 4 enables you to draw polygons and freeform shapes directly in a chart. You can draw objects quickly and efficiently, and you do not need any special artistic talent to achieve an attractive effect for your charts and slides.

Artwork frequently used is as a special effect to lend support and aesthetic appeal to a presentation. The new version of Graph offers a special toolbar with buttons that activate all its key drawing functions; this toolbar closely resembles the Drawing toolbar in the PowerPoint program.

Some shape-drawing features are not available in Graph. The AutoShapes toolbar, for example, is not available. Neither can you add clip art from PowerPoint's ClipArt Gallery directly to a chart. The buttons in Graph's Drawing toolbar enable you to draw filled objects, such as ellipses, rectangles, and freehand shapes. You can alter the color fills and borders of these objects as you would those of any other chart objects.

Before you draw shapes and other objects in the chart, you need to make sure that the Drawing toolbar is displayed in Graph. Follow these steps:

1. With Graph displayed, open the View menu and choose Toolbars. The Toolbars dialog box appears.

2. Choose the Drawing option.

3. Choose OK. The Drawing toolbar appears, as shown in figure 14.21.

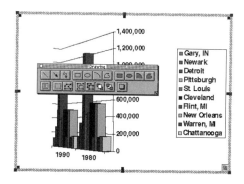

Fig. 14.21

After you display a toolbar, feel free to move it to your active work area.

Tip

To draw a perfect circle, hold down the Shift key while you draw. To draw a perfect square, hold down the Shift key while you draw.

Adding Ellipses, Rectangles, and Freeform Shapes to a Chart

To add an ellipse to a chart, follow these steps:

1. With the PowerPoint presentation open, double-click the chart to launch Graph.

2. With the chart selected, click the Ellipse tool in the Drawing toolbar. The mouse pointer changes to a crosshair pointer.

3. Click and drag to draw the ellipse.

4. Release the mouse button. The ellipse appears in the chart. The object is transparent (without a color or pattern fill), as shown in figure 14.22.

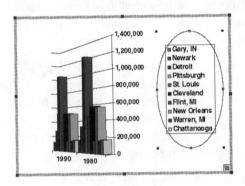

Fig. 14.22

This ellipse can be filled with color or outlined.

Tip

To draw an ellipse with a color fill, click the Filled Ellipse button in the Drawing toolbar and draw the ellipse again.

To add a rectangle to a chart, follow these steps:

1. With the PowerPoint presentation open, double-click the chart to launch Graph.

2. With the chart selected, click the Rectangle tool in the Drawing toolbar. The mouse pointer changes to a crosshair pointer.

3. Click and drag to draw the rectangle.

Tip

To draw a rectangle with a color fill, click the Filled Rectangle button in the Drawing toolbar.

4. Release the mouse button. The rectangle appears in the chart. The object is transparent (without a color or pattern fill).

You can see the pattern that is developing here. Drawing simple graphic objects is the same, whether you draw a filled shape or one without a color or pattern fill.

Drawing freeform polygons is a more complex process, but you can draw them with or without color fills, just as you can the other shapes in the Graph drawing toolbar.

To add a freeform polygon object to a chart, follow these steps:

1. With the PowerPoint presentation open, double-click the chart to launch Graph.

2. With the chart selected, click the Freeform or Filled Freeform tool in the Drawing toolbar. The mouse pointer changes to a crosshair pointer.

3. To draw a freeform object, click and drag the mouse, and then draw (as you would with a pencil) the desired shape.

4. Before you finish drawing the freeform shape, you have to close it. Release the mouse button, and drag the mouse to the point where you began drawing the shape. Click the mouse button again to close the freeform shape that you just drew. (If you omit this procedure, when you release the mouse button, Graph continues adding segments to the shape as you move the mouse over the chart object.)

The freeform object appears in the chart, as shown in figure 14.23.

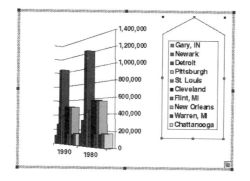

Fig. 14.23
Freeform shapes
are not limited to
regular shapes.

When selected, a freeform shape has a standard set of eight handles that you can use to resize or reshape it. To edit the shape in detail, follow these steps:

1. Select the freeform shape that you want to edit.

2. Click the Reshape button in the Drawing toolbar. Handles appear around the freeform shape (see fig. 14.24).

3. Drag a handle to change the shape.

Fig. 14.24
Drag handles to
change the shape
of a freeform
object.

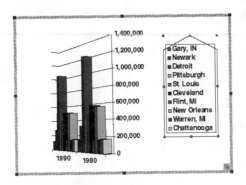

Changing Graphic Colors

Any of the shapes that you draw in a chart can have customized color or
pattern fills. When you draw a filled shape in a chart, you can change its
borders and areas the same way that you change any other chart object.

To change graphic colors in an object, follow these steps:

1. With the chart displayed in Graph, click the object to select it.

2. Open the Format menu and choose Selected Object. The Format Object
   dialog box appears, displaying the Patterns tab.

3. Choose color fill or border line options, as desired. (These options were
   described in detail in the section "Colorizing Charts" earlier in the
   chapter.)

4. Choose OK.

Troubleshooting

Can I apply shading to objects drawn in Graph?

Unfortunately, you can't. Neither can you apply shading to chart backgrounds or
series markers, such as bars or columns. To do so, you have to draw objects directly
in the PowerPoint slide; shading effects can be applied only there, not in Microsoft
Graph. Fortunately, although Graph has a substantial set of drawing tools,
PowerPoint offers a much larger set of drawing features.

*I have too many columns in my 2-D bar chart. Is there a way to fix this problem without
deleting important values from my datasheet?*

Absolutely. You can use a feature called Format (Chart) Group, which appears at the bottom of the Format menu. This dynamic menu option changes according to the chart type that you're dealing with. If you are working with a bar chart, for example, you would open the Format menu and choose Bar Group.

For this example, you change the overlap on a set of bars to save room in your chart. (You can use this process only for 2-D bar charts and 2-D column charts.) Follow these steps:

1. With your chart displayed in Microsoft Graph, open the Format menu and choose Bar Group. The Format Bar Group dialog box appears.

2. Click the Options tab, if it is not already displayed.

3. In the Overlap text box, type a value, such as **30**. This value represents the percentage of the width of each bar that is overlapped by its neighbor.

4. If you want to use gaps to set columns apart, choose a value for the Gap Width option.

5. Choose OK to execute your changes. Your 2-D columns are more closely grouped, resulting in a more spacious chart.

As you can see, there is much more to this feature than described here. Chapter 19 discusses the Format (Chart) Group and Format Chart Type commands in greater detail.

▶ See "Understanding Alternative Chart Types," p. 416

IV

Charts

From Here...

A book could be written just on PowerPoint's chart-customization capabilities. Although this chapter discussed many subjects, it barely scratched the surface. If you want to know more about associated charting and drawing subjects, read the following chapters:

■ Chapter 17, "Working with Color," offers a deeper discussion of basic color mechanics in PowerPoint.

■ Chapter 19, "Using Advanced Charting Features," offers more information about powerful chart-customization features.

■ Chapter 21, "Using Advanced Color, Text, and Drawing Features," discusses in greater detail the processes of changing colors, working with palettes, and using the advanced drawing features of PowerPoint.

Chapter 15

Creating Organizational Charts

Organizational charts are one of the many new features offered in PowerPoint 4. An organizational chart describes the structure of a company, including company officers, assistants, departments, and employees. Organizational charts resemble nothing so much as a computer programmer's flow chart.

OrgChart is a separate application that is bundled with PowerPoint 4. This application enables you to create organizational charts as graphical objects, which can be embedded in a slide and then cut and pasted to any slide in your presentation.

In this chapter, you learn the following things:

- The basic components of an organizational chart

- How to create and embed an organizational chart

- How to edit and change relationships in an organizational chart

- How to change the colors in an organizational chart

Understanding the Elements of an Organizational Chart

Organizational charts are quite straightforward: they basically consist of an organization tree of a company or department. OrgChart, however, offers many tools for creating organizational charts that can confuse the user. When you launch the OrgChart program for the first time, your screen looks like figure 15.1.

Fig. 15.1

A typical organizational chart, although fully editable, looks like this by default.

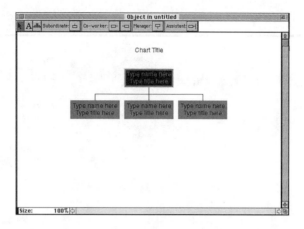

OrgChart is an application in its own right, and you can use it to create charts of remarkable complexity. You can customize any element of an organizational chart by applying different box and line styles and color fills; you also can add boxes of various kinds.

A toolbar at the top of the OrgChart window offers the buttons listed in the following table.

Table 15.1	OrgChart Toolbar Buttons	
Button	**Button Name**	**Description**
	Selection	Enables you to reactivate the arrow mouse pointer after you click another button in the toolbar
	Text	Enables you to type captions and notes anywhere in the chart window
	Reduce/Enlarge	Enables you to take a closer look at any box or section of a chart

Note

OrgChart offers three levels of magnification: Size to Window (⌘-I), 50% of Actual (⌘-J), and Actual Size (⌘-K). Pressing the appropriate shortcut key activates the desired magnification level.

	Subordinate	Enables you to insert a new subordinate box into the chart and attach it to a superior's box

Button	Button Name	Description
	Co-Worker Before	Enables you to attach another box for a worker at the same level in the organization to the left of the original box
	Co-Worker After	Enables you to attach another box for a worker at the same level in the organization to the right of the original box
	Manager	Enables you to insert a manager box above an employee box
	Assistant	Enables you to attach an assistant box to that of a manager or other employee box in the chart
	Perpendicular Line	Enables you to draw a straight line at 90 degrees, across or up and down
	Diagonal Line	Enables you to draw a line at any angle
	Connecting Line	Enables you to draw dashed lines between boxes in a chart to show special relationships
	Rectangle	Enables you to draw filled boxes for special entries in a chart (drawn boxes default to the same style as the boxes in the basic template)

Figure 15.2 shows a very basic organizational chart that contains several important elements.

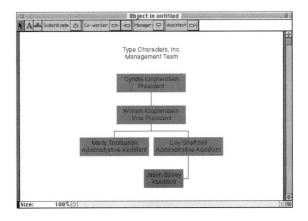

Fig. 15.2
Organizational charts are made up of manager, subordinate, co-worker, and assistant boxes.

Although figure 15.2 is a very simple organizational chart, it combines enough elements to convey the flavor and functionality of the OrgChart application. The highest level, president, is at the top of the chart. Connected to the president is the vice president, which divides into two boxes, each containing an administrative assistant. Finally, one assistant is listed at the bottom of the chart.

Creating an Organizational Chart

Tip
With any slide displayed, click the Insert OrgChart button in the toolbar to launch OrgChart and create an organizational chart.

You start by creating a new slide from an AutoLayout that contains an OrgChart object. To create an organizational chart, follow these steps:

1. With a PowerPoint presentation open on-screen, open the Insert menu and choose New Slide. The New Slide dialog box appears, displaying the AutoLayouts.

2. Choose the AutoLayout titled OrgChart. The new slide is displayed in PowerPoint (see fig. 15.3).

Fig. 15.3
The AutoLayout for organizational charts also has a placeholder for a slide title.

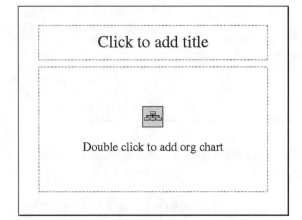

3. Double-click the OrgChart object in the slide. The OrgChart application launches, displaying a chart template.

> **Caution**
>
> When the OrgChart program appears, it is in its own window. A crucial difference between OrgChart and Microsoft Graph is that OrgChart is an OLE 1 application. This means that when you finish editing the organizational chart, you must open the File menu and choose Update to place the chart in the PowerPoint slide.

Editing an Organizational Chart

After you create an organization chart, you can start editing it. When you finish the chart and place it in a PowerPoint presentation, you still can edit the chart, but you need to return to OrgChart to make the changes.

Editing the Chart Title

To edit the title of an organizational chart, simply highlight the text and type the new text. The placeholder title is replaced by the characters that you type.

Adding Boxes to a Chart

To add boxes to an organizational chart, follow these steps:

1. To add a higher manager box to the chart, click the Manager button in the OrgChart toolbar.

2. Click the Manager box in the template to select it. The box is highlighted, and the mouse pointer changes to a small box called the Manager cursor (see fig. 15.4).

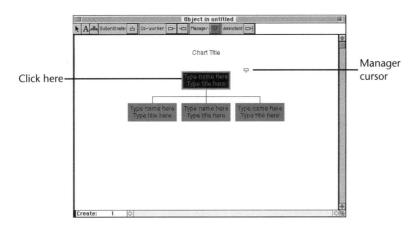

Fig. 15.4
The shape of the mouse pointer changes to reflect the selection.

3. Click inside the highlighted box. A new box is added on top, as shown in figure 15.5.

Note

The new box is highlighted, indicating that it is selected. When a box is highlighted, you can edit its text contents or attach another box to it.

Fig. 15.5
A manager box
always is added
above a selected
box.

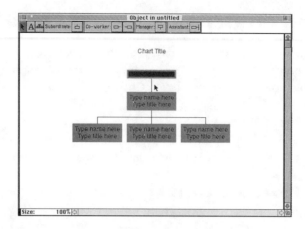

To add an assistant box, follow these steps:

1. Click an existing box in the chart to select it.

2. Click the Assistant button in the OrgChart toolbar. The mouse pointer changes shape again.

3. Click the previously selected box. An assistant box appears below it, as shown in figure 15.6.

Fig. 15.6
The mouse pointer
changes shape to
become an
assistant box.

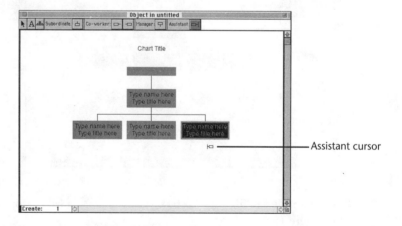

Now that you have added boxes, you're ready to edit the text entries for each box.

> **Note**
>
> Don't be fooled by the tiny sizes of boxes. When you select a box to type text in it, the box expands to accommodate the text.

Editing Organizational-Chart Boxes

You can enter up to four lines of information in each box of an organizational chart. Boxes automatically expand to accept the text that is entered.

To edit a box, follow these steps:

1. Double-click the box. The box expands, as shown in figure 15.7.

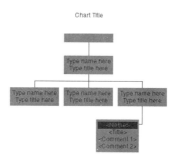

Fig. 15.7
An active box expands to accommodate the width and depth of the text.

2. Type a name in the <Name> line.

3. Press the down-arrow key to move to the next line (<Title>). You can also include any notes or remarks in the <Comment 1> and <Comment 2> lines, if you want.

4. Type the appropriate title for this employee.

5. Click outside the box that you just edited. The result may resemble figure 15.8.

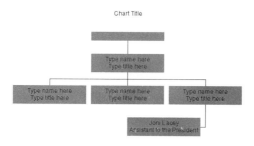

Fig. 15.8
Boxes expand to accommodate the longest line of text.

Changing the Color of Boxes and Backgrounds

Any box can be changed to reflect the special status of its occupant. You can change both the color of the box and the background. To do so, follow these steps:

1. Click the box for which you want to change the color. The box is high-lighted.

2. Open the Boxes menu and choose Box Color. A pop-up menu of 16 color choices appears, as shown in figure 15.9.

Fig. 15.9
Choose a background color from the Box Color pop-up menu.

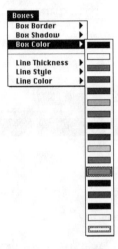

3. Choose a color that stands out against the default blue background.

4. Click outside the box that you just changed.

5. To change the OrgChart background color, open the Chart menu and choose Background Color. Another pop-up menu of 16 color choices appears, as shown in figure 15.10.

Fig. 15.10
You also can change the color of the chart's background.

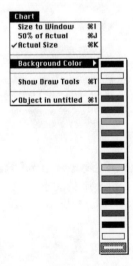

6. Choose a color that suits your taste.

Keep in mind that the background color that you choose in the OrgChart program affects the appearance of the chart in the PowerPoint slide, just like a chart created in Microsoft Graph. Choose your background color carefully so that it doesn't clash with the existing presentation's color scheme. You can eliminate the background color, making the chart background transparent, by choosing the None option from the Background Color menu.

Working with the Chart Levels

When you choose to work with parts of an organizational chart, you have access to a remarkably flexible set of options. OrgChart elements are denoted by the type of employees they represent and by specific sections of a more complex chart.

When you want to make changes to all the boxes in a certain level or levels of an organizational chart, you can use various selection options. In OrgChart, you can execute a normal Select All command by pressing ⌘-A, but that's just one of many options for selecting the chart levels.

To see the other options for selecting chart levels, open the Edit menu and choose Select; then choose one of the following options from the pop-up menu:

- *All:* selects all chart elements.

- *All Assistants:* selects all assistant OrgChart boxes. Assistants is a separate box type.

- *All Co-Managers:* selects all equivalent-level manager boxes.

- *All Managers:* selects all manager OrgChart boxes.

- *All Non-Managers:* selects all non-manager OrgChart boxes. Non-manager types include assistants and subordinates, both of which have specific boxes assigned to them.

- *Group:* selects a group of boxes.

- *Branch:* selects a branch of the chart.

- *Lowest Level:* selects the entire lowest level of the chart.

- *Connecting Lines:* selects all connecting lines in the chart.

Tip

You also can press ⌘-A to select all elements in an organizational chart, ⌘-G to select a group of boxes, and ⌘-B to select a branch.

You can select more than one box in a chart by holding down the Shift key while you click boxes.

Menu options such as All Managers, All Non-Managers, All Assistants, and Connecting Lines are exceptionally handy when you want to set those specific types of boxes apart, apply a different color to them, change their font formatting, or split them to another chart.

Changing the Chart's Style

OrgChart offers an innovative feature that enables you to rearrange charts yet retain their essential structure and relationships. This feature—the Styles menu—is unique to OrgChart. The menu combines the attributes of a pop-up menu with the qualities of a toolbar, as figure 15.11 shows.

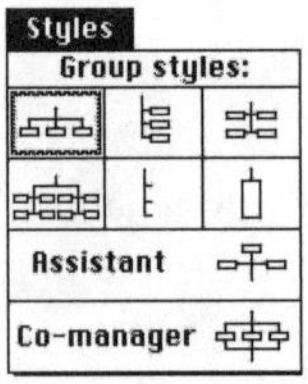

Fig. 15.11
The Styles menu is a combination of a menu and a toolbar.

Changing Styles

Three categories of styles are available. The Group Styles are six chart arrangements that you can apply to the entire chart. Clicking any of the six Group Styles buttons when the entire chart is selected rearranges the chart in a different style.

Selecting any box in a chart and then clicking the Assistant style button changes the selected box to the assistant style, which is denoted by a right-angled connecting line.

To adjust the style for an entire chart, follow these steps:

1. Open the Edit menu and choose Select; then choose All Boxes.

2. Open the Styles menu and choose one of the six Group Styles options.

Creating a New Level

Some levels cannot be selected at one time. In these cases, you may need to create a new level in your organization chart that allows you to group certain boxes.

To create a new level in the organizational chart, follow these steps:

1. Hold down the Shift key and click the boxes for which you want to establish a relationship.

2. Open the Styles menu and choose Assistant or Co-Manager. The organizational chart's connecting lines change to accommodate your selection and may resemble the example shown in figure 15.12. In this example, a co-manager level has been created.

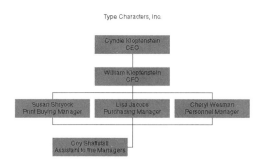

Fig. 15.12
The three managers were made true co-managers.

Notice that the three boxes are connected at the top and the bottom. The box styles were changed to create a single compact unit, as shown by the connecting lines at the bottom as well as at the top; these lines imply that the three are at exactly the same level in the corporate hierarchy. (Also notice that as a result, the assistant boxes have been moved to a position in which they are shared by all co-manager boxes.) Now the selected boxes are true co-managers or co-assistants and can be selected as such.

Adding Elements to a Chart with Drawing Tools

As noted earlier in this chapter, OrgChart offers a few drawing tools to help you add elements to a chart. To display the drawing tools, choose the Chart menu and Show Draw Tools. The four drawing tools appear in the toolbar.

The Perpendicular Line button is used for one purpose: to draw horizontal or vertical lines. Regardless of the position of the mouse, this button enables you to draw a straight line in a vertical or horizontal direction.

OrgChart's Diagonal Line button enables you to draw a straight diagonal line or to create a polygon shape, such as a diamond. Clicking this button and dragging the mouse between boxes or groups draws the diagonal line.

The Connecting Line button enables you to draw dashed connecting lines between any two boxes in a chart, adding angles where necessary. For example, the CEO may have a special working relationship with the Marketing V.P., who may report directly to him for various business purposes, bypassing the normal chain of command.

To draw a connecting line to show this relationship, follow these steps:

1. Click the Connecting Line button.

2. From the edge of the first box you want to connect, drag the mouse to the edge of the second box you want to connect. OrgChart draws a dotted connecting line between the two boxes, as shown in figure 15.13.

Fig. 15.13
Create extra connecting lines to show special relationships on the chart.

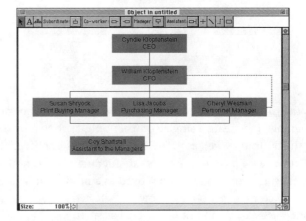

Embedding an Organizational Chart

The OrgChart program, unlike Microsoft Graph, is an OLE 1 application. The OrgChart toolbar and menus do not appear directly in the PowerPoint window; the OrgChart program appears in its own window. After you finish creating your chart, therefore, you must embed it in your slide.

To embed an organizational chart in a slide, open the File menu and choose Update (*Filename*). (*Filename*) is the name of the PowerPoint 4 file in which your OrgChart object is to be updated. Updating is the step in which the chart is actually embedded in the presentation. If the chart is the way you want it, you must perform this step after you create it, or the chart will not appear in your presentation.

IV

Charts

> **Note**
>
> Updating is not the same as leaving the program. You can update the chart in the presentation and remain in the OrgChart program.

After updating the chart, if you want to return to the presentation, open the File menu and choose Quit and Return to (*Filename*).

After you update the organizational chart in your slide and close the OrgChart program, you may discover that you need to edit the chart. To do so, simply double-click the organizational chart in your PowerPoint slide. The OrgChart program reappears on-screen, displaying the chart for editing.

Troubleshooting

When I double-click the organizational chart in my slide, the OrgChart program doesn't start.

Two different problems may have occurred. First, you may already have OrgChart running, with the chart that you tried to open already displayed. A tip-off: if the chart that you clicked in your slide is dimmed, it's already displayed in the OrgChart program. You can't reopen an organizational chart if it's already being edited in the OrgChart program. The second problem is that the OrgChart program may be corrupted or missing from your system. Use the PowerPoint setup program to reinstall OrgChart.

How can I add two or more subordinates to a single box in a chart?

Click the Subordinate button, and then click the box to which you want to add a subordinate. Click the Subordinate button again, and click the same box to which you added the first subordinate. A second subordinate box is added. You can add as many subordinates as you need.

Bear in mind that this chapter does not present a comprehensive discussion of the OrgChart program. Organizational-chart styles can be very flexible; you should handle them carefully to avoid confusing your viewers.

From Here...

The four chapters in this section covered the basics of charting in the PowerPoint 4 package. The next few chapters cover other major subjects, including the following:

■ Chapter 16, "Printing and Other Kinds of Output," discusses how to print your presentation in monochrome and color output; how to produce overhead transparencies and slides; how to use the Genigraphics slide-production service; and how to print notes pages, handouts, and outlines.

■ Chapter 17, "Working with Color," provides a more detailed discussion of basic color mechanics in PowerPoint.

■ Chapter 19, "Using Advanced Charting Features," offers more information about powerful chart-customization features.

Part V

Output and Color

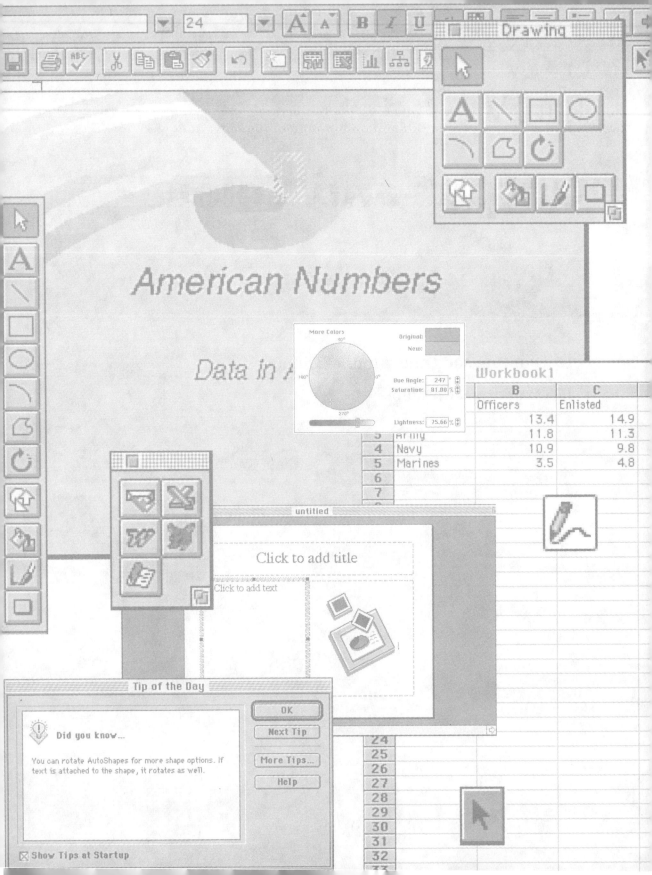

Chapter 16

Printing and Other Kinds of Output

With PowerPoint, you can produce a variety of presentation media. The simplest and cheapest output method, requiring no special equipment other than your printer, is printing your slides on paper. You also can print your outline, speaker's notes, and audience handouts on paper.

For a more professional-looking presentation, consider producing overhead transparencies, a computer slide show, or 35mm slides.

In this chapter, you learn how to do the following:

- Set up your slides

- Print your slides and supporting materials

- Send your slides to Genigraphics Corporation for quick processing

- Create and run a slide show

- View slide shows with the PowerPoint Viewer

Choosing an Output Medium

Following are some guidelines for deciding what kind of output is best for you:

- *Overheads.* If you have a laser or inkjet printer, you can load it with transparencies that are specially made for printers, such as 3M Scotch

Laser Printer Transparencies or 3M Inkjet Printer Transparencies (for Hewlett Packard DeskJets). You print on these transparencies as though they were paper. The result is a set of quality transparencies that you can project by using an overhead projector.

- *Slide show.* A slide show is an electronic presentation that uses your computer to show the slide presentation on-screen. You can use a variety of special effects, such as timings, transitions, and builds. To display your slide show, you can use a desktop computer, but only for a small audience of (at most) three or four people. For a larger audience, you need a *projection panel*—a transparent color computer display designed to fit on top of an overhead projector.

- *35mm slides.* If you can fully darken the room in which you will give your presentation, you can show the presentation in slide format. Create colorful 35mm slides by using a desktop film recorder or by sending your PowerPoint file to a service bureau capable of processing slides. Using 35mm slides is the best choice for a large audience, because you can project the slides on a large screen and the details remain clear. Be forewarned, however: you will need ample lead time. If any of the slides don't turn out or contain mistakes, you have to reshoot them and have them developed again.

You also can print to paper through a laser printer to create handouts or a flip-board presentation. This section describes various ways to output your presentation.

Printing to Genigraphics

PowerPoint comes with the printer driver and software that you need to send your PowerPoint files to Genigraphics Corporation. Genigraphics Corporation is a graphics service bureau that can transform your PowerPoint presentation into 35mm slides, 8-by-10-inch color transparencies, or 8-by-10-inch color prints. You can send your presentation to Genigraphics on disk by mail or, if you have a modem, upload your presentation using the GraphicsLink software provided with PowerPoint. You learn more about GraphicsLink later in this chapter.

When you install PowerPoint, the Genigraphics driver installs, as well. If the Genigraphics driver is not listed in Chooser, run the PowerPoint setup and choose to install the driver.

Outputting to a Printer

PowerPoint uses the default printer—the selected printer in Chooser—as the output device. Naturally, you can change the printer if you have a different printer attached and the appropriate software loaded. Use the Chooser to select a different printer.

You can choose a printer that will produce the output you want, as follows:

- If you plan to send your PowerPoint presentation to a graphics service bureau, choose the printer driver that the bureau prefers. You may need to drag the printer description file (PDF) into the System Folder, if it is not there already.

- If you plan to print your PowerPoint presentation at a different location, using a better printer (such as a laser printer), choose that printer's driver.

Setting up Your Slides

The next step in the output process is to set up your slides by using the Slide Setup command (File menu). This option enables you to identify your output medium (paper, on-screen slide show, or 35mm slides), as well as the orientation (portrait or landscape) of slides, notes, handouts, and outlines.

> **Note**
>
> If you are planning to produce on-screen slides or 35mm slides, size your slides for the output medium that you will use for your final presentation. Should you want to print drafts on paper, PowerPoint can temporarily scale the print output so that it fits on your printer's paper.

To set up your slides, follow these steps:

1. Open the presentation that you want to set up.

2. Open the File menu and choose Slide Setup. The Slide Setup dialog box appears (see fig. 16.1).

Output and Color

Fig. 16.1

Stop by the Slide
Setup dialog box
before you print.

Tip

To print overhead
transparencies,
choose Letter or
A4 in the Slides
Sized For pop-up
menu, and choose
Portrait orienta-
tion for your
slides.

3. In the Slides Sized For pop-up menu, choose the output medium that you plan to use—letter or A4 paper, on-screen slides, 35mm slides, or custom.

Each option presets width, height, and orientation settings, which are listed in the following table. The sizes are not actual but rather used for proportional purposes; slides, for example, are set to a 2:3 aspect ratio and the service bureau reduces them.

Option	Width	Height	Orientation
Letter paper	10 in.	7.5 in.	Landscape
A4 paper	10.83 in.	7.5 in.	Landscape
On-screen slides	10 in.	7.5 in.	Landscape
35mm slides	11.25 in.	7.5 in.	Landscape

Tip

You can choose
one orientation
for slides and
another for notes,
handouts, and
outlines.

4. If you want, change the orientation.

> **Note**
>
> In landscape orientation, the image is wider than it is tall. In portrait orienta-
> tion, the image is taller than it is wide.

The default settings—Landscape for slides and Portrait for notes, hand-outs, and outlines—are good choices for almost all purposes, with one exception. For overhead transparencies, you should choose Letter or A4 paper and then choose Portrait orientation.

5. If you want, change the width and height by clicking the arrows next to the Width and Height boxes or typing a number. If you make a change, the Slides Sized For box automatically displays the Custom option.

6. If you want to start slide numbering with a number other than 1, click the arrow button next to the Number Slides From box, or type the number.

> **Note**
>
> Numbers do not appear in slides unless you insert them by opening the Insert menu and choosing Page Number. An easy way to add page numbers is to use the Pick a Look Wizard.

7. To confirm your choices, choose OK.

The choices that you make in the Slide Setup dialog box affect only the presentation that is open when you choose the Slide Setup command.

> **Note**
>
> If you change the size or orientation of a presentation that you have already created, PowerPoint adjusts the layout of each slide to produce the best possible balance. You should review each slide individually to make sure that it still looks good. You may need to adjust the position of charts and text boxes.

Printing Slides, Notes, Outlines, and Handouts

After you select your printer and set up your slides, printing with PowerPoint is simple. Open the File menu and choose Print, or press ⌘-P; the Print dialog box appears. Choose options such as the number of copies or the range of slides to be printed; then choose OK.

To print slides, outlines, notes, or handouts, follow these steps:

1. If necessary, open your presentation and set up your slides.

2. If you want to print overhead transparencies, load your printer's paper tray with laser transparencies.

3. Open the File menu and choose Print, or press ⌘-P. The Print dialog box appears (see fig. 16.2). The Print dialog box varies, depending on the print driver selected in the Chooser.

Tip

If you're planning to print an outline, use Outline view to arrange it the way you want it to print.

V

Output and Color

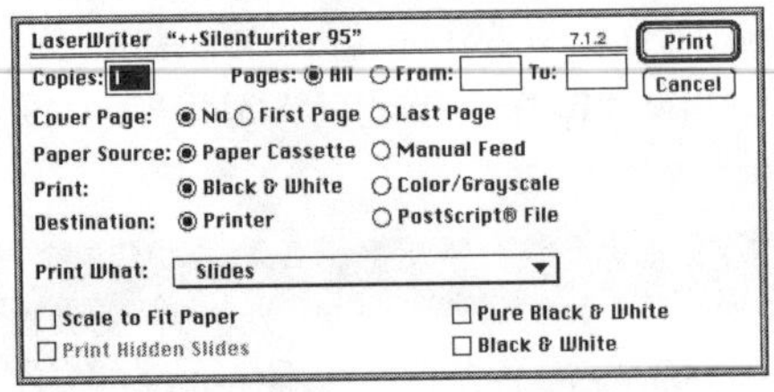

Fig. 16.2

The Print dialog box enables you to print slides, support material, or both.

> **Caution**
>
> If you have a laser printer, do not use heat-sensitive transparencies that are designed to be used with heat-transfer copiers. These transparencies will melt inside your printer and destroy the mechanism. Make sure that you get the transparencies from a box labeled *Laser Printer Transparencies*. If you are not sure where a transparency came from, don't use it.

4. From the Print What pop-up menu, choose the presentation component that you want to print.

▶ See "Setting Transition Styles and Transition Timing," p. 445

You can choose Slides, Notes Pages, Handouts (2 Slides Per Page), Handouts (3 Slides Per Page), Handouts (6 Slides Per Page), and Outline View. If you incorporated builds into your presentation, you see two additional options: Slides (With Builds) and Slides (Without Builds). The Slides (With Builds) option prints one page for each step of the build; the Slides (Without Builds) option prints just one page that shows all the build items.

> **Note**
>
> If you are printing handouts, the 3-slides-per-page option is a good choice. The slides are large enough to be easily legible, and one side of the page has space for notes.

Tip

Choose Current Slide to print the slide that currently is displayed.

5. If you want to print more than one copy, type a number in the Copies box.

6. If you want to print only a portion of your presentation, make a choice in the Pages section.

7. If you have hidden some of the slides in your presentation but want to print them, choose the Print Hidden Slides option.

8. If you are printing a draft, choose the Black & White option to print your slides quickly in black and white (with the exception of pictures, which are printed in grays). Choose Pure Black & White to print all components of your slides, including pictures, in black and white.

9. If you are printing draft copies of an on-screen or 35mm slide presentation, choose the Scale to Fit Paper option.

10. Choose OK.

Troubleshooting

I just printed my slides on my black-and-white printer, but they look dark and muddy and didn't photocopy very well.

Try choosing the Black & White or Pure Black & White option in the Print dialog box. These options remove color fills, which are replaced by white. The Black & White option turns all text to black and replaces all color fills with white, but it uses grayscale printing for some objects (such as decorative borders and clip art). The Pure Black & White option doesn't print any grays except for pictures.

I want to make a quick printout of my slides so that my assistant can double-check them. However, it's taking too long to print them. Isn't there a Draft printing option?

The reason why it is taking so long for your slides to print is that your printer is trying to capture the colors you used by printing gray tones. To speed printing, choose the Black & White or Pure Black & White option in the Print dialog box.

V

Output and Color

Printing to a File

If you plan to send your PowerPoint presentation to a graphics service bureau, you may be asked to print the presentation to a file.

When you do, you should choose the printer driver that the service bureau prefers. If you plan to send your file to Genigraphics Corporation, for example, you use the Genigraphics printer driver.

To print to a PostScript (EPS) file, follow these steps:

1. If necessary, open your presentation and set up your slides.

2. Open the Chooser, select the desired printer, and then close the Chooser by clicking its close box.

3. Open the File menu and choose Print, or press ⌘-P. The Print dialog box appears.

4. From the Print What pop-up menu, choose Slides, if necessary.

5. If you want to print only some of your slides, choose an option in the Pages section.

6. Choose the Print to File option. If this box is dimmed, the driver that you chose is preset to print to a file.

7. Choose Save. A Create File dialog box appears.

8. In the Create File text box, type a name for the PostScript file that you are creating.

9. Choose Save to confirm the output-file name and start printing the file.

If you chose the Genigraphics printer driver, you see the Genigraphics Driver Job Instructions dialog box (see fig. 16.3) instead of the Create File dialog box. The Genigraphics dialog box enables you to specify the output that you want (35mm slides with plastic mounts, 35mm slides with glass mounts, 8- by 10-inch overheads, and/or 8- by 10-inch color prints). You can order as many of these elements as you like, and you can order more than one set of each. You also specify how you will send the file (via modem or floppy disk). If you choose the modem option, you use the GraphicsLink software to upload your file to the nearest Genigraphics service center.

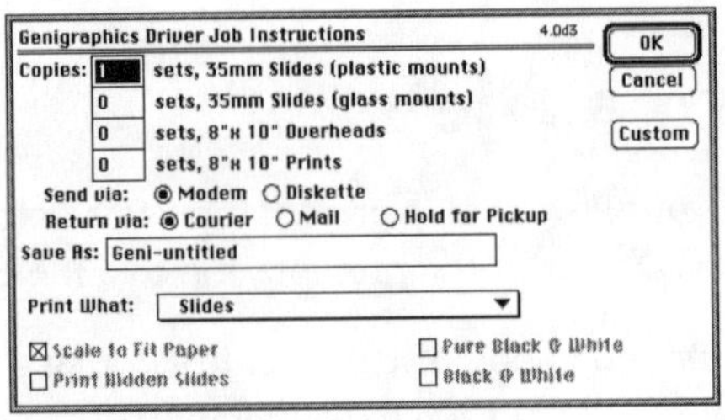

Fig. 16.3
The Print dialog box for the Genigraphics printer is quite different from the standard Print dialog box.

Next, you specify how you want your slides returned (via express courier or mail, or hold for pickup). Finally, type a name for your presentation in the Save As box, and choose OK to confirm your choices.

When the Genigraphics printer driver finishes printing your presentation, the Genigraphics Billing Information dialog box appears (see fig. 16.4). Using this dialog box, you specify where you want the slides, transparencies, or prints to be sent and to whom you want the charges billed. You also can specify how you want to pay for the services. (Genigraphics accepts American Express, Visa, and MasterCard, in addition to Genigraphics accounts and COD.) When you finish filling out the information, choose OK.

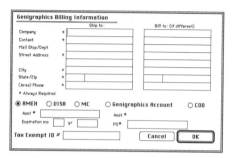

Fig. 16.4
Enter specific billing information in the blank text boxes.

Using GraphicsLink

If your computer system is equipped with a Hayes or Hayes-compatible modem, you can use the supplied GraphicsLink software to upload your PowerPoint presentation to the nearest Genigraphics service center. There is no charge for the telephone transmission, because GraphicsLink uses 800 numbers to upload your file. If you choose express courier delivery and rush service, your slides, transparencies, or prints can be delivered as quickly as the next business day.

> **Note**
>
> Before using GraphicsLink for the first time, you need to know the baud rate (1,200, 2,400, 9,600, 14,400, or 19,200) at which you're operating. GraphicsLink is preset to use a 2,400-baud Hayes modem, but you can change these settings.

If you need rush processing, call the nearest Genigraphics service center before using GraphicsLink and ask about rush services. You will receive a rush confirmation code that you will need to supply when you use GraphicsLink.

Note

You can use GraphicsLink with modems that are not Hayes-compatible, but you will have to specify the modem initialization, dialing, and termination strings.

To upload your presentation to a Genigraphics service center by using GraphicsLink, follow these steps:

1. Double-click the GraphicsLink application icon. (You find this icon in the same folder that contains PowerPoint.) The GraphicsLink dialog box appears (see fig. 16.5).

Fig. 16.5
The GraphicsLink application is modem software designed specifically for transmissions to Genigraphics.

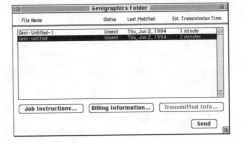

2. Open the File menu and choose Communications Setup. The Communications Setup dialog box appears.

3. Click the Modem Speed button to choose your modem's baud rate. You may have to adjust the other settings to conform to your specific protocol.

4. Choose OK. You return to the GraphicsLink dialog box.

5. In the Destination list, select the Genigraphics service center to which you want to send your presentation for processing, and then choose OK.

6. Select the presentation that you want to send. To select more than one presentation, hold down the Ctrl key and click the presentations that you want to send. To send all unsent presentations, open the Edit menu and choose Select Unsent.

7. Turn on your modem, if necessary.

> **Note**
>
> If you want to change the job instructions, or if you want to take advantage of rush service, click the Job Instructions button at the bottom of the screen. You see the same dialog box that appeared when you used the Genigraphics printer driver to print your file. Change your order, if you want. To supply the rush confirmation code, click Custom and type the code in the Rush Confirmation Code box. Choose OK to confirm your options.

8. Choose Send. GraphicsLink sends your presentation to the service bureau that you selected.

Troubleshooting

I tried to send my presentation, but a dialog box appeared, informing me that the transmission was unsuccessful.

GraphicsLink had trouble accessing your modem. Make sure that your modem is plugged in, turned on, and connected to your computer as well as to the telephone line.

I'm sending a big presentation file to Genigraphics, and it's tying up my computer.

Just switch to another application. GraphicsLink can send your presentation in the background.

I'm trying to send my file, but Call Waiting messes up my modem, and transmission ceases.

Most phone systems enable you to disable Call Waiting temporarily. If you have a touch-tone phone, try pressing *70. If you then hear a dial tone, you have disabled Call Waiting for the next call. Now use GraphicsLink.

Creating a Slide Show

If you want your presentation to feature the brilliant colors that you see on your color monitor, you have two choices: 35mm slides or a slide show. In a slide show, PowerPoint's screen elements—the menus, toolbars, and scroll bars—disappear, and the first slide fills the screen. When you click the mouse, the next slide appears.

A slide show has many advantages over other presentation media, including the following:

- You need not allow substantial lead time for film development. After you complete your presentation in PowerPoint, you can display the slide show immediately.

- You can give a presentation in a room that cannot be fully darkened (a necessity with 35mm slides).

- You can use the mouse pointer, which is visible on-screen during the slide show, to call your audience's attention to a particular element of the slide. You even can write and draw on the screen as you give the presentation.

- You can use professional-looking effects, such as transitions and builds. These effects add variety, interest, and emphasis to your presentation.

- With PowerPoint's multimedia capabilities and a sound-equipped system, you can include sounds and movies in your presentation.

- You can rehearse your presentation until you have it just right, and you can keep making changes until the moment your presentation begins.

- If you have embedded information, such as a worksheet, in a PowerPoint slide, you can open the source worksheet and make changes. For example, you can make a "what-if" analysis for the audience.

- You can give a continuous presentation—one that keeps running in an endless loop until you tell it to stop. This option is a good choice for exhibits.

- You can add buttons to your slides that enable you to branch to another presentation while the slide show is in progress.

The major disadvantage of slide shows is the computer's small screen, which limits the size of your audience to three or four people. Many organizations, however, have projection devices that enable you to project your computer's output by means of an overhead projector. When you use one of these devices, you can present a slide show to an audience of 50 or more people.

PowerPoint's slide-show capabilities are impressive and sophisticated, yet extremely easy to use. You can create a simple slide show with a click of the mouse. Creating a continuously running slide show also is very easy. As your understanding of slide shows grows, you can add special effects, such as sounds, builds, transitions, timings, branches, and movies.

Running a Simple Slide Show

With PowerPoint, it is very easy to create a simple slide show in which slides advance when you click the mouse button.

To run a slide show, using PowerPoint's default settings, follow these steps:

1. If necessary, open your presentation.

2. You can switch to the Slide Sorter by clicking the Slide Sorter View button at the bottom of the screen or by opening the View menu and choosing Slide Sorter if you want to change the slide order.

3. Select the first slide that you want to display in the slide show. To show all the slides, click the first slide.

4. Click the Slide Show button at the bottom of the screen. PowerPoint displays the first slide in your presentation.

5. To advance to the next slide, click the mouse button. You also can press the space bar, the N key, the right-arrow key, or the down-arrow key to advance to the next slide.

> **Note**
>
> Rather than leave a slide on-screen for a long time while you discuss a point, press B to black the screen. Press B again to return to your presentation.

6. To write or draw on the screen with the mouse, click the Freehand An notation button: the pencil icon in the screen's right lower corner (visible only when the slide show is in progress). Click and hold down the mouse button to write or draw. When you finish, click again to restore the mouse pointer. The writing or drawing that you produce this way is temporary; it does not affect the slide's appearance after the slide show is over.

7. To view all the slides in order, continue clicking the mouse button or pressing any of the keyboard equivalents (space bar, N, right arrow, or down arrow). To view the preceding slide, click the right mouse button or press one of these keys: P, left arrow, or up arrow.

   Table 16.1, which follows these steps, lists the key and mouse commands that you can use while viewing a slide show in PowerPoint.

8. Continue clicking until you have displayed all the slides. When the slide show is finished, the PowerPoint screen appears again.

Tip
To stop a slide show at any time, press Esc.

Tip
To erase an on-screen annotation, press the E key on the keyboard.

V

Output and Color

Note

So that your audience does not see the PowerPoint screen after you display the last slide, end your presentation with a black slide. To do so, add a blank AutoLayout slide after your last slide. Open the Format menu and choose Slide Background; the Slide Background dialog box appears. Deselect the Display Objects on Selected Slides option. In the Shade Styles section, choose None. Click the Change Color button to change the background color to black. Then click OK and choose Apply.

Table 16.1 Mouse and Keyboard Commands for Slide Shows

To...	Do This...
View the next slide	Use any of these options: ■ Click the mouse button ■ Press N ■ Press the right-arrow key ■ Press the down-arrow key ■ Press the space bar
View the next slide, even if it is hidden	Press H
View the preceding slide	Use any of these options: ■ Press ⌘-Shift-Tab ■ Press P ■ Press the left-arrow key ■ Press the up-arrow key ■ Press the Delete key
Go to a particular slide	Type the slide number and press Return
Black/unblack the screen	Press B or period (.)
White/unwhite the screen	Press W or comma (,)
Show/hide the pointer	Press A or equal (=)
Erase freehand annotation	Press E
Stop/restart an automatic slide show	Press S or plus (+)
Stop the slide show	Press the Clear key, or press Esc

Running a Slide Show in a Continuous Loop

At trade shows and conventions, you may have seen computers at booths that are running continuous slide shows. You can easily do the same thing with your computer and PowerPoint.

To create a continuous slide show, follow these steps:

1. If necessary, open your presentation.

2. Switch to the Slide Sorter by clicking the Slide Sorter View button at the bottom of the screen or by opening the View menu and choosing Slide Sorter.

3. Select all the slides in your presentation by opening the Edit menu and choosing Select All or by pressing ⌘-A.

> **Note**
>
> This step is necessary because the timings that you choose in step 5 affect only the slides that you select in the Slide Sorter.

4. Open the Tools menu and choose Transition. The Transition dialog box appears (see fig. 16.6).

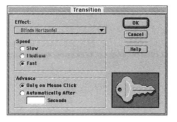

Fig. 16.6
The Effect pop-up menu provides an extensive selection of transition types.

5. In the Advance section, type the number of seconds for which you want to display each slide.

6. Choose OK.

7. Open the View menu and choose Slide Show. The Slide Show dialog box appears (see fig. 16.7).

8. If you want to display only some of the slides in your presentation, type the number of the beginning slide in the From box and the ending slide in the To box. If you type a number only in the From box, PowerPoint displays the presentation starting from that slide number.

Fig. 16.7

In the Slide Show dialog box, you can customize the rate at which your slide show advances.

9. In the Advance section, choose Use Slide Timings. PowerPoint uses the automatic timing option that you specified in the Transition dialog box (step 5).

10. Choose the Run Continuously Until COMMAND+. (period) option.

11. Choose Show to start your slide show.

Rearranging Slides

As you preview your slide show, you may find that one or more of the slides is out of sequence. You can change the order of your slides easily by using the Slide Sorter.

To change the order of slides, follow these steps:

1. If necessary, switch to the Slide Sorter by clicking the Slide Sorter View button or by opening the View menu and choosing Slide Sorter.

2. Click the slide that you want to move, and hold down the mouse button. As you move the slide, the mouse pointer changes to a pointer attached to two small slide icons.

3. Drag the slide to the new location. Release the mouse button and the slide appears in its new position.

Tip

To prevent viewers from disturbing the show, place the mouse and keyboard behind the computer while the show is running.

Tip

To undo any change that you just made in the slide order, immediately open the Edit menu and choose Undo, or press ⌘-Z.

Viewing Slide Shows with the PowerPoint Viewer

Suppose that you want to give a presentation while you are traveling. A computer is available, but PowerPoint is not installed. Does this mean that you can't present your slide show? No, and the credit is due to PowerPoint Viewer, an application included with your copy of PowerPoint. Bring with you a disk containing your presentation and PowerPoint Viewer, and you can display your presentation.

PowerPoint Viewer also comes in handy when you want to send your presentation to a computer user who does not have PowerPoint. Just include PowerPoint Viewer on the disk with your presentation.

You may duplicate PowerPoint Viewer and give it to other users freely without violating the law or your software license.

Creating Disks Containing PowerPoint Viewer and Your Presentation

You need two 1.44M (high-density) floppy disks to create a portable version of your presentation—one that you can take with you when traveling or that you can send to other users.

To create disks that contain PowerPoint Viewer and your presentation, follow these steps:

1. Make a copy of the PowerPoint Viewer disk included with your original PowerPoint program disks.

2. Copy your presentation to the second disk.

> **Note**
>
> If you are not sure whether the computer on which you will run your presentation has the TrueType fonts that you used, open the File menu and choose Save As to display the Save As dialog box. Choose the Embed TrueType Fonts option, and then save your presentation to the floppy disk. PowerPoint includes the fonts that you have used, and they will be available when your slide show is viewed.

Installing PowerPoint Viewer on Another Computer

PowerPoint Viewer runs too slowly from a floppy disk. For good performance, you or the person to whom you are sending your presentation should install both the Viewer program and your presentation on the computer that will be used for the presentation. The computer must use System 7.

To install Viewer and the presentation, insert the disk and drag the Viewer to any folder on the hard disk. Then insert the disk holding the presentation and open it. Drag the presentation file to the same folder the Viewer is in.

Using PowerPoint Viewer To View a Slide Show

After you install PowerPoint Viewer, you can display a slide show on a computer that does not have PowerPoint installed. All the features available in a

PowerPoint slide show—including the special effects that you may have included, such as builds and transitions—will be available.

To view a slide show with PowerPoint Viewer, follow these steps:

1. Start PowerPoint Viewer by double-clicking the PowerPoint Viewer icon. When PowerPoint Viewer starts, you see the PowerPoint Viewer dialog box, which is similar to the Open dialog box that you see in most Macintosh applications.

2. Select the PowerPoint presentation that you want to view, and then choose Show.

3. If you want the presentation to run continuously, choose the Run Continuously Until COMMAND+. (period) option.

4. At the conclusion of the slide show, the PowerPoint Viewer dialog box appears again. Choose Quit to exit.

From Here...

For more information on printing and producing output with PowerPoint, refer to the following chapters:

- Chapter 2, "Getting Acquainted with PowerPoint 4," introduces the Slide Sorter.

- Chapter 3, "Quick Start: Creating a First Presentation," introduces printing.

- Chapter 17, "Working with Color," helps you design your color PowerPoint presentations for maximum effectiveness.

- Chapter 20, "Advanced Presentation Management," covers advanced slide-show features, such as transitions, builds, multimedia effects, hidden slides, timing, and slide-show rehearsals.

- Chapter 22, "Customizing PowerPoint," shows you how to change the default print settings.

Chapter 17

Working with Color

You were introduced to PowerPoint 4's basic color palettes in earlier chapters. In many situations, applying colors simply because they offer a nice appearance is not enough. Many presentation elements, such as handouts and speaker's notes, don't require color of any kind; you need little or no knowledge of color to create them. Color is, however, a very important component of slide shows. Proper use of color can make the difference between a dull or boring presentation and one that excites, informs, and prompts a decision.

Improper use of color can actually lead to a negative reaction; used badly, color can irritate the viewer. Assigning the wrong color to text in a slide can make the text unreadable. Colors that do not match properly in a slide can produce eyestrain.

On the other hand, specific color combinations always seem to work because of their universal appeal and basic character. PowerPoint helps you keep your color schemes under control in subtle but effective ways.

This chapter covers color in detail and shows you how to do the following:

- Create new colors and place them in the palette

- Understand the relationship between template color schemes and color palettes

- Understand the 8-color and 90-color PowerPoint default palettes and how to change their colors

- Use color effectively

Understanding Color in PowerPoint 4

When you choose a template for use in creating a PowerPoint 4 presentation, you make a decision about the presentation's appearance. You have a specific set of colors to work with, but that doesn't mean that you cannot change them. PowerPoint gives you the flexibility to use any color that you desire, anywhere you want.

 The front-line tool for working with color in PowerPoint is the pop-up Fill Color palette in the Drawing+ toolbar. This tool actually is a combination of a menu and a color palette, as figure 17.1 shows.

Fig. 17.1
This floating palette is used primarily for drawing, but it also enables you to choose colors for any object.

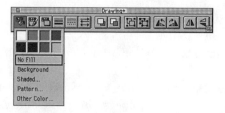

Notice the appearance of the same palette in the Font dialog box (see fig. 17.2), where it is used for assigning different colors to slide text. The same color set is used in several places throughout the program.

Fig. 17.2
You can use the Font dialog box to change text color.

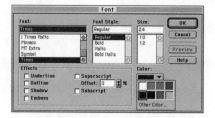

Studying PowerPoint's Basic Color Palette

The palette shown in the preceding two figures shows the eight basic colors for the selected template. Each color is assigned a specific place and is used for specific objects to ensure appropriate and proper use of each color in the slide show. (Believe it or not, eight colors usually is more than enough for any slide show.)

To view PowerPoint's color schemes, open the Format menu and choose Slide Color Scheme. The Slide Color Scheme dialog box appears (see fig. 17.3).

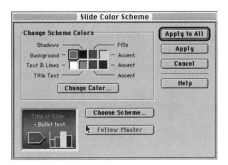

Fig. 17.3
The pop-up color palette appears in several places.

Effective color management begins with knowing the specific role of the eight colors in the Slide Color Scheme dialog box. The following list describes the color options:

■ *Background color:* used to create background fill colors for slides

■ *Shadows:* the shadowing color used for text, graphic objects, and other items in your slides

■ *Fills:* choose the color to fill drawn objects

■ Three *Accent* options: used primarily for chart series items in the default

■ *Text & Lines:* color assigned to body text and to the borders of drawn objects in slides

■ *Title Text:* color assigned to titles in your slides

You learned in chapters 3 and 4 how to change a slide background color and a Slide Master's background color. When you select a template, the background color sets the tone for the rest of the elements in your presentation. Although you can change the background color at any time, bear in mind that you may need to change other colors to compensate. The colors that usually need to be adjusted in such a case are the Text & Lines and Title Text colors.

When you select a new color scheme for your presentation, you choose the background and text colors; PowerPoint automatically assigns the other six colors.

Use the Slide Color Scheme dialog box to choose colors and color schemes. Table 17.1 describes the functions of the command buttons in the Slide Color Scheme dialog box.

Table 17.1	Slide Color Scheme Button Functions
Button	**Description**
Apply	Applies color changes to current slide and closes dialog box
Apply to All	Applies color changes to all slides in the presentation and closes dialog box
Change Color	Accesses color palette to assign new colors
Choose Scheme	Chooses a new color scheme (a full eight-color palette) for your presentation
Follow Master	Resets current color scheme to that of the Slide Master color scheme (handy when you select a new color and then decide that you don't want it after all)

You can activate the Slide Color Scheme dialog box when you are viewing any slide in your presentation, when you are viewing the presentation in Slide Sorter view, or when you are viewing the Slide Master.

Although the Slide Master governs the color scheme for the overall presentation, you can use the color-changing techniques that you learn in this section to change the color scheme for an individual slide. Any slide can have different background colors and different text colors than the rest of the presentation.

Note

A good way to manage multiple slide color schemes is to use Slide Sorter view. This view enables you to get an overall picture of where a different colored slide fits into the presentation. All the color-changing features that you normally accessed in Slide view or the Slide Master can be accessed in Slide Sorter view as well. For most of the examples in this chapter, Slide view or the Slide Master is used, but Slide Sorter view is used to illustrate the process of changing the color scheme for only one slide in a presentation.

Changing a Presentation's Color Scheme

Changing a color scheme is a separate process from simply changing a color. As noted earlier, changing a color scheme involves changing two key elements: the background color and the text color. Then, the rest of the slide elements follow along with similar color changes.

To change the color scheme for an entire presentation, follow these steps:

1. Open the View menu and choose Slides to change to slide view or click the Slide View button.

> **Note**
>
> Because you are changing the color scheme for the entire presentation, it doesn't matter which slide you're currently displaying.

2. Open the Format menu and choose Slide Color Scheme. The Slide Color Scheme dialog box appears.

> **Note**
>
> Do not be deceived by the title of this dialog box; you can use it to change the color scheme for a single slide or for an entire presentation.

3. Click the Choose Scheme button. The Choose Scheme dialog box appears, as shown in figure 17.4.

> **Note**
>
> When the dialog box appears, the Text & Line Color and Other Scheme Colors sections are blank.

Tip
Watch the Description area at the bottom of the Choose Scheme dialog box for information about the steps that you are performing.

V

Output and Color

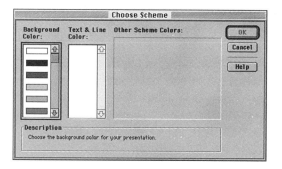

Fig. 17.4
In this dialog box, PowerPoint suggests colors that work well together.

The following list describes the elements of this dialog box:

- *Background Color.* This list box displays 90 colors that you can use as the background color.

- *Text & Line Color.* This list box is blank until you select a background color. When you do, the box displays a list of colors chosen by PowerPoint to match the background color. The number of colors offered varies according to the background-color choice.

Tip
Check the text-color results in the thumbnails to make sure that your text color stands out against the background color.

- *Other Scheme Colors.* After you choose a text and line color, a set of four thumbnails appears in this section of the dialog box. Each thumbnail displays a different color scheme, showing the other six colors that PowerPoint chose or each color scheme. Click one of the four thumbnails to select the complete color scheme.

4. Select a background color. You can choose among black, white, and 88 other colors.

   When you select a background color, a set of colors appears in the Text & Line Color list box. The number of colors varies, depending on the background color selected, but most lists offer 8 to 12 colors.

5. Select a text and line color. The Other Scheme Colors thumbnail set appears, as shown in figure 17.5.

Fig. 17.5
Based on the colors selected for the background and for text and lines, PowerPoint shows sample schemes.

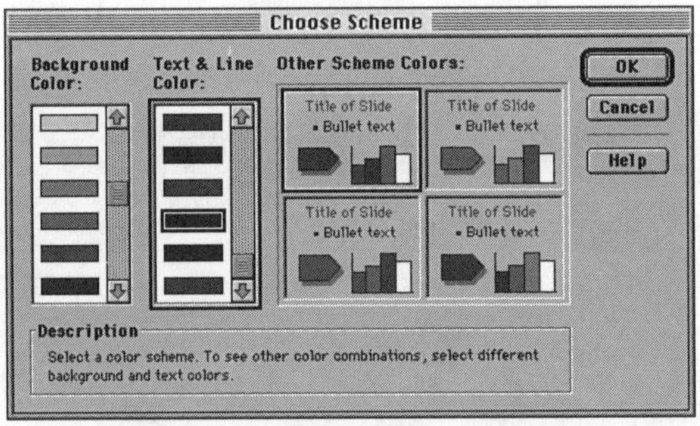

Note

Some colors are a good match for the background color and therefore produce readable body text on your slides. PowerPoint makes an effort to select a group of colors that work with the background color, but some colors do not work quite as well as others. Use the thumbnails in the Other Scheme Colors box to keep an eye on text-color choices.

Within each thumbnail, the three small columns represent the three accent colors that are automatically assigned to each scheme. The title at the top of each thumbnail reflects the new title color. The polygon on the left side of each thumbnail shows the default fill color for drawn objects. Finally, the shadow color appears behind the polygon as a shadow.

6. Click one of the four thumbnails to select it.

7. Choose OK. The Slide Color Scheme dialog box reappears. Notice that the color scheme has changed to reflect your choices.

8. Choose the Apply to All button to apply the new color scheme to the entire presentation. PowerPoint displays the message Charts are being updated with the new color scheme and closes the Choose Scheme dialog box.

> **Note**
>
> Choosing Apply to All is the key to changing the entire presentation. If, when you're in Slide view, you click the Apply button, the new scheme is applied only to the current slide.

9. If the color scheme doesn't quite fit your taste when you view the slides again, open the Edit menu and choose Undo, or press ⌘-Z.

Changing a Slide's Color Scheme

Changing a single slide's color scheme is essentially the same as changing the color scheme for an entire presentation. The example in this section uses Slide Sorter view to demonstrate the utility of that view for determining the placement of the slide that contains the new color scheme. You start by displaying the current presentation in Slide Sorter view. Follow these steps:

1. Open the View menu and choose Slide Sorter or click the Slide Sorter View button. PowerPoint displays the presentation in Slide Sorter view, as shown in figure 17.6.

2. Click the slide that you want to change.

3. Open the Format menu and choose Slide Color Scheme. The Slide Color Scheme dialog box appears.

4. Click the Choose Scheme button. The Choose Scheme dialog box appears (see fig. 17.7).

Fig. 17.6
Slide Sorter view shows thumbnail versions of your slides and is great for general maintenance.

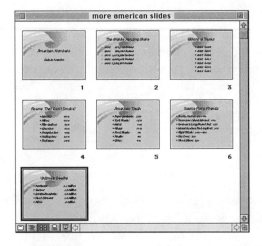

Fig. 17.7
Choose a scheme that applies to one slide.

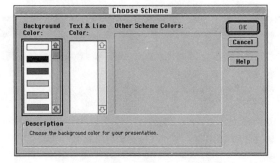

5. Select a Background Color. A set of colors appears in the Text & Line Color list box.

6. Select a Text & Line color. The Other Scheme Colors thumbnail set appears.

7. Click one of the four thumbnails to select it.

8. Choose OK. The Slide Color Scheme dialog box reappears.

9. Click the Apply button to apply the new color scheme to the slide selected in Slide Sorter view. PowerPoint applies the color scheme and closes the Slide Color Scheme dialog box.

The new slide is displayed alongside the others in Slide Sorter view. Now the slide has a different appearance, which can be an intelligent tactic to make it stand out and get the audience's attention. With a little imagination and discreet application of color, you can ensure that your audience is never bored.

Understanding Basic Color Theory

The color Macintosh System offers many temptations. Millions of colors are available. Also, almost every major software package offers hundreds of colors in the basic color palette. The quantity of colors may tempt the intrepid presentation-maker to excess. PowerPoint's basic palette offers the first antidote: only eight colors are available in the basic palette.

The crucial trick is not to please yourself; you must please your audience. The psychology of color is both subtle and powerful. Considering your audience and thinking ahead are the keys to getting that crucial purchase order signed and on your desk. Consider the psychology and world view of the people who will see your presentation, and you may well get the edge that you need to succeed.

Following are some rules to consider when applying color to your slide presentations.

Keep It Simple

The first rule—*keep it simple*—is nearly universal in any field of human endeavor; it definitely applies to presentation design and the use of color. Drowning a slide in vibrant colors can have precisely the opposite effect from the one that you intended. PowerPoint automatically provides some levels of effective color management; in most situations, it may be best to follow the guidelines and color schemes that PowerPoint offers.

Watch Your Color Schemes Carefully

The second rule is *govern your color schemes wisely*. You can apply a different color scheme to each slide, but in most cases, this is not be a good idea; too many color schemes can be confusing and disconcerting to the audience. The vast majority of your slides (perhaps 70 percent) will be simple text slides that contain bulleted lists; these slides are best displayed with simple, consistent colors.

A corollary to this rule is that assigning a different color scheme to a slide sometimes is a good idea, particularly if your presentation deals with different subjects and you want to provide effective transitions between subjects. This method also can draw attention to a chart that illustrates a crucial point of your presentation. Just don't go overboard.

Tailor Your Color Schemes to Your Audience

The third rule is *color schemes can be tailored to your audience*. If you are addressing an audience whose members are from a foreign country, try to make them feel more at home by using their national colors as a base for your presentation's color palette.

Different corporate environments can require different approaches. In general, you may expect marketing and public relations executives to respond more warmly to a flashy, strikingly colored presentation (at least within limits) than a board of directors or upper-management group of a Fortune 500 corporation. Also, company cultures vary widely, regardless of the department that you're addressing. Take a few minutes to get a general idea of the culture of the group that will view your presentation.

Watch Your Fonts and Color Schemes in Text Slides

Rule four is the most specific: *text slides work best with highly contrasting color schemes*. A good rule of thumb is to use white, yellow, or light-blue text against a dark background or dark text against a light background. Most important, make sure the text is readable. If the audience has to squint or strain, they won't read the text on the slide.

Go easy on the typefaces as well; use conservative typefaces that are generally accepted by Corporate America—for example, Times, Helvetica, Bookman, and Palatino. The Macintosh can accommodate every typeface conceived throughout the history of printing, and it is easy to succumb to the temptation to use ornate, striking typefaces for your slides. Use these types of fonts very sparingly.

PowerPoint uses two color-mixing systems to help you create new colors for your palettes: Hue-Saturation-Luminance (HSL) and Red-Green-Blue (RGB). The last section of this chapter, "Changing Palette Colors," describes the PowerPoint color systems and shows you how to create custom colors for your presentation.

Applying Colors to Individual Objects

◀ See "Using PowerPoint's Drawing Tools," p. 215

Unlike using more generalized color schemes, applying colors to individual objects can be considered to be an open field of play. Essentially, you can use every color that you can display on your color monitor, but ideally not all in one presentation.

You use the buttons in the Drawing and Drawing+ toolbar to apply colors to objects. The Drawing toolbars are not available in Slide Sorter view so you must switch to Slide view to display the toolbars. Table 17.2 describes the buttons in the Drawing+ toolbar.

Button	Button Name	Description
	Table 17.2 The Drawing+ Toolbar	
	Fill Color	Pop-up menu for applying a different fill color.
	Line Color	Pop-up menu for applying a different line color.
	Shadow Color	Pop-up menu for applying a different shadow color.
	Line Style	Pop-up menu for applying a different line style (thickness or line weight, or double line).
	Dashed Lines	Pop-up menu for applying a dashed line style.
	Arrowheads	Pop-up menu for applying an arrowhead at either end or both ends of a line (available only if a drawn line or arc is selected).
	Bring Forward	Layering tool used to bring a drawn object forward (handy when you have several objects in a stack).
	Send Backward	Layering tool used to send an object backward through a stack.
	Group	Tool that groups selected objects together into one selectable object. (PowerPoint's ClipArt Gallery contains many examples of this technique.)
	Ungroup	Tool that takes one object composed of several objects and breaks them into their individual parts. (You can use this tool to change PowerPoint clip-art objects.)
	Rotate Left	Tool that rotates the selected object 90 degrees to the left.
	Rotate Right	Tool that rotates the selected object 90 degrees to the right.

(continues)

V

Output and Color

Table 17.2 Continued		
Button	**Button Name**	**Description**
	Flip Horizontal	Tool that flips the selected object 180 degrees horizontally.
	Flip Vertical	Tool that flips the selected object 180 degrees vertically.

The key tools for altering colors in drawn objects are the Fill Color, Line Color, and Shadow Color buttons in the Drawing+ toolbar.

Changing the Color of an Object

Figure 17.8 shows a typical slide, designed for the purpose of adding graphic objects. Starting with this exercise, you go beyond the basic palettes to select colors from a wider palette.

Fig. 17.8
You can add any object to this AutoLayout to dress the slide up a bit.

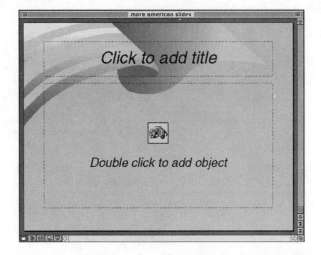
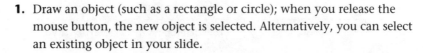

To change the color of an object, follow these steps:

◀ See "Drawing Basic Shapes," p. 216

1. Draw an object (such as a rectangle or circle); when you release the mouse button, the new object is selected. Alternatively, you can select an existing object in your slide.

2. Click the Fill Color button in the Drawing+ toolbar, and hold down the mouse button. The pop-up menu appears, as shown in figure 17.9.

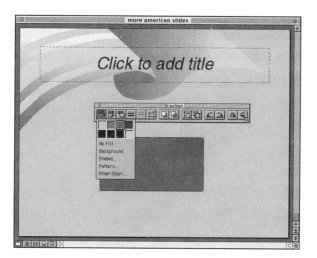

Fig. 17.9
You can move the
palette to the
active work area.

Note

Notice that in figure 17.9, the current Fill Color is highlighted in the pop-up palette. This color corresponds to the default color applied to the selected object.

3. Select a color, and release the mouse button. PowerPoint fills the selected object with the color that you chose.

or

Choose the Other Color option. The Other Color dialog box appears, as shown in figure 17.10. Double-click a color to apply it to the object.

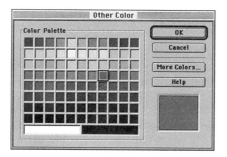

Fig. 17.10
You are not limited
to the default eight
colors.

The Other Color palette is arranged in 11 columns of eight color boxes each. Each set of eight color boxes falls under the heading of one color type, as described in table 17.3.

Table 17.3 Color Boxes in the Other Color Palette	
Color	**Column**
Gray	1
Red	2
Orange	3
Yellow–orange	4
Yellow	5
Yellow–green	6
Green	7
Blue–green	8
Blue	9
Violet	10
Red–violet	11

The rows are numbered 1 through 8, of course, but row 1 is at the bottom of the palette and row 8 is on top. Row 8 contains the basic hues for each color range; the colors in rows 7 through 1 increase in intensity as you progress down the column. When you click any color box, its name (`Red #8`, `Yellow #7`, and so on) appears in the status bar at the bottom of the PowerPoint screen.

Two larger color boxes—black and white—appear at the bottom of the palette for quick and easy selection.

Using Shaded Colors

In most situations, basic colors are adequate for any task. In other cases, you can employ special graphics effects, such as shading or pattern fills, to add an artistic touch to a simple drawing.

To apply shading to an object, follow these steps:

1. Select the object that you want to change.

 2. Click the Fill Color tool in the Drawing+ toolbar, and hold down the mouse button. The pop-up menu appears.

3. Choose the Shaded option. The Shaded Fill dialog box appears (see fig. 17.11).

Fig. 17.11
Use the Shaded Fill dialog box to add shading to the fill color.

4. Choose a Shade Style and then choose an option in the Variants section.

5. Choose OK.

The Shaded Fill dialog box contains two options that may be familiar to you from earlier chapters: the Shade Styles option-button section and the Variants section. The Shade Styles options enable you to choose the direction of the shaded fill. The Variants section displays four thumbnails that show four different variations on the shade style.

The Color button produces a pop-up menu that is the same one you display by clicking the Fill Color button. This menu gives you access to the basic eight-color palette and also to the Other Color palette, from which you can choose any color for the background and in which you can use the Dark–Light slider bar that enables you to change the brightness or darkness of the selected object.

> **Note**
>
> To add an embossed effect to a graphic, draw an ellipse or other shape on top of a rectangle that contains a shading variant and color (use the rectangle as a guide to ensure that the ellipse is in proportion to the rectangle), change the color of the ellipse to the same as that of the rectangle, and add a shading variant that runs in the opposite direction.

▶ See "Using Special Shading Effects," p. 467

Using Pattern Fills

PowerPoint offers 36 pattern fills that you can apply to any selected object. Pattern fills are applied from the Fill Color pop-up menu and can be combined with any color.

To add a pattern fill to a drawn object, follow these steps:

1. Select the object that you want to fill with a pattern.

2. Click the Fill Color button in the Drawing+ toolbar, and hold down the mouse button. The pop-up menu appears.

3. Choose the Pattern option. The Pattern Fill dialog box appears, as shown in figure 17.12.

Fig. 17.12
The patterns reflect your current fill and background colors, but they can be changed.

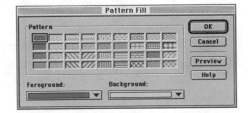

4. Choose the foreground and background colors from the respective pop-up menus. (You also can use the Other Colors dialog box for each option.)

> **Note**
>
> The foreground color is the color that the actual pattern assumes. The background color should be chosen so that the pattern stands out effectively. (In some cases, a well-chosen pattern and background color may actually resemble another color; you would need to do a great deal of experimenting to create such a combination.)

5. Choose a pattern from the palette.

6. Click the Preview button to view the effect of the pattern on the object before you apply it. If you do not like the results, you can change the colors again or choose the Cancel button to close the dialog box without making changes.

7. Choose OK.

> **Note**
>
> If you choose a pattern fill for a shaded object, the shading is canceled and cannot be recovered or combined with the pattern fill.

Changing Line Colors

To change line colors for an object, follow these steps:

1. Select the object.

2. Click the Line Color button in the Drawing+ toolbar. The Line Color pop-up menu appears (see fig. 17.13).

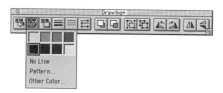

Fig. 17.13
The Line Color pop-up menu has the same eight default colors as the Fill Color pop-up menu.

3. Choose any of the colors in the palette.

   or

   Choose the Other Color option. The Other Color dialog box appears. Choose one of the 90 color swatches in the palette.

4. Choose OK.

Adding a Shadow and Changing Shadow Colors

Adding a basic shadow and changing the color of a shadow is simple. The latter process is almost identical to the process of changing the color for a regular drawn object. Just make sure that the shadow color you choose is appropriate for the effect that you are trying to achieve.

To create an embossed shadow effect, follow these steps:

1. Select the object and click the Shadow Color button in the Drawing+ toolbar; hold down the mouse button. The Shadow Color pop-up menu appears (see fig. 17.14).

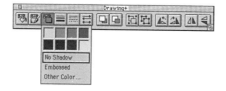

Fig. 17.14
This menu contains the eight default colors.

2. Choose the Embossed option. This option applies a subtle shadowing effect, based on the object's color, to the selected object.

V

Output and Color

Note

If you choose the Other Color option, you are in effect choosing the standard type of shadowing (not embossing), to which you can apply any color.

To change shadow colors for the selected object, follow these steps:

1. Click the Shadow Color button in the Drawing+ toolbar, and hold down the mouse button. The Shadow Color pop-up menu appears.

2. Choose any of the colors in the palette, or choose the Other Color option. The Other Color palette dialog box appears.

3. Choose one of the 90 color boxes in the palette.

Tip

You can add shading, shadowing, and other effects to text-object backgrounds, just as you can to graphic objects.

4. Choose OK.

To add a custom shadow effect to any graphic or text object, follow these steps:

1. Select the desired object.

2. Open the Format menu and choose Shadow. The Shadow dialog box appears (see fig. 17.15).

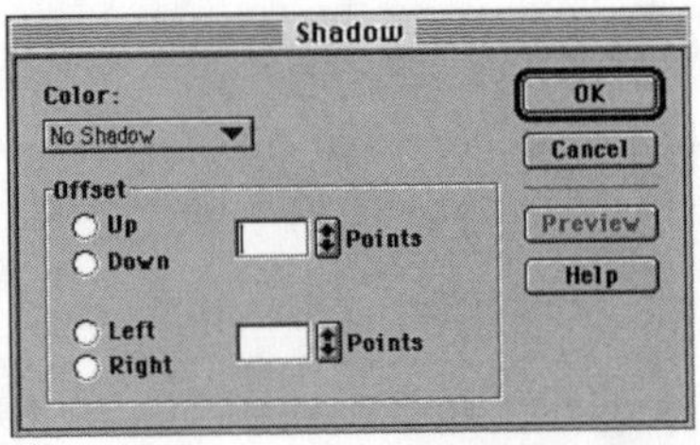

Fig. 17.15

Use the Shadow dialog box to create a custom shadow.

Shadow
Color: No Shadow ▼
Offset
○ Up ☐ ▲▼ Points
○ Down
○ Left ☐ ▲▼ Points
○ Right
OK
Cancel
Preview
Help

The Shadow dialog box contains the following Offset options:

- *Up:* raises the shadow offset above the object margin by the specified number of points

- *Down:* lowers the shadow offset below the object margin by the specified number of points

- *Left:* sets shadow offset to the left of the object margin by the specified number of points

■ *Right:* sets shadow offset to the right of the object margin by the specified number of points

> ### Note
>
> The Offset options specify how much shadowing to add. The up and down offsets and the left and right offsets are paired alternatives that you adjust up or down to lengthen or diminish the shadow.

3. Adjust the shadow to the desired level. (You may need to do some experimenting to get it right.)

4. If you want to apply a different color (different from the template default shadow color) to the shadow, select one from the Color pop-up menu or from the Other Color dialog box.

5. Choose OK.

Changing the Text Color

You can work with the color of text objects in two ways: change the color of the text itself; or add a color fill, shading, or pattern fill to the text-object background. In the first case, you are formatting the font itself; the second is a matter of applying a simple color fill.

To change the color of title or body text in a slide, follow these steps:

1. Select the text.

2. Open the Format menu and choose Font. The Font dialog box appears, as shown in figure 17.16.

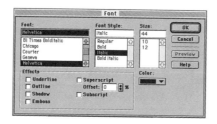

Fig. 17.16
In the Font dialog box, you can change text colors.

3. Select a color from the Color pop-up menu, or choose the Other Color option and follow the steps described in the previous exercises.

4. Choose OK.

V

Output and Color

To change the background color or fill of the text object, follow these steps:

1. Click the text object to select it.

2. Click the Fill Color button in the Drawing+ toolbar, and hold down the mouse button. The Fill Color pop-up menu appears.

3. Select a color from the pop-up menu.

   or

   Choose the Other Color option. The Other Color dialog box appears. Choose a color from the palette in that dialog box.

4. Choose OK.

Changing Palette Colors

The Other Color dialog box (refer to fig. 17.10) contains another option that this chapter hasn't yet explored in detail. Clicking the More Colors button takes you to the More Colors dialog box (see figs. 17.17 and 17.18), which offers an extremely flexible and sensitive method for adjusting colors to a precise value.

> **Note**
>
> The dialog boxes you see vary, depending on the Apple System software you have installed. The dialog boxes shown here appear if you have System 7.5 installed.

Fig. 17.17
You can choose more colors in this dialog box.

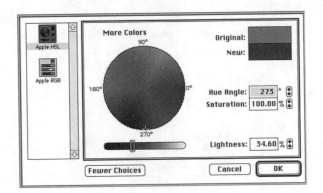

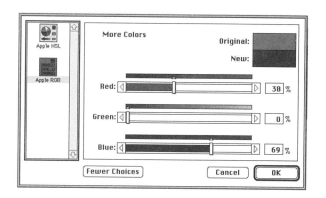

Fig. 17.18
You can adjust
colors in this
dialog box.

As noted earlier in this chapter, PowerPoint uses two color-mixing systems that enable you to create custom colors: HSL (Hue-Saturation-Luminance) and RGB (Red-Green-Blue). The following list describes the HSL method.

- *Hue.* The hue simply is the color shown in the color box. The hue determines the basic color: green, blue, orange, and so on.

- *Saturation.* The saturation setting determines the basic vividness or purity of a color. More gray in a color means less saturation; less gray means more saturation.

- *Luminance.* Luminance is the degree of lightness or darkness in a color, which is created by mixing black and white in differing degrees.

These three quantities are mixed to create the colors that you see in the Other Color palette and all colors that you see in PowerPoint.

HSL and RGB are very similar. RGB is the mixture of the pure red, green, and blue brightness values to produce a mixed color. The red, green, and blue values are measured from 0 to 65,535 in PowerPoint and adjust as the HSL values are adjusted. The HSL values are measured from 0 to 65,520. RGB essentially determines the brightness of the red, green, and blue light that is emitted and is a result of the relative brightness of these three values.

Think of a TV set, which uses the same system to produce its images. A TV set has three guns: red, green, and blue. Each gun shoots out light of the respective color. If a color gun fails in your TV set, you immediately notice the change in the color quality of your screen.

You can adjust individual HSL values by clicking the up- and down-arrow buttons next to each text box. You also can also type specific values.

Tip
When you mix a color that is pleasing to you, write down the red-green-blue values so that you can reproduce the color value in other work.

V

Output and Color

Additionally, you can use the mouse to adjust the color bar below the color wheel. Drag the scroll box or click the up or down arrow to adjust the brightness and red, green, and blue values. Use the color bar to make fine adjustments to your colors.

View the color changes in the rectangular sample box below the words "More Colors."

To add a custom color to a slide object, follow these steps:

1. Select the object.

2. Click the Fill Color button in the Drawing+ toolbar, and hold down the mouse button. The pop-up menu appears.

3. Choose the Other Color option. The Other Color palette dialog box appears.

4. Click one of the color swatches that most closely approximates the custom color that you want to create.

5. Click the More Colors button in the dialog box. The More Colors dialog box appears.

6. Click More Choices to see the Apple HSL and Apple RGB buttons.

7. Click Apple HSL to adjust the HSL values to the desired level. Notice that the crosshair in the color wheel moves as you adjust Hue and Saturation.

8. Choose OK. You return to the Other Color dialog box, which now displays the custom color in the thumbnail in the bottom-right corner.

9. Choose OK. PowerPoint applies the new color to the selected object. The custom color now appears in a new swatch in the Other Color color set of the Fill Color pop-up menu.

> **Note**
>
> Although you clicked a color box in the Other Color palette to begin creating your custom color, the original palette color box is preserved.

When you create a custom color, that color appears along the bottom of the Fill Color, Line Color, and Shadow Color palettes so you can quickly select a custom color to apply to another object.

Troubleshooting

I can't find all the color tools that I need.

Most of the tools that are used for applying color fills, shading, shadowing, line weights, line colors, and so on are located in the Drawing+ toolbar, which typically is not displayed when you start to use PowerPoint. To display this toolbar, open the View menu and choose Toolbars command. In the Toolbars dialog box, select the Drawing+ toolbar, and then choose OK.

I screwed up my color scheme by applying the wrong color to all my slides.

You probably clicked the Apply to All button when you changed a color in the palette for the current slide. The trick is understanding the difference between the Apply and Apply to All buttons in the Slide Color Scheme dialog box. If you click Apply to All, you can place the new background color, object color fill, or other palette color in many places where you don't want it to be.

When this happens, the system probably takes a minute to make all the changes. The screen message `Charts are being updated with the new color scheme` probably appears. After that's done, before you do anything else, open the Edit menu and choose Undo, or press ⌘-Z. The screen message reappears, and your changes are undone.

From Here...

Color is a sophisticated tool and a realm of knowledge unto itself. You learned some principles of color theory and techniques in this chapter, but you still have seen only the basics. For more information, read the following chapters:

- Chapter 19, "Using Advanced Charting Features," discusses increasingly sophisticated chart types and explains how to create and save custom chart types for use in future presentations.

- Chapter 21, "Using Advanced Color, Text, and Drawing Features," offers more tips about using color in your presentations. The chapter also shows you how to create a color scheme from scratch.

Part VI

Advanced PowerPoint 4

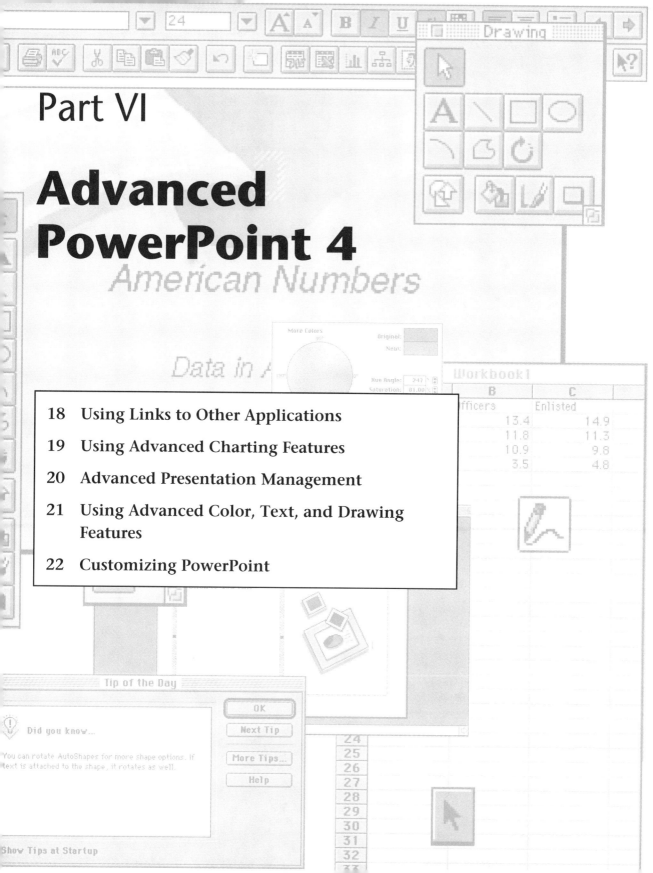

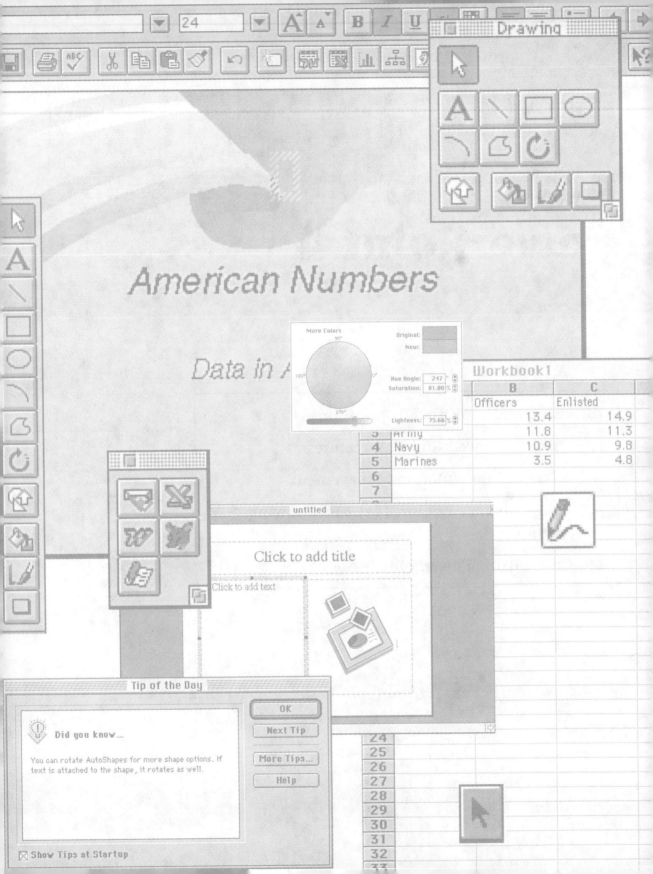

Chapter 18

Using Links to Other Applications

PowerPoint 4 offers enhanced capabilities for linking and exchanging different kinds of data from other applications to a presentation. If you change the data in the other application program, PowerPoint updates the linked data in the presentation file. The process is called *object linking and embedding* (OLE).

The term object can be quite deceptive and confusing. First of all, anything you work with in PowerPoint is an object, whether it is a simple piece of artwork, a chart created in Microsoft Graph, or body text in a slide. Objects in a PowerPoint presentation are held in place by placeholders. *Placeholders* reserve space in the slide for the particular object type they're supposed to hold. They are resizable and movable within the confines of the slide.

But objects aren't just items created in PowerPoint. Objects are also items that are created in other programs and either linked or embedded to the PowerPoint presentation or published and subscribed to a slide in the presentation. This is where the true power of objects in PowerPoint asserts itself.

In this chapter, you learn the following:

- How to understand the two versions of object linking and embedding

- How to link objects from other programs into your PowerPoint presentation

- How to embed objects from other programs into your presentation

- How to use Publish and Subscribe

- How to use drag and drop between files and applications in PowerPoint

Understanding Object Linking and Embedding (OLE)

Object linking and embedding enables users to combine various types of data into one document. OLE also allows users to have instant access to any of the applications that originally created that data—without the tedious starting and restarting of programs or repetitive cutting and pasting of data into the Clipboard.

◄ See "Working with Objects," p. 86

Object linking and embedding are two different processes that you use for different results. *Linking* is copying an object from one application to another while creating a connection between two applications. The data in the container application, therefore, is automatically updated whenever you change it in the source application.

> **Note**
>
> The *source* application is the one in which the object was created; the *container* application is the one to which the object is copied.

To edit linked data, you can open the source application by double-clicking the linked data in the container application. The source application appears in a separate window. When you are done editing the data, you save the document and choose the File Exit command to close the source and the container automatically updates. When you link an object, you are working with a copy of the object that you can link with many container applications and files.

Embedding, on the other hand, is creating a new object or placing an existing object within the container application. In PowerPoint, for example, you can insert an Excel chart by embedding it. When you embed an object, you open Excel within PowerPoint, create a new chart or insert an existing one, then close Excel.

When you want to edit an embedded object, you double-click it and the source application opens within PowerPoint. You can then update the object and close the source application without ever leaving PowerPoint. When you embed an object, you are working with only one object inserted into only one application and file.

One advantage of embedding objects into your PowerPoint files is that when you bring your presentation file to another location, all the embedded objects are taken along for the ride—without having to bring all the original object files. All the objects are lodged and present in your PowerPoint file. (This does create a much bigger and slower PowerPoint file, however.)

Please note that when you modify an object in its source application, that object must be re-embedded in the container, or the changes in the object will not appear in the container file.

Now let's add another level of complexity to this discussion—OLE 1 and OLE 2.

Using OLE 2

PowerPoint includes two types of OLE—OLE 1, which has been supported for a few years now, and the new OLE 2, also called editing in place. OLE 1 is basically described in the previous section. When you link or embed an object, you must open the source application to edit the object. OLE 2 provides an easier method of editing; however, OLE 2 is newer and not as widely available as OLE 1.

PowerPoint 4 supports OLE 2, which enables you to edit embedded objects from other programs in the same PowerPoint window. Microsoft's new versions of PowerPoint (4), Microsoft Word (6), and Excel (5) all support OLE 2; future versions of applications from other software companies may also support OLE 2.

When using OLE 2, PowerPoint's menus and toolbars are temporarily replaced by those of the source application. This is called *in-place editing*. You have already read about this technique many times in previous chapters. In creating charts in PowerPoint, for example, you used Microsoft Graph. Microsoft Graph is actually a separate application and an OLE 2-compliant program. Every time you use Graph to create and edit charts, it quickly replaces PowerPoint's menus and toolbars with its own set.

Editing in place means, in effect, that you can have one or five applications all using the same window, without having all the applications open at the same time. Editing in place saves time and system memory.

> **Note**
>
> When you produce an organizational chart, as you did in Chapter 15, "Creating Organizational Charts," you use Microsoft's OrgChart program, which is not an OLE 2 program. It's an OLE 1-compliant program.

Working with Other OLE 2 Applications

On PowerPoint's most basic level, it's easy to create and use objects from other programs. PowerPoint's Standard toolbar offers two quick tools for doing so: the Insert Microsoft Word Table and the Insert Microsoft Excel Worksheet tools.

 PowerPoint's Insert Microsoft Word Table tool enables you to create a table in Word and embed it into a PowerPoint slide. You must, of course, have Microsoft Word 6 installed on your system.

 PowerPoint's Insert Microsoft Excel Worksheet tool enables you to create a typical Excel worksheet to embed into a PowerPoint slide. Using this tool requires an installed copy of Excel 5 on your system.

Creating an Embedded Object

Assuming that the latest version of Word is installed on your system, you use the following method to embed objects from that program. It's a good example for two reasons. A tool is provided for fast access to the program from PowerPoint, and it provides a good demonstration of the power of OLE 2.

To insert a Word 6 table, make sure you're in PowerPoint's Slide view, and follow these steps:

 1. Click the Insert Microsoft Word Table tool in the PowerPoint Standard toolbar, and hold down the mouse button. A pop-up 4-by-5-cell grid appears, as shown in figure 18.1.

Fig. 18.1
Using the pop-up grid for a Word table will take you directly to Word.

2. Drag the mouse down and across from the top left cell in the pop-up tool. By doing so, you are defining the number of table entries to be created in the table. As you drag, the message cell at the bottom of the table tool shows the selected table size: 3×3, 4×3, or whatever the selection is.

3. Release the mouse button. After a moment, during which PowerPoint starts the Microsoft Word application, PowerPoint's toolbars and menu bar disappear and are replaced by Word's toolbars and menu bar, as shown in figure 18.2.

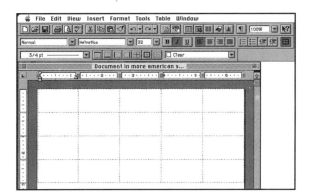

Fig. 18.2
The order of the
Word menus is
the same as for
PowerPoint.

The PowerPoint slide is still displayed on-screen, but the Word screen elements and a new Word table also appear on-screen.

4. Enter text in each cell of the table, and format the text if you like.

5. After editing and formatting the table, click the PowerPoint slide anywhere outside the table object you just edited, and the table is inserted into your slide as a text object with the color and font defaults assigned to it from within PowerPoint, as shown in figure 18.3.

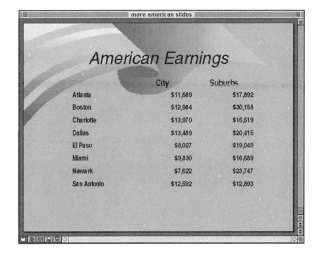

Fig. 18.3
The finished table
takes on the
assigned color
scheme and
layout.

The method of using Excel 5 to insert worksheet objects into a PowerPoint slide is identical to that for Word 6 except for the actual editing mechanics and data type of the program.

To insert an Excel 5 table, make sure you're in PowerPoint's Slides view, and follow these steps:

1. Click the Insert Microsoft Excel Worksheet tool in the PowerPoint Standard toolbar, and hold down the mouse button. A pop-up 4-by-5-cell grid appears.

2. Drag the mouse down and across from the top left cell in the pop-up tool. By doing so, you are defining the number of rows and columns of cells to be created in the datasheet. As you drag, the message cell at the bottom of the table tool shows the selected worksheet size: 3×3, 4×3, or whatever the selection is.

3. Release the mouse. After a moment, during which PowerPoint starts the Excel 5 application program, PowerPoint's toolbars and menu bar disappear and are replaced by Excel's toolbars and menu bar.

4. After editing and formatting the table, click the PowerPoint slide anywhere outside the datasheet object you have just edited. The datasheet is inserted into your slide.

You can also use the Insert Object command to create a new embedded object. To do so, follow these steps:

1. Open the Insert menu and choose Object. The Insert Object dialog box appears, as shown in figure 18.4.

Fig. 18.4
From this dialog box, you can choose the type of object to be inserted.

2. If not already selected, click the Create New option button. The Object Type list box in the dialog box shows the different types of objects (freeform drawings, Excel charts, datasheets, and so on) that are available to you.

3. From the Object Type list box, choose the file type you want to embed.

4. Choose OK.

If the application program is OLE 2-compliant, PowerPoint's menu bar and toolbars are replaced and you can create the new object.

If the application you selected is OLE 1-compliant, see "Using OLE 1" later in this chapter for more information on how to proceed.

5. Click anywhere outside the boundaries of the object to embed it in the PowerPoint slide.

The object has been successfully embedded.

Embedding an Existing Object File

It is possible to bring an existing file, like an Excel spreadsheet, into a presentation as an embedded object. Instead of creating a new object from scratch, as in the previous example, any drawing, chart, or other object from a program that supports OLE can be embedded. This stands to reason, considering that an embedded object is the actual file created by the other program. This is why presentation files with embedded objects are so easily transported.

To embed an existing file, follow these steps:

1. Display the PowerPoint slide in which the object is to be placed.

2. Open the Insert menu and choose Object. The Insert Object dialog box appears.

3. Click the Create From File option button. The file list is displayed in the Browse dialog box, as shown in figure 18.5.

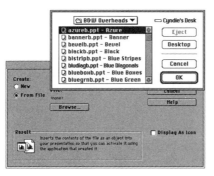

4. Using the familiar Macintosh interface, locate the desired file.

5. Choose OK. The desired file name should now appear in the file list.

6. Choose OK. The object file is embedded into the slide.

Tip
Existing PowerPoint 4 presentation files can be embedded as objects.

Fig. 18.5
With the Browse dialog box, locate the object to embed.

Tip
An embedded movie or animation sequence automatically runs in a presentation. Pictures and other objects automatically appear in your slide show.

VI

Advanced PowerPoint 4

Creating a Linked Object

Creating a link to a PowerPoint presentation from an object file of another type is as easy as copying and pasting between the programs. As noted earlier in this chapter, however, the relationship of a linked object to the OLE client program (such as PowerPoint) is different from that of an embedded one.

Tip

Linking places a copy of your linked data in the presentation, not in the actual file.

After an object is linked from another program to a PowerPoint 4 presentation, whenever the other program is used to change the source file for the object and the object changes are then saved, the changes to the object are shown in your presentation without re-embedding the object, regardless of whether PowerPoint is open or not. PowerPoint's Paste Special feature is the key to effective linking of objects within your presentation.

To create a linked object, follow these steps:

1. In the application that was used to create the source file, open the file containing the desired object for linking.

2. Select the data in the file that you want to link.

3. Open the application's Edit menu and choose Copy.

4. Switch to the PowerPoint window and display the slide in which you want to insert the linked item.

5. Open the Edit menu and choose Paste Special. PowerPoint's Paste Special dialog box appears, as shown in figure 18.6.

Fig. 18.6

The Paste Special dialog box allows you to choose what type of object to paste.

6. In Paste As, choose Object as the way you want to paste the contents of the Clipboard. Choosing Object establishes the link.

7. Choose OK to close the dialog box. The object appears on your slide.

If you want to edit the linked object, double-click the object and the source application appears in its own window. When you are finished editing, save the file and close the source application. The link is then updated in

PowerPoint. Additionally, you can open the source application at any time, edit the linked file and save it, and the updated data automatically appears in the PowerPoint slide, whether or not PowerPoint was open at the time.

To create a link between an existing OLE 2 object file and PowerPoint, follow these steps:

1. Display the PowerPoint slide in which the object is to be placed.

2. Open the Insert menu and choose the Object command. The Insert Object dialog box appears.

3. Click the Create From File option button. The Browse dialog box appears.

4. Choose the file you want from the Browse dialog box, and choose OK. The linked object appears in the slide.

Using OLE 1

Many applications, though they don't support OLE 2, are still extremely powerful and sophisticated and may offer capabilities that Microsoft application programs cannot match. Those who own and use Word or Excel 4 can still use these programs as vital tools in tandem with PowerPoint 4, by employing OLE 1 techniques to link and embed objects.

To embed a new OLE 1 object in a PowerPoint 4 slide, follow these steps:

1. Start PowerPoint 4 and open the desired presentation.

2. Minimize the PowerPoint window.

3. Start the OLE 1-compliant application program that offers the object type desired.

4. In the application program, create or open and select the drawing, datasheet, chart, or other object you want to embed.

5. Open the Edit menu and choose Copy to copy the object to the Clipboard.

6. Minimize or close the program.

7. Maximize the PowerPoint program window.

8. Open the Edit menu and choose Paste Special. PowerPoint's Paste Special dialog box appears.

9. Choose OK. The embedded object is placed into the presentation.

Double-clicking the picture brings up the original application in its separate window, displaying the picture for editing. After you do so, the picture shows as dimmed on the PowerPoint slide. This is a tip-off that its originating application is running with the object file.

> **Note**
>
> Whenever you double-click an embedded OLE 1 object, the slide displays that object in a dimmed box, indicating that the object is being edited by its original program.

◄ See "Manipulating Objects," p. 246

To modify an existing embedded OLE 1 object in PowerPoint 4, follow these steps:

1. Double-click the embedded object in the PowerPoint slide. The program that originally created the object appears. It is a separate window and does not replace the PowerPoint toolbars and menus.

2. Modify the object within the application program. When you're finished making your changes, save your work.

3. Open the File menu of the application and choose Exit. The program closes and the PowerPoint slide shows the changes you made to the embedded object.

Using Publish and Subscribe

Publishing and subscribing is another way of linking data and applications. You first create a *publisher*, which is similar to a source file. The part of the data you use to create the publisher is called the *edition*. You can then *subscribe* to that edition so the data is connected, or linked, to one or many applications. When changes are made to the publisher, the edition is updated and the changes are then made to the subscriber.

You can move, resize, and recolor the data in the edition but you can only modify the data in the source document. Additionally, if you cancel the subscription, or the link, the edition becomes a graphic so that it can no longer be updated through the source document.

Creating a Publisher

You create a publisher so you can share it with other files and applications. After you create a publisher, you can then subscribe to it.

To create the publisher, follow these steps:

1. Save the presentation you want to publish.

2. In the Slide Sorter, select the slide you want to publish.

3. Open the Edit menu and choose the Create Publisher command. The Create Publisher dialog box appears.

4. In the Name of New Edition box, type a name for the publisher.

5. Choose the Publish button. The slide is then published and ready to use in other presentations or in other applications.

Subscribing to an Edition

After the edition is published, you can subscribe to it from any number of applications or files.

To subscribe to an edition, follow these steps:

1. Open the presentation in which you want to insert the edition.

2. In Slide view, display the slide in which you want to insert the edition.

3. Open the Edit menu and choose the Subscribe To command. The Subscribe To dialog box appears.

4. Select the edition. The preview box displays the selected edition.

5. Choose the Subscribe button. The dialog box closes and the edition appears in the slide.

To edit the edition, open the source file and modify the edition. Save the file and close it. The subscriber automatically updates.

Canceling a Subscriber

You can cancel a subscriber to break the link between it and the publisher. When you cancel the subscriber, you can then edit the data in the destination document separately from the source.

VI

Advanced PowerPoint 4

To cancel the subscriber, follow these steps:

1. In PowerPoint, select the subscriber you want to cancel.

2. Open the Edit menu and choose the Subscriber Options command. The Subscriber Options dialog box appears.

3. Choose Cancel Subscriber. PowerPoint asks you to confirm the choice.

4. Choose Yes to confirm the action, and then choose OK to close the dialog box.

Canceling a Publisher

You can cancel a publisher if you find you no longer need to link the published data to other files or applications.

To cancel a publisher, follow these steps:

1. In the source file, change to Slide Sorter view.

2. Choose the publisher.

3. Open the Edit menu and choose the Publisher Options command. The Publisher dialog box appears.

4. Choose Cancel Publisher. PowerPoint asks you to confirm the cancellation.

5. Choose Yes to cancel, and then choose OK to close the Publisher dialog box.

Working with Placeholders

Essentially, a *placeholder* is a resizable container for objects of any description. Placeholders are interchangeable and generic. Although you can create new slides that have specified placeholders for charts, body text, organizational charts, and titles, any placeholder can be used for any purpose. By a simple trick with the mouse, a chart placeholder can be used to contain a graphic image, as in the example that follows.

To change placeholder types, follow these steps:

1. First, insert a new slide into your presentation by clicking the New Slide button and choosing an option in AutoLayout. Select, for example, a Graph slide, as shown in figure 18.7.

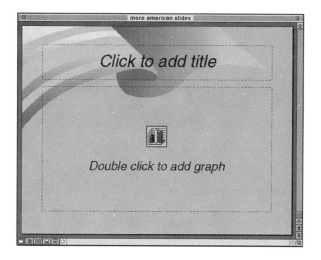

Fig. 18.7
The `Double click to add graph` area is the placeholder.

2. Click the border of the graph box. The border becomes thicker and screened and small black boxes, or selection handles, appear on the corners and sides of the box.

3. Open the Insert menu and choose Picture. The Insert Picture dialog box appears, as shown in figure 18.8.

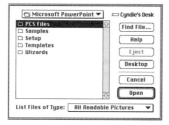

Fig. 18.8
The Insert Picture dialog box looks nearly the same as most other destination dialog boxes on the Macintosh.

PowerPoint supports four graphics formats—Act, MacPaint, TIFF, and EPS.

4. Choose the type of file to import from the List Files of Type pop-up menu, and locate the desired file, using the Macintosh interface.

5. Choose Insert. The Graph placeholder now contains a picture, as shown in figure 18.9.

VI

Advanced PowerPoint 4

Fig. 18.9
All placeholders can be converted to contain a different object than their title indicates.

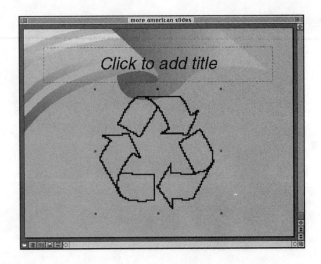

The key to the whole process of changing the placeholder type and inserting the graphic inside the placeholder is clicking the margin of the placeholder before you insert the picture or other object. If you don't, the new object is simply pasted on top of the existing placeholder. When you use the placeholder, the inserted picture is automatically resized to the dimensions of the placeholder.

Using Drag and Drop

Among PowerPoint's most important new features is its support of enhanced drag-and-drop features. In earlier chapters of this book, you looked at the basics of drag-and-drop features—especially how to drag and drop cells and rows or columns of data in Microsoft Graph datasheets, and text in PowerPoint slides and in Outline view. You can also drag and drop copy by simply holding down the Option key when you perform the operation. There's much more to it, however.

It's possible with PowerPoint 4 to drag and drop elements between open presentation files. You can even drag and drop data between applications. Drag-and-drop copying is also supported between applications. That particular feature is one of the key benefits available to Microsoft Office owners— those who own Microsoft Word 6, Excel 5, and PowerPoint 4 all in the same package.

Microsoft Office owners who are reading this book should keep a few things in mind:

- Drag and drop works the same way in all levels. In a document, between documents, and between programs that support drag and drop, the keystrokes and mouse actions are the same.

- Dragging and dropping between applications dramatically slows system performance. Usually, it is faster and easier to use the Copy and Paste commands.

What Programs Work with Drag and Drop?

The version numbers for the programs mentioned here (Word 6, Excel 5, and PowerPoint 4) are very important. Earlier versions of all three of these programs do not work with drag and drop in its present glory. You won't be able to drag and drop between files in the same program, or drag and drop between separate programs with earlier versions of Microsoft application programs. Only the very latest versions of the three programs included in Microsoft Office (or sold separately) work with the new drag-and-drop features.

With these caveats, the next two sections show you how to use drag and drop between PowerPoint documents and how to drag and drop a PowerPoint element from the PowerPoint program to another application (in this example, Word 6 will be used).

Dragging and Dropping between PowerPoint Presentations

To start, make sure you have PowerPoint 4 launched and you know two files you want to share data between. Then follow these steps:

1. Open each desired file.

2. Reduce the size of each of the two windows so that you can place them side by side, or one above the other. Either way, the goal is to be able to see both windows.

   The results may resemble figure 18.10. It's important that both files be displayed for drag and drop (between files) to work.

Tip

Slide Sorter view is required for dragging and dropping slides and their data between PowerPoint files.

VI

Advanced PowerPoint 4

Fig. 18.10
Only one window
can be active at a
time, but you can
have several open
simultaneously.

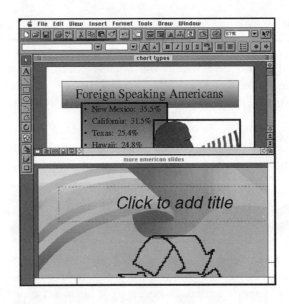

The next step is very important. PowerPoint 4 directly supports the
dragging and dropping of slides (with all the contents that the dragged
slide contains) between files. Dragging and dropping between
PowerPoint files only works if both presentations are shown in Slide
Sorter view.

3. Click each file, and for each, open the View menu and choose Slide
Sorter. The result may resemble figure 18.11.

Fig. 18.11
The open
windows are in
the Slide Sorter.

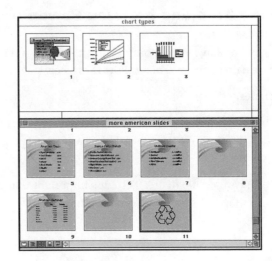

4. Click and drag the desired slide. As you drag, the mouse pointer changes to a tiny box with a down arrow attached to it, and a bracketing arrow travels along. Move the mouse over the other presentation to the location in the Slide Sorter where you want the slide to be dropped (see fig. 18.12).

Notice that the slide is removed from the first presentation and placed in the second. You also have the option of making a copy of the slide and placing it.

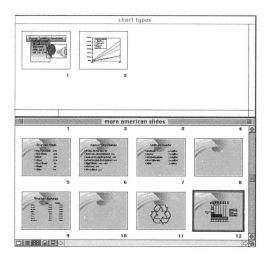

Fig. 18.12
The moved slide takes on the color scheme of the current document.

5. Release the mouse button. The slide has been dragged and dropped to the new file and is now slide number 12.

Note

You can also drag and drop copies of slides between presentations. Simply press and hold the Option key as you drag the slide thumbnail from one file's Slide Sorter to the other file.

Does this procedure look suspiciously familiar? It's almost exactly the same procedure as the simple act of rearranging slides in the Slide Sorter, which was discussed in Chapter 4. The major difference is that in dragging and dropping, the selected slide is moved to another file. To retain the changes, both files must be saved by choosing Save from the File menu for each file.

VI

Advanced PowerPoint 4

Dragging and Dropping between Applications

Dragging and dropping between applications is as straightforward as it is between files. Applications that support OLE 2 are the only type of program that can support drag and drop between programs; at the time of this writing the only packages that support this feature are PowerPoint 4, Excel 5, and Word 6. Almost certainly, others will follow.

In the next example, a PowerPoint file has an Excel datasheet copied to it. This can have some very interesting results, as you'll see when you follow these steps:

1. Display the PowerPoint file that you want to drag and drop to.

2. Open Microsoft Excel 5 and display a datasheet from which you want to drag data.

3. You may want to organize the two programs side by side or in another arrangement for easier viewing and dragging, as in figure 18.13.

Fig. 18.13

The same two windows, side by side.

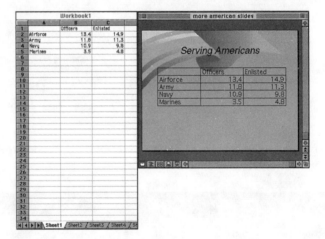

4. Display the PowerPoint presentation that you want to drag to. For the example, Slide view is sufficient.

5. In the Excel datasheet, select the data that you want to copy. Any selected data is highlighted.

6. Click and hold the mouse over the border of the selected data in the Excel datasheet. Hold down the Option key when you do this.

7. Drag the mouse over to the PowerPoint window, place it over the area of the slide, and release the mouse button.

Figure 18.13 illustrates the result after the Excel object was enlarged to fill the area.

The datasheet that's now in the PowerPoint slide is an Excel object. Double-clicking the copied datasheet in the PowerPoint slide starts PowerPoint's OLE 2 capabilities, in which PowerPoint's menus and toolbars are replaced by those for Excel 5; the datasheet can be edited, formatted, and resized as if you were actually using Excel. So, after the drag-and-drop copy is done, you're back to the process of in-place editing, which was described earlier in this chapter.

There's more. When you select the datasheet and drag and drop copy it from Excel to PowerPoint, any chart that's based on that Excel data comes along for the ride. You can drag on one of the handles on the new object in the PowerPoint slide to display more of its contents.

You can also copy and paste Excel datasheet rows and columns from the embedded Excel object into a Graph datasheet in your presentation.

You should notice the patterns that are emerging. In a move for ease of use, Microsoft has made sure that drag and drop copy works on all levels in the same way. Holding the Option key when you drag and drop copies the selected data or object from one place to another in the same document, between documents, or between applications.

From Here...

Despite the detailed discussion of object linking and embedding that's been offered in this chapter, there's quite a bit more about OLE that goes beyond the scope of this book. For more information on the subject, refer to Microsoft's PowerPoint 4 program documentation. Consider the following chapters for information on PowerPoint's effective features:

■ Chapter 19, "Using Advanced Charting Features," digs into more esoteric chart types and various advanced features of chart creation, plus looks into the importing of charts from PowerPoint 3, the previous version of the program.

VI

Advanced PowerPoint 4

■ Chapter 20, "Advanced Presentation Management," discusses adding special effects to your presentation, and some techniques for adding and embedding multimedia objects such as movie clips and sounds into your slides.

■ Chapter 21, "Using Advanced Color, Text, and Drawing Features," helps you exercise some of PowerPoint 4's more advanced tools for text rotation, recoloration of various objects such as clip art, and creation of new color schemes.

Chapter 19

Using Advanced Charting Features

Earlier in this book, three chapters were devoted to the process of creating datasheets and charts for use in PowerPoint slides. While those chapters covered a lot of ground, many features were passed by. PowerPoint 4, for example, offers many more chart types than were explained earlier, including 2-D and 3-D line charts, scatter charts, stock charts, the spectacular combination charts, 3-D area charts, and three types that are newcomers to the PowerPoint program: 3-D surface, 2-D radar, and 2-D doughnut charts. Although this chapter can offer only brief accounts of most of the additional chart types, you learn about how these charts can be used and the reasons for using them.

Other new features that are explained in this chapter include the use of Trendlines, a chart forecasting feature that enables you to extrapolate future values from current ones for display on a chart; the capability to create and save custom chart types for future use; and importing charts and data from Microsoft Excel. Chart selection and customization commands, that were bypassed earlier, also are covered briefly.

In this chapter, you learn about the following subjects:

- Understanding alternative chart types

- Understanding and using trendlines

- Saving custom charts and creating new default charts

- Exporting and importing charts to and from various applications

Understanding Alternative Chart Types

PowerPoint offers too many chart types to allow comprehensive coverage in this book. The following sections, however, give examples of many alternative chart types you might consider using.

Using 2-D Line (XY) Charts

In standard charting nomenclature, line charts, area charts, scatter charts, and stock charts are all examples of *XY chart* types. XY charts are so named because their values are calculated against both two-dimensional axes: x and y. In PowerPoint, unfortunately, Microsoft made the decision to split "Line" and "XY (Scatter)" charts into separate categories. There is no functional difference between them, because they are calculated the same way. This can confuse the user, because there are many redundant chart types offered between them. In this book, it's easier to split them into specific categories such as stock, line, and scatter chart types so that you can see the uses and subtle differences between them.

Line charts, for example, are an interesting and subtle option for helping your audience draw visual conclusions from your numeric data. Line charts are deceptively simple—messages can be found in line charts that may not be apparent in other types. In figure 19.1, you can see that facts such as growth or, in this instance, populous, are driven home with emphatic clarity. This is one major advantage of a line chart—multiple messages can be conveyed with a minimum of screen clutter.

Fig. 19.1
Line charts can make some data easier to understand than even a typical bar chart.

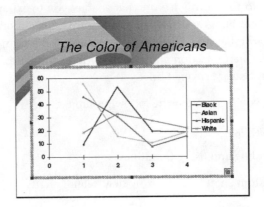

In PowerPoint 4, line charts are often called XY charts because their data is charted against two axes—the x- and y-axes—and because each point, line, or sized object needs to be measured against each axis to determine its location.

In figure 19.1, for example, each point on each line has a value. The common element across all XY charts is the requirement for two values for each data item used to create and locate the markers representing each series value.

> **Note**
>
> Graph's Clear command is a pop-up menu offering three options: All, Contents, and Formats. Selecting Contents removes the data, but retains the fonts or other formatting you applied in the selected cells for fresh data entry. Clearing Formats removes the fonts or other visual changes you applied to datasheet numbers and labels.

To create a line chart like the one shown in figure 19.1, follow these steps:

1. In PowerPoint, click the Insert Graph button on the standard toolbar. Microsoft Graph appears.

2. To delete the default data that appears in the datasheet, select the data, open the Edit menu, and choose Clear All. Type your data for the line chart.

3. Open the Format menu, choose AutoFormat. The AutoFormat dialog box appears.

4. Choose Line from the Galleries list box.

5. Select a chart type (#10 was used in the illustration).

6. Choose OK.

To beef up the lines and make them more visible, follow these steps:

1. Click a line in the chart.

2. Open the Format menu and choose Selected Data Series. The Format Data Series dialog box appears, displaying the Patterns tab.

3. In the Patterns Line section, choose a heavier line weight from the Weight pop-up menu.

4. Choose OK.

You can follow the same procedure for the other lines in the chart.

Understanding and Using 2-D Scatter Charts

Scatter charts are a handy and useful tool when you need to display a large number of series in a chart. Lines and points are the objects that are displayed in scatter charts. (As noted earlier, there is no functional difference between a scatter and a line chart.) *Points* represent the actual data values in each series, and the graphic shapes used to define those points are called *markers*.

In many cases, you don't use lines in a chart, but simply points or data markers. Markers create the scatter chart, in which the points show their relationships to each other by the common colors or shapes of the markers. In scatter charts, the height of the points along the line represents the data values in the chart. Scatter charts are plotted against two axes—the x- and y-axes—because each point, line, or sized object needs to be measured against each axis to determine its location. (Hence, they're a type of XY chart.)

Why do you use scatter charts? If you have more than four series, connecting lines may confuse the viewer or obscure some of the data markers on the chart. In that case, scatter charts without lines may be just the thing to display a large number of series. The nature of data markers (which are very small entities on the chart) enables the user to display almost as many series as he wants. Also, a scatter chart is suitable if you have only a few series, but also have a large number of values in each series.

Handled properly, a scatter chart can be used to bring together many disparate sets of data, such as demographic surveys of customers in the marketplace. Logarithmic scales can be used to tie together values from widely ranging statistical areas, such as surveys of different age groups.

The line chart from figure 19.1 is shown as a scatter chart in figure 19.2.

Fig. 19.2
XY scatter charts are a very good choice when you have many data series to show.

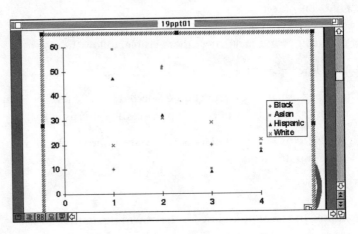

Scatter chart types are quite similar to several line charts in the Gallery. Scatter chart #2, in particular, is functionally identical. Most other scatter chart types add grid lines or, in the case of scatter chart #4, a logarithmic scale is automatically added to the chart. If you have a series whose values range between 10 and 15, and another series that shows values of another order of magnitude (say, 100 to 150), a logarithmic scale is a good option.

Scatter chart type #6 is a smoothed line chart without data markers. The same feature can be enabled on any line chart (or scatter chart displaying lines) by enabling the Smoothed Line check box option when you format lines under the Format Data Series dialog box.

Using Stock Charts

In Microsoft Graph, stock charts—charts that track opening and closing stock prices as well as high and low—are not offered as a separate section under the Graph Gallery; they are, instead, grouped with the line chart type in the PowerPoint program. Nonetheless, stock charts are so unique, and require such a different set of data, that they deserve their own space in this chapter. The same is true, of course, with combination charts, the building of which may be the most challenging chart-building task you undertake. They're described in the next section.

Stock charts require different data sets from those used in previous examples—one type, a *High/Low/Close* (HLC) stock chart, requires three series of data, one that represents a series of low stock price values, one that shows high values, and one that shows closing values. An *Open/High/Low/Close* (OHLC) chart requires four respective series. The open value is the price at which the stock opened trading for the given time period. A sample stock chart is shown in figure 19.3.

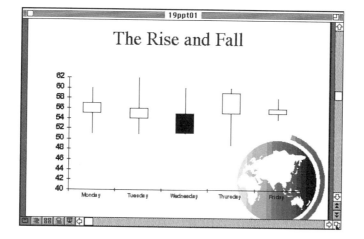

Fig. 19.3
You can use fluctuating stock prices to create an OHLC chart like this one.

VI

Advanced PowerPoint 4

What are the elements of stock charts? Some unfamiliar element names have popped up here, and they bear some explanation.

Hi-Lo lines are used to show the extent of stock price fluctuations. Hi lines extend above the up-down colored bar for each series. Lo lines extend below it.

Up-Down bars indicate the open and close values of the data series. Keep in mind that the Up-Down bar can represent a value that closes lower as well as higher; and that a high or low value and a close value can be the same: in such a case, no high or low line extends from the Up-Down bar. Up-Down bars only apply to one type of stock chart, the Open/High/Low/Close chart. In the High-Low-Close chart type, a short horizontal line pointing to the right is used to indicate the closing value. Hi-Lo lines are still used in HLC charts.

The open price is located on either the top or the bottom edge of the Up-Down bars for each trading day (or week, or year, and so on), and the open price value is measured against the y-axis. If a price went up for the time period, the open value is on the lower edge of the Up-Down bar. If it went down, it's the top edge of the bar.

The low price is located on the bottom end of the Hi-Lo line combination, and it's the lowest price at which the stock traded for the given time period. It is measured against the y-axis. The high price is located on the top end of the Hi-Lo line combination. It is the highest price level that the stock traded for during the given period, and it also is measured against the y-axis. The high value is not necessarily the value that the stock closed at; if it is, no high line extends beyond the Up-Down bar.

The closing price is located on either the top edge or the bottom edge of the Up-Down bars for each trading period, and they are measured against the y-axis. The closing price is the price at which the stock rests at the end of each given trading period. A closing price data marker can be placed to clearly mark its position for each trading day. If a price went up for the time period, the closing value is on the upper edge of the Up-Down bar. If it went down, it's on the lower edge of the bar.

To create a basic stock chart, follow these steps:

1. In PowerPoint, click the Insert Graph button on the standard toolbar. Microsoft Graph appears.

2. Select the default data in Graph's datasheet. To delete it, open the Edit menu and choose Clear All. Type the data set specific to your project. In our example, the series labels were Monday through Friday and the columns were Open, High, Low, Close.

3. Click the By Column tool on the Graph Standard toolbar.

4. Open the Format menu and choose AutoFormat. The AutoFormat dialog box appears.

5. From the Galleries list box, choose Line.

6. Select chart #9 (the OHLC chart option).

7. Choose OK. The OHLC chart appears.

It may be necessary to edit the chart for a clean, uncluttered slide. Return to Chapter 13, "Creating Basic Charts," if you need help with these tasks. There are many types of changes you can make to this chart and most others. They include deleting items, changing font size and style, adjusting the scale, and altering the color scheme. Chapter 13 can help you make all these edits.

As you see, you can add some interesting touches to a stock chart. Stock charts can display a huge number of series values, as anyone who's seen a Dow Jones stock price history chart can attest. (Appendix B shows a stock chart of this type.) HLC charts work much the same way, but discussions and examples of every chart type offered by PowerPoint are beyond the scope of this book. Nonetheless, with a little experimentation, any stock chart of either type can be customized and altered to suit your needs. They can also be added to a combination chart.

Using Combination Charts

Combination charts are especially powerful and complex chart types that primarily are used to define and illustrate relationships between different sets of data. Combination charts can have elements of stock charts, bar charts, line charts, and column charts within them.

Combination charts combine elements from many different types of 2-D charts and enable you to plot data in two or three different ways on the same chart. Charts of this type are often used to draw relationships between, for example, gross revenues and profits, where yearly gross revenues might be shown in columns and yearly profits in a line. Powerful and informative messages can be conveyed with this chart type.

Tip

Combination charts can display two x- and two y-axes on the same chart.

Combination (or overlay) charts are so named because one type of chart is overlaid on another chart. As a result, a combination chart displays, at a minimum, two y-axes and one x-axis. It's also possible to display two x-axes and two y-axes on the same chart. Combination charts, as you can imagine, also require a slightly different set of data than other charts. A sample set of data is provided to build the example in this section. Combination charts, incidentally, are only available in 2-D types. Figure 19.4 shows an example of a combination chart.

Fig. 19.4

Combination charts are used best when you have two data series that you want to compare overlapping.

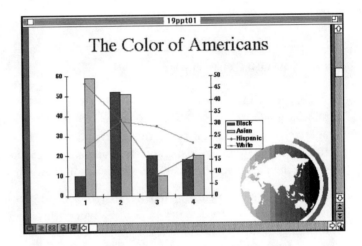

Tip

For combination or overlay charts, in many charting applications the y-axis is also called the Y1 axis.

For combination charts, PowerPoint 4 displays x-axis values on the horizontal axis, shown on the bottom of the chart. In line charts, the x-axis is used to denote categories and series labels. Figure 19.4 shows increments along the x-axis labeled as 1, 2, 3, and 4.

The y-axis is the second and vertical axis against which the numeric values of one series are measured. The increments and range of the y-axis are based on the values in your data. In figure 19.4, the y-axis is used to measure the columns; the y-axis is scaled from 0 to 60 and measured in increments of ten.

The Y2 axis is the third axis in this combination chart and is the basis by which the second set of data is measured. The Y2 axis is the vertical axis shown on the right side of the chart. Notice that the scale of values in the Y2 axis is different from the scale of values in the Y1 axis. In figure 19.4, the Y2 axis is scaled from 0 to 50 in increments of 5. The Y2 axis measures the lines that overlap the 2-D columns.

> **Note**
>
> In combination charts, it is a good idea to be explicit and generous with your axis labels—and to add a legend. A tremendous amount of information is conveyed in a chart of this type, and it's easy to forget a label that provides the viewer with the critical visual link to interpret the data.

Tip
As noted, the second y-axis in a combination or overlay chart is also called the Y2 axis. When Graph puts the Y2 in the title entry, it is leaving you a clue as to what axis you are adding a title.

You take a different approach to the creation of this type of chart; because the steps required are somewhat more complex and the details must be sweated to get the chart right. Also, because of the myriad possibilities of this type of chart and space considerations, only one exercise can be used in this section. One exercise is enough, however, to illustrate the power of this chart option, its complexity, and the tremendous number of customization options available.

The data set is deceptively simple. To properly create and customize the chart shown in figure 19.4, follow these steps:

1. In PowerPoint, click the Insert Graph button on the standard toolbar. Microsoft Graph appears.

2. Select the default data in Graph's datasheet and delete it. Type the data set specific to your combination chart. Where the data is entered into the datasheet determines which set of data is displayed as columns, lines, or shaded areas. For example, if you enter three rows of data and choose one of the columns and line combinations, the first two rows of data will be displayed as columns and the third as a line.

3. Open the Format menu and choose AutoFormat. The AutoFormat dialog box appears.

◄ See "Customizing Charts," p. 307

4. From the Galleries list box, choose Combination.

5. Choose a chart type from the Format thumbnails (#2 in the example).

6. Choose OK. A rough combination chart appears, which may be similar to the one shown in figure 19.4.

You now are ready to make fine-tuning adjustments to the chart. The colors of the bars, the font style and size, alignment of labels, applied patterns, and resizing of the entire chart are all available options. You can return to Chapter 14, "Customizing Charts," if you need step-by-step help with these edits. When you finish working with the chart, click outside the chart boundaries to place the chart on a slide while returning to PowerPoint.

VI

Advanced PowerPoint 4

It takes some work to build properly a readable and useful combination chart. You may need to add labels and change the width of lines, for instance. It's not an automatic process: you don't type the data set and get a fully functional, readable chart. It's necessary to strike a balance between conveying all the information required to deliver your message and avoiding cluttering your slide. That's why grid lines aren't used in this chart—they would only confuse the viewer.

> **Note**
>
> When you create your combination chart, take a look at your series data in the left margin of the spreadsheet. You see a white dot next to the Y2 series row. That white dot is the overlay chart indicator. It indicates that this data series forms the overlay chart, which, in this case, is a line chart with markers.

Combination charts require more planning and setup than other types, but their rewards are greater, because they can convey a great amount of information that would otherwise require two or three charts to depict.

You can use the Format Chart Type and Format Group commands to alter the overlays in your combination charts. A section near the end of this chapter, "Customizing Combination Charts," describes these techniques in more detail.

Using 2-D Radar Charts

Tip
Radar charts can benefit greatly from somewhat heavier line weights.

Radar charts also are called spider charts, because their general shape is like that of a spider's web. Radar charts are used best when you need to show multiple variables, such as ratings in different areas, performance levels of entities such as employees or corporate divisions, or progress in a project or other endeavor.

Radar charts require at least three categories and one series of data. They can also be somewhat perplexing to understand at first glance. Figure 19.5 shows a radar chart generated with the basic default labels and series names provided by PowerPoint.

The row labels are shown in the legend and the column labels in the datasheet are used to label each spoke. The rows represent the three series of data, and each series is shown as a geometric shape whose appearance is determined by the position of each series value on the spokes.

Radar charts are best viewed when the series are arranged to provide maximum visibility to as many series values as possible. This means that when using option 6 in the Radar charts, the series must be stacked like pancakes with the smallest shape on top, the next largest below that, and the largest on the bottom. If they aren't, entire series can be hidden from view and thus from analysis by the audience. If you aren't using option 6, the chart is made up of lines only and it makes no difference what order they are in.

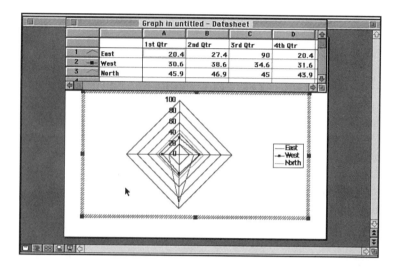

Fig. 19.5
This is the default graph data displayed as a radar chart.

Note

In figure 19.5, the series are arranged in such a way that all the series values can be measured along the spokes. Look closely at the datasheet in the figure. The East data set, which is on the top of the chart stack, is on the third row of the datasheet. Notice also that its values are consistently less than those of the next datasheet row up, the West row. Radar charts may require rearranging of chart values to get the best effect.

A standard datasheet can usually be made to work well with a radar-type chart; the key is to arrange your series for best visibility. Otherwise, axes and axis labels, series markers, grid lines, and other elements of radar charts can be selected and customized much as any other chart.

To create a simple radar chart, follow these steps:

1. In PowerPoint, click the Insert Graph button on the standard toolbar. Microsoft Graph appears.

2. Select the default data in Graph's datasheet and delete it. Type the data set information specific to your project.

VI

Advanced PowerPoint 4

3. Open the Format menu and choose AutoFormat. The AutoFormat dialog box appears.

4. From the Galleries list box, choose Radar.

5. Select a chart type (#2 in the example). This option is a radar chart without grid lines.

6. Choose OK.

The end result, given the relative sparseness of the chart, can be rather striking and visually attractive. Radar charts are also well suited for displaying a substantially greater number of series and data values than are given in this example. Up to six or eight data series can be accommodated in a radar chart without difficulty. They're worth considering for an offbeat and striking accent to your data—if you can ensure that your series values is visible.

Using 2-D Doughnut Charts

Tip
Doughnut slices, just like pie slices, can be pulled away from the chart.

Doughnut charts offer many of the same attributes of pie charts, which were described in chapters 13 and 14. The main difference between pie charts and doughnuts is the obvious visual one: the center of a doughnut chart is hollowed out. There is one more difference: unlike a pie chart, it's possible to display more than one series in a doughnut chart. Each series has its own doughnut, one inside of another.

A doughnut chart does provide much the same function that a pie chart does: to display the division of a finite quantity—such as a year's market share—from one series of data. The use of a doughnut chart is mainly a stylistic decision. Figure 19.6 shows a typical doughnut chart.

Fig. 19.6
Doughnut charts, like pie charts, are simple to understand when you have a single data set.

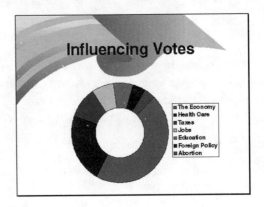

To create a doughnut chart, follow these steps:

1. In PowerPoint, click the Insert Graph button on the standard toolbar. Microsoft Graph appears.

2. Select the default data in Graph's datasheet and delete it. Type the data set specific to your project.

3. Open the Format menu and choose AutoFormat. The AutoFormat dialog box appears.

4. From the Galleries list box, choose Doughnut.

5. From the Formats thumbnails, choose a chart type. It appears as a doughnut chart.

6. Choose OK.

7. If the doughnut appears to be all one color, click the chart (to select it) and then click the By Column tool on the Graph toolbar. The series values should split the doughnut up properly.

The use of doughnut charts is quite straightforward—a 3-D doughnut type is not even available. They're a good substitute for pie charts if you want to break the monotony of a long series of chart slides.

Using 3-D Surface Charts

3-D surface charts are new to PowerPoint; they are a more specialized chart type that is generally not suited for many of the conventional business tasks used by other charts in this chapter. *3-D surface charts* closely resemble topographic maps—in fact, given enough series of data, you could actually construct a topographic map with geological data in PowerPoint.

Surface charts are used to show surface variations established over two or more evenly spaced values. Those evenly spaced values are the X and Y values in your chart, and there must be a minimum of two series of data and two categories of values to form a surface chart. The z-axis values in the chart determine the topography of the chart's surface. A fairly typical 3-D surface chart is shown in figure 19.7.

3-D surface is a chart type that can benefit from the use of major grid lines on each axis. The major grid lines for all axes are displayed on the chart, which greatly aids readability on an already difficult chart.

Fig. 19.7

A 3-D surface chart looks difficult to create, but actually takes just the click of a button.

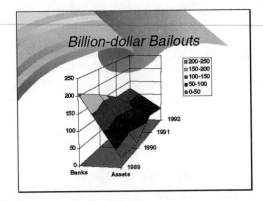

Each series label has a tick mark and a major grid line assigned to it to help show the values of each series as they move across the chart. Based on the surface altitudes, the chart assigns colors to each value range. On first glance, this can be confusing—what values do the colors signify? They actually don't signify any series values—just surface transitions from one series to another. The surface traverses up several ranges of altitude.

There is great scope for creativity and experimenting with this chart type. The chart in figure 19.7 shows a few adjustments, such as 3-D rotation, that have been made to render the chart's values more readable. The following example helps you create a typical 3-D surface chart:

1. In PowerPoint, click the Insert Graph button from the standard toolbar. Microsoft Graph appears.

2. Select the default data in Graph's datasheet and delete it. Type the data set specific to your project.

3. Open the Format menu and choose AutoFormat. The AutoFormat dialog box appears.

4. From the Galleries list box, choose 3-D Surface.

5. From the Format thumbnails, choose a chart type.

6. Choose OK.

To add height and depth to the graph, follow these steps:

1. Open the Format menu and choose 3-D View. The Format 3-D View dialog box appears, as shown in figure 19.8.

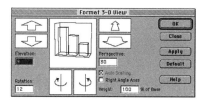

Fig. 19.8
Make adjustments
to the three-
dimensional view
here in the Format
3-D View dialog
box.

2. Enter values to make adjustments to the chart in the Elevation, Rotation, and Perspective text boxes.

3. Choose OK.

To add grid lines to the chart, follow these steps:

1. Open the Insert menu and choose Grid Lines. The Grid Lines dialog box appears.

2. Click the Major Grid Lines check boxes in the Category (X) Axis, Series (Y) Axis, and Value (Z) Axis dialog-box sections.

3. Choose OK.

To relocate the legend to a more convenient place, click the legend, and then follow these steps:

1. Open the Format menu and choose Selected Legend.

2. Click the Placement tab.

3. Click the Right option button under the Type option list to place the legend on the left side of the chart.

4. Choose OK.

Your surface chart may resemble the one shown in figure 19.7.

Surface charts can be heavily customized, and you just had a small taste of that in the preceding example. While they're a very specialized chart type, surface charts are also very attractive and if they're chosen properly for the subject matter, they can be a striking addition to a slide show.

Comparing 3-D Area and 3-D Line Charts

3-D area and 3-D line charts are two more options that you should consider for your slide shows. Both types are readily adaptable to the same kinds of data and can deliver the same message; the use of one over another is

VI

Advanced PowerPoint 4

generally a matter of taste. *Area charts* simply fill the areas below the lines with colors or patterns, but the values defined are the same. 3-D lines and areas are easily customized in much the same way that other 3-D charts are—for different chart depths, rotated views and different perspectives, gap widths between 3-D lines, different grid lines, and more.

Lines are generally easier to see in three dimensions than in 3-D area charts because you don't run the risk of hiding substantial areas behind other ones. Viewers see lines somewhat more distinctly, as separate series at different depths within the chart. Nonetheless, 3-D areas offer other advantages, such as a greater physical presence in the chart, particularly when one area is much greater than the others.

To get to this point, quite a few things may need to be adjusted beyond the basic chart. The rows of data in the chart datasheet may need to be rearranged to ensure that the largest area is in the "back" of the chart. The 3-D viewing angle may need to be adjusted for better area visibility. Axis label fonts may need to be readjusted.

To create 3-D area or line charts, follow these steps:

1. In PowerPoint, click the Insert Graph button on the standard toolbar. Microsoft Graph appears.

2. Select the default data in Graph's datasheet and delete it using the Clear All command from the Edit menu. Type the data set specific to your project.

3. Open the Format menu and choose AutoFormat. The AutoFormat dialog box appears.

4. From the Galleries list, choose 3-D Area. Eight thumbnails appear in the Formats area.

5. Choose a chart (#6 in this example.)

> **Note**
>
> 3-D area chart types #5, #6, and #7 are all quite similar, except for the grid lines that are displayed as their default. Also, several stacked area charts are offered that vary according to their use of grid lines, labels, and other chart elements.

6. Choose OK. The chart appears, as shown in figure 19.9.

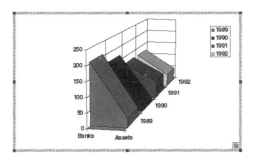

Fig. 19.9
The same data from the combination chart used to create a 3-D area chart.

After you look at the complete graph, you may find it necessary to change the position of some of the series to ensure that all of the statistics are visible. Follow these steps for moving series of data:

1. Click the Datasheet tool to display the datasheet, if it isn't already visible.

2. Drag-and-drop edit each series (by clicking the row button and dragging each row to its new position—make sure you don't erase any other rows) until the series with the smallest values are in the top row, and the progressively larger numbers appear successively down the datasheet.

   The chart results in a better view of the respective areas, as shown in figure 19.10.

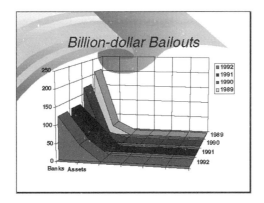

Fig. 19.10
Move the data series so that the smallest values are first.

For added readability and attractiveness, you may also choose to add depth and height to the chart. These steps walk you through that process:

1. Open the Format menu and choose 3-D View. The Format 3-D View dialog box appears.

VI

Advanced PowerPoint 4

2. In the Elevation text box, enter a value.

3. In the Rotation text box, enter a value.

4. If the Perspective feature is not displayed, click the Right Angle Axes check box. The X should be removed, displaying the Perspective feature in the dialog box. If the Perspective feature is already displayed, proceed to the next step.

5. Enter a value in the Perspective text box.

   For many charts, you need to play with the 3-D values to get it right. Also, don't forget that you can rotate a 3-D chart with the mouse.

6. Choose OK.

In the end, PowerPoint's chart types, plus the many customizing features that are available, offer many ways to deliver a chart-based message to your audience. There are other alternatives, however. If you're used to creating your charts and datasheets in Excel, it's quite easy to import them into your presentation and entirely bypass having to create charts in PowerPoint at all. (That procedure is described a little later in this chapter, in the section "Importing Excel Charts.")

You can also adopt a preferred chart as a new default type. That procedure is described in "Creating a New Default Chart" later in this chapter.

Troubleshooting

I can't get my stock charts to display properly.

The key to correct stock charting is twofold: having the correct number of series and displaying your series By Columns on the datasheet. An OHLC stock chart must have four series, one each for the Open, High, Low, and Close data sets, and an HLC chart must have three series. When your data series are properly entered, click the By Column button on Graph's Standard toolbar.

My scatter chart data markers are almost invisible on-screen.

This proves to be a difficult problem only because you have to do some work with the chart's color scheme (and very likely its slide as well) to make your scatter chart markers more visible. On many occasions, a scatter chart needs a different color scheme from the rest of the presentation because of the difficulty of making the markers visible.

A good rule of thumb is to use bold, bright primary colors for scatter chart markers, and to use a dark background color on the slide. First, click the scatter markers, each series in turn, and choose Format Selected Data Series. Change the marker colors to reflect your needs (making sure that each marker series is a different color). If you must use grid lines (which can be a good idea with a scatter chart) use black for their color to ensure that your markers show up. Then select a dark color for your slide background.

An example of the use of these techniques for a scatter chart appears in Appendix B of this book.

Creating a New Default Chart

Using a preferred chart as a default chart format has a number of advantages. First, it prevents the necessity of reentering the same set of data for a series of charts using the same datasheet, or even the tedium of clearing and pasting data between slides.

Second, every formatting specification you desire can be included in the default format, including axes, axis labels, types of grid lines, line weights, fonts attached to labels, colors, and anything else having to do with chart formatting.

To create a new default chart, follow these steps:

1. If you create a chart for your slides and you're pleased with the layout and want to use it as the new default format, make sure all the formatting changes are made that you want to include in the new default.

2. Open the Tools menu and choose Options. The Graph Options dialog box appears, as shown in figure 19.11.

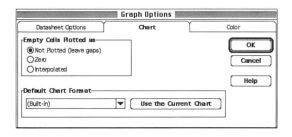

Fig. 19.11
In the Graph Options dialog box, set the defaults for slides.

3. Click the Chart tab.

Here, an entire list of new charts can be added for new default chart types. Under the Default Chart Format list, the Graph default is called Built-In.

4. In the Default Chart Format section of the dialog box, choose the Use the Current Chart button.

> **Note**
>
> The new default chart type is placed as an entry in the Graph folder. Whenever Graph is started up, it loads the new chart type from this file as the default format.

5. Choose OK.

Exporting a PowerPoint Chart to Other Applications

Though PowerPoint cannot directly export chart objects to other applications, it's possible to save a slide as a bitmap picture for display in other programs. It's a straightforward process, and it's described in the following steps:

1. Display the slide you want to export as a bitmap picture.

2. Open the File menu and choose Save As. The Save As dialog box appears (see fig. 19.12).

Fig. 19.12
This dialog box is a familiar Macintosh feature for saving, opening, and browsing files.

3. In the Save Presentation as text box, type the desired name for the file.

4. Choose the folder in which the file can be saved.

5. In the Save File as Type pop-up menu, choose Scrapbook (pictures).

6. Choose OK.

The slide is saved as a picture, or screen shot, to be viewed or placed in a different application.

Importing Data and Charts

PowerPoint 4 offers direct ways to import data and charts from Microsoft Excel. Versions 4 and 5 of Excel are supported. Although PowerPoint has a closer relationship to Excel 5 in terms of object linking and embedding capabilities, you can still include Excel 4 charts and datasheets. This short section describes the direct importing of data and charts from Excel files.

Importing Data

Importing Excel or Lotus 1-2-3 datasheets can be an extremely handy feature for PowerPoint users. You may want to create your own charts in PowerPoint but have most of your data committed in datasheets from another program. Importing them can save tons of work. Doing so requires only that you be in PowerPoint's Graph application. A good way to start is by displaying a PowerPoint default chart and datasheet in a new Graph slide. With the default chart and datasheet displayed in Microsoft Graph (not in PowerPoint), follow these steps:

1. Open the Edit menu and choose Import Data. The Import Data dialog box appears, as shown in figure 19.13.

Fig. 19.13

Another instance of the common Macintosh dialog box for choosing destinations or, in this case, sources.

2. Choose the folder in which the file can be located.

3. In the File Name list, double-click the desired file name to place it in the Graph document. A message box appears asking whether you want to overwrite the existing data.

4. Choose Yes. The Excel data is displayed in the Graph datasheet.

Importing Excel Charts

Importing Excel charts can also be useful for PowerPoint users. You may want to create your own charts in Excel because you're used to that program, and your data may be committed to datasheets in that program. Importing them is simple and doing so requires only that you be in PowerPoint's Graph application. A good way to start is by displaying a PowerPoint default chart and datasheet in a new Graph slide. With the default chart and datasheet displayed in Graph (not in PowerPoint), follow these steps:

1. Open the Edit menu and choose Import Chart. The Import Chart dialog box appears.

2. Choose the folders in which the file can be located.

3. In the File Name list, double-click the desired file name to select it and import it into Graph. A message box appears asking whether you want to overwrite the existing chart.

4. Choose Yes. The Excel chart is displayed in Graph, available for changing and editing in Graph's normal modes.

Importing Charts from PowerPoint 3

If you built a library of presentations and charts created in PowerPoint 3, you're in luck. It's a very simple matter to import charts from the previous version of the program into PowerPoint 4.

Essentially, all you have to do is load the old-format presentation into the PowerPoint program. Once you do so, double-clicking on a chart in a slide automatically converts the old Microsoft Graph charts to the new version. The major difference between the versions of Graph, of course, is that the older version uses OLE 1, while the current version uses OLE 2, or in-place editing. Graph data is converted automatically, invisible to the user. Here's how the procedure is done:

1. Start the PowerPoint program.

2. Open the File menu and choose Open, or press ⌘-O. The Open dialog box appears.

3. From the appropriate folders, choose the PowerPoint 3 file you want to load and then choose OK. (You also can just double-click the title to import the file.) After a moment, the program displays this message:

```
This presentation uses File Format 80. It will be converted
to Format 102 and opened as Read-Only.
```

4. Choose OK.

5. After the file is opened, save the open file as a new PowerPoint 4 format file (you cannot overwrite the old one).

6. Double-click a chart in the presentation. The conversion is finished.

To use an alternative method, follow these steps:

1. With your presentation displayed in PowerPoint, open the Insert menu and choose Slides from File. The Insert File dialog box appears.

2. From the appropriate folders, choose the PowerPoint 3 file you want to load.

3. Choose OK.

The slides from the PowerPoint 3 file (or PowerPoint 4 file, for that matter) are automatically converted and inserted into your presentation. You do not even see a screen message regarding file formats, but you may see a `Charts are being updated to the new color scheme` message for a moment as the computer does its work.

Saving Custom Chart Types for Later Use

Earlier in this chapter, you learned how to create a new default chart. Now, a similar procedure can be used to create new AutoFormats. Doing so enables you to reuse powerful new chart formats for any appropriate chart.

There are actually two different ways to perform this task. One is to use the same procedure as for defining a default chart. The other way is simpler and more efficient. The easier procedure is described here:

1. Display the chart, in Microsoft Graph, for which you want to make a new AutoFormat.

2. Open the Format menu and choose AutoFormat. The AutoFormat dialog box appears.

3. Under the Formats Used section of the dialog box, click the User-Defined option button.

4. Click the Customize button. The User-Defined AutoFormats dialog box appears, similar to figure 19.14.

Tip
You can delete any AutoFormat you previously defined here.

VI

Advanced PowerPoint 4

Fig. 19.14

The User-Defined AutoFormats dialog box allows you to define aspects of slide formats.

5. Click the Add button. The Add Custom AutoFormat dialog box appears, as shown in figure 19.15.

Fig. 19.15

Type the name and description of the custom layout in these text boxes.

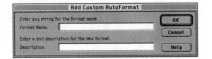

6. In the Format Name text box, type the desired chart name (make it an easily understood name that won't be confused with other chart types).

7. Type a description in the Description text box, if desired (it is not required).

8. Choose OK. The AutoFormat is added to the User-Defined list.

To apply the newly created AutoFormat, follow these steps:

1. Open the Format menu and choose AutoFormat. The AutoFormat dialog box appears.

Tip

If you're pleased with your current chart layout and want to save it as a new AutoFormat, make sure all the formatting changes are made that you want included in the new chart type.

2. Under the Formats Used section of the dialog box, click the User-Defined button.

3. In the Formats list, click the chart type you want. The dialog box displays a sample chart.

4. Choose OK. The AutoFormat you previously defined is applied to the chart.

Notice that all the proper text formatting and chart elements are exactly where they should be. Remember that specific chart types you define may also require a certain number of data series to display properly.

Customizing Combination Charts

PowerPoint offers other features to customize and change combination charts (and, for that matter, any chart type) by using two commands that haven't been discussed very much until now: the Format Chart Type command and the Format Group command. Neither command is particularly difficult and both offer another dimension to the conventional use of AutoFormats, which you've relied on for most of the charting examples in this book.

Both commands allow you to change the type of data markers that are applied to any data series in your chart. For example, if you have a combination chart that uses a line and an area, the area can be quickly converted to a set of 2-D columns. A chart of any type can be converted to any other type.

The Format Chart Type command and the Format Group command are closely interrelated, and they can both be accessed from one another (see fig. 19.16 and fig. 19.17).

Tip

Use the Format Chart Type and Format Group commands to experiment with combination chart types.

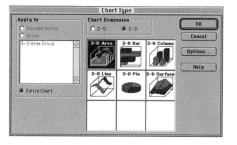

Fig. 19.16

Chart Type has direct access to the Format Group command.

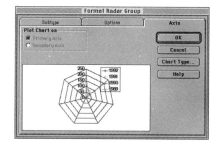

Fig. 19.17

You can reach Chart Type from within Format Group as well.

The Format Group menu option is a dynamic one that changes based on the chart type you select (see fig. 19.18). You see two Group commands on the Format menu only if you're using a combination chart. Otherwise, only one Group command is shown on the menu.

VI

Advanced PowerPoint 4

Fig. 19.18

Format Group is a dynamic menu listing that changes with the type of chart selected.

If you click the 1 Column Group or 2 Column Group menu commands, you bring up the Format Column Group or Format Line Group dialog box, each of which bears three tabs: Subtype, Options, and Axis. All of these add custom effects to your charts, and all three tabs dynamically change to offer different features depending on the chart type that's currently selected.

In all cases, clicking the Chart Type button in the Format Group dialog box brings up the Format Chart Type dialog box in turn (refer to fig. 19.17).

This is the place where you can change the chart type that's applied to the current chart or selected series (or a Group) in a combination chart. A Group is a group of data series used to create a chart, and a single series is obviously one set of data markers of the same color in the chart. You can have up to two groups in a chart, which results in a combination chart. Clicking one of the groups in the Group list and then clicking a thumbnail changes the chart type for the selected group.

It isn't as hard as it sounds. Be aware that you can change any chart to a 2-D or 3-D type (by choosing the 2-D or 3-D option button under the Format Chart Type Chart Dimension section shown in fig. 19.16), but you cannot apply 3-D chart types to groups in a combination chart. The other group is erased from view in the chart.

Click a thumbnail in the Format Chart Type dialog box to change the chart type for the selected chart or group. It's a great way to experiment with various combinations and chart styles.

Using Trendlines To Do Forecasting

Trendlines are a useful tool for forecasting and illustrating trends in your charts. You can apply trendlines to most 2-D chart types; they're very useful for 2-D column charts, but they can be applied to bar, scatter, line, and area charts as well. In fact, they can be applied to any chart type in the XY category. They can also be used with a combination chart, and in such a chart a trendline can be applied to each group. They cannot, however, be applied to an OHLC or HLC stock chart. You see a 2-D column chart used generically in the examples shown here.

Trendlines are a tool for forecasting possible future trends in your data. While they're simple to use, the concept behind trendlines is not. The theory behind trendlines is an idea called *regression analysis*. Without getting too technical, regression analysis is the basis for using your datasheet statistics to create the trendline. The math behind creating trendlines is not trivial, and you can choose between six different mathematical models to create your trendline.

Linear

Polynomial

Logarithmic

Exponential

Power

Moving Average

Depending on the nature of your datasheet numbers, you may need to try two or three math models to get the most accurate trendline. How can you tell if a trendline is accurate? Check the R-Squared value. All the calculation methods listed above yield a final value between 0 and 1. The closer a trendline's R-Squared value is to 1, the more accurate it is for the purposes of your chart. If it's closer to 0, the less accurate its trend calculations are.

Please note that many details are beyond the scope of this book; Graph's On-Line Help on this subject (which is found best by using the Search for Help On feature) is highly recommended for users who need more detail than can feasibly be provided here.

To apply a trendline, follow these steps:

1. Display your 2-D column chart in Microsoft Graph.

2. Click the data series (a set of columns of a specific color) to which you want to add a trendline.

3. Open the Insert menu and choose Trendline. The Trendline dialog box appears, as shown in figure 19.19.

VI

Advanced PowerPoint 4

Fig. 19.19
Use the Trendline
dialog box to plot
projections.

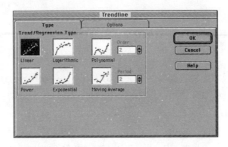

4. Six thumbnail types are displayed on the Type tab, showing the various trendline types that can be applied: Linear, Logarithmic, Polynomial, Power, Exponential, or Moving Average. Click any of them (it may take some experimenting to get the best trendline type for your chart).

You can add a name for your trendline and set other options for the trendline, such as displaying the R-Squared value.

5. Click the Options tab (see fig. 19.20).

Fig. 19.20
Customize the
Trendline in the
Options tab area.

> **Note**
>
> You need at least four series values to display the R-Squared value of your trendline to determine its accuracy.

6. To display the R-Squared value for your trendline, click the Display R-Squared value on Chart check box.

7. To display the formula used to create the trendline, click the Display Equation on Chart check box.

> **Note**
>
> The use of trendlines also offers a forecasting feature in which you can extrapolate from the data in your chart to a user-specified number of time periods based on the time periods reflected in your chart. Doing so extends your trendline beyond the scope provided by your basic chart. You can forecast backward or forward on your chart trendline. This feature is also called goal seeking.

8. To add forecasting to your chart, under the Forecast section of the Options tab, type a value in the Forward Periods or Backward Periods text box or use the mouse to increment them to a desired value. Both Forward and Backward forecasting can be used at one time.

9. The Trendline name is automatically added, or you can add your own by typing it in the Custom text box.

10. Choose OK.

By using trendlines, you can add a sophisticated element of forecasting and statistical trend illustration to your charts. It's recommended that you have some understanding of mathematics (or know someone who does) so that you can make the best choice for accurate forecasts. Nonetheless, displaying the R-Squared value is a good expedient for a quick assessment of the accuracy of each of the six types of trendlines, though it does require some experimenting.

Troubleshooting

How can I get all my axis tick mark labels to display properly? Some of them are erased when I display the chart.

Often, Graph does not display all your axis tick mark labels because the font that's assigned to the axis is too large. When that happens, labels sometimes overrun each other, and the Graph program tends to drop them. To fix this, reduce the font size by clicking the offending axis and choosing the Format Font command.

You can run into the same problem in a 3-D chart. There are two cures for this: change the font size and adjust the 3-D Rotation values in the ways described in this chapter.

(continues)

(continued)

Can I create combination charts using 3-D types—say, a 3-D column chart combined with a 2-D line?

No. It's not possible to combine a 3-D chart to create a combination chart type. The other chart type is automatically erased. Your series data in the datasheet is not removed, but Graph does not display it in combination.

Also, if you play around with the Format Chart Type command as described earlier in this chapter, you find it's possible to combine a 2-D pie chart with, say, a line chart, but the results are almost meaningless and you have a very hard time trying to define the relationship between such a combination of types. Nonetheless, the scope for experimentation is so great that even with a trial-and-error process, you may find combinations no one has thought of, and with customizing features even be able to pull them off.

From Here...

Despite the extensive looks at PowerPoint 4's powerful charting capabilities, there is much that has been skipped or glossed over due to simple space considerations. An entire book could be devoted to PowerPoint's charting features alone. Hopefully, ample information has been provided to you for further explorations of charting. There are some advanced topics remaining to be discussed in the following chapters:

- Chapter 20, "Advanced Presentation Management," shows you how to add special transition effects and their timing to a presentation, along with the use of multimedia effects such as sound bites and video clips.

- Chapter 21, "Using Advanced Color, Text, and Drawing Features," shows how to add special effects to slide text, text rotation, tricks with color, and the creation of new color schemes.

- Chapter 22, "Customizing PowerPoint," shows how functions you saw in this chapter can be added to a customized toolbar.

Chapter 20

Advanced Presentation Management

PowerPoint 4, along with its previous versions, offers many special effects that can be added to slide shows. No presentation, particularly if it includes special multimedia elements such as video and audio clips, is complete without a set timing structure that enables the user to seamlessly integrate various elements without unwanted foul-ups during the actual show. Even if you have never conducted a public talk in your life, PowerPoint's transition, timing, and rehearsal features can help you appear as a Norman Vincent Peale. For effective presentation management, you need to understand and use PowerPoint's rehearsal features.

You learn about the following PowerPoint 4 features in this chapter:

- How to create transitions between slides

- How to rehearse and set timings for events in your presentation

- How to integrate multimedia elements into your presentation

Setting Transition Styles and Transition Timing

When you run a slide show, it's quite simple to flip from one slide to the next on-screen—it's the typical 35mm slide show metaphor. It's just as easy, however, to provide graceful transitions between slides that add a more sophisticated effect with minimal trouble on your part. Transition styles can be assigned for any or all slides in your presentation with a few mouse clicks.

A *transition style* is the style in which a slide appears and disappears in an on-screen presentation. The concept is analogous to a slow fade, a "peeling" off the screen during a movie, or a fancy video effect applied to a screen message during a football game. It's a quick segue to the next slide in your presentation. PowerPoint 4 offers 46 different transition styles that can be applied to any slide in your presentation. Styles include vertical and horizontal blinds, in which segments of the slide are revealed to the viewer; Box In and Box Out, in which the information on the next slide appears to implode or explode onto the screen; Checkerboard Across and Checkerboard Down, in which the contents of the next slide appear in a checkerboard pattern; and Cover Left, Up, Down, Left-Up, Right-Up, Left-Down, and Right-Down, in which the slide is assigned a direction from which it appears to be placed down on top of the previous one. There are, of course, many more.

◀ See "Working with Outlines," p. 187

◀ See "Creating Speaker's Notes," p.176

When you rehearse a presentation, you're actually in the process of setting the timing for all the events in your presentation—when each slide appears, when text points in a list appear on-screen, and so on. Effective use of timing in a presentation, particularly in a long and complex one, is a vital tool in preventing your audience from losing interest in your ideas.

Knowing the timing of your slide show also points out the importance of the other parts of your presentation—the outlines, speaker's notes, and handouts that were discussed earlier in this book. With a few extra minutes of preparation, all these tools can be used to deliver your message intelligently and cogently.

Setting a Transition Style on a Slide

You can assign a transition to a slide in any PowerPoint view—Slide, Notes Pages, Outline, and Slide Sorter (see fig. 20.1). Although all views offer the same method for assigning effects, the Slide Sorter has advantages; its thumbnail display of all the slides enables you to keep visual track of all the slides to which you have assigned effects, and to interact with the entire presentation in a way that other views don't permit. Slides can be dragged and dropped in the Sorter to a different order, for example. You use the Slide Sorter to assign transition effects for the examples in this chapter.

Another solid advantage of using the Slide Sorter to apply transitions and other effects is its display of small Transition icons underneath each slide thumbnail indicating when a transition effect has been applied to a selected slide, as shown in figure 20.1. The icons do not appear if a slide has not had an effect applied to it.

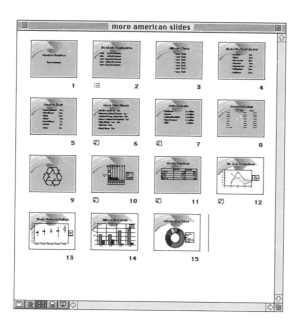

Fig. 20.1
The Slide Sorter
shows thumbnail
views of the
presentation.

Tip
For a fast transi-
tion assignment,
choose an effect
from the Transi-
tion pop-up menu
at the top of the
screen below the
toolbar. A transi-
tion icon appears
below the chosen
slide.

To assign transitions to slides in Slide Sorter view, follow these steps:

1. Open the desired presentation in PowerPoint.

2. Open the View menu and choose Slide Sorter. The Slide Sorter appears.

3. Click the slide to which you want to assign a transition.

4. Click the Transition button on the Slide Sorter toolbar to display the Transition dialog box, as shown in figure 20.2.

Fig. 20.2
Select a transition
style from this
dialog box.

VI

Advanced PowerPoint 4

5. Choose the transition options you want. (These are described in text that follows.)

    Remember that, as on the Slide Sorter toolbar, a transition effect can be applied from the pop-up menu in the dialog box.

An advantage of using the Transition dialog box in the Slide Sorter or in Slide view is that you can assign speeds and specific timings to transitions. This can be done with slides that already have assigned transitions, or with newly assigned ones.

Setting Transition Timing

To set the transition timing for a slide, follow these steps:

Tip
Select all your slides and choose a transition if you want to apply the same transition to every slide.

1. To assign a different speed to your transition, click on either the Slow, Medium, or Fast option button in the Speed section of the Transition dialog box.

   Slides can be advanced with a mouse click, or you can set the slide to advance automatically after a specified time.

2. Select an option for advancing your slides:

   - If you want the slide transition to advance on your prompting, click the Only on Mouse Click option button.

   - To set a custom slide timing, click on the Automatically After __ Seconds option button and enter the desired length in seconds (before the next slide appears) in the text box.

Managing Multimedia Effects

The last few years have seen an explosion of multimedia effects and applications in the Macintosh market. A few meaningful results have come of this wave of new technology; the most important additions to the roster of computer-based media are full-motion video and CD-quality sound. Both of these additional data types can easily be incorporated into your PowerPoint presentation. The standard that has emerged for the use of video on your Macintosh is Apple's QuickTime.

Understanding Video

Video comes from any of several sources. You can hook up a portable video camera or a VCR to your Macintosh and you instantly have new video clips to play with, or you can buy video clips on CD-ROM.

Recording video clips on your Macintosh can be an expensive business; video typically chews up hard disk space at an astonishing speed. Though it does have some drawbacks, it is most certainly one of the best ways to capture your audience's attention. A video clip can be played on a prompt by the user during the presentation, or the clip can be set to play automatically during the slide show, once or in a continuous loop.

A copy of QuickTime is packaged with the Macintosh System software. Several features of QuickTime can be used to ease the process of playing video during a presentation. Later in this chapter, you learn about the techniques for proper manipulation of video in your slides. The next section deals with the placement of video clips in your presentation.

Inserting Video Clips

You can insert video clips into any slide of your presentation. Doing so is a straightforward process. To insert video clips and other objects, you must be in PowerPoint's Slide view. Follow these steps:

1. If you're still in the Slide Sorter, choose Slides from the View menu.

2. With the Slide Changer, choose the slide into which you want to insert the video clip.

3. Open the Insert menu and choose Movie. The Preview dialog box appears (see fig. 20.3).

Tip
In the Slide Sorter, double-click the slide in which you want to insert a video clip. The slide is displayed in Slide view.

Fig. 20.3
This dialog box enables you to find the video clip to insert.

4. Locate the proper folder that contains your video file, and double-click its title. When you select the movie, the Open button changes to the Insert button.

5. Choose the Insert button. The new video clip appears on the slide as a poster frame of the first clip of the video. The video object can be resized and moved around the slide like any other object on-screen.

There are options for controlling and playing video clips and other multimedia data types. They are discussed a little later in this chapter.

VI

Advanced PowerPoint 4

Using the Play Settings Feature To Trigger Multimedia Events

PowerPoint 4 offers a simple but powerful way to manage the timing and triggering of multimedia elements in your presentation by using the Play Settings command.

It's easy to apply timing to multimedia events in your presentation. It's also a handy, or even essential, feature if you're not interested in clicking the mouse to control all aspects of your slide show when you deliver it. As with other timing events in your presentation, it's a matter of specifying a time delay with a couple of mouse clicks and typing a value into a dialog box. To do so, follow these steps:

1. Click the desired video object.

2. Open the Tools menu and choose Play Settings. The Play Settings dialog box appears (see fig. 20.4).

Fig. 20.4

In the Play Settings dialog box, set the timing and transition for the video clip.

3. Choose options in the dialog box. The options displayed in this dialog box are described in table 20.1, following these steps.

4. Choose OK.

Tip

To hide multimedia effects on an otherwise crowded slide, choose the Hide While Not Playing check box in the Play Settings dialog box.

Table 20.1 Play Settings Options	
Option	**Description**
Sound	Sound file (WAV); not available in PowerPoint 4
Movie	Video clip (AVI)
Other	Other objects, such as animation
Action	Performs a specific action

Option	Description
When Click on Object	Tells the program to play the object when it's double-clicked by the presenter
When Transition Starts	Plays the object at a specific time after the slide appears
When Transition Ends,	Plays object when the Plus *x* Seconds slide appears; specifies a time delay after the slide appears
Hide While Not Playing	Suppresses the view of the video clip until it is played

Note

If you have two or more multimedia objects in a slide, different timings can be assigned to each so that they trigger in sequence.

Multimedia objects are a fun way to dress up a slide, but don't go overboard with them. Many products, on disk and particularly on CD-ROM, are available and provide libraries of stock video footage that can be used freely. When you are importing video clips, remember not to use copyrighted material. You may be held liable for expensive royalties, or even criminal prosecution, if the unlikely chance occurs that you are caught using someone else's artistic or intellectual property to spice up your slide show.

Tip

When you cut and paste multimedia objects that have Play Settings applied to them, the settings migrate with the objects.

Managing Video Effects

The Edit menu allows you to set options for how your video clip will be played in your slide show. Figure 20.5 shows the menu movie options displayed, with a typical video clip.

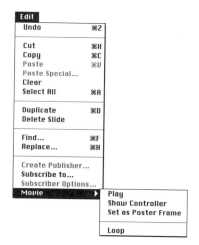

Fig. 20.5
The Edit menu contains video-clip play options.

VI

Advanced PowerPoint 4

To play an existing video clip, follow these steps:

1. Click the embedded video object to select it.

2. Open the Edit menu and choose Movie; then choose Play from the cascading menu. After a moment, the video clip begins to play.

Troubleshooting

My video doesn't play during my presentation.

Don't forget to take the video clips along if you transport the presentation. Make sure you bring all your multimedia objects with you when you deliver your presentation.

Another tip: when you embed video files into your presentation, make sure you bring them from your hard disk and not a CD-ROM. You need to think ahead on this issue, because the host computer on which you deliver your presentation may not have a CD-ROM drive. The safest bet is to place your multimedia object files directly on your hard drive before you embed them into your presentation. In other words, copy the desired files from the CD-ROM (if that's where they originate from) to the hard disk.

Then, when you bring the presentation and its multimedia object files in to the other site, you can be assured that the presentation will find them, because you can place the object files in the host computer. Most Macintosh computers have an internal hard drive, so you'll be safe in knowing that your presentation will find the files when it needs them.

Hiding Slides

PowerPoint 4 offers the capability to hide one or more slides in a presentation. Hidden slides are especially useful if you have created a large presentation that contains elements for several different audiences—some of whom may not need to see parts of the same slide show.

Creating Hidden Slides

Slides can be hidden when you are in Slide view or in the Slide Sorter. The Slide Sorter is recommended for this operation because Slide Sorter makes it easier to keep track of the slides.

To hide multiple slides with a single Hide Slide command, hold the Shift key as you click each slide in the Slide Sorter and then execute the Hide command (see fig. 20.6).

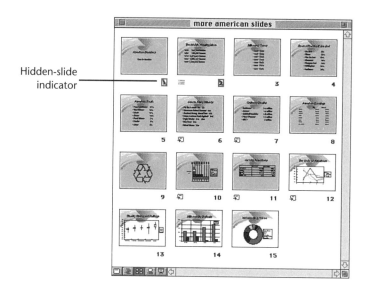

Hidden-slide
indicator

Fig. 20.6
A hidden slide is
indicated in the
Slide Sorter.

To create hidden slides in a presentation, follow these steps:

1. Display the presentation in the Slide Sorter.

2. Click the slide to be hidden during the presentation.

3. Open the Tools menu and choose Hide Slide.

The slide number at the bottom has a box icon stamped over it, signifying that it is hidden when the slide show is run. The hidden slide is skipped automatically.

If you change your mind about a hidden slide, simply execute the Hide Slide command again.

Displaying Hidden Slides

During a presentation, it may become necessary to display a hidden slide for an unanticipated reason. The procedure is a simple one and can be done during the slide show.

To display hidden slides, follow these steps:

1. Run the slide show.

2. When a slide appears during the slide show, move the mouse. If the slide after the current one is a hidden slide, an asterisk icon will appear at the bottom right corner.

By moving the mouse on-screen, the asterisk icon is displayed. The mouse must be moved by the presenter for the icon to appear. The icon can then be clicked for the next, otherwise hidden, slide to appear.

Building Text Effects

Text elements in your slides can have a feature applied to them called *builds*. Builds are similar to the transition styles described earlier in this chapter, except that they're applied to text objects. Individual build effects are applied to individual items in a bulleted list, or assigned to an entire selected bulleted list or text object at once. There are some limiting factors to build effects, however, that include the following:

■ You cannot apply build effects to slide titles.

■ You cannot apply build effects to drawn art, clip art, or any object other than a body text object.

■ You cannot apply one build effect to one bullet item, and then another build effect to a second or third bullet item in a bulleted list.

As with transitions, builds can be applied to slides in either Slide view or the Slide Sorter. For this example, the Slide Sorter is used. Figure 20.7 shows a Slide Sorter displaying several slides to which builds have been added.

Fig. 20.7
The icon at the bottom left indicates that a build has been applied to that slide.

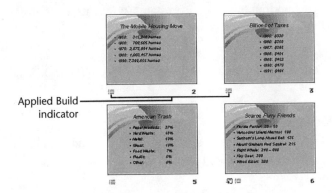

Applied Build indicator

Builds are normally applied to text slides—slides that contain a bulleted list as their main component. They're called *build slides* for this reason. Sometimes they also are termed Progressive Transition slides. Regardless of the semantics, follow these steps to create them:

1. Display the current presentation in the Slide Sorter.

2. Click the slide to which a build is to be added.

3. Click the Build button in the Slide Sorter toolbar. The Build dialog box appears (see fig. 20.8).

Fig. 20.8
The Build dialog box offers specific options for applied builds.

4. Choose the Build Body Text option, which makes the current slide a build slide, regardless of its contents. Although the slide may contain no body text, the build is attached to the slide. Nontext objects in the slide are not affected.

5. In the Effect pop-up menu, choose one of the various effects, which closely parallel the effects offered for slide transitions.

6. To dim previous bulleted items in the body text, click the Dim Previous Points check box, and choose a color from the pop-up menu.

7. Choose OK. The chosen build effect is assigned to the slide.

If the build is applied to body text in a bulleted list, each bullet item reveals itself in sequence using the chosen build effect. In the Sorter, a small icon appears denoting the slide as a build slide. The icon is the same as the graphic on the Build button on the Slide Sorter toolbar.

Rehearsing Your Presentation

Now that you have learned about transitions, builds, multimedia events (at least, the basics thereof), and merging and branching presentations, it's time for the finishing touch—rehearsing presentation timing and events. PowerPoint's rehearsing tools are among the best in its field.

Rehearsing is a vital step in creating an effective presentation; it's also much simpler than it sounds. Why is it important? When you apply build and transition effects, and include numerous multimedia elements, it's important to keep control of the timing of all the various elements to, simply put, keep

VI

Advanced PowerPoint 4

yourself from messing up in front of your audience. Rehearsing is another tool that puts you in control, and with speaker's notes, handouts, and outlines, it is one that should not be neglected.

In figure 20.7, notice that a callout points to some numeric entries under certain slides. Those numbers indicate the number of seconds for which that specific slide is displayed during the presentation.

To rehearse your presentation, follow these steps:

1. Display the first slide in your presentation.

2. Open the View menu and choose Slide Show. The Slide Show dialog box appears (see fig. 20.9).

Fig. 20.9
You customize the slide presentation advancement in the Slide Show dialog box.

3. Choose rehearsal options, which are described in table 20.2 following these steps.

4. Choose Show. The slide show starts, and a timer is displayed at the bottom of the screen, showing elapsed seconds.

Click the mouse, or press the space bar, Return, or Enter to trigger each successive event in the slide show. You can press Esc at any time to stop and go back to the PowerPoint screen.

Table 20.2 Rehearsal Options	
Option	**Description**
All	Rehearses entire presentation
From	Specifies range of slides to rehearse
Manual Advance	Uses mouse click or keystroke to advance to the next slide
Use Slide Timings	Uses default slide timings in template

Option	Description
Rehearse New Timings	Uses keystrokes and/or mouse click to set timings and trigger the events of the presentation
Run Continuously until COMMAND+'.'	Presentation runs in endless loop until you press ⌘-period (.)

Remember that when you rehearse a presentation, you're rehearsing all the events that compose it—builds, multimedia event triggers, and the length of time that each slide is displayed.

Annotating Slides

While you're conducting a slide show, you might find it handy to emphasize points, like a teacher at a chalkboard. PowerPoint 4 offers an easy way to do this.

When you run a slide show, you see a small pencil icon in the bottom-right corner of the screen, as shown in figure 20.10.

American Trash

———Annotation icon

Fig. 20.10
The pencil icon in the bottom-right corner of a presentation is for marking annotations on the slide.

Click the icon while in the slide show. Drag the mouse across the screen. You can draw circles around items, and draw arrows to point to slide elements.

To move on to the next slide, or the next event in the current slide, press the space bar or Return.

From Here...

Many tools for effective presentation management are presented in this chapter. Some subjects, such as multimedia objects, have been extensively discussed, but out of necessity, many detailed touches have been left out. Exploring the features described in this chapter should give you a much stronger feel for how an entire presentation is tied together. For information on other advanced topics, see the following chapters:

- Chapter 21, "Using Advanced Color, Text, and Drawing Features," shows how to add special effects to slide text, text rotation, tricks with color, and the creation of new color schemes.

- Chapter 22, "Customizing PowerPoint," discusses how many functions covered in this chapter can be added to a customized toolbar.

Chapter 21

Using Advanced Color, Text, and Drawing Features

No matter how powerful an application program is, there probably will not be a day when one program can perform every task a user needs to get a job done. This is true even of PowerPoint 4—as flexible and useful as it is for presentations—and it can't hurt to expand PowerPoint's capabilities to add sizzle and pop to your slides.

There are many powerful and inexpensive tools that PowerPoint users can use for brilliant presentations. This chapter introduces you to a few of them.

In this chapter, you learn the following advanced tasks:

- Use colors and patterns effectively

- Use shading effects

- Handle fonts

- Create and edit tables

- Use the Equation Editor

Tips for Using Colors and Patterns Effectively

◀ See "Applying Colors to Individual Objects," p. 378

Several chapters in this book emphasize that color is an important tool for creating successful presentations. Besides making attractive pictures, color provides many elements in a presentation. Color can add emphasis to items in a slide and lend balance to a slide's appearance.

Your first impulse may be to use lots of color mixes to break the monotony of a long presentation. In most situations, you should resist that impulse. Using the same colors throughout a presentation can give unity to an overall concept.

Why learn more about how color works? Slide and chart readability can be aided greatly by the proper use of color. Therefore, colors should be chosen carefully when you build a color scheme. In black-and-white overheads, patterns and shades of gray aid in readability and must be chosen with even more care.

Colors and patterns can be used to direct attention to important points, data, graphics, and chart elements. For emphasis in color printouts or overheads, a bold color can be applied to the most important series. Lighter shades of the same color can be applied to other series in a chart. For on-screen presentations, light or bright colors can be used for emphasis. For black-and-white overheads and slides, the most important series should be shown in the darkest pattern.

A good rule of thumb for text slides (which probably constitute the majority of the slides you make) is to use color rather than text style for emphasizing lines or values in text.

Understanding good color relationships can be very useful in creating a successful presentation. Warm colors, such as red, orange, and yellow, draw the eye's attention by offering more visual punch and activity. Cool colors, such as greens, blues, and violets, provide rest for the eye. They can be used for backgrounds to set off areas of warmer colors, such as a movie clip depicting a bright outdoors scene.

Tip

Avoid red-green color combinations because a substantial portion (almost 10%) of the population is red-green color-blind.

Colors also have complementary relationships. On a color wheel, for example, the colors of the rainbow are drawn, each occupying a segment of the wheel. Colors that are located on opposite sides of the wheel from each other are *complements*. Color complements illustrate how certain colors get along with each other most effectively, regardless of their essential character. That's why dark blue and yellow have such frequent use in presentations.

Blue is a more restful color than yellow, yet the two colors mesh quite well. They are located opposite one another on the color wheel. Light greens and violets, and reds and light blues are also complementary color combinations. These combinations please the eye when used properly. Generally, one of the complements is used in a large area (such as a slide background) or with a high saturation, while the other color is used as an accent, such as text color.

Another aspect of using color is a *split complement*. Split complements expand on the range of complementary colors for a more subtle effect. For example, on the color wheel, light green is located next to yellow. Light green is a split complement color that can be used well with dark blue, which is normally the complement of yellow. Thus, a complementary color can have a color substitute (split complement) that is adjacent to it in the color wheel but that still works as a combination. The color templates offered in PowerPoint 4 universally follow the concepts of using complementary colors and split complements for their color schemes.

The simple use of complementary colors is not always enough. Physiological and psychological changes take place in people when they're exposed to certain colors. People are capable of finding a room that's painted a blue color to be colder in temperature than a room painted a mild peach color, even if both rooms are the same temperature. Red is known as a color that can raise the tension of the viewer, or even raise his blood pressure.

By the same token, if you have large areas of complementary colors (or split complementary colors) bordering each other, the effect is visually disturbing and annoying. It's an effect known as *simultaneous contrast* and should be avoided. It happens, for example, if you have an area of bright red and one of bright green bordering each other. The contrast leaps out at you and is hard to look at.

> **Note**
>
> To avoid the problem of simultaneous contrast, a good technique is to place a black, gray, or white border around the color object. An even better technique is to avoid having two large areas of complementary colors present. You can also lower the saturation of each color to produce a milder effect.

With some basic tips for good color relationships behind you, it's time to take a closer look at PowerPoint's color mixing system.

Understanding PowerPoint's Color Matching Systems

While Chapter 17, "Working with Color," discussed color and PowerPoint in some detail, the attributes of color in PowerPoint need some further explanation.

◀ See "Studying PowerPoint's Basic Color Palette," p. 370

As seen earlier, PowerPoint relies on two color mixing schemes for color creation: RGB and HSL. They are more than sufficient for any color work in a presentation and touch upon several basic concepts and definitions of color. As used in PowerPoint, the two color mixing systems cooperate with each other, and when one mix is adjusted, the other adjusts to match. The two color models are mathematically identical.

◀ See "Working with Color," p. 369

As you saw in earlier chapters, the Red-Green-Blue color model defines how much of each of the three colors is added to the mix in order to arrive at the final color. PowerPoint provides an unusually generous scale for mixing RGB-based colors, with the range for each color being from zero to 65,535 in brightness values. The brighter each of the three colors is, the closer the mix is to white—the brightest possible color. If all three values (red, green, and blue) are zero, the end color is black.

The *hue* is the basic color of the mix—red, green, blue, yellow, or any of the other basic colors in the spectrum. *Saturation* and *luminance* affect the actual purity and brightness of the color, respectively. Luminance actually represents the effect of light on the color, and is shown when you adjust the brightness values of the red, green, and blue mix. The more saturated a color is, the more purity it displays.

The More Colors dialog boxes provide several important tools for creating new colors and for understanding exactly how color works in the program (see figs. 21.1 and 21.2). These dialog boxes appear if you have System 7.5 of the Apple System software installed. Earlier versions of the System software use a single dialog box.

Fig 21.1

The More Colors dialog box enables you to adjust colors.

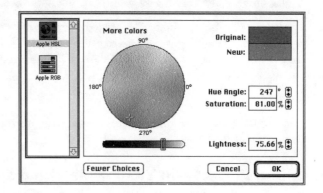

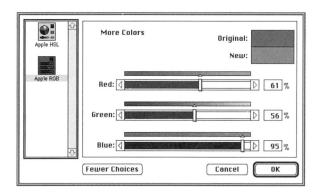

Fig. 21.2
Change RGB
values in this
dialog box.

To open the More Colors dialog boxes, follow these steps:

1. Select an object and then click the Fill Color button on the Drawing+ toolbar.

2. Choose Other Color from the drop-down menu. The Other Color dialog box appears.

3. Click More Colors. The More Colors dialog box opens.

4. To see the HSL and RGB icons, click More Choices.

The wheel in the More Colors dialog box, which is displayed when you click Apple HSL, displays the range of colors available at the current lightness setting. To change the color, click anywhere on the wheel. The color selected is displayed in the New box. To go back to the original color, click the Original box. To make fine adjustments, click the up and down arrows for Hue and Saturation. As you click the arrows, the crosshair in the wheel moves to show the change in the color. You also can type values in the Hue and Saturation boxes.

Clicking the arrows to adjust the value in the Lightness control box does not affect the position of the crosshair. This box displays the value of lightness for the color currently indicated by the crosshair. Lightness means how close the color is to black or white. You can click the slider bar below the wheel to adjust lightness, or you can drag the slider left or right.

To view the RGB values, click the Apple RGB icon. When you adjust the Hue, Saturation, or Lightness controls, the values in the Red, Green, and Blue control boxes adjust simultaneously.

VI

Advanced PowerPoint 4

Keep in mind that when you make adjustments to any value, you may not see the color adjust on the monitor. This relates to the color range that can be displayed by your monitor.

Using Adobe Fonts

If you've ever worked in publishing, and if you've worked with computers extensively, you've probably heard of Adobe. Adobe Systems was the inventor of the PostScript language for laser printers, which is very widely used today. A massive library of computer fonts has been created by Adobe and a host of other font manufacturers.

You can use Adobe fonts for slide titles, body text, and outlining in the same ways you use TrueType fonts. Adobe fonts are special because they're the standard for service bureaus, particularly in the publishing realm. Thus, many professionals prefer them for computing tasks.

Almost invariably, when you send any kind of file to a service bureau for output, you are asked to use Adobe fonts in your files. That's partly because Adobe font names are accepted as the standard names for typefaces. (TrueType fonts usually have imitative names—not identical names—because of copyright restrictions.)

Adobe fonts are installed in many laser printers; some people have a PostScript laser printer on their desk. Those who don't can use another alternative, called Adobe Type Manager. Adobe Type Manager, or ATM, is a high-quality font control program that allows your application to display and print industry-standard Adobe fonts whether or not you have a PostScript-type printer. Additionally, PowerPoint comes with a small selection of TrueType fonts for your use.

> **Note**
>
> If you use Adobe fonts in your presentation, you may have to bring them with the presentation when you deliver it to the service bureau for output. Call the service bureau first to ensure that it has the fonts you use in your presentation; if not, take the fonts along.

Using Alternative Table Editing Techniques

Instead of building table creation features into PowerPoint 4, Microsoft elected to enable users to take advantage of Microsoft Word 6 to build complex row/column tables. However, there's one hitch: if you don't own Word 6, there's no way to make use of PowerPoint's OLE 2 features to embed a table from Word into a slide.

The same is true if you don't own Microsoft Excel 5. PowerPoint 4 offers a tool for editing and inserting row/column datasheets using Excel 5. The process, as with Word, uses OLE 2. PowerPoint does not offer a native method for editing and creating datasheets for display in a slide—even Graph's datasheets are used only to create charts and cannot be directly displayed in the program. Essentially, you only can take full advantage of PowerPoint's table creation and datasheet creation tools if you also own Word 6 and Excel 5.

Tip
Use the Object command from PowerPoint's Insert menu to help create a new data sheet or table object with other Macintosh programs.

Creating Tables Directly in PowerPoint

Simple tables can be created directly on the PowerPoint slide. Though typing and editing a simple table on a slide is fairly inflexible and doesn't offer the formatting capabilities of a sophisticated word processor like Word, WordPerfect, or MacWrite, there are a few advantages:

- There's no need to run another application program.

- All of PowerPoint's basic editing tools are available, including line spacing, text formatting, and ruler tab setting.

- Because you're typing unformatted text for your table, it's considered just another PowerPoint object. Background coloring and shading can be applied, as well as shadowing and text colors.

When you want to create a table directly in PowerPoint, follow these steps:

1. In PowerPoint's Slide view, display the slide where you want to write your table.

2. Open the View menu and choose Ruler. PowerPoint's ruler appears.

3. Click the Text tool in the Drawing toolbar.

4. Click the slide to position the insertion point.

5. Type your tabular data. Press the Tab key between each text box of data. At the end of each table row, press Return.

As you enter your data, the ruler changes its appearance to reflect the growth of the table, as shown in figure 21.3.

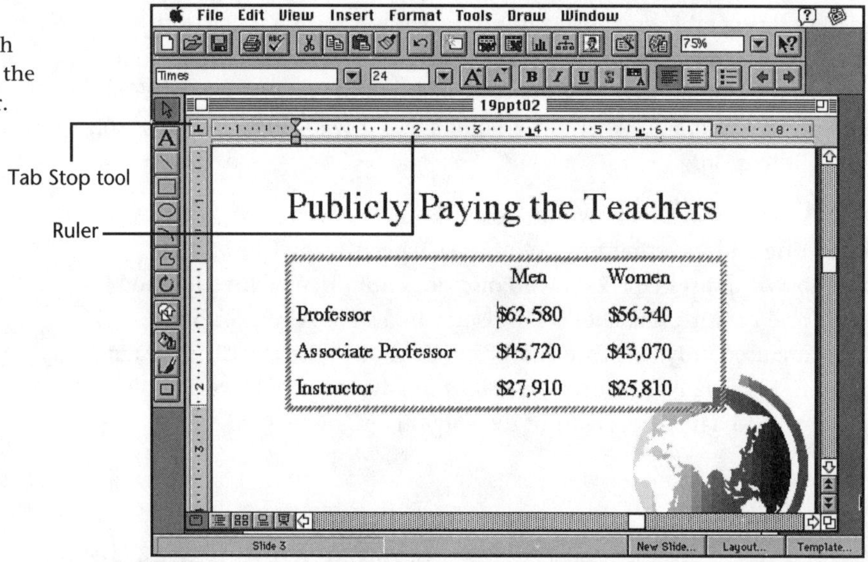

Fig. 21.3
The ruler width keeps up with the data you enter.

You can use four different types of tab stops in a table format: Left, Right, Center, and Center with Leader. The Tab Stop tool in the top left corner of the document window (adjacent to both rulers) allows you to cycle between the four tab types to select the one you want.

6. To add tab stop formatting on columns in a table, click any text item in the desired column. Do not select any text, because then tabs cannot be set.

7. Click the Tab Stop tool to select the tab style you want.

8. Click inside the top ruler to place the tab markers. The entire column adjusts. Figure 21.3 shows a table with two tab markers used to align the values.

Colors also can be set for borders of a table because it is just another text object. The column heads can be boldfaced and underlined. Fill colors also can be set, lending a bit more emphasis to a table.

There's no provision for adding borders to individual table cells. Because the table you're typing onto the slide is only a simple text object, there's no easy way to structure a table with borders around each value.

Using Special Shading Effects

PowerPoint offers some interesting shading effects beyond those used for most of the examples in this book. In all, PowerPoint offers 22 specific shading effects that can be applied to a slide. First, let's review briefly what's involved in changing shading effects.

To change shading effects for one or more slides, open the Format menu and choose Slide Background. Shading styles are split into six discrete Variant categories:

Vertical	4 styles (shading is oriented vertically)
Horizontal	4 styles (shading is oriented across the slide)
Diagonal Right	4 styles (shading is oriented from left to right diagonally)
Diagonal Left	4 styles (shading is oriented from right to left diagonally)
From Corner	4 styles (shading effect is directed from a corner of the slide)
From Title	2 styles (shading radiates from slide title)

One of the most interesting shading styles is the From Title variant set. By itself, the style is quite distinctive, as shown in figure 21.4. The flag is part of the background and the shading shows mostly on the right top corner down to the bottom of the screen, producing a distinctive effect.

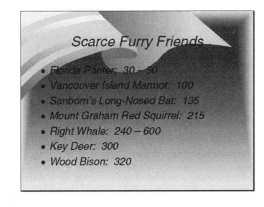

Fig. 21.4
The gradient screen of the background begins at the title and fades to the edges outward.

Wherever you move the title, the shading adjusts to match. The From Title shading style should be used sparingly because it tends to draw attention to the title, which can be a detriment to the clarity of the message conveyed in the slide. Nonetheless, the effect is very striking, because the eye is also drawn downward to the object below the title, in a spotlight effect.

Using the Equation Editor

The Equation Editor is another separate application program, or applet, that is provided with PowerPoint for the creation and insertion of mathematical equations into your slides. If you're a math major, this is a program that you'll appreciate. Only a short section describing its basic features is offered here, but if you are knowledgeable about advanced math topics, Equation Editor has a lot to offer.

1. Open the Insert menu and choose Object.

2. When the Insert Object dialog box appears, choose Microsoft Equation 2.0 from the Object Type list.

   The Equation Editor toolbar and menus appear, as shown in figure 21.5 (Equation Editor is an OLE 2 application).

Fig. 21.5
Equation Editor has a toolbar much like those of PowerPoint, Word, and Excel.

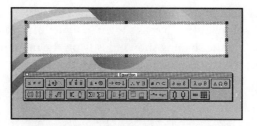

An editing area in white surrounded by a grayed border also appears, displaying a blinking insertion point. This is where you edit your equation.

When the Equation Editor screen appears, you can immediately begin entering your equation.

3. For the current example, type a value.

   Now, you enter a template. The Editor's toolbar is divided into two sets of tools. The top row of buttons on the toolbar is a set of Symbol Palettes used to enter mathematical value symbols, and the second or bottom row of buttons is a set of Template Palettes that are used to insert mathematical templates for fractions, matrices, integrals, brackets of various types, and other elements of math equations.

When you click an Equation Editor button, a pop-up menu of symbols attached to the button type appears. For example, figure 21.6 shows the template menu list attached to the Fraction and Radical Templates symbol button.

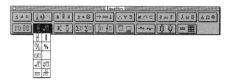

Fig. 21.6
The buttons of the toolbar access pop-up menus.

4. Click the Fraction and Radical Templates button as shown in figure 21.6. (It's the second button from the left in the bottom row of the toolbar.) This toolbar button offers formatting for fractions, radicals, and long division.

5. To add a fraction symbol to your equation, you can click any of several template buttons on the pop-up menu.

   Each button on every pop-up menu is actually a template for formatting numbers with mathematical symbols. When you choose a fraction template, it's inserted into your equation. Fraction templates automatically contain two placeholders for numbers that you can type in to finish the mathematical expression.

6. Type a number in the top half of the fraction template, press the down arrow key to advance the insertion point to the bottom of the fraction template, and type another number.

   The results may appear somewhat like figure 21.7.

Fig. 21.7
Built-up fractions, like this one, are a button click away.

The fraction template was applied and numbers were added to create the fraction.

VI

Advanced PowerPoint 4

Tip

The crucial feature of the Equation Editor is its toolbar, which is split into two rows: Symbol Palettes on the top row and Template Palettes on the bottom row.

To add a multiplication sign or other operator to your equation, click the Operator Symbols button on the Equation Editor toolbar (it's the fourth button from the left on the top row). Choose the multiplication symbol from the pop-up menu. The multiplication symbol is inserted into the equation.

To change the point size, follow these steps:

1. Drag the mouse to select the equation text.

2. From the Size menu in the Equation Editor, choose Define.

   The Sizes dialog box appears. This is where you define the default point sizes for the fonts in your equations—the full-size font in the equation, subscript and superscript fonts, the point size of mathematical symbols, and the point size of math subsymbols.

3. In the Full text box, enter a size (we used 40pt).

4. Choose OK.

The results may appear similar to figure 21.8.

Fig. 21.8

Changing size and other attributes of equations are done at the menu level.

To embed the equation into the slide, click anywhere outside the editing area in Equation Editor. To edit the equation again, simply double-click the equation object. The Equation Editor appears, displaying the equation for further work.

There's a great deal more about Equation Editor that cannot be explained in this book; Equation Editor is, in fact, a powerful and complex application program all by itself, and a book could be written about this subject alone. The last steps in this exercise show you how to resize the equation to a larger font.

Troubleshooting

I can't get the Equation Editor to start. It's not listed in the Insert Object dialog box.

You probably didn't install it. Fortunately, it's easy to do. Use the PowerPoint 4 Setup program and choose to install components that weren't previously installed in your computer. Double-click the PowerPoint Setup icon in the PowerPoint folder, choose the Add/Remove button when the Setup screen appears, and follow the instructions from there.

What can I do to ensure an effective black-and-white or grayscale presentation?

Colors don't always translate well into grayscale or black-and-white. A good practice is to use more patterns in your objects to help visually distinguish them. This is particularly useful for laptop users.

Believe it or not, the vast majority of PowerPoint users rely on either overhead transparencies or black-and-white handouts for their presentations. According to Microsoft, only 2 to 3 percent of PowerPoint users employ on-screen slide shows for their work. You are probably dealing with the issue of using grayscales on a frequent basis. That's why Microsoft provides a large selection of black-and-white overhead templates in the program, along with color slides and overhead transparencies.

From Here...

Congratulations! From the simple to the complex, all the chapters up to this one covered many important issues about creating your own presentations. You are now very likely to have a lot of your co-workers asking you how to use features of the PowerPoint 4 application program. Go forth and wow the corporate masses!

For information on other topics, see the following chapters:

- Chapter 22, "Customizing PowerPoint," the final chapter in this book, discusses how to customize PowerPoint's user interface.

- Chapters 13, 14, and 19 discuss charting and graphing from the simple to the complex.

- Chapter 17, "Working with Color," digs into many of PowerPoint's color handling features.

- Chapter 18, "Using Links to Other Applications," discusses object linking and embedding issues in more detail.

- Chapter 20, "Advanced Presentation Management," discusses special effects, presentation rehearsing, and adding multimedia elements.

VI

Advanced PowerPoint 4

Chapter 22

Customizing PowerPoint

PowerPoint allows you to change your work environment to suit your needs. You can change toolbars by adding, removing, or rearranging their contents. You can even create your own custom toolbar. Default settings associated with your presentations, such as color and text, may also be changed. When you finish customizing PowerPoint, you can save changes and apply them to future presentations.

In this chapter, you learn to do the following:

- Change PowerPoint's defaults

- Create custom toolbars

- Modify existing toolbars

- Change PowerPoint's default editing options

- Set PowerPoint to prompt for summary information

Note

For the instructions in this chapter, it is assumed that PowerPoint 4 has been installed in the PowerPoint folder. If you have installed PowerPoint in a different folder, please substitute your folder name in the following examples.

Understanding PowerPoint's Defaults

Defaults are initial settings used by PowerPoint that can be changed at any time. If you've used other Macintosh applications such as Word, then you're already aware of the advantage of defaults: they allow you to start using the product immediately to create results. In the case of Word, you can create a document without first choosing the page size, layout, typefaces, and so on; Word's default settings create a basic, all-purpose document for you. Similarly, PowerPoint's default settings cover all aspects associated with creating, viewing, and outputting a presentation. Specifically they are:

- Printing defaults

- Viewing defaults

- Text editing defaults

- Color defaults

- Object defaults

- Options defaults

Note

Defaults allow you to get up to speed quickly by automatically using standard settings. Until you get comfortable with PowerPoint, create your presentations using the default settings.

Because you don't have to assign default settings before creating your first presentation, you can get acquainted with PowerPoint's commands at your own pace. It's a good idea to do so before changing default settings. PowerPoint's defaults are saved in a file called default.ppt. Later in this chapter, you learn how to customize this file.

Printing Defaults

PowerPoint can use any printer installed to your system. Printer settings are determined by the type of printer currently selected for use in PowerPoint. To determine which printer is currently selected, open the Apple menu and select the Chooser (see fig. 22.1). If you want to change the default printer, select the new printer name from the list in Chooser.

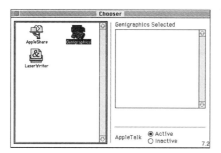

Fig. 22.1
The Chooser is a Macintosh interface for selecting a printer.

To view the current printing defaults, open the File menu and choose Print. The Print dialog box appears (see fig. 22.2).

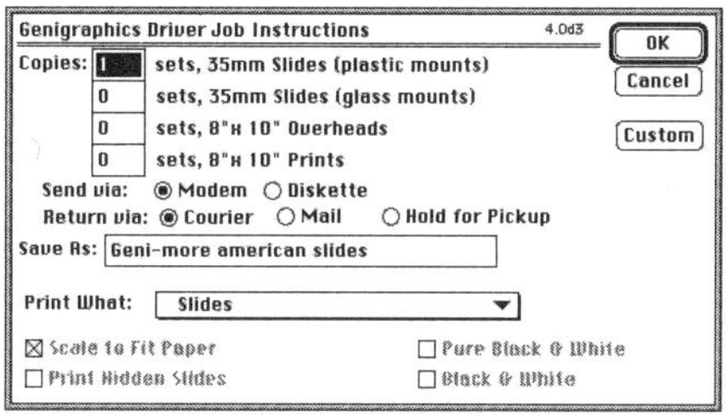

Fig. 22.2
The current printer is the Genigraphics driver.

Viewing Defaults

PowerPoint allows you to switch between four presentation views. The Slide view is initially scaled to 50 percent of full view. The Slide Master has a centered title at the top, set in Times 44 Regular (if available). The Notes Master centers a reduced (50 percent scaled down) slide at the top of the notes page. The Outline Master displays a blank outline page, scaled down to 33 percent of its full size. The default handout page contains no text or objects.

Text Editing Defaults

Title objects in PowerPoint have a default text style of Times 44 Regular, while body object text uses Times 32 Regular. Initially text is centered. Text boxes automatically receive the Adjust Object Size to Fit Text feature.

To change the default text editing settings, change the text size and style as desired. Then follow one of the two methods described later, in the "Changing PowerPoint Defaults" section, to save the default settings.

VI

Advanced PowerPoint 4

Color Defaults

The following eight color settings are available in the default color scheme:

Element	Color
Background	White
Lines & Text	Black
Shadows	Gray
Title Text	Black
Fill	Blue
Accents	Green
Accents	Red

◀ See "Studying PowerPoint's Basic Color Palette," p. 370

To change the default color scheme settings, select new color schemes by using the Color Scheme option on the Format menu. Then, follow one of the two methods described later to save the default settings.

Object Defaults

Drawn objects are transparent (not opaque), framed in black, filled with white, and unshadowed. The default line style is the thinnest line in the menu, without arrowheads.

To change the default object setting, select new object attributes and follow one of the two methods described next to save the default settings.

Changing PowerPoint Defaults

PowerPoint defaults for all presentations are stored in the default.ppt file. You can save default settings for all future presentations or only for the current presentation.

To save new default settings for all future presentations, follow these steps:

1. Open a new presentation and use the commands on the Format menu (Font, Slide Layout, Slide Background, and Slide Color Scheme) to select the setting you want to change.

Or, open an existing presentation that contains the settings you want to use as defaults.

2. When all settings are correct, choose Save As from the File menu. The Save As dialog box appears.

3. In the File Name box, type **default.ppt** and click OK to save the file. The next time you open or create a presentation, the settings you selected will be the defaults.

To save default settings for only the current presentation, follow these steps:

1. Select the Selection button on the Drawing toolbar. Doing so ensures that no objects or text in the active presentation are selected.

2. Use the commands on the Format menu (Font, Slide Layout, Slide Background, and Slide Color Scheme) to select the settings you want to change.

Because you change the settings without selecting text or an object first, PowerPoint automatically saves the new settings as defaults for the active presentation.

Customizing Toolbars

PowerPoint allows you to display, modify, and create toolbars to suit your needs. Specifically, you can:

■ Add or remove buttons from any of the supplied toolbars

■ Rearrange the buttons on toolbars

■ Create a custom toolbar

Adding and Removing Buttons on the Toolbar

To add a button to a toolbar, follow these steps:

1. Click the toolbar area, pressing and holding down the Ctrl key and the mouse button, and then choose Customize from the shortcut menu, or choose Customize from the Tools menu. The Customize Toolbars dialog box appears, as shown in figure 22.3.

Tip

You can add the same button to more than one toolbar. If you find that you're using a particular button frequently, add it to the Drawing toolbar as well as the Standard toolbar. Next time you need to access the button, you can click the one that is closest.

VI

Advanced PowerPoint 4

Fig. 22.3
Use the Ctrl key, hold the mouse button down, and click any toolbar to access the Customize Toolbars dialog box.

> **Note**
>
> There are several ways to display the Customize Toolbars dialog box. You can display the dialog box by choosing Customize from the Tools menu, or by choosing Toolbars on the View menu and then clicking Customize in the dialog box that appears.

2. Select a button category from the Categories list. Notice that each selection determines the items shown in the Buttons area in the dialog box.

3. Select the desired button, and then drag and drop it onto the toolbar.

4. Add more buttons by repeating steps 2 and 3.

Tip
When you remove a button from a toolbar, it's not gone forever. You can always put it back by following the steps for adding buttons to toolbars.

To remove buttons from a toolbar, follow these steps:

1. Click the toolbar area, press and hold the Ctrl key and the mouse button, and then choose Customize from the shortcut menu, or choose Customize from the Tools menu. The Customize Toolbars dialog box appears.

2. Drag the button you want to remove from its toolbar. As you drag, the button's outline follows the mouse pointer.

3. Release the mouse button when the button is no longer on the toolbar.

4. Remove more buttons by repeating steps 2 and 3. You can close the Customize Toolbars dialog box after you have finished removing buttons.

Rearranging the Contents of a Toolbar

You may wish to organize buttons in groups by inserting spaces between buttons, or simply move a button to a new location on the toolbar. To move a button on a toolbar, follow these steps:

1. Move the mouse pointer to the toolbar you want to modify, press and hold the Ctrl key and the mouse button, and choose Customize. The Customize Toolbars dialog box appears.

2. While the Customize Toolbars dialog box is on-screen, move the mouse pointer to the toolbar and drag the button to its new location on the toolbar.

3. Release the mouse button to complete the operation.

To group tools together, do the following:

1. Move the mouse pointer to the toolbar that you want to modify, press and hold the Ctrl key and the mouse button, and choose Customize. The Customize Toolbars dialog box appears.

2. While the Customize Toolbars dialog box is on-screen, move the mouse pointer to the toolbar and click the button at the end where you want to insert a space.

3. Drag the button to the right and release the mouse button to complete the operation. A space should exist between the dragged button and the button to its left.

Tip
It is helpful to group similar tools together.

Creating a Custom Toolbar

Create your own toolbar by following these steps:

1. Click View on the menu bar and choose Toolbars. The Toolbars dialog box appears (see fig. 22.4).

Fig. 22.4
The Toolbars dialog box allows you to choose those toolbars that are opened.

2. Click the Custom setting and choose OK to close the dialog box. An empty custom menu appears on-screen.

3. Move the mouse pointer to the empty Custom toolbar, press and hold the Ctrl key and then click the mouse button, and choose Customize from the shortcut menu. The Customize Toolbars dialog box appears.

Tip

Toolbars may slow down PowerPoint, especially if you are using just 4M of RAM. To increase performance, remove all unnecessary toolbars and create and display a custom toolbar.

4. Select a button category from the Categories list. Notice that each selection determines the items shown in the Buttons area in the dialog box.

5. Select the desired button and drag and drop it onto the Custom toolbar.

6. Add more buttons by repeating steps 3 through 5.

Note

As you create and customize toolbars, you may find it helpful to *float* the toolbar on the PowerPoint screen. To float a toolbar, drag it away from the top or sides of the screen until its outline changes to a rectangular shape.

Troubleshooting

I can't see some of the buttons on a toolbar when the toolbar is placed on the sides of the screen.

Change the toolbar to a floating toolbar by dragging the toolbar near the center of the screen until its shape changes to a rectangle.

I accidentally removed a button from a toolbar.

Select Tools, Customize to display the Customize Tools dialog box. Select the name of the toolbar missing the button from the Categories list. Locate the missing button and drag it to the toolbar on the PowerPoint screen.

I wanted to remove a button from a toolbar by dragging it, but I just selected the button.

Display the Customize Tools dialog box by pressing and holding the Ctrl key and the mouse button while the pointer is on the toolbar. You can now drag the button to remove it.

I tried to swap the position of two buttons on a toolbar, but I just get additional space between the two buttons.

Make sure you drag the button past the center of the adjacent button. Be careful not to drag the button off the toolbar; you'll remove it completely.

Changing PowerPoint Options

In addition to defaults associated with presentations, you can set preferences by using the Options dialog box, shown in figure 22.5. You can set options for editing, spelling, viewing, saving, and some general items. Choose Options from the Tools menu to display the Options dialog box. All nine options in this dialog box are enabled by default. To disable an option, simply choose it.

Fig. 22.5
PowerPoint
program options
are set in this
dialog box.

The options are described briefly in table 22.1, and then in more detail in the sections that follow.

Table 22.1 Options in the Options Dialog Box	
Option	**Result**
Replace Straight Quotes	Replaces straight quotes with *Smart Quotes* (quotes that curve in the appropriate direction to either open or close the quote).
Automatic Word Selection	Selects text a complete word at a time as you drag. Turning off this option causes words to be selected one character at a time.
Use Smart Cut and Paste	Text pasted from the Clipboard is pasted with appropriate spaces between words.
Always Suggest	Always suggests an alternative word in the Spelling dialog box when encountering a spelling error.
Status Bar	Displays the status bar.
Prompt for Summary Info	Always prompts for summary information when saving a presentation for the first time.
Show Startup Dialog	Displays the Startup dialog box when you start PowerPoint.
Show New Slide Dialog	Displays the New Slide dialog box when you start PowerPoint.
Recently Used File List	Displays a list of recently used files on the File menu. You can specify the maximum number of files to be displayed in the Entries box.

VI

Advanced PowerPoint 4

Replace Straight Quotes with Smart Quotes

Smart Quotes are special characters used by typesetters. This option is enabled by default in the English version of PowerPoint.

When Smart Quotes are enabled, the double (") and single (') straight quote marks you type are replaced with the corresponding Smart Quotes. Also, existing quotes are not affected; any existing quotes must be changed manually after enabling Smart Quotes.

> **Note**
>
> The Smart Quotes feature also controls apostrophes to make sure they curve in the proper direction.

Automatic Word Selection

Marking this option enables the Automatic Word Selection feature of PowerPoint. Automatic word selection causes entire words to be highlighted as you drag the I-beam pointer into the word. This feature is helpful if you tend to reword titles or bullet text frequently. If this option is not marked, the letters of words will be highlighted one at a time.

Use Smart Cut and Paste

When Smart Cut and Paste is enabled, PowerPoint pastes text from the Clipboard with some intelligence. That is, PowerPoint adds or removes the necessary spaces between words as needed. To illustrate this feature, consider the following sentence:

The quick fox jumped over the lazy dog's back.

Now suppose you have copied the word brown from another sentence onto the Clipboard. With Smart Cut and Paste disabled, pasting the word directly after the word quick would yield the following:

The quickbrown fox jumped over the lazy dog's back.

With Smart Cut and Paste enabled, pasting the word after quick yields:

The quick brown fox jumped over the lazy dog's back.

The feature added a space after quick to make the sentence read properly. The feature will also remove extra spaces between words, as necessary.

Spelling

When Always Suggest is enabled, the Spelling dialog box always suggests an alternative when a misspelled word is encountered.

Status Bar

Select the Status Bar option to remove the status bar from the bottom of the screen.

> **Caution**
>
> Disabling the Status Bar option makes you rely on your memory. If you have difficulty remembering which slide you're on, or how to perform a procedure, turn the status bar back on.

Prompt for Summary Info

The Prompt for Summary Info option, which is enabled by default, displays the Summary Info dialog box whenever you save a file for the first time. You can disable this option and access the Summary Info dialog box whenever you want by choosing Summary Info from the File menu. Use this dialog box to enter descriptive information about your presentation.

Whenever a file is saved for the first time, PowerPoint prompts you for descriptive notes or summary information that make finding the presentation easier later on.

> **Note**
>
> You can add summary information any time to a presentation. To do so, first make sure the presentation is open and choose Summary Info from the File menu to display the Summary Info dialog box. Type descriptive text in the text boxes (up to 255 characters) and then choose OK.

Show Startup Dialog

Enabling the Show Startup Dialog option displays PowerPoint's startup dialog box each time you start PowerPoint. The startup dialog box gives you options for creating new presentations and for opening existing presentations. If you become proficient at locating and using options such as the AutoContent Wizard and the Pick a Look Wizard, you'll speed your startup process by disabling the Show Startup Dialog feature.

Show New Slide Dialog

Enabling the Show New Slide Dialog feature displays a New Slide dialog box each time you start PowerPoint—if you're not using the AutoContent or Pick a Look Wizards to begin your presentations. The New Slide dialog box allows you to choose the layout of the tiles and text of your slides.

Recently Used File List

If you frequently use the same set of files, the Recently Used File List option will save you time. By default, PowerPoint displays the last four files that were opened and closed at the bottom of the File menu. Select the Recently Used File List option to hide the list, or adjust the number of files displayed on the list by specifying a different number in the Entries box.

From Here...

In this chapter, you explored PowerPoint's defaults and customization options. Refer to chapters throughout this book for more details about the many PowerPoint features mentioned here. After you've used PowerPoint for a while, you may want to come back to this chapter to customize the program to best meet your needs.

Other chapters you may now want to review include:

- Chapter 2, "Getting Acquainted with PowerPoint 4," gives you more information about the various toolbars and how to display them.

- Chapter 16, "Printing and Other Kinds of Output," explains how to choose a default printer.

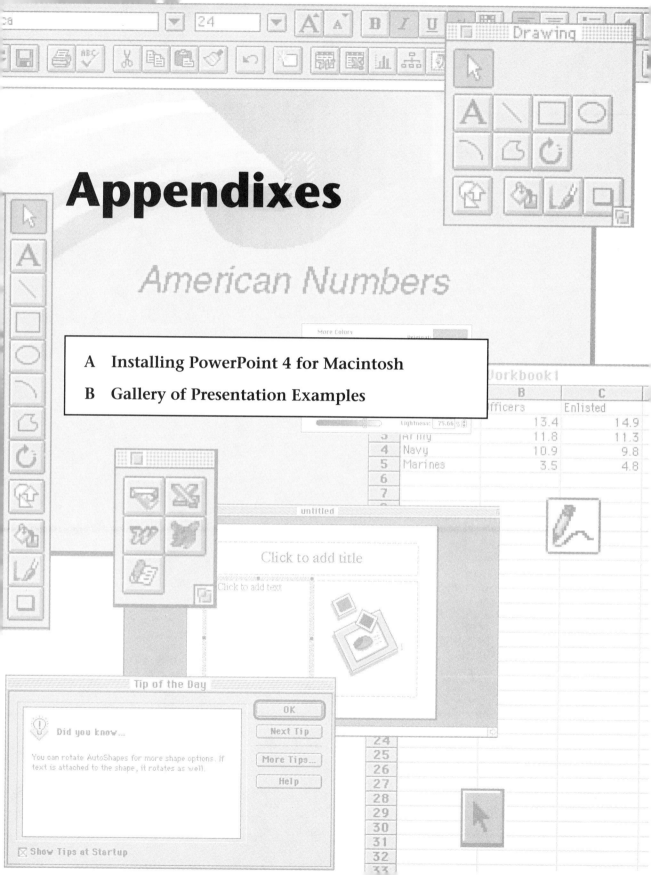

Appendixes

American Numbers

Installing PowerPoint 4 for Macintosh

When you install PowerPoint (or any other software program) on the Macintosh, you get the best results by holding down the Shift key as you restart your computer. This action suppresses the Extensions, which may conflict with the installer program in Microsoft PowerPoint. Also make sure that no other applications are running and that any virus-detection software is suspended.

Checking System Requirements

PowerPoint 4's base requirements are:

- System 7.0 or later

- Minimum 4M of RAM (more is recommended)

- Hard disk

- 3.5-inch (1.4M) floppy disk drive

A color monitor is recommended, as is QuickTime (if you want to play QuickTime movies).

Full installation of PowerPoint requires a little less than 40M of disk space. Given the depth and richness of the program's features, this requirement shouldn't be any big surprise.

Checking System Recommendations

For serious work with PowerPoint 4, you should have 8M of RAM (or more) in your Macintosh. Particularly when you begin adding movies to your slide shows, your presentation files can get very large in a short period of time. Pictures and bitmapped images also expand a presentation file rapidly.

Given the size of the PowerPoint program on your hard disk, having a large hard disk is a very good idea. Hard drive prices have been going through the floor recently; stores in Southern California, for example, have been selling 340M hard drives for $200. So if you've been waiting for disk storage to become affordable, the time has come.

PowerPoint can run on any Macintosh that is equipped with enough RAM and hard disk space. The faster the Macintosh, however, the faster you can work. Also, you most likely will want to use a color monitor (which eliminates the Plus, Classic, and SE-series machines). If you have a Mac II or later, you'll be happy with the performance and capabilities of PowerPoint.

Copying Source Disks

Before installing PowerPoint, you should make a backup set of your PowerPoint installation disks for use in case anything goes wrong. Keep the original disks in a safe place, and use the copies to perform your installation. (Don't worry; this procedure is legal.)

You need 11 high-density, 3 1/2-inch floppy disks to copy all the PowerPoint installation disks. Label the target disks (the disks on which you are placing the copies) PowerPoint Disk 1, PowerPoint Disk 2, and so on.

Many disk-copying applications are available, but none is necessary. Simply insert the original disk into your drive and then eject the disk by pressing ⌘-E (don't drag the disk to the Trash). This method leaves a ghosted icon on the Desktop. Insert the target disk, and drag the ghosted icon directly on top of the target disk. You will be asked whether you are certain that you want to replace the entire contents of the target disk with the contents of the original disk. Click OK to continue. Repeat this procedure until you have copied all the disks.

You now can use the copies to install PowerPoint 4, as described in the following section.

Installing PowerPoint

During the installation process, you are asked to choose the type of installation you want. You can choose one of the following options:

- *Complete.* The Complete option installs PowerPoint and all its support files, including Equation Editor and the ClipArt Gallery. This installation requires 35 to 40M of disk space.

- *Custom.* You should choose the Custom option only if you need to conserve disk space, because you must make decisions about what to install and what to leave out.

- *Minimal.* The Minimal option installs only those files that are needed to run Microsoft PowerPoint. Features such as Equation Editor, WordArt, the ClipArt Gallery, Cue Cards, and Wizards are left out, but you can install them later at any time.

To install PowerPoint, follow these steps:

1. Insert PowerPoint Disk 1 (your working copy) into your floppy disk drive, and double-click the Setup icon. A welcome screen appears.

2. Click the Continue button, type your name and company name (if applicable), and click Continue again. A message appears: `Please wait while Setup copies its working files to your hard disk.`

3. Choose an installation option: Complete, Custom, or Minimum.

If you need to clear some more disk space for the program, click the Exit Setup button.

PowerPoint advances through the installation from this point; you provide no additional help other than inserting the correct disk when you are prompted.

Tip

If the installation is your first glimpse of PowerPoint, watch the on-screen dialog boxes, which provide tidbits of information about application features.

Note

Installation takes quite some time—remember that a full installation is about 40M—so pour a cup of coffee and sit back.

Gallery of
Presentation Examples

High-Low-Close Stock Chart

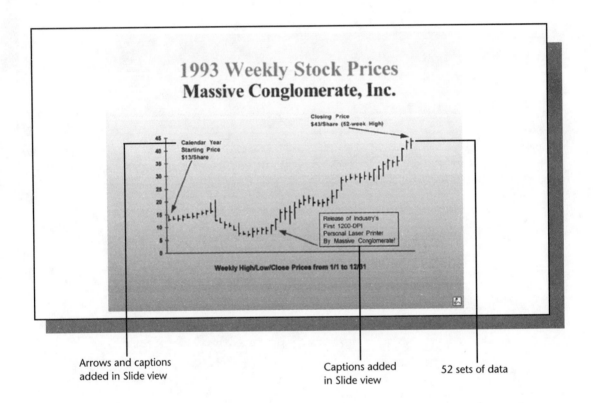

Arrows and captions
added in Slide view

Captions added
in Slide view

52 sets of data

Line-Column Combination Chart

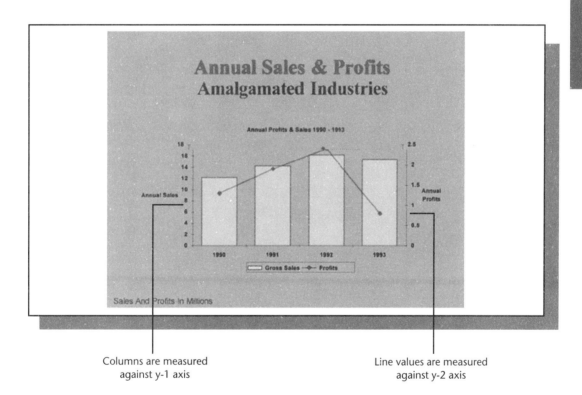

Columns are measured
against y-1 axis

Line values are measured
against y-2 axis

Combination Chart—Same Contents, Different Charting from Preceding Chart

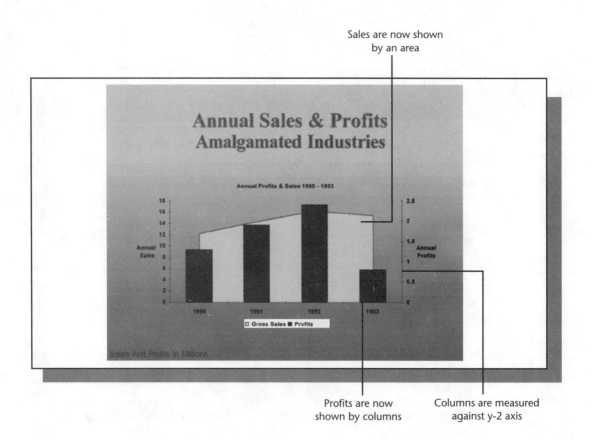

Sales are now shown by an area

Profits are now shown by columns

Columns are measured against y-2 axis

Another Combination Chart—This Time Showing Annual Sales (Columns) and Stock Prices

High-Low-Close markers
with markers crossing

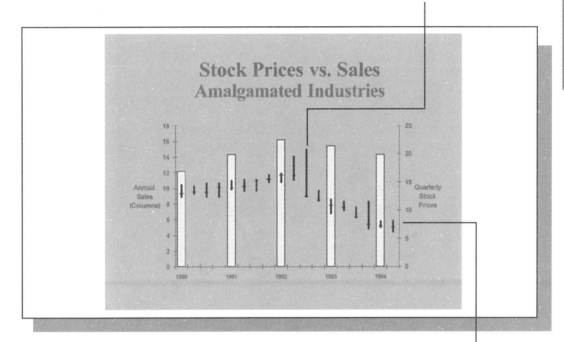

HLC markers are measured
against y-2 axis

Simple Text Slide with Clip Art

3-D Line Chart

Elevation of 5

Perspective of 30

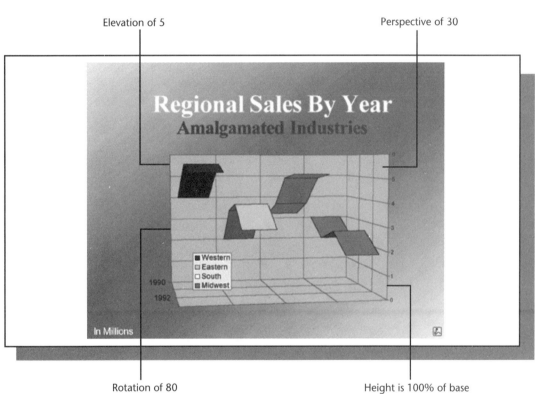

Rotation of 80

Height is 100% of base

2-D Scatter Chart

Logarithmic scale
applied to y-axis

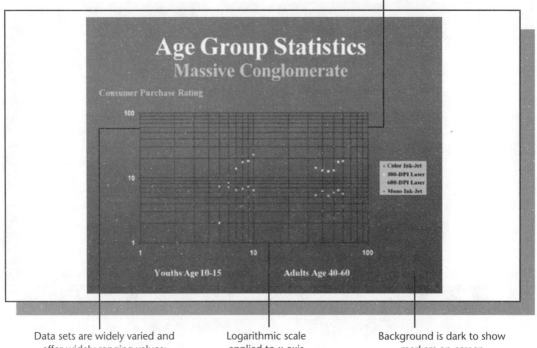

Data sets are widely varied and
offer widely ranging values;
hence, a logarithmic scale is
applied to each axis

Logarithmic scale
applied to x-axis

Background is dark to show
markers on-screen

A Table Created with Word 6

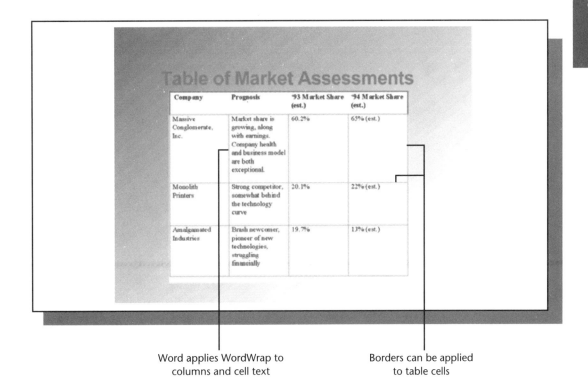

Word applies WordWrap to
columns and cell text

Borders can be applied
to table cells

3-D Pie Chart

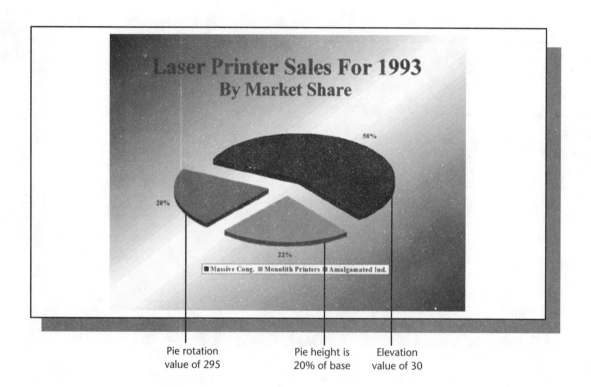

Pie rotation value of 295   Pie height is 20% of base   Elevation value of 30

Custom 3-D Column Chart

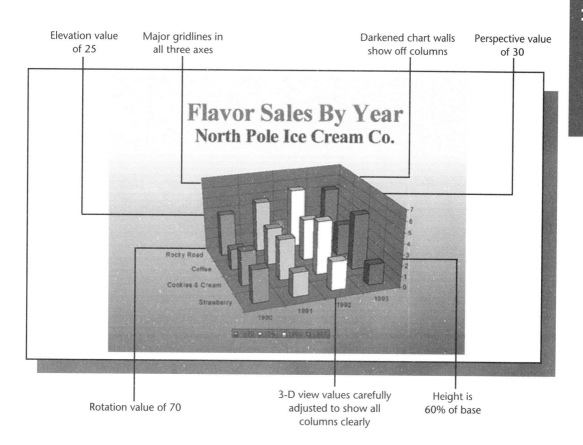

Elevation value of 25

Major gridlines in all three axes

Darkened chart walls show off columns

Perspective value of 30

Flavor Sales By Year
North Pole Ice Cream Co.

Rotation value of 70

3-D view values carefully adjusted to show all columns clearly

Height is 60% of base

3-D Surface Chart

Legend (shows
"altitude" values)

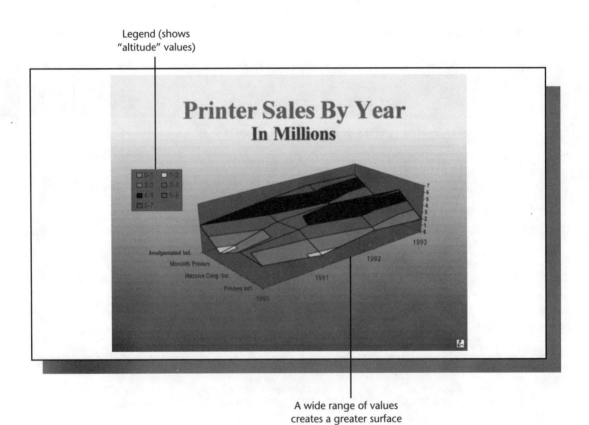

A wide range of values
creates a greater surface

Multimedia

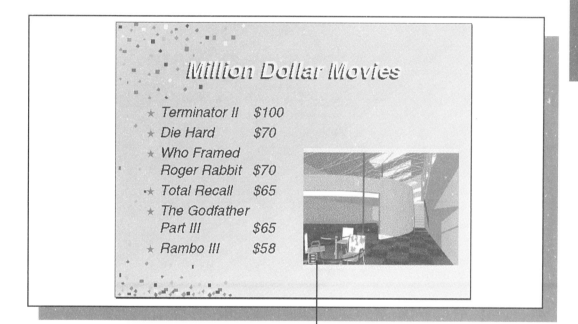

Click-and-play movie object

Index

Action Index